Trinity
A PORTRAIT

Trinity

A PORTRAIT

Edited by Edward Stourton
and John Lonsdale

THIRD MILLENNIUM
PUBLISHING, LONDON

Editor's Note

When John Lonsdale asked me to edit this book I was daunted by what it might involve; Trinity is one of the greatest academic establishments in the world and, with its size, history, achievements and wealth, it is scarcely a subject to be taken on lightly. But you cannot say 'no' to your former tutor.

I had reckoned without the really remarkable enthusiasm the College inspires among its members. Editing this book has turned out to be a very great pleasure.

Almost everyone we asked to contribute agreed to do so; some of the essays you will find here are works of real scholarship, some are serious journalism. All have required substantial time and effort from people with busy lives. Memories of College life have poured in from alumni and alumnae, and they span eight decades of Trinity life (matriculation dates – or, for those who were not undergraduates, the year of election to the Fellowship – are given after contributors' names). They reveal engaging differences and developments over the years, but they also suggest that some of the essential elements of the Trinity experience endure unchanged.

John Lonsdale and I felt we needed the guidance of an editorial committee. I am grateful to Richard Serjeantson and Tim Gowers, who represented the Fellows, and to Daisy Goodwin and Nicholas Coleridge, who represented the wider Trinity community and brought their considerable journalistic and publishing experience to bear on the task. Hugo Gye ensured that the book includes a good range of voices from today's Trinity (and put in the time while he was preparing for his Finals), and Lynne Isaacs of the Alumni Office has been tirelessly efficient and miraculously creative in tracking down past members of the college.

Corinne Lloyd was the Head of Alumni Relations at the time the book was commissioned, Tony Bannard-Smith holds the post today; both were as supportive as they could have been. The beautiful look of the book says everything that needs to be said about the work of the publishers, TMI. I am especially grateful to Chris Fagg, who was relentlessly thorough in driving the production process. Our thanks are also due to the Choir and Stephen Layton, the Director of Music, for the CD which is included inside the back cover.

But the two people who deserve most credit for this achievement are Catharine Walston and John Lonsdale. Catharine, as Managing Editor, shaped the text, researched the wonderful collection of images, caught the howlers and spotted the areas where we had fallen short. Professor Lonsdale has been the driving force behind the project from first to last.

The Trinity that looks out from this Portrait is supremely confident of its vocation, proud of its past and determined about its future; but there is just enough of the eccentric, the louche and the disreputable here to suggest an institution that does not take itself too seriously. I hope you enjoy reading this book as much as I have enjoyed editing it.

ES, May 2011

Contents

Preface

PROFESSOR DAME ALISON RICHARD,
VICE CHANCELLOR 2003–10

Collegiate Cambridge has good reason to join in this celebration of Trinity College.

Those who visit Trinity's stunning buildings as tourists, or read about the College or its alumni in books, will discern the trappings of distinction: royal origins, venerable age, connections (historical and contemporary) with some of the world's greatest minds and leaders. Less evident but no less impressive, however, are Trinity's extraordinary ability to see what the future has in store and the generosity with which Trinity helps to ensure that Collegiate Cambridge is ready to respond, adapt and innovate.

Consider the following few examples of contemporary relevance:

Graduate students and Darwin College

In 1900 there were scarcely any graduate students in Cambridge; in 1964 there were 2,000. Trinity saw that the trend was accelerating, realised that the existing colleges would struggle to accommodate such numbers, and – with St John's and Caius colleges coming to the call – founded Darwin College as the University's first graduate-only college, and also the first to admit both men and women. Now there are nearly 6,000 graduate students in Cambridge. They enhance the life of the community during their sojourn here, and they carry their talents to many endeavours thereafter. Crucially, they are also the lifeblood of the University, creating the academic enterprise anew in each generation. Trinity not only saw all this clear sightedly but acted to support the growth of the graduate student body. The current shape, size and well-being of the Cambridge student population owe much to Trinity College.

Knowledge exchange and the Cambridge Science Park

Growth in research student numbers has been strongly driven by the growth of research itself. Particularly during the last 50 years, the links between university research and technological and societal change have become more evident, and the

economic benefits of investment in research coupled with rapid and effective 'knowledge exchange' are much emphasised today. Cambridge was an early leader in this development, with increasingly permeable institutional boundaries.

It was Trinity College, however, that spotted the transformational opportunity: in 1970 Trinity established the Cambridge Science Park, the first in the country, where research-based industry could thrive in close collaboration with University academics, with flexible space and a supportive infrastructure. There are now over 60 tenant companies of varying size.

The investment has been very successful for the College, and the activity catalysed thereby has rippled widely through the University and the region. Let me here pay tribute to Sir John Bradfield, whose brainchild the Science Park was, and who shares with King Henry VIII the distinction of making the College rich – a wealth that enables the far-sighted projects I am describing.

Bursaries and access

The first philanthropic gift to Cambridge as recorded in the annual Commemoration of Benefactors service was the 13th-century donation by Queen Eleanor, wife of Edward I, of 50 marks 'for poor scholars'. Cambridge's academic prowess has always been at its peak when the importance of supporting gifted students from all backgrounds through their studies has been best recognised.

In our own times, Trinity saw a growing need for bursary support and – building on the long practice of awarding the sort of bursary that funded Isaac Newton as a student – created the Isaac Newton Trust in 1988, with a remit to support undergraduate students in need throughout collegiate Cambridge. As a result, when the comprehensive Cambridge Bursary Scheme was set up in 2006, a model and an administration already existed and the Trust now administers the scheme on behalf of the whole community. It is surely partly due to this support that Cambridge has the lowest drop-out rate in the country, at around 1 per cent.

Sustaining diversity

Every Cambridge college is distinctive. Colleges differ markedly in age, history, size, traditions and, to an extent, purposes. This diversity is a strength, with the colleges' unique identities providing a range of options for students as well as nurturing intense loyalties – and a certain competitive spirit!

Trinity College plays a crucial role in helping to iron out the wrinkles that are a consequence of this diversity, particularly with respect to differences in endowment. Notably, Trinity supports research fellowships and teaching officers at other, less well-endowed colleges, and indeed makes substantial contributions to the Colleges Fund, thereby sustaining the vitality as well as the diversity of Collegiate Cambridge.

Looking to the future, the University is expanding physically by developing the extensive North West Cambridge site, bringing major questions about how to accomplish this in the best long-term interests of Collegiate Cambridge. I see Trinity with its thinking hat on once more, and I am grateful.

Trinity is a college like other colleges, providing attentive pastoral and academic care to generation after generation of students and supporting a Fellowship of academics – hallmarks of the Cambridge college system. It is also a college like no other. Trinity's size, distinction and wealth equip it to be a leader in that system, and its innovative and generous spirit lead it to act like one. In consequence, the College is a brilliant asset, not only to Cambridge, but to the world.

Foreword

THE MASTER, LORD REES OF LUDLOW

'Some books are to be tasted, others to be swallowed, and some few to be chewed and digested.' So thought Francis Bacon, one of Trinity's greatest alumni. This book may be savoured in all these ways, distilling Trinity's intellectual history across the centuries, our members' memories down the decades.

Trinity has helped to educate more than its expected share of the traditionally 'great and good' – judges, generals, cabinet ministers, business leaders and the like, but also those in wider walks of life – the arts, journalism, sport. And the College has a global reach: Jawaharlal Nehru, his grandson and great-grandson were all at Trinity. Our members, their memories, their influence, their friendships, are international.

I hope this book will remind all who were once at Trinity of their years here – not just of their lectures, supervisions and the tripos, but also of their College life: TCSU, May Balls, Magpie & Stump, the Lake Hunt, First and Third, choral singing, and so forth. Many will also learn things they never knew. Our undergraduate years were so crowded that we missed a great deal – we had no idea of the eminence of that elderly man who shuffled down our stairs in his slippers; we had only the sketchiest knowledge of the College's history, or of the treasures in the Wren Library.

Folk memories, too often lost but preserved here, show how much has changed since the dark days of the 1940s. More recent, easier decades have seen the admission of women, the rise in graduate-student numbers, and the succession of new buildings which have allowed us to house all junior members;

landladies and 'digs' are now extinct. Older members who remember coal hods and bootblacks will read of an unfamiliar new world – but one still recognisable. Younger members will probably not envy how things were done in their parents' and grandparents' day. The College depends on the loyalty and expertise of its staff – who feed us, watch over us, clean our rooms, or maintain our fine buildings and gardens. It is good that they too feature here. We celebrate all those who, remembered each year at Commem, 'by patient continuance in well-doing have brought honour to this house.'

We are all stewards of a legacy that stretches back to our foundation in 1546 – and further still, to the origins of our precursor college, King's Hall, in 1317. But this book does not claim to be a full history of the College: it supersedes neither the familiar slim volume by G. M. Trevelyan, nor Robert Nield's excellent financial history, *Riches and Responsibility*, but a comprehensive, scholarly, history of Trinity is even now under way.

Trinity's story, like that of any great institution, is a paradox. It seems governed by tradition. In fact, it changes with each new year of undergraduate and graduate students, with each new intake of research fellows and lecturers, with broader social changes not only in the United Kingdom but across Europe and the world.

The cumulative achievement of those who have taught here is colossal. Newton is pre-eminent – perhaps the greatest intellect

of the last millennium. But he is one among the extraordinary roll-call of scholars whose work is here outlined. There can be few other patches of ground, anywhere, on which so many great ideas have germinated as the few precious acres on which Trinity stands. The whole world has learned from those who spent their formative years here.

I have been privileged to be Master since 2004. My firmest impression is of how dedicated my colleagues are to sustaining the quality of all the College does. Trinity can also be proud of its role in the wider university, as our Vice Chancellor Emerita acknowledges. The College cannot flourish unless within a university that continues to be world-class, with a collegiate system that offers the special educational experience which, as this book shows, has offered so much to so many generations. Sharp transitions in the way students are funded are under way. Trinity, although ancient, remains a 'work in progress' and must respond to these changes, to see to it that our future is worthy of our past.

CHAPTER 1

Trinity Minds

PHILIP ALLOTT *(1955)*

There is no such thing as a characteristic Trinity Mind. For almost 700 years, there have been minds that contain the spirit of the place occupied by Trinity College. And the spirit of a place contains the spirit of the times. The *genius loci* of a university reflects and refracts the *Geist* of the *Zeit*. The intellectual history of Trinity College is an integral part of the general history of a particular civilisation.

Founded in the 13th century, the University of Cambridge was the product of a series of intellectual revolutions extending over a period of almost 2,000 years, originating in ancient Greece and ancient Israel. The medieval universities of Europe reflected a new intellectual flourishing over the course of several centuries, culminating in what has been called a 12th-century renaissance.

In 1318, responding to a petition from King Edward II, the Pope recognised the University of Cambridge as a *studium generale*, an approved institution of higher education. In 1317 Edward had established in Cambridge a Society of the King's Scholars (*scolares regis*, in Latin). By Letters Patent in 1337, his son Edward III established the King's Scholars as a Hall – *aula scolarium regis*, shortened to *aula regis*, or the King's Hall. The King's Hall was financed under 11 successive monarchs (until 1546) from the royal Exchequer.

It has been suggested that the King's Hall was the first university college in the modern sense – a residential establishment with Fellows and graduates and undergraduates, and with a tutorial system of academic and personal supervision of the students. Between 1317 and 1352, perhaps attracted by

the royal presence in the University, seven more colleges were founded in Cambridge, including Michaelhouse (1324). In 1546 the King's Hall and Michaelhouse became Trinity College.

The King's Hall, cradle of public servants, and Michaelhouse, a private foundation by Hervey de Stanton for the education of clerics, provided what the society of 14th-century England needed from higher education. The King and the Church were the pillars of the established social order. But it was a society in which the very idea of higher education contained the seeds of social change.

In subsequent centuries, there would be a series of revolutions – social, political, religious, legal and intellectual – epochs in the unceasing process of human social evolution. People whose minds have contained the spirit of the place occupied by Trinity College have played a significant part in those transforming events.

By the later 15th century the King's Hall had lost its position as the largest college in the University. For a brief period, from 1446 until he was deposed in 1461, Henry VI seemed determined to make the King's Hall into a mere adjunct of his new Eton College–King's College nexus (both founded in 1441).

Henry of Lancaster returned from refuge in France and defeated Richard III, the last of the Plantagenet kings, at the Battle of Bosworth Field in August 1485, taking the crown as Henry VII, the first of the Tudors. He brought with him from France Christopher Urswick, his chaplain and confessor, a former Fellow of the King's Hall. Three months later Henry appointed Urswick as Warden of the King's Hall, reasserting its independence from Henry VI's college.

In 1545 King Henry VIII had procured an Act of Parliament for the dissolution of the university colleges, which had been spared from the dissolution of the abbeys and monasteries following the Act of Supremacy of 1534. But people of influence in the universities and

at court, and not least his wife Katherine Parr, hastened to do what people of influence are expected to do. They exercised influence. Queen Katherine told friends in Cambridge that, in her opinion, the king 'being such a patron to good learning' would 'rather advance and erect new occasion therefor' than get rid of the colleges. Henry appointed two commissions to look into the matter, consisting of three leading officials of the two universities, including John Redman, Warden of the King's Hall and friend of Katherine Parr. We may not be surprised that they advised against dissolution. On the contrary, what the colleges needed was more money and better organisation.

Left: *Thomas Nevile (c.1548–1615) Master of Trinity (1593–1615) and Dean of Canterbury (1597–1615), by an unknown artist in about 1600. Provenance unknown.*

Far left: *Francis Bacon (1561–1626), 1st Baron Verulam and Viscount St Albans, by a painter of the English school 1611–27. Given by Peter Burrel, Esq. in 1751.*

Ecclesiastical revolutionary and doctrinal conservative and Christian humanist – and public sinner larger than life – King Henry may have seen a last opportunity favourable to the redeeming of his troubled soul in founding sister colleges at Oxford and Cambridge. Cardinal College, Oxford, was reborn as Christ Church. The King's Hall and Michaelhouse were reborn as Trinity College. The King's Letters Patent (19 December 1546) dedicated the College to the Holy and Undivided Trinity, declaring that it was to be a college of literature, the sciences, philosophy, good arts and sacred theology – that is, the new humanist agenda for higher education. It was to be called 'Trynitie College … of Kynge Henry the Eights Fundacion'. The King died on 28 January 1547.

In official documents in the 1330s, Edward III had called the King's Hall 'our college at Cambridge'. It is his royal standard, with its French *fleurs de lys* redolent of the Hundred Years War, that the College still raises above the Great Gate, formerly the gate of the King's Hall. Mary and Elizabeth, the daughters of Henry VIII – the half-Spanish and very Roman Catholic Mary and the more English and less Roman Catholic Elizabeth – both contributed to the building of the new Chapel, which was almost complete by the time of Elizabeth's state visit to Cambridge in 1564. In documents relating to that enterprise, they both referred to 'our new college in Cambridge called Henry the Eighth's College'. During a visit to the College by Queen Victoria, the Master (Whewell) asked whether the Queen would like to take a rest in 'my house' (the Master's Lodge). The Queen corrected him: '*my* house.'

It is a strange fact that it was at Trinity College in 1571 that a first volley was fired in an unholy holy war that would have very big consequences – a Puritan exodus to settlements in North America, a civil war in which a king was executed and a theocratic Cromwellian republic briefly established, the restoration of a monarchy which would display Roman Catholic tendencies leading to the removal of another king in the so-called Glorious Revolution of 1688 and the determining by Parliament of the succession to the throne (the Act of Settlement of 1701) subject to conditions, including those set out in the Bill of Rights of 1689.

In 1571 John Whitgift, Master of Trinity College, contrived to have Charles Cartwright dismissed from the Lady Margaret Professorship of Divinity and deprived of his Trinity Fellowship. Whitgift became a forceful Archbishop of Canterbury, present at the deathbed of Queen Elizabeth, placing the crown on the head of James I. Cartwright became the relentless leader of the Presbyterian opponents of the establishment of the Church of England.

Whitgift and Cartwright clashed over two perennial theological problems which had become crucial issues in the making of Reformation Christianity throughout Europe. Is personal salvation pre-determined by God? Do we have the power to determine freely our actions, independently of the will of God? But the *casus belli* was also institutional. For the Presbyterians, the Reformation had been designed to remove the corrupt hierarchical structure of the Roman Church, whereby its bishops owed allegiance to the Bishop of Rome known as the Pope.

Page from the Junior Bursar's Admissions Book, showing the signatures of the first 16 Masters of Trinity.

It seemed that the English Church, under the leadership of Whitgift, was now reproducing the same thing in a structure of bishops under the ultimate authority of the monarch as Supreme Head of the Church in England. The title was changed under Elizabeth to Supreme Governor of the Church of England. The word 'head' had seemed to imply that the monarch, like the Pope, was part of the Church hierarchy.

Whitgift was the cause of a profound long-term unintended consequence. He commissioned Richard Hooker (of Corpus Christi College, Oxford) to write a scholarly defence of the integration of the Church of England into the English constitutional structure. Hooker did so at great length in his *Of the Laws of Ecclesiastical Polity* (1593). Hooker's brilliant amalgam of the best of medieval political philosophy and the best of English constitutionalism fed directly and powerfully into the mind of John Locke (of Christ Church, Oxford) whose ideas were used to explain and justify the constitutional anomalies of 1688–9 – the Glorious Revolution – and to inspire and guide the making of the United States of America.

Six Fellows of Trinity were members of the team of scholars who created the masterpiece of English literature that we call the King James Bible of 1611. Their pragmatic instructions told them to use, so far as possible, five existing translations. Some of the most familiar and beautiful passages in this new Authorised Version were taken from those earlier translations.

John Winthrop entered Trinity College in 1602 during Thomas Nevile's magnificent architectural transformation. Not for the last time, the College must have seemed like a permanent building site. His father was the annual auditor of the College accounts. John married, for the first time, at the age of 17 and could not continue as a student. Later he said that the universities – 'the fountains of learning and religion' – had become corrupt and too expensive for students of modest means.

Winthrop became a charismatic leader of the Puritans of East Anglia, the region that provided a remarkable number of those who made the exodus to America. The Puritans had seen a threat of counter-Reformation in what seemed to be a Romanising tendency in the Church of England led by William Laud (Bishop of London from 1628; Archbishop of Canterbury from 1633), enforcing High Church doctrinal and liturgical orthodoxy.

The House of Commons showed signs of resisting the Laudian movement, and Charles I accordingly dissolved Parliament in 1629. Needing money, he recalled Parliament in 1640. An obscure and haphazard civil war followed in which Parliamentarians opposed Royalists. The tinder had been religion; but it was a conflict that reflected more general social transformations.

In 1629 Winthrop convened a meeting in Cambridge of potential sponsors of a self-governing settlement in Massachusetts. While still in England he was elected as the first Governor of Massachusetts. He preached a sermon to his ship's company of future colonists, which included John Cotton, a close friend from Trinity. His sermon would resonate throughout American history to the present day. 'For we must consider that we shall be as a City upon a Hill. The eyes of all people are upon us.'

His use of the familiar New Testament image (Matthew 5:14) would come to be seen as epitomising America's special destiny. John Cotton also preached a still-quoted sermon to the emigrating group. They were, he said, such as 'dream of perfection in this world'. The Puritan exiles declared themselves to be loyal members of the Church of England, apostles of a purified Anglicanism. Cotton was the grandfather of Cotton Mather, whose name is associated with the Salem witchcraft trials (1692) and whose vigorous teaching would usher in an 18th-century American religious revival, the first Great Awakening.

Winthrop was re-elected as Governor several times. In 1636 the General Court of Massachusetts decided to establish a 'school or college'. It was to be located at Newtowne which, in 1637, was renamed Cambridge in honour of the place where many of the leading colonists had studied. The college was renamed Harvard College (1639) in honour of John Harvard, an alumnus of Emmanuel College, Cambridge (founded in 1584 as a Puritan college), who had provided Harvard College's first main private endowment. Its first President (at the time called 'Schoolmaster') was another Trinity graduate, Nathaniel Eaton, who ruled the College controversially and was removed (1639). Its third and much respected President (1654–72), Charles Chauncy, had been a Trinity undergraduate and Fellow.

If Winthrop's attachment to his college had been closer, Harvard College might well have been called Trinity College. Adam Loftus evidently felt more warmly towards his college. Archbishop of Armagh, Archbishop of Dublin, Lord Chancellor of Ireland, he was one of a small group who obtained from Queen Elizabeth a charter (1592) establishing a university for Ireland. Loftus became the first Provost of Trinity College, Dublin. Charles Perry, Senior Wrangler, Smith's Prizeman, Fellow of the College, first Bishop of Melbourne, was one of the founding sponsors of Trinity College, the first college of the University of Melbourne (1872), and of Geelong Grammar School (1855).

Edward Coke left Trinity in 1570 and was called to the Bar (Inner Temple). He became a major actor in the great constitutional transformations of the first decades of the 17th century which would determine the whole future of the British constitution and of other constitutions inspired by the British constitution.

Coke was, at different times, a member of all three organs of the constitution – the House of Commons (Speaker in 1593), the government (Attorney General, acting as a servant of the king as much as of the courts) and the judiciary (Chief Justice of the Court of Common Pleas). The significance of this fact is that Britain's evolutionary constitutionalism would be organised, from then until now, as a trilectical struggle among the three focuses of ultimate public power.

Locke and Montesquieu and the makers of the American constitution of 1787 would recognise that the fine tuning of the checks and balances among the three great organs and functions of the constitution is the great challenge of democratic constitution-making.

Coke, in his role as a relentless judge and in his immense work of legal scholarship, including a massive series of law reports, affirmed a decisive principle. The relationship of all forms of law must be determined finally in the courts. This idea became a fundamental principle of liberal democracy, a principle which we now call the Rule of Law. All public legal power is ultimately subject to the law as determined and enforced by the courts.

Francis Bacon left Trinity in 1575 and was called to the Bar (Gray's Inn). Thomas Jefferson said (1811) that Bacon, Newton and Locke were 'my trinity of the three greatest men the world had ever produced'. Jefferson cannot have had in mind Bacon's legal career, which was as scintillating as Coke's and also included an intellectual effort to bring order to the morass of English law. However, as Lord Chancellor, he was impeached and convicted of bribery. His charming defence, which he did not present to the House of Lords committee in person, having told them that he was not well enough to attend their deliberations, was that the bribes had not affected his judgments. He was removed from his public offices in 1621.

Trinity had been useful for Bacon. It had taught him to despise what he called 'professory learning' whose practitioners 'resemble spiders, who make cobwebs out of their own substance'. For the young Bacon, the Cambridge mind had been corrupted by an Aristotelianism filtered through the medieval scholarly mind to form an arid and useless intellectualism. For the mature Bacon, the task was to take up again the intellectual challenge of the ancient Greeks – 'a total reconstruction of sciences, arts and all human knowledge, raised upon proper foundations'.

Baconism, a distinctly British form of humanism, had an important effect on the Continental European mind in the 18th century. It impressed Voltaire, who purported to idolise Bacon, Newton and Locke, using and overusing them in his devastating criticism of the old regime in France. Diderot and d'Alembert paid tribute to Bacon ('one of England's foremost geniuses') as a primary inspiration of their *Encyclopédie, ou dictionnaire raisonné des sciences, des arts et des métiers* (1751–72), a monumental work of the French Enlightenment, ordering all human knowledge in the new spirit of free thinking. The Bacon–Locke–Berkeley–Hume axis of British philosophy awakened Continental philosophers from what Immanuel Kant called 'dogmatic slumbers'. He dedicated his *Critique of Pure Reason* (1781/87) to Bacon.

Baconian humanism is not merely, or primarily, about the method of the natural sciences. It sets out a universal intellectual principle. Tradition and authority and convention are not sufficient grounds of truth. After the intellectual convulsions of the Renaissance and the Reformation, the time had come for an intellectual revolution led by the Baconian watchwords of truth and utility, treating reason as a force of mind rather than a source of truth. 'From a natural philosophy pure and unmixed,' Bacon said laconically, 'better things are to be expected.' Even he could not have foreseen the amazing achievements of the natural sciences.

In the last decade of the 17th century Charles Montagu, a close Trinity friend of Isaac Newton and sometime Fellow of the College, played a part in another kind of revolution. England had been seen as a country of 'great wealth' (the first Venetian ambassador, 1497) and London as a 'mighty city of commerce' (a German royal visitor, 1592). Britain was now leading the way into a new form of capitalism, with the accumulation of personal wealth, a market economy, industrialisation, flourishing urbanism, energised by an ancient spirit of intense individualism. It was giving birth to a new kind of human society, even a new kind of human being.

The financial system lagged far behind. Montagu, later 1st Earl of Halifax, was a lord of the Treasury from 1692 and Chancellor of the Exchequer from 1694. A Bank of England was established under the Bank of England Act 1694, creating a sound basis for paper money. The Bank, using moneys originally subscribed by private investors against the hypothetical security of receipts from taxation, lent money to the government – the beginning of the National Debt, the Consolidated Fund and government borrowing in general. A real power of Parliament over the public finances, as opposed to theoretical claims of the so-called supremacy of Parliament, had been established. The

Lampada Tradam ('I hand on the torch'), the motto and arms of William Whewell in Whewell's Court. It was also adopted as one of the magical mottoes of the poet Victor Neuburg while involved in the occult practices of another notorious Trinity alumnus, Aleister Crowley.

masters of the British economy were now materially committed to the post-1688 constitutional settlement.

Seventy years after Nevile's great work, the *genius loci* of Trinity College was disturbed again. Isaac Barrow – first holder of the Lucasian Professorship in Mathematics, Master of the College (1672–7) and a theologian with an unusually benign view of human nature – was a man of robust character. He resigned the professorship, allowing Isaac Newton to be appointed, at the age of 27. A meeting of the University central body rejected his proposal for a stately building, at least as good as that at Oxford, for ceremonial occasions. He was 'piqued at this pusillanimity' and, that very afternoon, marked out the foundations of a building 'more magnificent and costly' than the building he had proposed to the University.

His friend Christopher Wren designed a library inspired by Jacopo Sansovino's Library of Saint Mark's in Venice. Wren's matchless building, the formal lawns and peripheral planting and cheerful fountain of Great Court, the cloistered calm of Nevile's Court and the green oasis of the Fellows' Garden reflect an ancient aesthetic ideal of *lucidus ordo*, a product of mind acting in conjunction with nature, which Trinity minds contain as a lifelong spiritual possession. In the luminous ante-chapel, beneath the loquacious clock, six Trinity minds embodied in marble tell us that thought defeats time.

Richard Bentley was Master of the College from 1700 until 1742 or, more strictly speaking, until 1721 when he was removed from the mastership by the Bishop of Ely as Visitor, following protracted legal proceedings, including proceedings in the High Court, stemming from what some Fellows saw as his high-handed abuse of his magisterial power. Ignoring his dismissal, he remained in the Lodge until his death.

Statue of Byron by the Danish sculptor Thorvaldsen in the Wren Library.

Bentley arrived from London with a public reputation for combative scholarship. A Trinity tradition of classical scholarship continued from Bentley through Porson and Jebb to Housman and Cornford in the 20th century. Leading classical scholars seem to see themselves as scholarchs, laying down the law imperiously on matters of scholarship. Housman said: 'I wish they would not compare me with Bentley … Bentley is alone and supreme.' Of a translation by the apparently omniscient Benjamin ('it isn't knowledge if he doesn't know it') Jowett, Master of Balliol College, Housman said: 'the best translation of a Greek philosopher which has ever been executed by a person who understood neither philosophy nor Greek.'

The relative passivity of the two universities in the 18th century had a surprising incidental effect on the general development of British social life. Britain would be a land of connoisseurship. Not least at Trinity, which included among its undergraduates an exceptional number of the sons of the most privileged social classes, the youths studied, no matter how superficially, the literature of Greece and Rome. They peppered their writings and their speeches in Parliament with Latin and Greek quotations and allusions. They travelled to the European Continent, sometimes with a College Fellow as cicerone, learning to admire the splendid remains of ancient Greece and Rome and the new achievements of European art and architecture inspired by the Greek and Roman examples.

With this higher education in pan-European taste they formed the desire to create reservoirs of great beauty, in their town-houses and on their estates in the country, and in museums – for example, in the Fitzwilliam Museum, magnificently endowed by the 7th Viscount Fitzwilliam (1816), who had been an undergraduate at Trinity Hall. Although the British might not be able to equal the best Continental masters in the fine arts and music, they became connoisseurs and sponsors and consumers of high culture to a degree unsurpassed in Europe.

George, 6th Baron Byron, came to Trinity (1805) with a romantic family story – Norman immigrants, soldiers with Edward III at Calais and with Henry VII at Bosworth Field; a Scottish maternal grandfather descended from James I. His significance in the transformation of European consciousness exceeded even his own self-dramatising. Byron challenges Nietzsche's designation of Rousseau as the first modern man. Rousseau's self-exposing correspondence has been edited, and published in 52 volumes, by a Fellow of Trinity, R.A. Leigh (1915–87).

There is a link between Byronism and Baconism. The intense individualism and passionate subjectivity of Romanticism in the arts and literature meant that a new basis had to be found not only for knowledge but also for morality, religion and social order. Tradition and authority and convention were no longer enough. To his contemporaries throughout Europe, Byron seemed to embody energising ideas of liberty, personal and social, the profoundly ambivalent legacy of 18th-century Enlightenment and Revolution. Giuseppe Mazzini, a progenitor of modern Italy, said: 'the day will come when Democracy will remember all that it owes to Byron.' The frenzy of the modern world had begun.

By 1800 British constitutionalism had been transformed. In the relative constitutional calm of the 18th century important features of the modern constitution – cabinet government, a Prime Minister, party politics, public opinion – had emerged organically out of a miasma of structural and opportunistic corruption. By the end of the century Britain found that it had absent-mindedly acquired a worldwide empire and negligently lost the American colonies.

The intelligent Elizabethan religious settlement had saved the country from the religious wars that ravaged much of northern Europe and delayed social progress. The constitutional settlement cobbled together at the end of the 17th century had liberated the creative and energetic classes of society, fatally undermining ossified political and social structures which persisted in many other European countries.

After the Europe-wide trauma of the French Revolution and the Napoleonic Wars, it seemed to some that 'there is a feeling, becoming daily more general and confirmed … in favour of some undefined change in the mode of governing the country' (Robert Peel, the Tory, writing in 1820). Others spoke of a possible 'British Revolution' (Francis Place, the radical, writing in 1830).

The peaceful establishment of a new social order saved Britain from the social turbulence of so many Continental European countries in the 19th century. The Duke of Wellington, Napoleon's nemesis, standard-bearer of the old order, called it revolution by process of law. Two Trinity minds played a significant part in the first stages of that process. In 1832, under Earl Grey as Prime Minister (1830–4), the Reform Bill, reforming elections to the House of Commons, finally ended its dramatic passage through Parliament. The Abolition of Slavery Act 1833 ended the institution of slavery in the British Empire, a reform that, like the abolition of the slave trade (1807), responded to a grass-roots movement in public opinion.

Earl Grey shares with two other Trinity minds – the 4th Earl of Sandwich and Henry Rolls – the distinction of having useful products named in their honour: a tea, a snack food and a motor car, respectively.

Thomas Macaulay left his Trinity Prize Fellowship in 1826 and was called to the Bar (Gray's Inn). Elected to Parliament in 1830 at the age of 30, he made the most influential speeches in the Commons debates on the Reform Bill. He characterised the question of the reform of Parliament as a struggle between the young energy of one class and the ancient privileges of another. It was time to bring the legal order of society into harmony with the natural order. To oppose reform was to go against the spirit of the age – a phrase then much in vogue. And the spirit of the age was, above all, the spirit of the new world-transforming industrial age.

Macaulay told the House of Commons to remember that English history is a story of the natural progress of society towards liberty. He used this tendentious argument in support of the abolition of slavery and the removal of the civil disabilities of Catholics and Jews. It was a recurrent theme of his historical writings. Like Voltaire and Hume, he seemed to treat history-writing as a form of national self-imagining which is useful in the task of managing social change.

Macaulay's enthusiasm for social progress had a spectacular world-historical consequence. In 1835 he went to India as the legal member of the Supreme Council of India. Official British India was beset by a dramatic struggle about the future of education in India. Macaulay immediately lent his formidable rhetorical force to the side of the Anglicists, led by Charles Trevelyan, his future brother-in-law, who wanted Indian

Statue of Thomas Babington Macaulay by Thomas Woolner in the Ante Chapel.

education to be conducted in English with an essentially English curriculum, as opposed to the Orientalists who wanted to retain the existing form of education conducted in the Indian languages with a curriculum reflecting the diverse religious cultures of India. It was a struggle about the whole future of India.

Writing in 1835, Macaulay was crudely dismissive of the merits of the cultures of India and spoke lyrically of the achievements of Western civilisation. Only a progressive English-speaking India could take an effective part in the future of the world. The Anglicists won the battle. Whatever judgement one may make of the decision and its consequences for the people of India, it is good that Trinity minds would include minds from India, from the rest of the Empire and Commonwealth and, with the rise of English as a universal language, from the rest of the world.

Meanwhile, Lord Melbourne, a Trinity Prime Minister (1834, 1835–41) succeeding another Trinity Prime Minister, shared his Trinity mind with the mind of the young Queen Victoria. In affectionate *tête-à-têtes* he told her about the nature of British politics and the mysteries of the British constitution. R.A. Butler (Master, 1965–78) would share his unrivalled experience of government with the young Trinity mind of Charles, Prince of Wales.

In the two ancient English universities the great 19th-century march of progress was a thing of fits and starts. After parliamentary commissions of inquiry and much vigorous debate, the universities began to converge with the very new world, teaching all the necessary scholarly disciplines at the college level and now, at last, with lectures and libraries and laboratories at the university level.

Pivotal and emblematic in the transformation of the universities was the remarkable William Whewell (Master, 1841–66) – 'science his forte, omniscience his foible', according to the irreverent cleric Sydney Smith.

Whewell ruled the College remotely and pugnaciously. He occupied his mind with everything from mineralogy to moral philosophy. Using the new words 'scientist' and 'physicist', he proposed a philosophy of the inductive sciences (1840) that seems close to the everyday understanding of the matter among scientists themselves. Philosophy of science was central to the work of C.D. Broad, Knightbridge Professor of Moral Philosophy (1933–53), who was also prominent in a Trinity speciality, the serious study of paranormal psychic phenomena.

Whewell founded and endowed the Whewell Professorship and Scholarship in International Law, having himself produced an English translation of one of the foundational treatises of international law, *De iure belli ac pacis* (1625) by Hugo Grotius. In the tradition of Nevile and Barrow, he added substantially to the College buildings, at his own expense.

God was a problem for the 19th century. Defying Nietzsche, God was certainly not dead. Religion was still refuge and strength for many people throughout the century. For others it had become a focus of anguished doubt, Evangelical seriousness struggling with itself. The writer George Eliot, translator from the German of two of the most influential religion-troubling books (Strauss's *The Life of Jesus Critically Examined*, 1835; Feuerbach's *The Essence of Christianity*, 1841), articulated that troubled state of mind. As told by F.H. Myers, a Fellow of the College and her host on this occasion, she had a moment of sombre clarity (*c*.1868) in the avenue in the Fellows' Garden. 'God, Immortality, Duty … how inconceivable [is] the first, how unbelievable the second, and yet how peremptory and absolute the third.'

Religion had provided an answer to the problem of evil raised by the Book of Genesis. If you could no longer accept the religious answer, what other possible basis could there be for morality? In the 19th century the philosophical market was flooded with possible strategies for putting morality back on a sound basis.

As Knightbridge Professor of Moral Philosophy (1838–55), William Whewell published his own treatise on moral philosophy, as did three other powerful Trinity minds: William Clifford, mathematician, moral philosopher and philosopher of consciousness; Adam Sedgwick, Woodwardian Professor of Geology; and Henry Sidgwick, Knightbridge Professor of Moral Philosophy from 1883. Sidgwick and Eleanor Balfour, whom he married in 1876, played a leading part in the founding of Newnham College, of which Mrs Sidgwick was the second Principal (1892–1900). She was a sister of Arthur Balfour, whose Trinity mind would be the intellectually serious mind of a Prime Minister (1902–5) and Foreign Secretary (1916–19). Balfour's Gifford Lectures, published as *Theism and Humanism* (1915), influenced the thinking of C.S. Lewis.

Under the influence of Whewell, a Moral Sciences Tripos was introduced in 1851, a small event with a vast cultural background. Auguste Comte, French intellectual leader in the field, proposed

to discover 'the essential laws of human nature'. Saint-Simon, his mentor, had proposed (1813) *la science de l'homme* (human science), using a method analogous to that of the natural sciences, with the human world being seen as also manifesting the phenomenon of causation. Comte called the new movement positivism (1840) and gave the name sociology (1847) to a new intellectual discipline. In his *System of Logic* (1843) J.S. Mill discussed the prospects of what he called the moral sciences.

For Friedrich Nietzsche, for whom the problem of mankind's moral pathology was a lifelong obsession, the only possible solution was to fashion a new kind of human being, an *Übermensch*. A Trinity mind, Francis Galton, cousin of Charles Darwin and a human scientist of the scientific kind, suggested that selective breeding might be used to make better human beings.

To understand better the inherited human condition might help in making a better human future. In the new spirit of scientific historiography, Frederic Maitland (1868) created the modern discipline of British legal history. His groundbreaking work on the legal and economic development of medieval English society, and on the history of British constitutionalism, provided a rich source for the study of Britain's long-term social history and for understanding socio-economic modernisation in general. His most influential book was published (1895) with Frederick Pollock, a former Fellow, as co-author. Pollock, Professor of Jurisprudence at Oxford, was a close lifelong friend of the remarkable US Supreme Court Justice Oliver Wendell Holmes Jr. Pollock set the pattern of writing for the study and teaching of law in universities.

It may seem improbable that a small group of friends meeting mostly in rooms in Nevile's Court in the first decade of the 20th century could convince themselves that they had found the answer to the problem of moral philosophy, a conviction that would have significant social consequences.

Those present might include George Edward Moore, Lytton and James Strachey, Maynard Keynes and E.M. Forster (both from King's College), Clive Bell, Thoby Stephen, Leonard Woolf, Bertrand Russell, Desmond MacCarthy and George Trevelyan, who became an influential historian in the style of

Thomas Macaulay, his great-uncle, and Master of the College (1940–51). The friends were joined, on her frequent visits from London, by Virginia Stephen, Thoby's sister, who, in 1912, married Leonard Woolf.

Some of the friends were members of the Apostles, a Trinity-centred discussion society founded in the 1820s in conformity with the poet-philosopher Coleridge's idea of a *clerisy* of the most intellectually advanced people who would, it was supposed, redeem the world from its moral imperfections.

G.E. Moore, a Fellow of the College since 1898, was a dominant presence in the group. It was he who had, so it seemed, solved the eternal problem of moral philosophy. He was a philosopher who had briefly been tempted by a British form of the German idealism of Kant and Hegel taught, in particular, by John McTaggart at Trinity and by F.W. Bradley at Oxford. Moore taught a way of thinking (*Principia Ethica*, 1903) in which our intuitive capacity to interpret an ideal of the good can regulate our personal life and, especially, our relationships.

Opposite: *Henry Sidgwick, Knightbridge Professor of Philosophy from 1883 to 1900 and promoter of higher education for women.*

Right: *The Moral Sciences Club, 1910. Bertrand Russell is seated fifth from the left. G.E. Moore is standing in the middle row third from the right.*

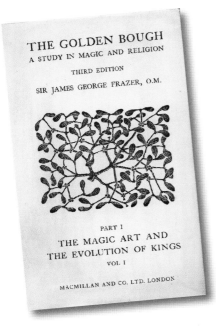

Left: *The Golden Bough by Sir James G. Frazer.*

Right: *Cartoon commemorating the Sultan of Zanzibar stunt of 1905, when Trinity undergraduate Horace de Vere Cole fooled the Mayor of Cambridge into giving 'his majesty' a civic reception and a tour of the University. De Vere Cole became a celebrated prankster, aided and abetted by both Adrian Stephen, who played the Sultan, and Adrian's sister, Virginia Woolf, who formed part of the entourage of the 'Emperor of Abyssinia' in the later Dreadnought stunt.*

His ideas had a powerful effect on all those who came in contact with him. In taking those ideas to the wider world, including the rather narrow world of Bloomsbury, his friends promoted a version of Moore's philosophy which Moore himself might not have recognised – a form of moral and aesthetic subjectivity which seemed to be a refined hedonism. Lytton Strachey had done much to dethrone Victorian values. His brother James brought into Britain a new spirit of the age contained in the writings of Sigmund Freud.

His Trinity mind was psychoanalysed by Freud himself in Vienna. He became general editor of the 24-volume Standard Edition (in English) of Freud's works. It was Strachey who, controversially, used the Latin words *ego*, *super-ego* and *id* to translate Freud's German terms *Ich*, *Über-Ich* and *Es*.

Moore was certainly no hedonist. To Russell he seemed to have 'a kind of exquisite purity'. Russell claimed to have caused Moore to tell the only lie he had ever told. Russell: 'Moore, do you *always* tell the truth?' Moore: 'no.'

Ludwig Wittgenstein was brought to Cambridge by Russell. His mind became, formally at least, a Trinity mind. Russell and A.N. Whitehead, Fellows of the College, had proposed a philosophy of mathematics (*Principia Mathematica*, 1910–13) identifying the fundamental mathematical principles that make mathematics possible. Wittgenstein proposed a philosophy of philosophy. His work is dealt with elsewhere in this volume by one of his successors as Professor of Philosophy, Simon Blackburn.

James Frazer spent almost all his academic life at Trinity. *The Golden Bough: A Study in Magic and Religion* (1890–1915), his vast work of descriptive and comparative anthropology (12 volumes in the third edition), suggested to some people that all religions, including Christianity, are miscellaneous permutations of perennial and universal mythic materials. T.S. Eliot said (1922) that Frazer's *Golden Bough* 'has influenced our generation profoundly'. It certainly influenced both Sigmund Freud in his probing of the unconscious individual mind and Carl Jung in his daring hypothesis of a collective unconscious mind of the human race.

With the apparent collapse of capitalism in the 1930s and the failure of democracy in several countries, some people began to look for an alternative social system. The problem was that the obvious alternative system was Marxist communism; but something purporting to be Marxist communism was being enacted in the Soviet Union in a ruthlessly totalitarian form. J.K. Galbraith, waiting for Keynes, excoriated free-market capitalism. Maurice Dobb (1948) and Piero Sraffa (1939) treated Marxian economics with scholarly seriousness. Some Trinity minds even treated the Soviet Union itself with a perverted form of loyalty, with dire consequences.

Edward Hallett Carr certainly took the Soviet Union seriously. He published a *History of Soviet Russia* in 14 volumes. He had been a diplomat from 1916 to 1936. Like Maynard Keynes and the Trinity historian J.R.M. Butler, he had been a member of the British delegation to the Paris Peace Conference which produced the Treaty of Versailles (1919), a searing experience. As Woodrow Wilson Professor of International Politics at the University of Aberystwyth, and as a Fellow of Trinity, he was a leader of a 'realist' school of international studies, treating relations between states as a ruthless struggle of competitive power.

Bertrand Russell's radical mind was deceived neither by Stalinist Russia nor by the rhetoric of the Cold War. In the tradition of Bacon and Macaulay, he spoke directly to the public mind, in favour of causes ranging from opposition to the First World War in 1916 to nuclear disarmament in the 1960s. He combined the analytical mind of the philosopher with a burning moral intensity.

In 1945 the world changed fundamentally. Trinity College's deepest roots are in a nation emerging into the new civilisation of the 14th century, a nation and an institution that would live through seven centuries of evolutionary change. Now a new world is emerging, presaging some kind of unstable and uncertain global civilisation. The human mind must respond yet again to new existential challenges.

The function of a university is to generate ideas at the highest level about the natural world and the human world and to share those ideas with succeeding generations of young minds. It is a function which is more crucial than ever in the making of the challenging new world of the 21st century.

We may be tempted to find ground for hope in the fact that, through seven centuries, minds affected by the spirit of this particular place have practised an unspoken trinitarian faith – a belief in the power of the human mind, in the power of the human mind to change the world, in the power of the human mind to make a better world.

––––––––•◆•––––––––

TRINITY WAS, ALWAYS IS, ABOUT TWO ELEMENTS: THE FRIENDS YOU made – and learned from – and the dons, who you learned from and made friends with. Both processes, both experiences, occurred side by side, in parallel. Trinity was filled with opening minds and opened doors.

Applying for entry and being interviewed by Kitson Clark in his rooms over Great Gate was the promise of things to come. Ideas were to be set out, challenged, shared; supervisions were times of engagement, bafflement, incomprehension, but always pointing to a time when, with effort, you might understand things you thought you never would. Peter Laslett – he of the illegible handwriting and incomprehensible lecturing style – stretched you mercilessly over theories of political thought; Walter Ullmann – his Mill Lane study strewn with hand-ground coffee beans – brought you almost face to face with the daunting abstractions of the medieval papacy; Michael Vyvyan – his rooms like a blood-strewn battlefield – intimidated you with his destruction of your essays. However, it was usually possible to remind yourself that they only spoke as they did because they assumed you might be capable of thinking as an equal – one day. It was certainly painful but also flattering and inspiring.

And there was a democracy of scholarship, or rather of knowledge. Did you want to know more about *Les Philosophes*? Call on Ralph Leigh, and he welcomed you. Did you need to test an unlikely theory about Marx? There was that young Amartya Sen living in New Court who you could talk to. Or the Chaplain, Hugh Dickinson, always ready to untangle points of religious contention.

You also learned that dons were human, fallible, vulnerable, with needs and desires. If 'sharing their weaknesses' meant that the Dean of Chapel, Father Harry Williams, dispensed gin liberally in his Great Court rooms; if such occasions often included the historian Jack Gallagher, this does not demean them as teachers and exemplars of the young. I risk sentimentality in saying that those fortunate enough to have experienced that informal circle learned a great deal from it, very enjoyably too. We were not corrupted by the experience. But it demonstrates that Trinity may have been properly hierarchical intellectually but was vastly inclusive in every other sense.

And there was and remains something awe-inspiring and chastening about belonging to an institution with such a high opinion of itself. Seated in the middle of a national culture that springs all too instinctively into the posture of the apologetic

Matriculation, 1967. Richard Chartres, now Bishop of London, poses at the start of his final year for a photograph in the Library, taken by the Sub-Librarian, Arthur Halcrow.

cringe – the apologies ranging from the intellectual (am I too clever?) to the cultural (am I too elitist?) to the social (am I too posh?) – Trinity was always openly proud of being superb at what it stood for. If it meant being better than someone else then so be it. This too was a lesson. Never apologise for being excellent.

These are abstractions. There was nothing abstract but rather intensely physical about the winter mists on the Backs, the wide, cold night skies framed by the magnificent profiles of Great Court, the summer seductive somnolence of Nevile's Court's classical perfection. Blessed, undoubtedly; privileged, of course; unforgettable, oh yes.

Sir John Tusa (1956)

I GRADUATED IN '68 SO TECHNICALLY I AM A SOIXANTE-HUITARD. There was some political turbulence in the University at the time, a dull echo of *les événements* in Paris, but Trinity under the sagacious hand of Rab Butler conducted its disagreements with good humour and decorum.

The Trinity I entered in 1965 was still part of Churchill's Britain. It was still possible to enjoy the thrill of climbing in after the Great Gate was locked for the night. Undergraduates were expected to dine regularly, be-gowned in Hall, although what was known as 'Trinity rubber chicken' made the meals somewhat less than Lucullan feasts. There were rumours that other colleges fared better but the real pleasure was in the conversation.

I had never lived away from home and I was astonished by some very simple revelations in my first year in New Court. Communal dining was a quite new experience and I discovered that people were often invited to stay in other people's houses during the 'vacs'. I was particularly innocent, but in many ways we all came up with much less experience than today's undergraduates. The College was, like most of our schools, all male, and there did not seem to be much pressure to prove one's sexual prowess.

My kindly and tolerant bedder in Bishop's Hostel explained the rules which she hoped would carry us through the year in harmony. She explained that she turned a blind eye to 'young gentlemen who had young ladies in their rooms'. She was easy about 'young gentlemen who preferred young gentlemen – if you get my meaning'. But then she said sternly, 'What I won't put up with is vegetarians'. The previous occupant of the set had been an anthropologist whose vegetarian cookery learned in North Africa had ruined the saucepans. Many years later, in an act which was possibly delayed adolescent rebellion, I did become a vegetarian.

I experienced great kindness at Trinity, not least from the hospitable Dr Robson. I remember a somewhat aggressive fresher demanding to know, 'Dr Robson, have you ever really lived?' To which he made a mild response, 'Well, there was that one year in Whewell's Court.'

Both the buildings and the story of the College conspired to elevate thought and widen horizons. The ante-chapel with its marmoreal giants still voyaging 'o'er strange seas of thought' worked powerfully on the imagination, while the preaching of that most undeanly Dean, Harry Williams, helped so many of us to begin that exploration of the shadow side within, which plays such a significant part in sustaining creativity throughout life.

(Richard Bishop of London) Richard Chartres (1965)

THERE IS THE SAME MAGIC NOW ABOUT ENTERING THE tranquillity of the Great Court that there was when I first arrived as a Trinity undergraduate some 43 years ago.

Those of us born shortly after the Second World War have sometimes been referred to as the lucky generation – and perhaps we were. Gone, or nearly gone, was the post-war austerity of the

1940s and 1950s and there undoubtedly was a whiff of change in the air. Yet, although there were the normal exams to be worked for with their attendant periods of anxiety, there was also time for wide-ranging discussion and perhaps rather less angst about employment prospects.

The 1960s were on occasions a difficult period of transition but, at the time, Trinity was particularly fortunate to have as Master Rab Butler who, in partnership with his incomparable wife Mollie, was able to defuse any potentially explosive issues, having already proved himself well versed at national level in 'the art of the possible'. And while there were rumblings of student protest, there was also a reassuring sense of continuity, epitomised by some highly colourful resident Fellows whose exploits were often the subject of undergraduate gossip and mirth. Who can forget the sight of F.A. Simpson ruthlessly decapitating any excessive plant growth with his secateurs (when not engaged in a stand-off with A.S.F. Gow), or of Besicovitch on his meandering, but well-trodden path across the grass of Great Court?

Equally memorable was the Chapel where we were inspired by two successive Deans at the forefront of theological thinking, Harry Williams and John Robinson – a succession marked by Bob Robson in one of his self-mockingly named 'Last Poems':

What shall we do without Harry?
What shall we do when he's gone
And we're left to be buried and prayed for
By 'Honest to God' Bishop John?

And then there was the multitude of extraordinarily loyal and understanding College servants – the porters, the bedders, the kitchen staff – whose cheery greeting and down-to-earth common sense were able to inject a welcome reality into our sometimes surreal existence.

E6 New Court was my home for my first two years. A small, communal bathroom had recently been installed on the first floor of the staircase which spared passing tourists or visitors the alarming sight of my pottering across New Court in my bathing towel. It was a quiet corner of the College, where the early-morning silence was broken only by the weekly refrain of 'O come

Prince Charles entering Great Gate as an undergraduate with the Master, Rab Butler, pursued by a throng of photographers, 1967.

all ye faithful' from the local refuse collector who, poor man, may well have been rebuked when news about his dawn chorus was leaked to the newspapers. He did, however, form the basis of a sketch in which I featured in a dustbin in the Trinity Revue. These annual shows enabled a number of us to make complete fools of ourselves (I seem to remember once coming on to the stage under an opened umbrella, uttering 'I live a sheltered life'), as well as poking fun at Establishment figures both within and outside the College; indeed, one or two of the College Fellows were alleged to have harboured secret hopes that they would gain further prominence by being pilloried in these performances.

My final year was spent in Great Court. Here, occasionally, the peace was disturbed by late-night revellers piling out of the College bar and attempting to sprint round a full circuit of the Court while the clock was still striking midnight. But my abiding memory is one of the silence at night-time 'when the busy world is hushed', punctuated only by the rhythmic chimes of the clock and the gentle flow of water cascading from the fountain. Magical. Yes, we were all very lucky.

Charles, HRH The Prince of Wales (1967)

MOTHER TERESA SMILED SERAPHICALLY. THE DUKE OF Edinburgh guffawed, 'Why on earth would you want to do that?' Rab Butler had just informed them that, having graduated that day, I now hoped to become Prime Minister of Jamaica. Not an odd ambition for a Trinity man, I thought, although in our previous chats Rab warned of the pitfalls of politics. The point was that Trinity encouraged us to believe everything was possible, and I did over the years get to do many journalistic assignments in and about the West Indies, so fulfilling my adolescent dream another way. And the conversation with distinguished interlocutors, surrounded by hooded contemporaries, that June 1979 day in Nevile's Court was a fine finale to Trinity, which had given us three years of enlightening interactions.

History was stimulating and fun, but most of the golden memories arose elsewhere. It was good preparation for life as a broadcaster and journalist, which in turn prepared me well for the last four years of making key decisions about London as Chairman of the Heritage Lottery Fund's Committee for the metropolis.

In 1976 I was not the typical Oxbridge undergraduate. Trawling old papers and diaries, I found a cutting from the *Sunday Express* of December 1970 with the headline 'Coloured boy from foster home wins free place at Winchester': 'Wesley, 12, who has overcome every obstacle says, "I want to go to university – Cambridge if possible".' May 1975's diary records 'a very wet day'. On that first visit I felt Trinity was the place for me. The physical impact of being in Great Court, imposing yet intimate, and the English Baroque splendours of Nevile's Court: where better to study history than in a place oozing it? Good enough for Prince Charles, too. I also felt a connection with Rab Butler, having swotted up his sagacious memoir *The Art of the Possible*. What I didn't know until 35 years later was that Rab had already helped shape my life; one of his wartime educational reforms produced a scheme (the Fleming Boys – after the Scottish judge who fleshed out the details) for state-school pupils to get county-council funded places at public schools (Winchester also paid half), and I was one of the last beneficiaries of this scheme. I was a bit of a social experiment but in that era poorer students all benefited from a full subsistence grant and universities didn't charge UK nationals for tuition; we could join the elite through ability, luck and hard work. 1976 was the penultimate all-male year, living and dining in a style handed down from the Tudors. So much has changed.

One privilege of those undergraduate days, through both the Union and the Fabian Society, where I became an elected committee hack, was encountering the leading political figures of the day. Sunny Jim Callaghan, the defenestrated Ted Heath, grumpy and silver; Thorneycroft, Williams, Foot, Owen in their pomp. Spending time with world historical figures like Margaret Thatcher, Indira Gandhi and Benazir Bhutto. Or perambulating with cultural stars such as Quentin Crisp and C.P. Snow. You learn more than you realise at the time from such encounters and they give an extra perspective to meetings with today's politicians and cultural grandees.

The dons were equally distinguished; like the great medievalist Walter Ullmann, a refugee from Nazi Austria, who himself looked and sounded like an ultramontane pope. We learned the history of the world with Jack Gallagher, Anil Seal, John Lonsdale; 19th-century Britain with Boyd Hilton; the origin of modern wars with Norman Stone; social history with Roy Porter (whose book on London is very useful for speeches). You could be up all night reading Plato or Marx.

I've come across Trinity men and women throughout my career, such as the policeman Wilf Knight who saw me on the other side of the lines during the Brixton riots (although a local resident, I was actually there in peace for *Newsnight*). Later I had great fun doing a consumer show, *Value for Money*, with Trinity's own Vanessa Feltz, where we both imagined we were dumbing down as the cameras

Wesley Kerr as an undergraduate in 1976

filmed us at crazy angles while we simplified complex issues. What we all have as Trinity alumni is a way of looking and a confidence in asserting. And lots of random memories of late-night chats round gas fires, and ambitious gatherings, as I found in a letter to my late foster mum Gertrude Hilleard from March 1979. 'I gave a party/bop, in my rooms for 30/40 people preceded by dinner for 8 (*cooked on the single gas ring*). I asked people to bring bottles and the whole thing (with chicken paprika for dinner) only cost £10 and went on from 7.30pm – 4am.'

I recently asked my sister Fiona how I changed in those years at Trinity, and she said simply, 'you became an adult'.

Wesley Kerr (1976)

Blue Boar Court.

I WAS FORMALLY AT TRINITY ON AND OFF FROM SEPTEMBER 1988 until June 1993, when I did a PhD in modern and medieval languages.

The first thing I would like to say about that time is that *there was* time. There was time for everything – more time than I have had before or since. Doing a PhD at the age of 21, being unmarried and not having a job, living alone, I spent three hours a day perhaps on the thesis and the rest of the time I was free to think; to read and to study other topics by myself in my beautiful new room in Blue Boar Court (with its own bathroom and kitchenette); to pray; to exercise and to socialise with my small circle of friends. Trinity left me alone. My tutor, the late Dr David Kelley, who was very kind and obliging in anything I needed, saw me only once or twice a term. He asked: 'Everything all right?' I would say, 'Yes, great, thank you,' and we would proceed to talk about everything and anything else but my thesis. At the end of the first year I passed my 'viva', at the end of five years I received my PhD and there were no complications. I appreciate that approach because in those five years I sowed the seeds for many of the things I would think about, or write about, or do, in later life. I did not have to attend courses, or punch in time somewhere or learn someone else's artificial curriculum and canon of shifting information. I had time for myself, and for meditation and contemplation, and that was what I most needed.

The second thing I would like to say is that Trinity made everything easy and available: procedures were easy, administration was neat, and my needs were catered for (I had to leave after my first year for military service and I was allowed to do that; and then I had to leave again during my fourth year to attend to my brother who had cancer, and I was allowed to do that too, with no questions asked and no fuss). Also, academically speaking, if I wanted the best library one could imagine; the best minds to engage with (students and teachers alike); the best lectures one could hope for – all were available. If I did not (and usually I just wanted to be alone) that too was facilitated. The Fellows, the porters, the staff were all very kind and discreet.

The last thing I would like to say is that the Fellows and students at Trinity College in particular seemed much less 'particular' than those of other Colleges: they seemed as if they had less to prove; they were more genteel; less politicised; less anxious; less worried about labels; less worried about outwardly affirming their own individual identities. Doubtless this was due to Trinity's illustrious history, its beautiful architecture and its great wealth. For me this was a relief; I always felt comfortable at Trinity, among the many students passing through who were bonded precisely by their lack of need for artificial bonds. I shall ever be grateful to God for my time there.

HRH Prince Ghazi of Jordan (1988)

CHAPTER 2

College Staff

HARRY EYRES *(1976)*

There is about one [bedmaker] to each staircase, that is to say, to every eight rooms. For obvious reasons they are selected from such of the fair sex as have long passed the age at which they might have had any personal attractions.

From C.A. Bristed, *An American in Victorian Cambridge*, Exeter, 2008 (first published 1852)

Trinity undergraduates tend to think the world and the College in particular revolve around them. They are not entirely wrong, because teaching young people is at the heart of Trinity's activity and mission, but they tend to underestimate their transience. They may in particular fail to notice or take for granted some of the more permanent and less showy aspects of the College's life: the people who keep the place ticking reliably like a good old clock; who ensure that the precincts are kept safe and beautiful and calm and quiet for learning, and all the other things that go on here; that there is food to eat; that rooms are kept clean, services maintained and mail delivered. An analogy is the world of the theatre where those who strut their stuff on stage are supported by the essential backstage crew of stage managers, technicians, prompters, who do not get the limelight but without whom the show would never start.

Undergraduates spend three or four years at Trinity, but others, not just Fellows, make their lives here: gardeners, porters, bedders, handymen. Sometimes jobs are passed down from father to son or mother to daughter. These are the people who can form a steadier view of College life, who can see changes

Previous pages: *Trinity bedmakers and porters, 1884.*

Right: *The Fellows' Bowling Green and King's Hostel.*

and continuities over decades. They can also see themselves in the light of an even longer history, carrying on traditions and occupying posts going back 700 years, to the very beginnings of the University and the College, before it even became Trinity.

Gardeners have been working the plots of land which now comprise Trinity for much longer than the 460-odd-year official history of the College. The recently retired head gardener George Thorpe has a particular interest in and affection for the strip of garden behind the Chapel, between the Master's Garden and the wall of St John's, now known as the Fellows' Bowling Green, with its south-facing wall and 25-foot-high beech hedge, and in between them the alley of mown grass for bowling. This was part of the original garden of King's Hall, one of the two houses or colleges which merged to form Trinity, and so dates back to the 14th century.

Thorpe was put in charge of it when he came to Trinity and discusses the changes he has made, and the care taken over upkeep, with quiet pride. 'I proposed increasing the width of the border from five feet to nine feet, based on Gertrude Jekyll's ideal dimension of a border. Nine feet allows three different layers of planting, one behind the other, and so a long season of flowering.' The cutting of the outsize hedge requires a lightweight scaffold tower three decks high which can be moved around on castors. Perfectionism at Trinity is not just the preserve of fussy dons.

Thorpe is a thoughtful man with an idiosyncratic outlook and a sly sense of humour; you would not be surprised to learn he was a practitioner of Zen Buddhism. He is a local man, brought up in Grantchester (his father did a wartime degree), who showed an interest in plants from a very young age ('I was meant to work here'). He is also a graduate of Jesus College, a fact he did not immediately reveal at his job interview with the members of the garden committee, fearing he might be considered over-qualified. When he disclosed the fact and voiced his fear, his interviewers told him tartly, 'We'll be the judges of that.' But Thorpe noticed that they began to speak in polysyllables.

His eye for history ranges from the distant past to the more recent. He likes to show visitors the bowls used by Fellows (fewer and fewer, it seems) in sets of three, with different biases, some

200 years old and resembling ancient Gouda cheeses. But some Fellows' habit of sending errant bowls deep into the herbaceous border is recalled less affectionately.

A door in the wall leads from the Fellows' Bowling Green into the Master's Garden. This provides an opportunity for Thorpe to reflect frankly on different occupants of the Lodge and their spouses. 'Rab Butler had his own gardener; the garden committee were unsure of their ground but it seemed the Master had autonomy.' Among spouses Lady Huxley is recalled with particular affection: 'She was a keen gardener and came from a family which had servants so she was easy dealing with gardeners. She used to weed the border herself.' Amartya Sen 'enjoyed figs'.

A walk down the Avenue, with its double rows of limes planted originally in 1780, across the river and into the Fellows' Garden, a 19th-century creation, allows Thorpe and fellow gardener Peter Rocket, with an Irish lilt in his voice and a keen Hibernian wit, to reflect on the idiosyncratic habits of Fellows, not always to the gardens' advantage.

Rocket is happy to point out Simpson's Hampton (use your knowledge of Cockney rhyming slang to navigate to 'wick' and then beyond), a yew tree which the eccentric theologian Dr F.A. Simpson used to prune with his own pair of secateurs. Then there was a certain Dr Sraffa, who used to wander around on the Backs chatting to tourists, especially young female ones, whom he used to invite back to his rooms and regale with manuscripts.

Spending time with these gardeners (and Trinity employs no fewer than 11) opens up long vistas of time and suggests a much slower rhythm, attuned to the seasons and the lifespans of trees, than the frenetic rush of undergraduate terms. These people are guardians of something you could almost call sacred, Trinity's greatest hidden expanse and resource, part of the College's soul, and seem sure of their calling.

The Porters' Lodge is hardly a hidden part of Trinity; it is of course the first port of call, the essential point of entry and reference, occupying the right side of the Great Gate. Nothing, in theory, gets in or out of the College without the porters' cognisance and approval. But what really goes on in the Lodge, and the varied and interesting lives the porters live, is often a mystery to undergraduates. Trinity porters, the only ones at Cambridge still to wear the traditional garb of bowler hats, are the most recognisable of Trinity's staff. Once upon a time they were the most feared, and some still find them intimidating.

The porters' main job may be keeping students and dons safe but they are also, of course, charged with maintenance of discipline. The late Head Porter George Hales and fellow porter Jim McCristal caught Prince Charles cycling across New Court in 1967. 'I told him to get off the grass,' McCristal is reported to have said. On this occasion, and probably unusually, porter's authority did not prevail. The Prince smiled but did not dismount: 'He was trying to get away from his private detective and he was taking a short cut down to Queen's Avenue. Well, once he was on that we couldn't touch him. It belonged to his mother.' There were no hard feelings between the Prince and the Head Porter – quite the reverse. They kept in friendly contact until Hales's death.

George Thorpe, who retired as Head Gardener in 2010, with Peter Rocket.

Opposite: *David Phillips, Senior Porter.*

Below: *George Thorpe accompanying the Queen in the Avenue in 1996.*

More serious disciplinary issues can arise – broken windows, a small clique of vandals – but on the whole the emphasis, and the image of the porter, have shifted. In the old days most porters were ex-military and 'students had to be careful', as Hales put it. Now, with the huge increase in tourism, the emphasis is more on public relations. More than one porter has said that 'we like to keep things friendly'.

Certainly you would not find a less overbearing or martial character than senior porter David Phillips, who has worked at Trinity since 1978. If the porters represent part of Trinity's hinterland, then Phillips's own personal hinterland is remarkably extensive. As well as his day (and night) job, Phillips is President of the Trinity Sports and Social Club, and his serious hobbies include photography and writing.

His writer's and photographer's eye gives him a keen insight into changes and continuities. 'Things have changed, slowly but surely. The students have certainly changed; they're under more pressure to get a good degree, not just a degree, and spend more time studying and less enjoying themselves.' A particular change is the move away from parties and discos – 'discos have died a death' – towards socialising in smaller groups. 'A lot of that is cost, I suppose.'

He also reports a decline in the kind of high jinks once associated with Trinity undergraduates, which might have made porters' lives difficult, but which they also sneakingly admire. These, as recalled by the College handyman Trevor Mitchley,

included painting all the saddles of the bicycles outside the Porters' Lodge pink; placing traffic cones on the heads of the four statues on the roof of the Wren Library; and the periodic moving around of the decoy duck kept up in the rafters of Hall.

The job of the porter has evolved also. 'I came here when I was young,' Phillips continues. 'There was a group of us who were young, which was good because the job was more physical, dealing with parties and so on. Perhaps we related better to students because we weren't so stuck in our ways.'

One unfortunate development has been an increase in break-ins, especially the theft of laptops. 'It's a difficult balance to strike,' reflects Phillips, 'between security and ease of access for everybody. You don't want to make the place like a prison.' Far from becoming a prison, Trinity has become a major tourist attraction. 'We started charging 18 years ago; it was a way of controlling numbers. Of course once you admit tourists they're all going to come to Trinity and ignore the other colleges,' he says with pardonable pride. 'We got to the point where the floors were getting worn down – and how do you replace them?'

Other changes include the decrease in the volume of post and computerisation. 'We used to have to do the postage accounts by hand – everything had to be entered in ledgers. That was drawing the short straw! Now the computers make it all much easier.'

But portering remains a very human job, and that is the side Phillips finds satisfying. 'I like to put myself in the shoes of the person on the other side of the counter – they're visitors, probably feeling a bit lost. I find it rewarding to help them out.' Porters all have first-aid training, and the occasional health incident is also an opportunity 'to help somebody'. It might surprise many to learn that porters, renowned for their combative spirit, have a touchy-feely side. David Bush, an assistant porter, who did a PhD in history at Clare Hall under the supervision of Jack Gallagher and went on to work for 20 years in special-needs education, says that undergraduates increasingly see porters as people they can talk to about personal matters. From bulldog to unofficial counsellor; an unexpected transformation.

Obviously something has kept David Phillips, a man of very lively mind and multifarious interests, in the job for over 30 years. Part of it is the variety of the duties, 'dealing with students,

Trinity bedmakers, 2010.

it were. Not many secrets can be kept from them. Some may feel that the supposed novelty and shock value of Tracey Emin's *My Bed* was rather old hat; they have to deal with that kind of thing every day. The distinguished Cambridge Professor of Philosophy and Trinity Fellow Simon Blackburn reports that when he was an undergraduate, his bedmaker discovered in his wastepaper basket the evidence of a sexual encounter and told him off (or congratulated him) in the following terms: 'Ooh Mr Blackburn, you dirty bugger!'

Once again there is more to the job of bedmaker than meets the eye. The cleaning is one thing – not very interesting in itself, as Janet Taylor, bedmaker for many years in the Wolfson Building, admits. But the quasi-maternal 'looking after' of students, the unofficial pastoral care, the real enduring friendships, are quite another. Some undergraduates may choose to keep their bedmaker at a distance. But to those prepared to open up a bit, there could be presented one of the best surprises of College life, with benefits to be reaped on both sides.

Janet Semple, bedmaker on E staircase New Court from the 1960s until the 1990s, is unabashedly nostalgic. 'They were gentlemen, gentlemen,' she enthuses. 'We called them Mr and they called us Mrs, but I didn't like that. And I remember when it changed: there was an undergraduate whose name was Aston, and he said, "If you call me Mr Aston once more I'm not letting you in my room. My name is Clive. And I'm not calling you Mrs Semple any more. What's your name?" And so I told him my name was Janet. And from then on they all started it.'

That seems to have been a high point of student–bedmaker relations. In general, though, Janet Semple tells a story of a decline of cordiality, perhaps an overall decline of sociability. 'They used to do a lot of banter; in those days you could have a nice laugh and a chat. Nowadays they're so full of themselves, they don't take notice of anybody. If you tell them to keep their room tidy they'll give you a look.' As for the coming of women, Mrs Semple is forthright: 'It was the worst thing ever when the girls came in. It should never have happened. Give me boys any day!'

You can tell that Janet Semple, now in her 70s, was once both very pretty and quite formidable. One of her biggest challenges came with the arrival of Prince Charles on her staircase in

with the Fellowship, with the general public'. He reflects that portering 'is one of those jobs that on the outside looks easy but there's a lot more to it than meets the eye. You've got to be a good man manager, you've got to be able to deal with such a wide range of people, people from all walks of life.' As far as the students are concerned, 'a lot of people think it's still *Brideshead Revisited*. It's not; those days have gone.'

Another attraction is the camaraderie of the Porters' Lodge, which brings together a bunch of people from different working backgrounds but with many shared interests. 'When you're in the team working nights, and you get quiet patches, you've always got something to talk about. One of the lads is learning French – he wants to move to France when he retires. We have one or two computer geeks.' Not all porters are 'lads'; until recently the deputy head porter at Trinity was a woman, Helen Stephens.

Undergraduates may be increasingly coming to see porters as friends rather than fearsome figures of discipline, but the chummiest relationship with a porter is unlikely to match the potential closeness of the bond an undergraduate can have with his or her bedmaker. Bedmakers see undergraduates in the raw, as

Waiting staff at an alumni event.

New Court. It was decided that the Prince should have his own bedmaker, of more homely aspect than the attractive Mrs Semple, and as she continues, 'We were told we had to move off. And I said, "We're not moving".' She threatened to go the *Cambridge Evening News* to reveal how the Prince, contrary to official statements, had been given special treatment (an enlarged kitchen); she kept her staircase, and friendly relations with the heir to the throne.

Other bedmakers echo Mrs Semple's regrets about a change to more instrumental relationships. Shirley Matthews recalls: 'Students were more jolly and friendly towards each other as well as towards the bedmaker. They used to make us cups of tea; sometimes they took bedmakers out on punts. And they gave us presents, not that we asked for them or expected them. Nowadays the students are more separate.' Mrs Matthews also remembers that 'students used to have lots of parties. There were bottles, bottles, bottles.'

But relationships between bedmakers and students are not all about banter and cups of tea. Bedmakers can see students at their best and their worst, and at their most vulnerable. Everyone knows that student life can be a roller coaster of great highs and

deep troughs. Often, it seems, the bedmaker is the first person to notice the danger signals and raise the alarm.

Janet Taylor recalls: 'You had to use discreet ways of making sure they were OK. There was one Australian girl who became very anxious over exams; when she was distressed she used to pull her eyebrows out so I knew that was a danger sign. But she did very well in the end.'

Sometimes it was a case of excessive parental pressure. Janet Taylor again:

I had this really nice Chinese boy who was studying medicine and at the end of his third year he got a 2:2. I went into his room on graduation day and saw he was packing to leave. I said, 'You can't do that, that's such a waste.' He said, 'My parents are so disgusted they're not even coming to graduation day.' He went to graduation day with a friend and while he was out I decorated his room with congratulations cards, and then I left. I didn't find out he'd stayed until years later when I went to Addenbrookes Hospital with my husband, who had cancer. This student had done well and was working there and he said to my husband, 'Your wife used to make such nice chocolate cakes and bring them in for us. She spoilt us.'

Maria Liston, Manciple.

Some stories are still more dramatic: Shirley Matthews tells one of 'a girl who took a massive overdose. When she came back from hospital my friend and I gave her a good talking-to. We said, 'Life is so precious, there's more to it than getting the best mark. Go out and enjoy it.' And she became a Fellow of another College.' Some of the wisest, most helpful and consoling words a student could hear might come from a bedmaker rather than an academic.

The rewards of the job for bedmakers and other members of staff do not just come from interaction with students. There is also the collegiate camaraderie of clubs and outings. Bedmakers recall with affection the annual outing to Yarmouth: lunch, and then a wander, then the theatre and supper afterwards, and 'a good sing-song'. But even here one of the strangest traditions of Oxbridge's largest college came into play. Janet Semple refers to the bedmakers of Whewell's Court as 'that side of the road'. For Janet Taylor, speaking of the tribal division of bedmakers on different sides of Trinity Street, 'It was them and us. There was no malice, just we never saw them and they never saw us. But we all congregated at Yarmouth.' Presumably they did at least exchange some words with each other. Bedmakers now retired regret the change from the Yarmouth outing to the larger, combined College staff excursions to different resorts such as Skegness and Brighton.

In summary, is it change or continuity which dominates the picture? For Trevor Mitchley, 'Trinity hasn't changed a great deal. Its heart still beats the same.' Surveying the immaculate expanse of Great Court, seeming to contradict Heraclitus's assertions that 'everything flows' and 'you cannot step into the same river twice', or the beautiful and hidden gardens, it is hard to disagree. But David Phillips reckons that in the 30-odd years he's been working at Trinity 'it's changed a heck of a lot'. He is referring not just to the computerisation of the Porters' Lodge, the coming of smart cards and tourists, but to more profound changes. Society 'is more egalitarian. But Trinity still should be elitist – elitist because people are bright, clever, talented. You need an elitist university. As for ethnic minorities, we just see them as students.' He does not mention the admission of women, the most dramatic change in the entire history of the College.

A further paradox is that the emergence of a more egalitarian society has not necessarily made relations between staff, students and Fellowship more fraternal. It could even have introduced new tensions. But at least there are opportunities for women in places no one would have expected a few decades ago. Who, for example, would have predicted the coming of a female Manciple, occupying a post, in charge of the service of food at High Table, whose title sounds positively Chaucerian?

Maria Liston's personal journey, leaving her home town of Orense in northwest Spain as a 20 year old, coming to work at Trinity first as a casual waitress, and then becoming the first female Manciple in the College's history, is worthy of a chapter in itself. She believes 'Trinity changes slowly, but it does change. The College has become much more family-oriented. We have Sunday lunches now for Fellows and their families.' Some Fellows 'treat you like an equal, and I have some very good friendships with Fellows, but some treat you like a servant. It will take a long time to change that.' All the same, she recalls one particular Master who showed uncommon humanity. 'There was a bakers' strike, or a flour-millers' strike, in the late 1970s and who would have thought Lord Butler would say, "Maria, have you got enough bread at home? Because there's no reason for you not to take the leftovers when we've finished." Who would have expected that from a man in his position?'

This highly capable, intelligent and articulate woman wanted to be a doctor, but 'at that time, coming from a working-class background in Spain, it was possible to send only one child to university'. That child was her brother, who became a historian. But Mrs Liston, from early on, has regarded Trinity as a kind of home from home. 'It reminded me of Santiago, which is an important university town in my part of Spain, Galicia. Still sometimes I watch the sunset from Great Court and say to myself, "Wow!" Or there are frosty winter mornings, when Great Court looks fabulous. I will never become a doctor now, but I am happy with what I'm doing. If I had my time over again, knowing what I know now, I'd do some things differently, but I'd do it all over again.'

AFTER COMING DOWN IN 1953 I LEFT FOR THE UNITED STATES to work for an American company. In the latter part of 1971 I was in England on business and was looking for a boarding school for my son. One school was near Cambridge so I asked the driver to take me to Trinity. Some months before I had had a very serious accident so hobbled into the Porters' Lodge on crutches. The Head Porter looked up and said, 'I have not seen you lately.' I told him that I had not been back to Trinity since going down in 1953. He then amazed me by saying, 'Would you be interested in seeing your rooms? You know that Prince Charles had rooms above yours.' He turned to a porter and said, 'Please give the keys to P1 to Mr Crawford.' When visiting Trinity a number of years later I recounted this story to a porter, who said, 'Oh, that was Mr Prior. He remembered everyone who graduated from Trinity.' What a prodigious memory and what a great College servant.

Douglas Crawford (1950)

I WAS LUCKY ENOUGH TO HAVE ROOMS IN GREAT COURT IN MY third year at Trinity (1964–5), on the second floor of G staircase, at parapet level. The staircase was unusual in that G1, ground floor, left, harboured the Junior Bursar, Dr Glauert's office, reached principally through the College Office, while over him on the first floor, in G3, was the Rev. F.A. Simpson, by then in his 80s, crusty and deeply eccentric. My set (main room and bedroom off), G5, was in turn immediately above Simpson's, while another student lived in G6 across the top landing, with whom I shared a kitchen and a WC.

Life on G staircase was different, to say the least. Simpson had been in his set of rooms since the days when Trinity's electricity supply was 110 volts. When the College was rewired for 240 volts, he refused point blank to allow the electricians into his rooms. So, in the 1960s, the rest of Trinity and Cambridge ran on 240, while a transformer above the entrance to G staircase dropped the voltage down to 110 just for Simpson and the two top-floor rooms. The maintenance department kept a supply of 110-volt bulbs for our lights and, because I had a record player, I was given a small transformer to step the current back up to 240 volts.

It was at night that Simpson was at his most alarming. Terrible groans and bellowing noises would periodically rise up from the room below, such that the first time I heard them I was sufficiently concerned to go and tell the night porter in the adjoining gatehouse in case Simpson was in his death throes. The porter merely replied that that was what Simpson did. A soul in turmoil and despair it seemed to me.

Mornings were not without incident either because G staircase had a bedder who had a cleft palate and a severe speech impediment. Unfortunately, I don't remember her name, but understanding her took practice and patience. Simpson loathed her and could be heard hurling insults at her most mornings, while she shouted back equally forcefully. Stomping up the stairs, she would bring me all the post for the staircase. When she had done this several days in succession, saying (I eventually decoded) that she had forgotten her glasses and could I please tell her which was whose, it dawned on me she could not read.

After I'd been there for a few weeks, one of the porters asked me with a grin how I was getting on with Simpson and the bedder. Apparently she was the only person prepared to put up with him. It seems his rooms were pretty dirty because he hated interference, and she couldn't care less, so they were well matched! The porter (I think it was Mr Nix) went on to tell me about her night out, which was to go to the Rex cinema when they had live wrestling on stage. He said it didn't do to sit too near to her because she would get very rowdy and excited, egging on the wrestlers and if she was clutching a bottle of cider or something, it would get sprayed around!

So life on G staircase was quite special really. Oh, and there was another advantage. The Junior Bursar had a couple of secretaries who sat in the window of a small office next to his as you walked from Great Gate. The tall one with her hair pulled back from her face was called Maggie. Maggie, oh Maggie, where are you now ….

Alan Lloyd (1962)

I was part of the last Trinity generation to lodge with landladies. During my stint, many of us spent at least one year out in Portugal Street or another of the Trinity-owned terraced houses behind the Round Church, where we boarded under the beady eye of formidable College-appointed minders. These were generally retired College porters or bedders, who knew everything there was to know about Trinity and ran their establishments in the spirit of seaside landladies in a McGill cartoon, with much twitching of curtains and numerous petty rules ('Gentlemen are requested NOT to SMOKE in the bathroom').

I spent my second year lodging with a legendary couple, Mr and Mrs Dunn, who ran 19 Portugal Street for two decades. I never knew their Christian names, they were only ever Mr and Mrs Dunn. Mr Dunn had retired as a porter from the Great Court Porters' Lodge; his bowler hat remained a prized possession, displayed on a hatstand in their basement sitting room. Timid Mrs Dunn wore a flowery housecoat over her dress. The Dunns seldom left their cramped basement quarters; the two upper floors were given over to a pair of bedrooms and sitting rooms for 'undergraduates' (Mr Dunn rejected the term 'student'). It was considered something of a privilege to secure

rooms at 19 Portugal Street, and these were passed on by word of mouth, gentleman to gentleman, as Mr Dunn put it.

Mr and Mrs Dunn saw their chief role as ensuring no 'women' entered the premises after 8pm. If they heard tinkling female laughter or the tread of a stiletto, they soon appeared on the upstairs landing. Mr Dunn did not altogether approve of the concept of female undergraduates, and particularly not at Trinity. He regarded their admission as 'a rare mistake by the Master'.

One summer evening I had chapped lips and covered them before going to sleep in cherry chap-stick. The next day I was accosted by Mr Dunn, who had been waiting for me to return from lectures. He needed to speak to me 'on a highly sensitive matter, Mr Coleridge'. It turned out that Mrs Dunn (who made my bed each morning) had discovered a perfectly formed, cherry-coloured lip shape on my pillowcase and suspected a 'woman' of staying overnight. I protested my innocence, but am not sure they ever believed me.

Mr Dunn's proudest memory was when the Prince of Wales had once come to breakfast at 19 Portugal Street, the guest of one of my predecessors, Alexander Russell. HRH had been an undergraduate at the time, and Mrs Dunn had served him eggs, bacon, sausage, tomatoes, mushroom, brown toast and a cup of coffee. I can remember the full menu since Mr Dunn used to reminisce about it, several times a week. 'Did I ever tell you, Mr Coleridge, about the occasion when the Prince of Wales took breakfast in your very rooms?'

'Actually you did tell me, Mr Dunn.'

'What a day it was! Mrs Dunn cooked him eggs, bacon, sausage …'

I became very fond of the Dunns, who represented a side of Cambridge, and indeed of Britain, now almost entirely disappeared. They were Tom Sharpe characters, for sure, but with a fierce loyalty to Trinity.

Nicholas Coleridge (1976)

I read law at Trinity from 1986 to 1990 and had the privilege of being in Great Court rooms when the re-enactment of the Great Court run as shown in *Chariots of Fire* took place with Sebastian Coe taking part. My two guests that day were

Mr Prior leading a procession in 1980, followed by the Vice Master, Jack Gallagher, and the Senior Fellow, Tressilian Nicholas.
The Dean of Chapel, behind Professor Gallagher, is the Right Revd John 'Honest to God' Robinson.

Jack Nicholson and Dodi Fayed, who were friends of my father who was a film producer. Dodi Fayed had been an executive producer on *Chariots of Fire*. Jack Nicholson was in the UK at that time in autumn 1988 filming *Batman* and was one of the biggest stars in the world. None of this cut any ice with Trinity's porters. First, Dodi Fayed turned up in his limousine and, of course, the porter on the Backs would not let him in without authorisation, which clearly he did not have. Consequently, the two of them had to finish their journey by foot. The second memorable moment was Dodi Fayed and Jack Nicholson trying to watch the race from the roof outside H5 Great Court which was my room at the time and the porter coming up and telling them that no one was allowed on the roof. An argument then ensued for a good ten minutes between another porter and Jack Nicholson, which ended with Jack Nicholson giving way. The day ended in the Garden House Hotel with us being served in the restaurant by the entire staff of the hotel seeking his autograph. Jack Nicholson was noted for his courtesy and openness – even giving an interview to *Varsity* newspaper on his way to lunch. Dodi Fayed was much more distant. However, my abiding memory of the day was the vigilance and officiousness of the porters who were not willing to give any ground to either of the two.

K.R. Sasha White (1986)

CHAPTER 3

Trinity and Mathematics

BÉLA BOLLOBÁS *(1963)*

The mathematician's patterns, like the painter's or the poet's, must fit together in a harmonious way. Beauty is the first test: there is no permanent place in the world for ugly mathematics.

G.H. Hardy

Mathematics before the foundation of Trinity

Throughout the Middle Ages mathematics was a vital part of a university education. Students entered a medieval university when they were very young, and during their first four years of residence they studied the trivium, comprising Latin grammar, logic and rhetoric: this earned them a bachelor of arts degree. Those who continued their studies earned master's degrees by studying the quadrivium, comprising arithmetic (numbers absolute), music (numbers applied), geometry (magnitudes at rest) and astronomy (magnitudes in motion). In turn, the quadrivium prepared the student for the serious study of philosophy and theology. In the quadrivium, students were taught at least some of the 13 books of Euclid's *Elements*: indeed, until about a hundred years ago, all educated men had studied the *Elements*. In spite of this apparent mathematical slant to the curriculum, the students learned only a smattering of what could remotely be called real mathematics, such as had been known to the Greeks over a thousand years earlier.

The 12th century saw the revival of learning in Europe, and with that the resurgence of mathematics through the assimilation of Arabic texts and of Greek works derived from Arabic sources.

Mathematics in the early days of the College

In England the medieval curriculum was terminated by a royal decree in 1535: the king ordered that Greek, Latin and divinity should be taught in addition to the trivium and quadrivium, and that the scriptures should be read. After this breakup of the medieval system of education the number of students fell considerably: in the year 1545, just before the foundation of Trinity, Cambridge had only about 30 new students and Oxford only 20. After the five Regius Professorships established by Henry VIII, the foundation of Trinity and the Edwardian statutes of 1549, the numbers increased again. The new statutes declared the central importance of mathematics in a university education and recommended certain sound textbooks.

The first Trinity mathematician of note was one of the most colourful academics ever, John Dee. In 1545 he was elected to a Fellowship in St John's, but on the foundation of Trinity a year later he was named as one of its original Fellows and made assistant lecturer in Greek. While at Trinity he studied mathematics, and on going down in 1548 he gave his scientific instruments to the College. Sadly, today there is no sign of them.

An amazing stage trick in which he appeared to levitate during a performance of a tragedy by Aristophanes in the Hall gave rise to the rumour that he was a sorcerer, an image that was not entirely uncultivated. It was said that he discoursed

Dr Dee's Magical Mirror in the British Museum.

with angels, dealt with evil spirits and could transmute metals; his *speculum* or mirror, a piece of solid pink-tinted glass, is preserved in the British Museum.

Mathematics did not rule Dee's life, although he taught arithmetic and astronomy at Louvain, geometry in Paris (in English!) and was invited to Oxford to lecture on mathematics. His petition to Queen Mary to form a royal library from the dispersed libraries of the monasteries went unheeded. When Elizabeth ascended the throne, Dee was taken into the royal service. In 1585, three years after the introduction of the Gregorian calendar in the Catholic countries on the Continent, he recommended its introduction in England in his report to the Government; his recommendation was not accepted, and the calendar was reformed only in 1752. He died in 1608 in the greatest poverty, aged 81.

Dee's successors at Trinity (and Cambridge) were not major players on the world stage of mathematics, but John Pell, born in 1610, was nonetheless an important mathematician. He entered Trinity at 13 and received his MA in 1630. After taking his degree, he continued his mathematical studies, and his reputation became so great that he was appointed to the very desirable chair of mathematics in Amsterdam. A spell in the diplomatic service ended when he took holy orders and became chaplain to the Archbishop of Canterbury. Nevertheless, he kept up his interest in mathematics all his life; it was to him that Newton explained his invention of fluxions. Today he is widely known for Pell's equation, $x^2-ny^2=1$, although this attribution is mistaken. The problem is to solve this equation in integers x and y, given a square-free integer n; this was only done by Lagrange over 100 years later, in a very elegant way.

The middle of the 17th century saw the birth of a new school of mathematics. Descartes published his *Geometry* in 1637, and a year or so later Cavalieri described his method of indivisibles, the forerunner of integration. Fermat used algebra to solve geometric problems, and Pascal worked on probability theory and projective geometry. Trinity's Isaac Barrow (1630–77) straddled the old and the new. He entered Trinity in 1644 and was elected

Isaac Barrow, Master of Trinity 1672–7 and first occupant of the Lucasian Chair of Mathematics.

published a book on the mathematics of Archimedes, Apollonius and Theodosius. From 1672 until his death five years later he was Master of Trinity.

Dee, Pell and Barrow were worthy mathematicians, but Newton, the next Trinity mathematician we should talk about, is on an entirely different level. As he is such a giant (and straddles mathematics and physics), we have a separate section on him later in this volume.

The Newtonian school

Newton's discoveries profoundly affected the study of mathematics in England. By the end of the 17th century the Newtonian philosophy was widely accepted in Cambridge, and not only because of the mathematicians who fought his corner in his dispute with Leibniz. When in 1692 Richard Bentley delivered the first course of Boyle lectures, he devoted several of his sermons to Newton's discoveries, expressing them in non-technical language and so reaching a wide audience.

Of the mathematicians following Newton, Roger Cotes (1682–1716) stands out. He came up to Trinity in 1699; in 1705 he was elected to a Fellowship, and in 1707 he was named the first occupant of the chair of astronomy that Dr Plume of Christ's had just founded. Bentley urged Cotes to establish an astronomical observatory. As the university was unwilling to give any financial assistance, Trinity erected one on top of the Great Gate; the Plumian professor was allowed to occupy the nearby rooms. The observatory was pulled down in 1797.

By 1700 there was a great need for a new edition of Newton's *Principia*, since the first edition had been out of print since 1690. Although Newton had collected some material for an enlarged edition, he was disinclined to undertake the task of producing a new edition: he delegated the task to Cotes, but went through it line by line. The two spent over three years collaborating on the 1713 second, revised edition, which contains not only Newton's lunar and planetary theory but also much new work by Cotes.

In his own research, Cotes worked on the decomposition and integration of rational algebraic expressions, and found a theorem in trigonometry based on forming the quadratic factors of $z^n - 1$.

to a Fellowship in 1649. He translated Euclid's *Elements* into Latin in 1655, and five years later into English; the latter became a standard English textbook for a long time. One of the most charming books in the Wren Library is Newton's copy of the Latin translation, with his notes in the margin. In 1660 Barrow was appointed to the Regius Professorship of Greek and three years later was chosen to be the first occupier of the Lucasian Chair of Mathematics. He worked on new ways of determining the tangents of curves and the areas under them; in particular, he proved the fundamental theorem of calculus that integration and differentiation are inverse operations. In 1669 he resigned from his chair and moved to the court in London; from then on he devoted most of his time to theology, although in 1675 he

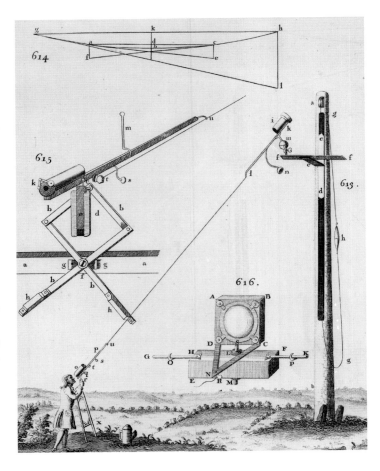

Christiaan Huygens' aerial telescope from Dr Smith's Compleat System of Opticks *in four books, 1738.*

His early death was a severe blow to Cambridge. As Newton remarked: 'If he had lived we would have known something.'

Cotes was succeeded in the Plumian Chair by Robert Smith (1689–1768), who came up to Trinity in 1707 and spent the last 26 years of his life as the Master. He wrote up his research and lectures in two books which had a great influence on the teaching of mathematics in Cambridge: these were *Opticks* and *Harmonics*, the first being on optics and hydrostatics, and the second on sound.

In his will Smith founded two annual prizes for excellence in mathematics and 'natural philosophy'. Over the years these became important milestones in the lives of aspiring mathematicians: being the First Smith's Prizeman was a guarantee of a Fellowship and an almost certain flying start to an academic career.

Sadly, in the next hundred years or so Cambridge failed to produce a mathematician of note. A great many reasons have been put forward for this. One was the acrimonious debate between Newton and Leibniz, who differed not only in their methods, but also in the notation they used. To the mathematicians of the day, the question as to which one to use was inextricably mixed up with the question of whether Leibniz had discovered the fundamental ideas of calculus for himself or had been led to them by reading some papers of Newton. Understandably, the mathematicians in Britain sided with Newton and did not care enough about the developments on the Continent. Another reason could have been that Newton's notation was unwieldy and his concepts were vaguely explained so that for mortal mathematicians (unlike Newton) it was very difficult to carry on in that style. Also, perhaps the mathematicians in Britain were so much in awe of their hero that they considered his style of mathematics above any criticism. Yet another reason that has been suggested is that, although Newton never gave a really precise explanation of his fluxional calculus and the English textbooks presenting it were shoddy, he strongly discouraged mathematical debate. This was in stark contrast with the open and free discussions on the Continent. Compared to France and other Western countries, England produced rather few mathematicians. Although in 18th-century England it seemed sensible to remain faithful to the geometric, synthetic arguments that provided a firmer foundation of mathematics than the dubious methods of Continental calculus, it was a great handicap to ignore them.

The Mathematical Tripos

In the early medieval universities there were no examinations; to receive a master's degree, the student made only a declaration that he knew the required subjects or perhaps took an oath that he had attended the appropriate lectures. Later, public disputations were required for a degree; in the early days these disputations were on scholastic questions and theology, later on philosophy, and subsequently on mathematics.

In about 1725 the system changed considerably: the 'moderators' (examiners) questioned all the candidates at the same time so that they could compare them with each other. This came about partly because in 1710 the Senate House, where the disputations were held, was turned into a library to house the 30,000 volumes given to the University by George I, and partly because it was felt that a fairer examination was needed. It took 20 years to build a new Senate House, and by then the new system of examination was in place, albeit tentatively. From the beginning, this 'Senate House examination', conducted in English rather than Latin, was mostly on mathematics, and to a much smaller extent on logic, philosophy and religion. It also led to an exact order of merit, with a number of 'brackets' for lower ranked candidates. Soon this Senate House examination

Mathematical Tripos examination paper, 1884.

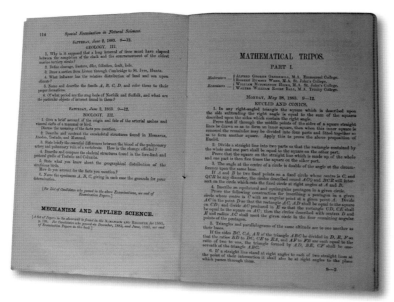

was well established: from 1748 the final lists were printed and were made available to the general public. A little later the first class was divided into two, called wranglers and senior optimes, respectively. The man at the top of the list was the Senior Wrangler and was followed by the Second Wrangler. Thus a candidate could be 'bracketed Sixth Wrangler'.

In the middle of the 17th century the examination was held in January and lasted for three days, with eight or nine hours of exams a day, divided into five or six papers; there was a fourth day dedicated to fine-tuning the order and producing the final list. From the end of the 18th century the questions were dictated and required the answers to be written. In 1824 an examination in classics was introduced for those who had already taken honours in mathematics, and henceforth the Senate House examination was known as the Mathematical Tripos.

The race to become the Senior Wrangler and then the First Smith's Prizeman became more and more intense so that already in the 18th century there were coaches to help prepare the students, and from the first half of the 18th century the use of a coach became a sine qua non for doing well in the Mathematical Tripos. As Littlewood wrote in his *Miscellany*: 'To be in the running for Senior Wrangler one had to spend two-thirds of

the time practising how to solve difficult problems against time.' There were legendary coaches like W. Hopkins (1793–1866), the 'Senior Wrangler maker', and E.J. Routh (1831–1907), who was himself a Senior Wrangler, beating the great physicist James Clerk Maxwell into second place. Hopkins coached 17 Senior Wranglers, and in 22 years from 1862 Routh coached the Senior Wrangler in every year. Hopkins, Routh and many of the other coaches over the years were substantial mathematicians in their own right, who became Fellows of the Royal Society. The last of the great coaches was a Fellow of Trinity, R.A. Herman, who coached J.E. Littlewood (1885–1977) and the man he was bracketed with as Senior Wrangler, James Mercer (1883–1932), also from Trinity.

In 1909, after a century and a half, the strict order of merit in the Mathematical Tripos was brought to an end by the combined efforts of two Fellows of Trinity, Andrew Forsyth (1858–1942), the Sadleirian Professor, and G.H. Hardy (1877–1947), who was a College lecturer at the time. They firmly believed that the Tripos was detrimental to pure mathematics in England, especially to analysis, and so were determined to abolish it rather than reform it.

A feature of the Mathematical Tripos was the competition between St John's and Trinity. St John's got off to a flying start, but towards the end of the 19th century Trinity started to close the gap. Until 1887 there was always one Senior Wrangler, but in that year four men were bracketed Senior Wranglers: two from St John's and two from Trinity. Until the abolition of the order of merit in 1909, there were four other occasions with brackets at the top, with all eight students coming from Trinity. Counting a bracketed Senior Wrangler as ½ (or ¼ in 1887), by 1908 Trinity and St John's were in a dead heat. According to legend (false, of course), St John's scoured America for a man who would be sure to be the Senior Wrangler in the last order of merit and so would ensure the victory of St John over Trinity, and found him in the person of Louis Mordell. Although Mordell was the undisputed star of his year, in the last order of merit in 1909 he was beaten by two Trinity men, and so Trinity nipped St John's at the line. As Mordell remarked later: 'I blotted my copy-book and was only Third Wrangler. I think I could have done better.'

The Analytical Society

The sorry state of mathematics in England, due to its isolation from Continental ideas and insistence on geometric proofs and Newtonian notation, was exacerbated by the excessive idleness of the mathematicians. For example, William Lax of Trinity (Senior Wrangler in 1785) held the Lowndean Chair of astronomy and geometry (established in 1749) for over 40 years, but neither lectured nor taught, and published only a handful of mediocre works.

Towards the end of the 18th century, mathematicians at Cambridge started to recognise that Britain's isolation was a serious handicap. Unfortunately, the adoption of analytical methods and of the Leibniz notation of differential calculus were fiercely opposed by the senior members of the Senate, who regarded any change as sacrilege, a sin against the memory of Newton.

The first man who started a movement to change the system was Robert Woodhouse (1773–1827) of Caius. From 1820 he was the Lucasian professor, but in 1822 he resigned it in exchange for the Plumian Chair. Although Woodhouse was eager enough to bring continental mathematics to Cambridge, he did not have much influence on his colleagues. The movement would have died away if in 1812 three undergraduates, Peacock and Babbage of Trinity and Herschel of St John's, had not decided to form the Analytical Society for the promotion of analytical methods and the differential notation. As Herschel put it, their aim was 'to do their best to leave the world wiser than they found it'. As the first step on the way to reform, in 1816 the Society published the first book in English on the 'continental type' of analysis, a translation of Lacroix's *Elementary Differential Calculus*. Next came the introduction of the 'new' notation into the Senate House examination. From 1817 Peacock used the differential notation in the examination whenever he was a moderator, and in 1820 Whewell did the same. By the early 1820s the notation was well established, and from then on the language of fluxional calculus rarely appeared in the examination. The reform was greatly helped by books by Peacock, Herschel, Whewell and Airy on the differential and integral calculus and its applications, so by the middle of the 1820s the victory of the reformers was just about complete. Not surprisingly, the use of analytical methods quickly spread from Cambridge to the rest of Britain.

Let us say a few words about two of the more important Trinity men who brought about this vital change to end the mathematical isolation of the country. George Peacock (1791–1858) was a great reformer: not only was he determined to reform analysis in Britain, he was also eager to reform the teaching of algebra. Although he exerted a great influence on the mathematicians of his day, he produced rather little original work. He was one of the most successful tutors Cambridge has ever seen. An old pupil of his wrote: 'While his extensive knowledge and perspicuity as a lecturer maintained the high reputation of his College, and commanded the attention and admiration of his pupils, he succeeded to an extraordinary degree in winning their personal attachment by the uniform kindliness of his temper and disposition, the practical good sense of his advice and admonitions, and the absence of all moroseness, austerity, or needless interference with their conduct.' Another remarked: 'His insight into character was remarkable.' He was instrumental in establishing the University observatory. In 1836 he succeeded Lax in the Lowndean Chair, but resigned it three years later to become the Dean of Ely.

William Whewell (1794–1866) graduated as Second Wrangler and Second Smith Prizeman in 1816 and spent his life working for his University and College, first as a tutor, and then from 1841 as Master. Until the age of 30 he devoted his life to mathematics in research, teaching and writing; in particular, he wrote the first book in English on applied mathematics using the analytic techniques. In recognition of his work on mathematics he was elected a Fellow of the Royal Society. Later his interests widened: he wrote on mineralogy, architecture, astronomy, philosophy and theology; in fact, in 1828 he became the Professor of Mineralogy, and in 1838 the Professor of Moral Philosophy. As his good friend John Herschel said: 'A more wonderful variety and amount of knowledge in almost every department of human activity was perhaps never in the same interval of time accumulated by any man.'

In February 1866 he was badly injured by a fall from his horse, and a few days later died in the Lodge. As his biographer wrote: 'Whilst his life was ebbing away fast on that last morning,

blinds and curtains were drawn wide apart in compliance with his wish, that he might see the sun shine on the Great Court of Trinity, and he smiled as he was reminded that he used to say the sky never looked so blue as when fringed with its turrets and battlements.' He was buried in the ante-chapel.

The early days of computing: Charles Babbage
Another member of the Analytical Society, Charles Babbage (1792–1871), is rightly considered to be the grandfather of computing. Although he did not have a particularly close connection to Trinity, the importance of his work justifies his inclusion in this gallery of Trinity mathematicians. He was not only a mathematician, but also a philosopher, engineer and inventor. Before coming up to Trinity he had already read works by Leibniz, Lagrange and Lacroix, so upon his arrival in 1810 he was greatly disappointed by the mathematical education offered by Cambridge. He gave the Analytical Society its name; as he stated, this society was formed to advocate 'the principles of

Charles Babbage's Difference Engine No.1, a 19th-century model built by Babbage's son, Henry Prevost Babbage, to his father's design.

Arthur Cayley.

pure *d*-ism as opposed to the *dot*-age of the university.' He also wrote the first paper in the memoir published by the Society in 1813. The same year he migrated to Peterhouse, as he had a premonition that in the Senate House examination he would be beaten by Herschel and Peacock – as indeed he was, becoming Third Wrangler.

In 1828 Babbage was appointed to the Lucasian Chair but, abusing his position, neither resided nor lectured. Nevertheless, he was a founding member of the Astronomical Society in 1820 and the Statistical Society in 1834. At Cambridge he saw that 'computers' (men performing calculations in order to produce numerical tables) were slow and prone to error, so from 1819 he set himself the task of constructing a mechanical computer. By 1822 he had published a note on his invention. His 'difference engine' was designed to compute values of polynomials by the method of finite differences. The construction of the first engine, weighing 15 tons and consisting of 25,000 parts, was never completed, although he had received ample funding for it. Later he designed and started to build an improved version of his machine. When this project also failed to bear fruit, he started a more complex machine he called the 'analytical engine', on which he worked until his death. His aim was to construct a machine that could be programmed by number cards, the forerunners of punch cards.

Babbage's numerous inventions for everyday life included the pilot (also called a cow-catcher), designed to clear a railway track in front of a locomotive, the dynamometer car he tested in about 1838 and the ophthalmoscope.

Amazingly, the basic architecture of the analytical engine was rather similar to that of today's computers. Following Babbage's plans, in 1991 the London Science Museum built two working models of the difference engine, using tolerances achievable in the 19th century. These machines, which can perform calculations up to 31 digits, show that Babbage's machine would have worked had he finished building it.

Algebra

In 1830 George Peacock published a *Treatise on Algebra*, the first book in Britain that attempted to place algebra on a sound footing. Later, while he was the Dean of Ely, he followed this up with a two-volume textbook on algebra. Peacock's efforts were continued by the Scottish mathematician Duncan Gregory (1813–44), who came up to Trinity in 1833 and became a Fellow in 1840. He was a founding editor of the *Cambridge Mathematical Journal*, to which he also contributed many articles. Gregory had a great influence on George Boole, one of the few giants of mathematics who had no formal training, best known for Boolean algebra, an essential tool for modern computer science.

The first truly world-class British mathematician since Newton was Arthur Cayley (1821–95), one of the founders of modern algebra. For his range, inventiveness and the introduction of a host of new and fertile theories he has been compared to Leonhard Euler, the Swiss giant of mathematics.

Although he was born in Richmond, Surrey, the first eight years of his life were spent in Saint Petersburg, Russia, where his father worked as a merchant. From the age of 14 it was clear that the young Arthur had great mathematical ability. In 1838 he entered Trinity as a pensioner and became a scholar in 1840; during his undergraduate days, George Peacock was his tutor and William Hopkins his coach. While still an undergraduate, he published three influential papers in the *Cambridge Mathematical Journal* in which he continued Cauchy's work on permutations, took the first steps towards defining an abstract group and was the first to use today's standard notation for determinants. In 1842 he graduated as Senior Wrangler and First Smith's Prizeman.

In the year he took his degree, Cayley was elected a Fellow of Trinity and became an assistant tutor. Making good use of the freedom his Fellowship gave him to do research, in the next four years he published 28 important papers. In 1843 Hamilton had found a way of 'multiplying' the vectors of four-dimensional space and so defined the space $\mathbf{H}$ of quaternions; continuing Hamilton's work, Cayley expressed rotation in three-dimensional space as a conjugation $x \rightarrow q^{-1}xq$ of quaternions; this led him to the Cayley–Klein parameters. He also showed that the construction of the quaternions from the complex numbers can be imitated to define a suitable multiplication in eight-dimensional space; the elements of this space $\mathbf{O}$ are the octonions, also called Cayley numbers. Later it was shown that the only dimensions in which there is a natural notion of multiplication (giving us the so-called normed division algebras) are one (the real numbers $\mathbf{R}$), two (the complex numbers $\mathbf{C}$), four (the quaternions $\mathbf{H}$) and eight (the octonions $\mathbf{O}$). These notions have turned out to be important in mathematics and physics; in particular, they lie behind the notion of the 'spin' of an elementary particle. Perhaps most importantly, Cayley started to work on invariant theory, a subject which revolutionised algebra.

As Cayley did not take holy orders, his Fellowship had limited tenure and he had to choose a profession. He chose law and in 1846 he entered Lincoln's Inn. In 1849 he was called to the Bar and spent the next 14 years of his life working as a lawyer, specialising in conveyancing. Although he earned his living as a lawyer, during those 14 years he continued his mathematical research and published about 250 mathematical research papers, many more than most great mathematicians publish in a lifetime. During his years in London, he had many deep mathematical discussions with his good friend J.J. Sylvester (1814–97), the great Johnian mathematician, who was at that time an actuary in London.

In 1863 Cayley was elected to the newly established Sadleirian Chair of Pure Mathematics: he willingly gave up his large income and the prospect of a great career in law in order to devote all his time to mathematics. He got married at once and settled in Cambridge to live there for the rest of his life. His home life was very happy; as relaxation he loved to travel, read novels and paint, especially watercolours.

As Sadleirian professor, Cayley's duties were to explain and teach the principles of pure mathematics and to apply himself to the advancement of that science. He published close to 1,000 papers, more than any other pure mathematician up to that time. In 1872 he was made an Honorary Fellow of Trinity, and three years later he became an ordinary Fellow, so that he received a stipend from the College.

Cayley made spectacular contributions to mathematics, creating beautiful theories. He held that 'as for everything else, so for mathematical theory: beauty can be perceived but not explained'. In 1889 the Cambridge University Press invited him to prepare for publication his collected papers. This enterprise took about a decade to complete: 13 quarto volumes were published, of which the first seven were edited by Cayley himself and the rest by Forsyth, his successor in the Sadleirian Chair.

In 1854 Cayley wrote two ground-breaking papers on algebra. In those days the only groups mathematicians knew were permutation groups: Cayley was the first to define an abstract group and to realise that certain matrices and certain quaternions formed groups. He proved the Cayley–Hamilton theorem, that every square matrix is a root of its own characteristic polynomial, a result which gave him great satisfaction. He discovered Cayley's formula and Cayley's law for binomial forms.

He contributed much to geometry. Justifying his view that 'projective geometry is all of geometry', he showed that Euclidean geometry can be viewed as part of projective geometry and introduced the idea of a projective metric. His work on higher dimensional geometry and matrices aided the foundation of quantum mechanics in the 1920s. He worked on the singularities of curves and surfaces the classification of cubic surfaces and on elliptic functions. In addition to pure mathematics, he worked on general and theoretical dynamics. In 1876 he published his only book, on elliptic functions. Many areas of pure mathematics can be traced back to Cayley, including the theory of knots, fractals, dynamic programming and enumerative combinatorics. In particular, Cayley's tree formula on the number of labelled trees led him to count isomers in organic chemistry and to propose questions about the existence of certain chemical compounds, many of which have been found since then.

He received nearly every possible academic honour, and a crater on the Moon was named after him. The combination of his noble and generous nature and his eminence in mathematics gave him much influence in the University. He took a great interest in the education of women: he helped in the teaching of the undergraduates of Girton College after its foundation in 1869, and for some years he was the chairman of the council of Newnham College. In 1874 his friends formed a committee to commission his portrait by Lowes Dickinson to be placed in the Hall. As his obituary said, 'It is difficult to do justice to Cayley's merits as a mathematician, so great and varied were his powers, and so wide the range of subjects to which they were applied.'

Another great algebraist of the 19th century was William Kingdon Clifford (1845–79). He came up to Trinity in 1863, having finished at King's College London, was Second Wrangler and Second Smith's Prizeman in 1867, and became a Fellow a year later.

He had a great influence on mathematics, with many concepts and results named after him. Perhaps he is best known for Clifford algebras, which generalise Hamilton's quaternions: he used them to study motion in non-Euclidean spaces and in various surfaces. He was the first to assert that physical matter could be viewed as a curved ripple in a generally flat space. As he wrote in 1870: 'In the physical world nothing else takes place but

this variation [of the curvature of space].' Indeed, today it is often claimed that the person who most anticipated the conceptual ideas of General Relativity was Clifford, not Riemann.

In 1871 Clifford moved to London to a chair at University College London. Although he was a man of enormous physical strength, in 1876 his health broke down and he died three years later, just 11 days before Einstein was born. Most of his work was published posthumously.

Logic and the foundation of mathematics

That logic became a part of mathematics is due in no small measure to Augustus De Morgan (1806–71) and George Boole (1815–64). As we have already remarked, Boole did not have any university education, although he was greatly encouraged by Gregory. De Morgan came up to Trinity at the age of 16, and he soon became a good friend of Peacock and Whewell. Peacock urged him to develop algebra and Whewell asked him to put logic on a firm footing; De Morgan spent most of his life pursuing these aims.

Because of his wide interests, which included playing the flute, he was only Fourth Wrangler in the Tripos in 1827. His non-conforming nature became evident when he refused to pass a theological test and thereby ruled himself out as a candidate for a Fellowship. His refusal was not due to any objection to the Church of England; rather, he objected to the test being compulsory.

After Cambridge he moved to London to go to the Bar, but kept working on mathematics. In 1826 London University was founded, and a little later the 22-year-old De Morgan was appointed as its first Professor of Mathematics. (Ten years later London University became a part of the newly founded University of London as University College.) He held that 'the moving power of mathematical invention is not reasoning but imagination'. Through his lectures and research, De Morgan single-handedly established his department as the home of high-class mathematical education in London. In 1865 De Morgan became the first President of the newly founded London Mathematical Society (which has become the main mathematical society for the whole of Britain). Although he loved to lecture and was very good at it, he resigned his chair twice on principle, the second time when he was already 60. Although his pupils secured for him a generous pension, misfortunes followed that hastened his death: first his very talented mathematician son died, and then so did his daughter.

De Morgan was a prolific writer on algebra and the foundations of formal logic, about which he corresponded extensively with Boole. Concerning the need to formalise logic, he wrote: 'Every science that has thriven has thriven upon its own symbols: logic, the only science which is admitted to have made no improvements in century after century, is the only one which has grown no symbols.' Today he is best known for De Morgan's Laws, which he first published in 1858. These 'laws' are the basic identities concerning operations on sets: if A and B are subsets of a fixed ground set then $(A \cap B)^c = A^c \cup B^c$ and $(A \cup B)^c = A^c \cap B^c$, where $\cap$ denotes intersection, $\cup$ denotes union, and the superscript c denotes the complement with respect to the ground set. He was also the first to make rigorous the idea of mathematical induction, perhaps the most general tool in pure mathematics; even the term 'mathematical induction' is due to him.

Bertrand Russell, from the Trinity Review, *1970.*

Unlike most 'serious' mathematicians, he wrote an enormous amount for the general public. Throughout his life, he revelled in being different: he never wanted to become a Fellow of the Royal Society, never voted in an election, and never visited the Tower of London or Westminster Abbey. As he said: 'I don't quite hear what you say, but I beg to differ entirely with you.'

After De Morgan, Boole and their followers had brought logic into mathematics, a movement was started in the second half of the 19th century with the opposite aim, that of making mathematics a part of logic by laying a rigorous logical foundation of mathematics. It was towards this enterprise that two Trinity mathematicians, Whitehead and Russell, made major contributions through their monumental treatise, *Principia Mathematica*, on which they worked for about ten years and which they published in three volumes from 1910 to 1913.

Alfred North Whitehead (1861–1947) came up to Trinity in 1880, graduated as Fourth Wrangler in 1883 and became a Fellow in 1884. For some years he concentrated on teaching and even accepted a teaching position at Girton; later he spent seven years on a book on algebra, which was published in 1898. In 1910 he had a disagreement with the College over the Forsyth affair – the Cambridge Professor Forsyth had to resign his chair because he was named a co-respondent in the divorce of the woman he promptly married – and resigned his Fellowship. After four years without a proper job, he was appointed to a professorship of applied mathematics at Imperial College, London; ten years later he moved to Harvard to take up a chair in philosophy.

Bertrand Arthur William Russell (1872–1970) was the grandson of Lord John Russell, who had twice been Prime Minister. Russell came up to Trinity in 1890, graduated as Seventh Wrangler and became a Fellow in 1895. From the beginning, he was greatly influenced by Whitehead, who recommended him to the Cambridge Apostles. When in 1916 he was convicted for anti-war activities, the College did not continue his Fellowship, although by then he had been an Fellow of the Royal Society for eight years. Two years later he was convicted a second time and was imprisoned for six months; while in prison he wrote an introduction to mathematical philosophy. After the First World War he concentrated on political activism and

writing, receiving the Nobel Prize for literature in 1950. In the last two decades of his life he was a prominent public figure. Together with Einstein, in 1955 he released a manifesto calling for the curtailment of nuclear weapons, and later became the founding president of the Campaign for Nuclear Disarmament.

At the Paris Congress in 1900, Russell and Whitehead heard Giuseppe Peano's lecture on the foundation of mathematics and were immediately attracted to the area. A year later Russell thought up his famous paradox showing that the naive set theory of Dedekind, Cantor and Frege is untenable. Russell's paradox (also known as the Russell–Zermelo paradox) has a great many variants – here is its original form. Frege's theory implies that one can define a class X as the class of all classes that do not contain themselves. So far so good. But does X contain itself? It is easily seen that whether the answer is 'yes' or 'no' we are led to a contradiction, so Frege's system is inconsistent. (To illustrate the definition of x, note that the class of all things that are not round contains itself, while the class of all things that are round does not contain itself.)

Russell wrote a polite note to Frege informing him of his paradox and its implications, which the latter received when the second volume of his work was about to appear. As Frege honestly wrote in the hastily added Appendix in which he tried to salvage his work: 'Hardly anything more unfortunate can befall a scientific writer than to have one of the foundations of his edifice shaken after the work is finished. This was the position I was placed in by a letter of Mr Bertrand Russell, just when the printing of this volume was nearing its completion.' Not surprisingly, Frege's attempt to shore up his edifice was unsuccessful, although this was shown only some years later.

Soon after this, Russell and Whitehead joined forces to write *Principia Mathematica*, their huge treatise on the foundation of mathematics, which is not only one of the most important books on mathematical logic and philosophy, but also one of the most important books ever. To avoid the pitfalls that plagued Frege, they constructed an elaborate system of types. Unfortunately, because of its unyielding notation and language, the great work of Russell and Whitehead was soon superseded, and now its original form is very rarely consulted.

Analysis and number theory

In analysis, the harmful (and certainly not splendid) isolation of Britain, which followed the rift with the Continent that dated back to Newton, came to an end only after 1900. Up to that point, Britain (really, the Mathematical Tripos) had produced several great applied mathematicians and physicists and, as we have seen, some world-class algebraists and logicians, but no analyst of the highest calibre. All this changed with the arrival of two extraordinary Trinity mathematicians, Hardy and Littlewood. Each was a giant in his own right and what was even more remarkable was that they formed a formidable partnership, the greatest in the history of mathematics. They wrote about 100 joint papers in an age when joint work of any kind was rare: they proved a host of ground-breaking results in hard analysis and number theory, and by the 1930s they had created a school of mathematics second to none. That Cambridge became, and still remains, one of the major centres of mathematics in the world, owes much more to Hardy and

Littlewood than it does to anyone else – even to Newton, the icon of Cambridge mathematics.

Godfrey Harold Hardy (1877–1947), always known as G.H. Hardy, came up to Trinity in 1896, and after only two years of study was Fourth Wrangler in the Mathematical Tripos. It irked him that he did not come top, as he had expected to, and it is not inconceivable that this relative failure contributed to the implacable hostility he felt towards the Tripos later. Strangely, throughout his life he held those who had beaten him in unreasonably high esteem.

In 1900 Hardy was elected to a Fellowship in Trinity, and in 1906 he was appointed lecturer. As a Fellow, he found a soulmate in Russell, his senior by five years, whose political views he shared, and who introduced him to the Bloomsbury Group and the Cambridge Apostles. Until 1911 his research was far from

Right:
J.E. Littlewood.

Far right:
G.H. Hardy.

Srinivasa Ramanujan (1887–1920), who became in 1918 the first Indian Fellow of Trinity College and the youngest ever Fellow of the Royal Society.

spectacular, although it earned him a Fellowship of the Royal Society in 1910. As he said later: 'I wrote a great deal … but very little of any importance; there are not more than four of five papers which I can still remember with some satisfaction.' During this period his greatest contribution to mathematics was his textbook *A Course in Pure Mathematics*. This book, which he wrote like 'a missionary talking to cannibals', was the first rigorous introduction to analysis in English, and as such remained *the* text used in Cambridge (and in other universities in England) for decades, influencing many generations of mathematicians. His enthusiasm for rigour and his delight in mathematical proofs stayed with him all his life. As he once told Russell: 'If I could prove by logic that you would die in five minutes, I should be sorry you were going to die, but my sorrow would be very much mitigated by my pleasure in the proof.'

Hardy's research leaped to the highest level when in 1911 he started his collaboration with Littlewood. That partnership continued for the rest of his life, ending with a paper published a year after his death. Hardy and Littlewood worked on several topics in analysis and number theory, especially convergence and summability of series, inequalities, additive number theory, including Waring's problem and Goldbach's conjecture, and Diophantine approximation. In 1914 Hardy brought to Cambridge Srinivasa Ramanujan, and for the next five years he did much joint work with the Indian genius. When in the 1930s Paul Erdös asked Hardy what he considered to be his greatest contribution to mathematics, he promptly replied that it was the discovery of Ramanujan: he considered their collaboration 'the one romantic incident' of his life.

Although Hardy was always proud to be a pure mathematician whose research would never be applied, in 1908 he used very simple but elegant mathematics to give an extension of the Mendelian law about the proportions of dominant and recessive characters. This law, which later became known as the Hardy–Weinberg law, refuted the idea that a recessive character should tend to die out and has proved to be of major importance in blood group distribution.

The Russell affair during the First World War soured Hardy's relationship with Trinity, and in 1919 he moved to Oxford as the Savilian Professor of Geometry. After 12 happy years in New College he returned to Cambridge as the Sadleirian Professor of Pure Mathematics, mostly because he considered Cambridge the centre of mathematics in Britain, and because in Trinity he was allowed to keep his rooms after retirement.

Shortly after Hardy's return to Cambridge, Hardy and Littlewood announced weekly meetings of a 'conversation class' in Littlewood's rooms, in which mathematicians of all kinds gave informal talks about their own work. According to Titchmarsh, 'This was a model of what such a thing should be. Mathematicians of all nationalities and ages were encouraged to hold forth on their own work, and the whole exercise was conducted with a delightful informality that gave ample scope for free discussion after each paper.' Later this class turned into a larger meeting run by Hardy, at which Littlewood never appeared.

For decades, Hardy was the unrivalled leader of the British mathematical community: not only was his research outstanding, but he was also a wonderful writer and lecturer. Many results and notions have been named after him: Hardy's inequality, Hardy's

A Disappearing Number, *an award-winning play by the Complicité company and Simon McBurney about G.H. Hardy and Srinivasa Ramanujan. Photograph by Tristram Kenton.*

theorem, Hardy spaces, etc. Through his papers, books and numerous students he changed the landscape of mathematics in Britain. In Cambridge he led a move to destroy (not reform!) the Mathematical Tripos, and succeeded in having the strict order of merit abolished. He was a great supporter of the London Mathematical Society and twice served as its president.

Hardy was fiercely proud to be a 'pure' mathematician, saying, 'I have never done anything "useful". No discovery of mine has made, or is likely to make, directly or indirectly, for good or ill, the least difference to the amenity of the world.' We know now that in this he was badly mistaken: number theory has found numerous applications in coding theory and cryptography, and his asymptotic formula with Ramanujan has been widely applied in physics to find quantum partition functions. Hardy's concession to applied mathematics was that he considered those applied mathematicians whose work has permanent aesthetic value, such as Maxwell, Einstein and Dirac, 'real' mathematicians as well.

In addition to mathematics, Hardy had another passion: ball games, especially cricket. Although in school he was not coached in any games, as an adult he was an ardent follower of cricket, which he also played a little. He played real tennis, and bowls on the Bowling Green of the College, whose scoring he codified, creating the system we still use. During his year in Princeton in 1928–9 he fell in love with baseball and, especially, American football, writing, 'American football knocks other spectacles absolutely flat … I shall go hysterical when it comes to the big matches.'

Hardy was a real eccentric: he disliked having his photograph taken and could not abide mirrors. He was a staunch atheist, who never entered a church or chapel, even for the election of new Fellows. He was fond of viewing God as his personal enemy, who worked at denying him happiness, whether in mathematics or in cricket. When he was about to cross a stormy Channel, he would send a postcard to his friends announcing that he had just solved the Riemann Hypothesis, as he had no doubt that God would not let him drown if the result would be that after his death he would be known as the man who proved the Riemann Hypothesis.

He loved to compile lists of outstanding people, often in the form of cricket teams. On one occasion, his First Eleven was as follows: 'Hobbs, Archimedes, Shakespeare, Michelangelo, Napoleon (capt.), H. Ford, Plato, Beethoven, Johnson (Jack), J. Christ, Cleopatra.' He also liked to rate mathematicians by comparing them to cricketers; for many years his highest praise was 'in the Hobbs class', but when Bradman came along, he felt obliged to revise his scheme.

Sadly, he did not benefit much from Trinity's generosity towards its retired Fellows. Soon after his retirement from the Sadleirian chair in 1942, his health deteriorated; he felt that he had lost his creativity and became deeply depressed; he even tried to take his own life. In this period his great contribution to mathematics was a little book, *A Mathematician's Apology*. In this melancholic masterpiece, Hardy gives a poetic account of what it means to be a mathematician. He died a broken man

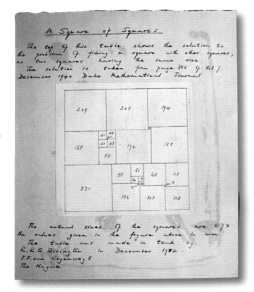

Below: *The top of a teak table in the College Bursary, given by a benefactor and showing the squared square, the logo of the Trinity Mathematical Society, founded in 1919 to 'promote the discussion of mathematical subjects of interest'. The explanatory piece of paper* (right) *is stuck to the underside.*

on 1 December 1947, on the day the Copley Medal, the Royal Society's highest honour, was to be presented to him.

John Edensor Littlewood (1885–1977) was the Trinity Fellow *par excellence*: he spent almost all his working life in Trinity and for over 60 years lived and worked in the same set of rooms in D Nevile's Court. He made great contributions to analysis and number theory; he took delight in tackling hard problems and was one of the best problem solvers the world has ever known. His collaboration with Hardy dominated the mathematical scene in England for a third of a century.

Although he was born in Rochester, from the age of seven he grew up in South Africa, where his father (who had been Ninth Wrangler) was a headmaster. The beauty of South Africa stayed with him all his life. After a few years at the local school, he went on to the University of Cape Town, the oldest, and at that time best, university in South Africa. By 1900 his father realised that even that was not good enough to nurture Littlewood's great talent in mathematics, so he sent his son to St Paul's School in London, where he was taught by an exceptionally able mathematician, F.S. Macaulay, who later became an FRS.

In 1903 Littlewood went up to Trinity and after only two years was bracketed Senior Wrangler with James Mercer, who was his senior by two and a half years and had attended the University of Liverpool before coming to Trinity. In those days the Senior Wranglers were celebrated by the general public and their photographs were sold during May Week. When one of Littlewood's friends tried to buy his postcard, he was told: 'I'm afraid we are sold out of Mr Littlewood, but we have plenty of Mr Mercer.'

In 1906, after only three years in Cambridge, Littlewood took Part II of the Mathematical Tripos, and started research under E.W. Barnes, then a Fellow of Trinity and later Bishop of Birmingham.

It says much about the isolation of British mathematics of the day that after an introductory project which Littlewood could complete easily, Barnes suggested that he should prove the Riemann Hypothesis. For close to a century, this problem, which is still open, has been considered the most important in all of mathematics: a proof of it would have important implications about the distribution of primes. The Riemann Hypothesis appeared on Hilbert's famous list of 23 problems for the 20th century and is also one of the seven Millennium Prize Problems for which the Clay Mathematics Institute is offering one million dollars.

In 1907 Littlewood accepted a lectureship in Manchester, and although he was awarded a Fellowship the next year he returned to the College in 1910 to fill the lectureship vacated by Whitehead. In 1928 he became the first occupant of the Rouse Ball Chair, founded from the benefaction of his former tutor. He retired in 1950. He proved deep results by himself and, from 1911, with Hardy. He also did important joint work with Cartwright, Offord and Paley.

Let us illustrate Littlewood's achievements with one of his results. The celebrated prime number theorem states that $\pi(x)$, the number of primes up to a number x, is approximated by a certain logarithmic integral, $\mathrm{li}(x)$. Furthermore, in 1914, based on numerical evidence, everyone believed that $\pi(x)$ is always less than $\mathrm{li}(x)$; indeed, we know now that $\pi(x) < \mathrm{li}(x)$ for all x up to 10^{14}. Then came Littlewood: using the zeta function, he proved the striking result that the difference $\pi(x) - \mathrm{li}(x)$ not only fails to be negative for all x, but changes sign infinitely often. And he proved this without being able to give any bound for the smallest x with $\pi(x) > \mathrm{li}(x)$.

Unlike Hardy, Littlewood had no objection to applied mathematics, saying: 'Before creation God did just pure mathematics. Then He thought it would be a pleasant change to do some applied.' In fact, in the First World War he served in the Royal Garrison Artillery: to the amazement and delight of the gunners, he found a formula to forecast precisely the positions of shellbursts. Before the Second World War, the problems arising in radio research led Littlewood and Mary Cartwright to work on nonlinear differential equations: using novel methods, they produced deep results about van der Pol's equation.

Before the First World War Russell, Hardy and Littlewood often holidayed together in a house they rented on the Cornish coast. In later years, in the vacations he shared a house with the Streatfeild family. He did mathematics, swam and climbed his favourite rocks; most importantly, he was staying with his daughter by Mrs Streatfeild, Ann. Not surprisingly, in light of the experience of Professor Forsyth, Littlewood never admitted that Ann was his daughter: calling her his 'niece', for decades he took Ann for long skiing holidays in Switzerland.

From about 1930 he suffered severe bouts of depression, often spending entire afternoons in various cinemas. His depression was probably exacerbated by his doubts about his decision to sacrifice family life for the life in College devoted entirely to mathematics. In spite of his severe depression, he went on producing work of the highest calibre, gave excellent lectures and looked after his research students. His uneasiness about meeting people outside the circle of his mathematical colleagues and Fellows of the College was deepened by his depression. He never suffered fools gladly: for many years he was considered the rudest man in Cambridge. Later in life he was proud to say that

he had never been secretary or chairman of any committee: even when he was the President of the London Mathematical Society, he never took the chair. In College he invariably arrived late for dinner so that he would not have to preside, and he refused to preside even in the Combination Room.

He was cured of his depression in 1960, ten years after he retired from his chair, when an excellent neurologist, Beresford Davies, prescribed for him a suitable combination of drugs. This enabled him to travel to the United States: altogether he made eight extensive tours between the ages of 75 and 83. He remained very active in old age: his last technical paper, on probability, was published when he was 84, and his very last paper appeared at 87. Remarkably, he did his last climb in Cornwall when he was 80.

From his mid-80s Littlewood's life revolved even more around the College. He spent most of his time in his room, listening to Bach, Beethoven and Mozart, as 'life is too short to waste on other composers'. For many years he was the Senior Fellow, but in spirit he was young: for example, unlike most of our older Fellows he was keen to admit women. After most dinners in Hall, he went up to the Combination Room to drink claret – as he was an excellent raconteur, he turned every evening into a special occasion: even the most eminent academic guests, like Dirac and Crick, were honoured to be entertained by him.

Littlewood's standing in mathematics was aptly summed up when in 1943 he received the Sylvester Medal of the Royal Society: 'Littlewood, on Hardy's own estimate, is the finest mathematician he has ever known. He was the man most likely to storm and smash a really formidable problem; there was no one else who could command such a combination of insight, technique and power.'

The Hardy–Littlewood partnership produced amazing results. As Edmund Landau, the eminent German number theorist, said: 'The mathematician Hardy–Littlewood was the best in the world, with Littlewood the more original genius and Hardy the better journalist.' For example, in a series of papers entitled *Partitio Numerorum*, Hardy and Littlewood broke new ground by introducing the 'circle method' to tackle a host of difficult problems. This was an analytic technique whose origins can be traced back to the work of Hardy and Ramanujan. They also obtained deep results about the analytic properties of the zeta function. Another of their great results, the Hardy–Littlewood maximal theorem, they first formulated in terms of the 'satisfaction' of a batsman – a clear sign of Hardy's pen. Together with Pólya, they also wrote a very influential book, *Inequalities*.

The partnership was shrouded in mystery: people wondered how two such giants could collaborate in great harmony for decades. As Littlewood shunned public appearances and never went to conferences, as a joke it was rumoured that Littlewood was invented by Hardy only to have someone on whom he could blame his mistakes. The rules for the collaboration were eventually revealed by Harald Bohr in 1947: when one wrote to the other, it was completely immaterial whether what they wrote was right or wrong. When one received a letter from the other, he was under no obligation to read it, let alone answer it. Although it did not really matter if they both simultaneously thought about the same detail, still it was preferable that they should not do so. It was quite immaterial if one of them had not contributed the least bit to the contents of a paper under their common name. What a set of negative axioms on which to build a glorious collaboration!

A great many mathematical talents were nurtured by Hardy and Littlewood; the greatest two were Ramanujan and Paley, both of whom died young.

Srinivasa Aiyangar Ramanujan (1887–1920) was an amazing self-taught Indian genius who, as Littlewood said, 'was the personal friend of every natural number'. He was born in Erode, a small village southwest of Madras, and fell in love with mathematics at an early age. He came across a vast collection of exercises written by a Cambridge coach, G.S. Carr, and eventually worked his way through all of them. Unfortunately, Ramanujan could not pass the necessary examinations needed to be admitted to the University of Madras, and so he became a clerk in the Madras Port Trust. While a clerk, he persevered with his research on his own, with guidance only from Carr's book, and proved a huge array of results including identities, infinite series, continued fractions and approximations. In January 1913 he sent a collection of his results to Hardy. After a fair amount of discussion, Hardy and Littlewood decided that Ramanujan was

an extraordinary mathematician, and Hardy proceeded to arrange a scholarship for Ramanujan to come to Trinity.

Ramanujan was an undoubted mathematical genius, but in several respects he knew less than an ordinary undergraduate: because of Carr's treatment of mathematics, he was not even sure what a proof was. As Hardy wrote:

The limitations of his knowledge were as startling as its profundity. Here was a man … whose mastery of continued fractions was … beyond that of any mathematician in the world, who had found for himself the functional equation of the zeta function and the dominant terms of many of the most famous problems in the analytic theory of numbers; and yet he had never heard of a doubly periodic function or of Cauchy's theorem, and had indeed but the vaguest idea of what a function of a complex variable was.

Ramanujan's lack of formal training made little difference to his creative genius: soon after his arrival in Cambridge in April 1914, not only did he prove great results on his own, but also embarked on an intensive collaboration with Hardy. Perhaps their most famous result is an asymptotic formula for the partition function; the method they used to prove this astonishing result was the basis of the Hardy–Littlewood circle method. Ramanujan's name is attached to many results and notions: in addition to the Hardy–Ramanujan formula, there are Ramanujan theta functions, Ramanujan tau functions, Rogers–Ramanujan identities and Ramanujan graphs, to name but a few.

In 1918 Ramanujan was elected a Fellow of the Royal Society, and a little later he became the first Indian Fellow of Trinity. Unfortunately, his health was never robust: in England he was diagnosed with tuberculosis and vitamin deficiency and was sent to sanatoria for long periods. When towards the end of 1918 his health seemed to have improved, he decided to return to India. As Hardy wrote: 'He will return to India with a scientific standing and reputation such as no Indian has enjoyed before, and I am confident that India will regard him as the treasure he is. His natural simplicity and modesty has never been affected in the least by success – indeed all that is wanted is to get him to realise that he really is a success.' However, Ramanujan's recovery did not last long, and he died a year after his return to India.

It is often held that in terms of 'natural' talent, Ramanujan had no equal: Hardy (as ever, fond of lists), when rating mathematicians on the basis of pure talent on a scale from 0 to 100, gave himself a score of 25, Littlewood 30, Hilbert 80 and Ramanujan 100.

Raymond Edward Alan Christopher Paley (1907–33) was Littlewood's outstanding student; he proved important results with Littlewood on harmonic analysis. He was a Smith's Prizeman in 1930, and was elected a Fellow of Trinity in the same year. He had an exceptional talent for collaboration: in addition to doing joint work with Littlewood, he worked with Zygmund, Wiener and Pólya. As Wiener wrote: 'Possessed of an extraordinary capacity for making friends and for scientific collaboration, Paley believed that the inspiration of continual interchange of ideas stimulates each collaborator to accomplish more than he would alone.'

Paley would certainly have become one of the leading analysts in the world, had he not died in an avalanche a few months after his 26th birthday. His death was a tremendous blow to analysis in Britain. To quote Wiener again:

[Paley] was already recognised as the ablest of the group of young English mathematicians who have been inspired by the genius of G.H. Hardy and J.E. Littlewood. In a group notable for its brilliant technique, no one had developed this technique to a higher degree than Paley. Nevertheless he should not be thought of primarily as a technician, for with this ability he combined creative power of the first order. As he himself was wont to say, technique without 'rugger tactics' will not get one far, and these rugger tactics he practised to a degree that was characteristic of his forthright and vigorous nature.

The Second World War and beyond

Of the many mathematicians who contributed to the war effort, perhaps none had a greater impact than William Tutte (1917–2002). Although he came up to the College as a chemist in 1935, he quickly gravitated to mathematics. Indeed, as an undergraduate he collaborated with three other Trinity students, Brooks, Smith and Stone, to solve a celebrated problem, that of squaring the square. After the outbreak of the Second World War, he went to Bletchley Park as a code-breaker. His greatest achievement there was his breaking of Fish, the code used by the German High Command. This was even more impressive than the celebrated breaking of Enigma, because not even the machinery for coding Fish was known. Memories of other Trinity code-breakers appear later in this volume. After his PhD in 1948, Tutte did fundamental work in combinatorics; in particular, he constructed the Tutte polynomial, which has found wide-ranging applications.

Frank Adams (1930–89) and Sir Michael Atiyah (1929–) contributed much to the development of algebraic topology, helping to turn it into one of the most respected branches of mathematics. Adams, one of the founders of homotopy theory, was the Lowndean Professor of Astronomy and Geometry at Cambridge from 1970 until his death. He is best remembered for the Adams spectral sequence, the Adams–Novikov spectral sequence and the Adams operations in K-theory. One of his major results concerned linearly independent vector fields on spheres, a problem closely related to Clifford algebras.

Atiyah, who is one of the most important mathematicians of our age, has been the President of the Royal Society, and Master of Trinity. He has collaborated with a host of major mathematicians, including Raoul Bott, Friedrich Hirzebruch and Isadore Singer, and has proved many important theorems. Perhaps his best known result is the Atiyah–Singer index theorem, a deep result with a host of applications, including the study of differential equations.

Alan Baker (1939–), who has been a Fellow of Trinity since 1964, has continued the tradition of the College in number theory. He is one of the founders of transcendence theory, which he has used to obtain effective methods in number theory: with his work he has revolutionized Diophantine theory.

Richard Borcherds (1959–) has proved deep results connecting group theory with other branches of mathematics. In particular, he introduced vertex algebras, which he later used, together with methods from string theory, to prove the monstrous moonshine conjecture of Conway and Norton. With this result Borcherds

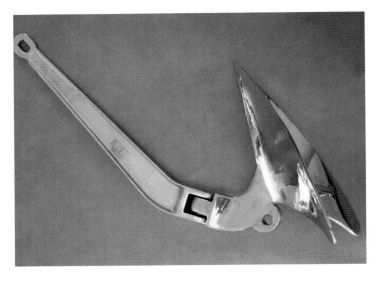

The CQR anchor was designed in 1933 by G.I. Taylor, its hinged shank allowing it to dig in immediately after 180 degree changes in wind or tide direction. It remains one of the strongest and most versatile bluewater anchor designs.

established a connection between the monster group, a very large simple group, and mathematical physics.

Timothy Gowers (1963–), the Rouse Ball Professor of Mathematics since 1998, shot to fame when he used combinatorial methods to prove several old conjectures of Banach; in particular (with Maurey) he solved the unconditional basis problem. He has also done ground-breaking work in combinatorics related to Szemerédi's theorem on arithmetic progressions.

Ben Green (1977–), who has been the Herchel Smith Professor of Mathematics at Cambridge since 2006, has proved very important results in combinatorics and number theory. He is best known for the Green–Tao theorem, that the sequence of primes contains arbitrarily long arithmetic progressions, proved by transferring Szemerédi's theorem to a sparse setting.

The greatest prize in mathematics, comparable to (but even rarer than) the Nobel Prize, is the Fields Medal: every four years since the middle of the 20th century, up to four of these have been awarded to mathematicians under the age of 40. Of the six Fields Medals received by British mathematicians, four have gone to Fellows of Trinity: Atiyah, Baker, Borcherds and Gowers. This is perhaps the strongest indication that the College has maintained its pre-eminent position in mathematics in Britain.

Applied Mathematics
Michael Proctor (1968)

A survey of mathematics at Trinity would not be complete without some description of three outstanding mathematicians of the 20th century whom we would call 'applied mathematicians', using advanced mathematics to describe physical phenomena, and in particular fluid dynamics – though 100 years ago the distinction between pure and applied mathematics was not as stark as it is today; for example, J.E.Littlewood, in his appealing memoir *A Mathematician's Miscellany*, discusses work he did in the First World War on ballistics.

Sir Geoffrey Taylor OM FRS (1886–1975) (always known as G.I.) was a pioneer in the study of waves and turbulence in fluids. His father was an artist, but his mother was from the mathematical Boole family. He began research in quantum theory with J.J.Thomson but soon switched to wave motion and turbulence,

winning the Adams Prize for an essay on the subject in 1915. He was always keen for practical experience, and while involved with propellor design during the First World War he learned to fly and do parachute jumps, and later became an accomplished sailor. Between the wars he was a Fellow of Trinity and a Royal Society Research Professor, which allowed him to concentrate on research without the distraction of teaching, which he disliked. While continuing his work on turbulence, he was also instrumental in developing models of fracture and plasticity in solids. Perhaps his most famous work is that on the structure of turbulence, where he elucidated the importance of the 'Taylor microscale' (at the interface between dynamic and viscous transfers of energy between scales of motion). His practical bent came to the fore again when he developed the so-called CQR anchor, which has found wide use for many small water craft.

During the Second World War he became an expert on blast waves and was part of the British delegation to the Manhattan project. It is said that by watching a film of a nuclear explosion, and applying simple dimensional analysis to the evolution of the blast wave, he was able to predict the energy released. This got him into trouble with the authorities, since the yield of the bomb was supposed to be classified! He was also very influential in the study of rotating fluids and of the instability of the interface between two immiscible fluids under gravity.

His technique was to combine careful but simple experiments with elegant theory, and his work and methods were the inspiration for the burgeoning field of fluid mechanics research in Cambridge, starting in the 1950's. That development was guided and led by George (G.K.) Batchelor FRS (1920–2000). Batchelor was from Australia and arrived soon after the war to work with G.I.Taylor on turbulence, only to find that Taylor had lost interest in the subject. Undeterred, Batchelor built on G.I.'s

The University's new Centre for Mathematical Sciences, Wilberforce Road.

work and that of the powerful Russian school. Among many other contributions he wrote the influential monograph *Homogeneous Turbulence*, published in 1953, still a standard work today. Later on in his career he switched to the industrially important problem of the mechanics of suspensions, and again made important contributions, using some of the same mathematical techniques that he had used in his turbulence work. His publications show that while he was very much at home with sophisticated mathematics, he disapproved of 'clever maths' for its own sake and always sought to address problems of practical importance. He is chiefly remembered for his founding of the Department of Applied Mathematics and Theoretical Physics (DAMTP), first in the Cavendish and then in somewhat more salubrious premises in Silver Street. Here he took full responsibility for everything, from the design of the seminar room to the careful selection of research supervisors. Under his 20-year leadership DAMTP became the foremost applied mathematics department in the world, not only in fluid mechanics but in relativity and cosmology as well. He also founded the *Journal of Fluid Mechanics*, which became and still remains the most prestigious journal in that subject.

The last of the trio is Sir James (M.J.) Lighthill FRS (1924–98). Lighthill was a pioneer in the field of aeroacoustics, and developed the theory of aircraft noise, showing that the noise output from a jet is proportional to the eighth power of the jet speed. He also made other important contributions to wave theory, which proved useful in such diverse areas as floods in rivers and traffic flow. Phenomenally quick to grasp new ideas, he believed with some justification that he could master any field – for example in later life while Provost of UCL he would don a white coat, visit the University College Hospital wards and pretend to be

an ENT consultant, using his knowledge of the human cochlea. His seminars were tours de force, often accompanied by visual demonstrations of the phenomena: his imitation of fish swimming was especially memorable. Lighthill was an outstanding student at Winchester, then an undergraduate at Trinity from 1941–3 before doing war work at the National Physical Laboratory in Teddington. Subsequently, he went to Manchester, becoming a professor at the age of 26. Thereafter he became Director of the Royal Aircraft Establishment at Farnborough before returning to Cambridge to take up the Lucasian Chair in succession to Dirac (the first Trinity man to hold the post since Charles Babbage, the computer pioneer), before going to UCL as Provost. Away from mathematics, Lighthill was a prodigious swimmer, with a speciality of swimming (on his back) around islands. He died while trying to swim round Sark (something he had done on a number of earlier occasions).

———————

In the late summer of 1940, I received my results in the Higher School Certificate at a grammar school in suburban London. As a result, the mathematics master suggested I compete for a Cambridge scholarship, something that few pupils of the school had ever done, let alone successfully. My parents agreed, despite the extra cost they would incur, partly because success would, at least for a while, avoid my National Service. We knew nothing of Cambridge; to us it was just the place that won the boat race every year, as it did in those days. My parents had only the vaguest idea of what a university did.

As a result, I worked with the master, a lot of the teaching being conducted in air-raid shelters, and in December 1940 went

Opposite: *The installation of Professor Edgar Adrian as Master in October 1951. Prominent in the front row of spectators is a future Master, Michael Atiyah (third from left in front row with spectacles), then an undergraduate, with his friends John Polkinghorne (to his right) and James Mackay (to his left).*

to Cambridge to take the scholarship examination. I arrived at Trinity on a Sunday, to be greeted by a helpful porter, who showed me to my room, told me where to eat and where to go for the examinations on Monday morning.

Sometime on Monday I called on my tutor, the Revd Burnaby. I had been looking forward to meeting him because rumour had it that his brother was Davy Burnaby, a radio comedian I had enjoyed. The result was a disappointment since he appeared to me to be a surly, unwelcoming individual. Looking back I realise that he had little experience of meeting lower middle-class children, and I had none of religious academics, so that unfamiliarity was the likely reason for the frigidity of our meeting. I left Trinity feeling that the best people there were the porters.

Shortly after my return from Trinity, a telegram came while I was at school. To my social class, a telegram always meant a disaster and I arrived home to find my mother in a panic. But the content of this one was joyous, simply saying, 'Congratulations, awarded exhibition, Burnaby'. This astonished everyone, not least me, because my maths was not all that good after only three months of scholarship preparation. In addition to the maths exams, we had to write an English essay, and I had spent a happy time writing about the English parish church; a hobby of mine had been to explore on my bicycle the churches of Surrey. I have often wondered whether that essay helped secure the exhibition.

My memory of October 1941 is poor but Burnaby was my dour tutor and the delightful Besicovitch supervised me in pure maths. Many dons were away because of the war, so for applied maths I had to go to Frank Powell at Caius, and my schoolmaster was disgusted. To have got an award at the best College and then be farmed out was, he said, unsatisfactory. In fact, it was brilliant for me, since Frank had been a suburban-London grammar-school boy like me and we understood one another.

Wartime regulations meant that one could only stay up for two years, so I omitted part I and went straight to part II of the Mathematical Tripos, which was taken in 1943, gaining a first. This meant enjoyable, hard work. In addition I had to do Home Guard and fire-watching duties. Some time in 1942–3 I was told that if I went to some additional lectures on statistics, not a subject in the Tripos, there was a possibility of a reserved post in the Ministry of Supply afterwards. These occupied yet more time, but to my parents' relief led to a post in London until 1945, and as a result, I became, courtesy of the war, a statistician.

There was a return to Trinity with a Senior Scholarship for the academic year 1946–7 to take part III of the Tripos. Now, for the first time, I really enjoyed Trinity and Cambridge. There were still shortages as in wartime and Rattenbury had replaced Burnaby, but I could go to a lot of brilliant lectures on topics of my choice and have more time for social activities. When I say the lectures were brilliant, the reference is to the content, not to their delivery. Now I knew why one went to Cambridge, to sit at the feet of leading figures in their fields.

Early in 1948 I had a letter from Wishart, then Director of the Statistical Laboratory in the Faculty of Mathematics, saying that from the autumn there was to be a new post of demonstrator, essentially the term for an assistant lecturer in a laboratory subject, and would I like to apply for it. There was no welcome from Trinity, even a letter about housing to Rattenbury elicited a cool, unhelpful reply. I remained at Cambridge until 1960, eventually becoming Director of the Laboratory, before taking up a chair first at Aberystwyth and then at UCL. I bear Trinity no ill will for the way it treated me. It provided board and lodging while the University made and encouraged me. The difficulties between us initially were likely due to the disparity between a grammar-school boy who had had little culture at home, and the public-school ethos that pervaded the place. Later there may have been a problem because statistics was not a Trinity subject. At least until my retirement from academia, no Fellow that I am aware of has specialised in the subject, unlike John's, King's and other colleges. This denial of the subject may exist even today because the present Master has written a fine book on the uncertainties that face us in the 21st century that makes no use of probability, the language of uncertainty, and the basic tool of statistics.

Dennis V. Lindley (1941)

I CAME FIRST TO TRINITY AS AN APPLICANT FOR A SCHOLARSHIP in the group of colleges of which Trinity was one. In 1947 this involved a two-day series of papers written in the Guildhall. I arrived late one night and was given a room in Bishop's Hostel, used during the term by the great mathematician Professor Swinnerton Dyer. Next morning I went out for breakfast to Hall which led me into Great Court for the first time in the light of a beautiful frosty morning. I shall never forget that awe-inspiring view.

When I was due to come up to Trinity in 1950 my mother became terminally ill. It was then I realised the value of the tutorship system. H.O. Evenett was my tutor. I was an only child and the situation was difficult but what marvellous support he gave me. My mother died at the end of October and he kindly arranged that I should come into residence in the following January. There I made good friends: John Aitcheson who had been a student with me in Edinburgh and became a distinguished professor of statistics, Michael Atiyah, future Master of the College and Fields medallist, and John Polkinghorne, later a distinguished theoretical physicist, theologian and president of Queens College.

There were many societies that one could attend. I became a life member of the Union, which I much enjoyed but at which I was too shy to speak. We had a mathematical society, but my most entertaining memory is of the Magpie and Stump, which was the Trinity Debating Society. When the Stone of Destiny or as it is also called 'The Stone of Scone' was stolen from Westminster Abbey the Magpie and Stump appointed as its question for debate 'stones are borne but scones are bred'.

One of Trinity's many great figures was Professor Besicovitch who had rooms above the arch leading from New Court to the Backs. He used to invite perhaps six undergraduates to his rooms for games of chess round a large oblong table. He would play a game with each undergraduate, moving round the table as the opponent in all the games at once. I never beat him and I cannot remember any undergraduate who did.

James Mackay (1950) (Baron Mackay of Clashfern)

Admissions

DAISY GOODWIN *(1980)*
WITH ADRIAN POOLE *(1967)*

My interview for Trinity started with me falling flat on my face. There was a step down into Dr Seal's rooms in Nevile's Court which I hadn't anticipated. It wasn't the most auspicious beginning – it's hard to discuss the historiography of colonialism when you have skinned both knees. I am not alone in losing my balance – Eleanor Scoones, a history candidate, recounts a similar experience:

> *A friend of mine who was also being interviewed for history on the same day as me tripped in her high heels at the top of the stairs when she was about to go into Boyd Hilton's rooms and fell down the stairs, hitting her head on the flagstone floor. Boyd heard the crash and came out of his rooms to find her lying at the bottom of stairs, skirt round her waist and legs akimbo, so his first question to her was 'Shall I call you an ambulance?' An ambulance came, but she insisted on going through with the interview. I went to collect her after the interview and give her a hand down the treacherous stairs, Boyd insisting on going ahead of us so that if she fell again at least she'd have a soft landing (this was before he lost loads of weight). When we went back to school a rumour was started that it was me who pushed her down the stairs ... obviously, this was completely untrue.*

Both girls got places.

Professor Adrian Poole, Admissions Tutor from 1989 to 1994, would admit that dexterity is not an essential quality for admission, given the graceful way that clever girls can fall down

Previous pages: *The BA Society Garden Party, 2010.*

Left: *In July 1982 Colin Philpott and Hilary Jarvis became the first couple to be married in the College chapel where both bride and groom were Trinity graduates. Hilary was one of the first women to study at Trinity, matriculating as a postgraduate student in Pharmacology in 1978, while Colin was President of TCSU.*

stairs. As a cricket enthusiast, however, he enjoyed being able to admit the then captains of the Young England (John Crawley) and Young Zimbabwe (Andy Whittall) teams around 1990, both of whom went on to play Test cricket. Tantalisingly, he was unable to admit the captain of Young India, who failed to meet the conditions set him, saying, 'This does show how high-minded even cricket-loving academics can be.'

So it seems that hand–eye coordination is no prerequisite for admission to Trinity. But I wouldn't recommend clumsiness as a strategy to the thousand or so applicants for the College's 210 places. Even if the average Cambridge economics graduate can expect a starting salary of £50,000, the risk of permanent injury is too great, probably. But the competition is fierce and straight-A grades at A level are commonplace, so how does the College pick the best people out of so many well-qualified candidates?

There was a time before the Second World War when the admissions process was like something out of Anthony Powell's novels, where one of five tutors would talk to the house masters of the leading public schools and make their selection based on a quiet word. Before the war the only qualifications for entry to Trinity were 'family connections' and 'money'. No formal qualifications were required for commoners, although scholars had to sit an entrance exam. 'Colleges would compete with each other to get the right sort of chaps.'

Times have changed. Applicants not only come in both sexes, they also come from all over the world, with 25 per cent of the intake coming from overseas, the biggest increase in students coming from the EU. British students are competing with the best and brightest from Germany, the Czech Republic and Hungary. According to Dr Paul Wingfield, who became Admissions Tutor in 2002, 'European students want to come here because of the one-on-one tuition. Cambridge is more expensive, but they think it is worth it.' This brain drain appears to be one way: 'I don't think we lose many of our students to the University of Bialystok.'

So how do you pick the very best? Being able to find the Admissions Office is the first test. One former admissions tutor reflected: 'It's amazing how many successful candidates have a good sense of direction.' Some colleges rely on performance at interview but high scores at GCSE, AS and A2 are a more reliable indicator of tripos performance than interview, according to Dr Wingfield. His interviewers are told not to rely on their own judgement, 'but to look at the paperwork'. There are practical reasons for this – brilliant academics are not always the most perceptive interviewers.

The challenge for the interviewers is to come up with questions that test skill and judgement rather than knowledge. Adrian Poole used to ask candidates the meaning of ten words like 'nadir' or 'impermeable': 'This was a test they could not possibly have prepared for but it is a good indicator of the depth of their reading.' Paul Wingfield, as a musician, would play them Beethoven's weirdest piece, 'which forces them to think on the spot in ways they cannot have anticipated'. In maths they have to be very careful not to recycle questions from previous years, 'as so many of the candidates have eidectic memories; they can all remember everything'.

The admissions procedure clearly seems to work. Trinity regularly tops the Tripos tables, with a clear ascendancy in maths and science. Although, if you are reading this with a respectable

Catalina Laserna came to Trinity in 1978 to study for a PhD in Social Anthropology. A native of Colombia, she was also interested in bull-fighting.

2:1 from the 1980s, Paul Wingfield accepts that Cambridge Firsts have got easier. A quick look at the Oxbridge admissions site reveals that candidates are attracted to Trinity for a variety of reasons, from 'my teacher said it was the only place to go if you are serious about maths' to ' it's like Hogwarts, nuff said'.

The College's ratio of admissions from the state versus the independent sector hovers around 55:45 per cent. This is not so very different from the social make-up of the College in the 1980s when I was there. This is not for want of trying on the College's part – Paul Wingfield's policy has been that 'at the margins we will give the benefit of the doubt to the kids with the least educational opportunities'. The College pays for coaching for promising maths students from state schools. It sponsors such initiatives as the national cyber challenge. It takes part in the University-wide initiative to encourage more applications from the maintained sector – with special responsibility for Milton Keynes, Hampshire and the Isle of Wight. But still the social make-up of the College has not changed as much as Paul Wingfield would like. 'No one could accuse us of being prejudiced against private schools,' he admitted to me rather ruefully. The feeling among private school heads and fee-paying parents that their children are discriminated against is not borne out by the statistics. The real change in the composition of the College, however, will come in the number of students admitted from the European Union. While there is a cap on students from outside the EU, European students currently have an unlimited right of entry. Paul Wingfield predicts a time very soon when one-third of the College's undergraduates will come from abroad. Even now in schools from Saigon to Sydney, Berlin to Budapest, there are students setting their sights on Great Court.

Applicants sweat blood over their personal statements (or they pay to download them) but Paul Wingfield is rather dismissive of these miracles of self-expression: 'They are only a starting point. I am more interested in their marks. There is nothing worse than a pretentious personal statement with no foundation in knowledge.' He does admit to being intrigued by the applicant who professed a deep passion for Ezra Pound's music. 'Luckily he knew his stuff.' Some candidates take the personal in personal statement very literally indeed: 'One girl, who was applying for law, decided to come out as a lesbian in her personal statement. We were surprised to say the least, but she was a strong applicant and she did in fact get a place.' College connections make absolutely no difference to an admissions tutor, although when I visited, Wingfield and his colleagues were deciding to admit a candidate who would be the seventh generation in her family to attend Trinity.

It is ironic that even in the Thatcherite 1980s, students like me from comfortable middle-class homes went to university unencumbered by tuition fees and with a minimum grant. Gradually, we are returning to the pre-war days when colleges were financed by fees (although Trinity has always had other sources of income – see the money chapter), and only the richest students could afford to go to university. The average student in 2010 graduated with around £23,000 of debt. The fees have not lessened the numbers of applicants – the demand for places is still around 5 to 1.

But the introduction, or rather the reintroduction of fees, has had another effect. Because parents are now paying for their children's education, according to Paul Wingfield, 'They are much more demanding than they used to be. I had one student who was despondent because her first wasn't as good as her parents were expecting.' What used to be an informal arrangement between tutors and schools has now turned into high drama: admissions tutors have to deal with helicopter parents who can't quite accept that this final hurdle is out of their hands. 'The largest bribe I have been offered was £30,000,' says Paul Wingfield. Some parents come with their children to the admission interviews and are surprised to be turned away. 'Parents are quite likely to ring up and complain if their child hasn't been accepted. Dealing with disappointed parents has become an occupational hazard,' says Wingfield.

But while you could argue that the social make-up of the College hasn't changed that much in the last 50 years, it is in one respect totally different. Girls were first admitted to Trinity in 1978. Trinity was among the second wave of colleges to admit women – King's and Clare were the first. According to my sources in the Common Room, the transition was a smooth one, one don enthusing: 'The first year with women went like a bomb – it became a much more human society pretty much overnight.' I arrived in the third year of Trinity women and I can vouch for the fact that it was pretty well integrated – even harassment was gender neutral – the same don made advances to me and then to my brother two years later. (I should add that said don is no longer at the College.)

The College seemed to take the admission of girls more or less in its stride. Like obnoxious male undergraduates before me, I was thrown into the fountain after the Matriculation Dinner. They certainly didn't spend any money tarting the place up. I remember the bathrooms were pretty grim in my day. I was one of two girls on a staircase of not very well housetrained men. At least they didn't go in for hour-long baths.

When I was there it felt like a smattering of women rather than full integration. It has taken a while to get the balance up. One-third of the Fellows are now women and the male–female ratio among the undergraduates is 53 per cent:47 per cent – the slight imbalance is a reflection of the preponderance of male mathematicians. I can't help feeling as I wander around Trinity and talk to some of the present undergraduates that, even if A levels have got easier and Firsts are no longer like gold dust, the undergraduates today are far more impressive than I was at that age. In fact, with my tawdry two As and 2 Bs at A level, these days I wouldn't have got in at all.

———— ·•· ————

AT MY GIRLS' BOARDING SCHOOL THE HEIGHT OF SUCCESS WAS a career in flower arranging followed by marriage to a rich man. When I moved to a boys' school I found expectations were very different. I was taught history by Christopher Coker, now Professor of International Relations at the London School of Economics, then a recent graduate from Trinity. He suggested that I applied to his old college. This was something that would never have crossed my mind, and the audacity was thrilling. In its 450-year history, no woman had ever done such a thing.

My subject was early medieval history, the hordes of Goths and Visigoths cutting a swathe across Europe, and I felt like one of those barbarians at the gates of Rome as I prepared my own assault on this bastion of masculinity. But I was no Vandal: I loved what little I knew of Trinity's past and customs, and simply wanted to be part of them myself.

In fact I knew almost nothing about Trinity. I didn't bother with the questions that today's students are encouraged to ask: quality and price of accommodation, ratio of tutors to students, contact hours. I found out nothing about the course, or even if Cambridge was a good place to study early medieval history. All I knew was that Trinity was the biggest, the richest, the most beautiful and the best. You could walk from Cambridge to London, I was told, without leaving Trinity land. The fully stocked wine cellar reputedly stretched all the way under Great Court, Trinity Street and Wolfson Court. Yet there was also an appealingly monastic asceticism, the pale blue quality, tucked away as it was in this remote flat fenland. I didn't apply to any other university, or any other college.

I was interviewed by the historian Robert Robson in his Great Court rooms. This was my world, I decided. The ancient courtyards with their mix of intimacy and grandeur, the Backs and gardens, and Dr Robson himself: clever, courteously aloof, and as pale and dry as the pale dry sherry he served. He was just what I expected – and hoped – of a Cambridge don. I didn't discover until later that he had been vociferous in opposing the admission of women into the College.

A subsequent interview with Boyd Hilton could not have been more contrasting: low 1970s brown corduroy armchairs in which you reclined rather than sat, an informal conversation and a sense that women would, after all, be made welcome.

On only a few occasions was the scale of our minority exposed: the odd feast in hall, the matriculation photograph – although the longish hair of 1978 makes it hard to distinguish male from female. There were 70 of us 'undergraduettes', as we were coyly known, among some 1,000 men in Trinity as a whole, but partly because of the size of the College we were easily absorbed. I was never made to feel strange. Other than the quaint prefix 'Miss' appended to our staircase names, no concessions were made to our sex – rightly, I thought. When I lived in Great Court I had to go outside like everyone else and cross the courtyard, clutching my washbag, to have a bath. I didn't mind. I felt privileged to be there at all.

Inevitably we were in huge demand for parties and relationships. At times it seemed as if we were elevated almost to goddess-like status, and the pressure was intense, but I don't think any of us mistook our popularity for a sudden mysterious increase in our charms. We knew it for what it was: sheer desperation.

By the time I graduated four years later, nearly 300 women had joined Trinity. In 2008 36 per cent of the College, including postgraduates, was female. There are female voices in the choir, and thanks to some refurbished staircases not many women now have to tiptoe outside in their dressing gowns. Other than that, I don't suppose much has changed. While enriching the life of the College, our monstrous regiment of women has, above all, blended in. Nay-sayers, you need not have worried.

Helena Drysdale (1978)

Life as a graduate student
William Kynan-Wilson (2004)

Trinity's graduate students form a community which has served to enrich and enliven the complexion of the College. The inception of the PhD degree at Cambridge in 1919 represents one of the great developments at the University during the 20th century. In 1938 Trinity's graduates numbered 75 in total, a mere 10 per cent of the College's junior members. Since then this figure has steadily increased, save for a few exceptional years. In 1960 a Tutor for advanced students (now expanded to two Tutors and known as Side F) was created in reflection of the growing number of research students. In 1993 the number of graduates at Trinity reached the 300 mark, and only a decade later this figure had reached a high of 400 research students. As a percentage of the student body, graduate numbers have remained steady at around 35 per cent since 1999.

Issues of funding always affect the numbers of graduates. As national funding is pinched ever more tightly, Trinity has increasingly borne the financial burden. All members of Trinity will have benefited from the College's largesse, but perhaps none more so than those pursuing research here. The level of financial support offered to graduates here is exceptional in its breadth and depth. I can say with confidence that this beneficence is a blessing all graduates are ever conscious of and grateful for.

The emergence and prominent increase in research students at Trinity must rank as one of the most notable, albeit least dramatic, developments in the College's history. The graduate body is increasingly diverse and international, with some 47 different nations represented in recent years. The first female members of College were graduate students admitted in 1976, some two years before female undergraduates.

At the heart of today's thriving graduate community is the College's graduate student union, known as the BA Society. The Society is generously supported by the College and run by a student committee whose roles cover all aspects and concerns of student life. Just over half of the graduates at Trinity are new to the College and enter as students of Side F; the care and attention given to new graduates is a matter of pride. The significant number of students who continue their studies at Trinity to postgraduate level and beyond attests to the strong bonds of College kinship.

Life as an international student
Argyro Nicolaou (2008)

To say that Trinity is a 'very English' college is to perpetrate a rumour that is longstanding but most certainly false. After having chosen the College for its architectural grandeur and its reputation as one of Cambridge's wealthiest, I was expecting to feel like an outsider – at least to begin with: a poor islander staring dumbfounded at a monument to British tradition. Come freshers' week, however, I realised that Trinity is much more culturally diverse than people usually give it credit for. I found out a year later – as Overseas Welfare Officer of Trinity College Students Union – that actually *half* Trinity's student population is international.

This isn't a new trend at all – Cambridge has always attracted a multicultural group of people who add to the University's prestige and allure. To think that as a student of Trinity you can get a room on Wittgenstein's staircase or walk through courts that inspired the genius of Nabokov is, to say the least, overwhelming.

You can celebrate the Chinese New Year, watch French films while munching on Brie and wine, and talk to people who can tell you first hand what the political situation is like in different countries of the world. You can even join forces with a crowd of students cheering their countries on during the Eurovision song contest and not feel like an idiot. Or, at least, be one of a crowd of idiots.

And all this happens while you get acquainted with British culture – in my first year I found myself having port in my room and loving it. Observing the British accent for an ADC play. Patiently queuing for a coffee at Starbucks. Learning to say 'loo' instead of 'toilet'. Lounging on the Backs with a Pimm's in the summer. Trying to come to grips with the rules of rugby while juggling two pints of beer at the Varsity Match at Twickenham. Life as an international student at Trinity opens your mind to the everyday pleasures of so many cultures that it is hard to figure out where all your habits come from by the end of your time at the university.

I faced no problems integrating in the Cambridge community; on the contrary, I found that my culture was not only accepted, it was embraced and wondered at. People were genuinely interested in where I came from; the focus of conversation is never on the cultural divide, but on the unique things people have to offer. These become springboards for some of the most stimulating relationships one can have. In the Lent term of my first year, I talked to a friend about Greek tragedy, explaining Aristotle's unities and different versions of myths, while he filled me in on Swinburne's talent and his criticism of Shakespeare. There's a place for everything in the daily life of a Trinity student.

Studying at Trinity changes you. When I go back home for the holidays, I can't stop talking about May Balls, supervisions and Formal Hall; I take a part of that back with me. In Cambridge, I can't and don't want to stop showing my true colours and sharing the history and culinary delights of Cyprus with my English and foreign friends. The experience of being at Trinity, and being an international student, makes you a more complex, mature person, informed by a vast range of cultures and sensitivities. Trinity can undoubtedly be called a college of the world, and the worldly.

The BA Christmas party invitation.

of female time, amounting in effect to a degree course in Social Relevance, which some people were bound to fail miserably (eg those pallid maths boffins scratching out equations in their Great Court kennels, pebble-thick lenses rising to gaze through casement windows in parched marvel as some garbed Godiva flounced unavailably past). Yes, we were all sex-starved and betwitted by the pitiless Darwinian odds, and if Darwin hadn't clocked natural selection in the 19th century I would have bloody well noticed it in 1978. The inevitable romantic disappointments and dismal drunken accidents mixed a bitter cocktail of yearning and fatalism. Aged 18 I was mature and balanced and innocent. By 20 I was a professional cynic.

Conrad Williams (1978)

I WAS THERE AT A PARTICULARLY SALIENT POINT, THAT PERIOD of transition from men's preserve to an initial, minimal, parched co-residence when the College's legions of undergraduate males were served 50 girls, and a monolithic male redoubt with its hearty sportsmen, science nerds, squinting maths geeks, smug lawyers, representative epitomes of the great public schools surfing around on a sense of entitlement became a frontier of co-residence, thus concentrating within Trinity's crenellated Empyrean the problematic imbalance between the sexes in the university at large.

One gal for every seven chaps was the nail-hard statistic we bit down on in the College bar every night as we arrayed the beer mugs and fag cartons. Oh, actually, that was the Varsity average. Trinity's ratio was an eye-blistering 50 girls to 1,000 men, a teaspoonful of parmesan on a cauldron of swirling minestrone. Anybody like me, coming from a progressive co-ed school, would have found the statistic dismal and the reality worse. The odds on any kind of romantic luck took a knee jab to the vitals, but the much bigger problem was the regressive effect of such a yin yang imbalance on the College atmosphere. I had been airlifted out of co-ed heaven and dropped into a medieval-themed testosterone park.

I caricature this Dark Age because it was tinged with comic desperation. We had to adapt, like it or not. Suddenly, all of us were working terribly hard at being 'interesting' to girls, worthy

IN 1979 I MATRICULATED AS THE FIRST EVER WOMAN MATURE student at Trinity, so I am unique in College history in that respect. However, even more remarkable was the fact that I was from a deprived social background with a small child in tow.

I recall my interview with Dr Seal. I felt it was going reasonably well until he asked what I should do if I did not get into Trinity – would I consider a polytechnic? Heart sinking, and somewhat hardening in the plummet, I was honest (as in my mind I did not feel destined to go anywhere else) and replied that I should just have to try again next year and, sort of, see how that went …

After my matriculation I used to joke as to why I had aimed so high: escape from my 20th-floor tower-block council flat; the grant was better than the social; if it was good enough for the Prince of Wales, it was good enough for me, etc. The core reason was to prove it needed only courage and hard work study-wise to gain entry to Cambridge no matter what your gender or social circustance. Even if you had left school without any qualifications, it was not too late. Trinity had no prejudices against my Cockney accent and lack of social graces in my application. I hope this hasn't changed and my message all those years ago still hold true today. Access? In 1979 I was a sign of the times, the result of a free education system as well as equal opportunities legislation and a feminist movement. Today the grant has gone but today is another story altogether.

Margaret Priaulx (née Hall) (1979)

Bedders' Garden Party.

I WAS NEARLY 40 YEARS OLD WHEN I MATRICULATED AT Trinity, a working man raised in a Glasgow council flat with no qualifications. I had followed my dad onto the railways at the age of 14 and in time became an activist for the National Union of Railwaymen. Having missed out on secondary education as an evacuee in the Highlands, I was keen to learn and managed to complete a number of correspondence courses through the Union before leaving to seek a less physically demanding career. Eventually I ended up working for the Gas Board and joining the National Union of General and Municipal Workers. Through the TUC, I was awarded a scholarship at Ruskin College, Oxford, to study for a Diploma in Economic and Political Science. At the end of my first year I won a scholarship from the Imperial Relations Trust to spend a year in Australia. On my return to Oxford for the second year of my diploma, I discovered that two of my first-year friends were now studying in Cambridge. I duly applied to

Trinity and to King's. On the same day as I visited King's to sit the entrance test, I was interviewed at Trinity by a much respected Fellow, Dr Pryor. We went round to a small local pub and there talked about welfare economics and other topics. Much to my surprise he took me round the College to the Wren Library and there became involved in a conversation with some workmen working on the stonework in front of that magnificent building, and he actually climbed up a long ladder to make some important point or other. He later told me that Trinity would offer me a place to study British Constitutional History and Economic History and give me the right to use the Senior Common Room, the privilege not to wear a gown if I so desired and the right to dine in the College on certain Friday nights each month. I promptly accepted this generous offer because of his trust in accepting me on the basis of our conversation and also because I had read a book by a certain Maurice Dobb who, from what I could gather, had been a tutor in Trinity. Since he was a Marxist historian, I simply admired a college that would encourage the free flow of ideas even though the ideas might well be unacceptable to the Establishment.

Some might say Trinity tends to be too paternalistic. I had a moral tutor even though I was a happily married man, living in a College flat. I also had a financial tutor and a fine academic tutor in Dr Anil Seal. Robert Robson took an especial interest in my progress and needs. On one occasion I was told that I was £64 underspent in the bar and they requested me to make sure I used my turns on the punts. Two of my children were born in Cambridge so we were busy and there were tutors who were happy to have my little son playing on their carpet while I took my tutorial, my wife's hands being full with the baby.

At the end of two years with a wife and family to support, I was anxious to get out into the world again. Dr Seal informed me that if I worked the summer vacation I could sit the Tripos Examination after two years. My qualifications were good enough to ensure a career in higher education teaching in Australia and later in Britain, for the Open University. I was a very lucky man the day I went for an interview at Trinity and I simply feel the College has to be admired for giving someone like me a chance to improve their lot.

John Inglis (1964)

I HAVE TO SAY, APPLYING TO CAMBRIDGE WAS NOT REALLY A major issue for me. I knew of the prestigious reputation that Cambridge carries so well and even though I personally knew I was a very hard worker, I thought my chances were slim. However, the fact that I was a state-educated black female did not even cross my mind as being a reason. I just thought, 'I might as well – what's the harm? It just meant I had to fill in my UCAS application a lot quicker!' Cambridge had the perfect course for me – a scientist who did not know exactly what she wanted to do. Headed by some of the world's top names, the Natural Sciences Tripos provided me with the content and flexibility I was looking for in a course; slowly funnelling me towards what was the right concentration for my individual passion for science.

When it came to choosing a college, I only really had Trinity in mind. When looking around the College, I was amazed by its vast beauty, especially Great Court (and later, seeing it covered in snow was even more breathtaking). The one person I knew

Maurice Dobb.

my gown opened my eyes to what I had achieved and I could not wait to get stuck in. But I could not have predicted what struggles lay ahead. Between Monday to Saturday lectures (which I thought was a myth), practicals and evening supervisions, I had to fit in training six days a week and competitions. This was even harder in the winter as the University athletics track didn't have floodlights at the time and it was near impossible to see where you were going after 4pm. But somehow, with the help of friends, understanding supervisors and a Dictaphone (oh yes), I completed my three years and graduated with a degree I can be proud of.

Phyllis Agbo (2004)

Phyllis Agbo, competing for Great Britain in 2009. She remains the most successful Varsity athlete of all time, winning seven different individual events two years running and setting three match and two grounds records.

attending Cambridge was a Trinitarian 'mathmo' and athlete. He told me I could not go wrong applying to the biggest and richest college in Cambridge. As well as being an educational haven for scientists and mathematicians, the sheer size of the College meant it would be hard not to find someone you could get on with. I have to say that the numerous grants available also helped make my decision easy. I did not know about the apparent preconceptions some people have about Trinity as being home to mainly privately educated white 'rich kids' or extremely bright timid guys.

The application process was interesting to say the least. Having applied for natural sciences, I had an exam paper to complete before my interview and it was one of the most baffling hours of my life. I was faced with questions such as 'how far away is the horizon?' and 'why can't you unboil an egg?' I remember looking over it thinking that this was going to be a whole new way of thinking for me.

Ten months later I was a member of Trinity College, standing in Nevile's Court taking my matriculation photo. Posing in

P T ECKERSLEY	D R F HAVILAND	C G D LANCA
P R EDGCUMBE	J C A HAYES	J G H LANDE
H S ELGAR	P HAZELL	P L LANDER
J L H B ELIOTT	D M HENDERSON	J R LANGLEY
H H ELLIOT	F R W HENDERSON	M P LATTER
VISCOUNT	W J HENDERSON	H R LAUREN
ELVEDEN	P W HERBERT	C H LAWREN
M J EUGSTER	R H B HERBERT	W N LEACH
P G EVELYN	G S P G HOARE	J T LEACOC
B V FANSHAWE	J M H HOARE	E D W LEAF
E V M FAVELL	H P E HODGSON	H H J LEIGH
E B M FISHER	F U HOLLINS	J H LEWIS
P G W S FOLJAMBE	J W HOPKINS	M G LILLING
J C FOSTER	R J HORN	H E J LISTER
P S FOWLER	A R L HORNBY	J H LITTLE
D GAME	M P G HOWARD	T D LITTLE
K C GANDAR DOWER	A J E HOWEY	H LIVERSID
P H GASKELL	I HOWITT	R de M C LLE
J A GAUNT	T W G HULBERT	W G LUCAS
J GELDARD	C S HUMPHR	C LUXMOOR
J GEORGE	F W JACKSON	M LUXMOOR
T A GLOSTER	T R E JACKSO	R J W McAL
A S T GODFREY	D H JACOBSON	R E MacCAW
T E GODMAN	J S W JARVIE	J R McCOSH
R P GOSNELL	M JEBB	ACGR
R J V GOSS	E G JEFFERY	INT
P L GOSSAGE	B E JEFFREY	CKE
K W GRAHAM	A A JESSUP	
R F S GRIGG	M A JOHNS	PH
B GRIMSTON	E C KAUFF	W
B D GRIMSTON	H W KEAR	
J StG GUNSTON	J KEE	MA
J P HADRILL	D W KENT	
J H V HALL	R G G KEI	
D H T HANBURY	J F KINGS	
J M HARGREAVES	O C KISCH	
F L HARPER	C M KNAG	
R A I HARRISON	VISCOUNT	
MARQUESS OF	KN	

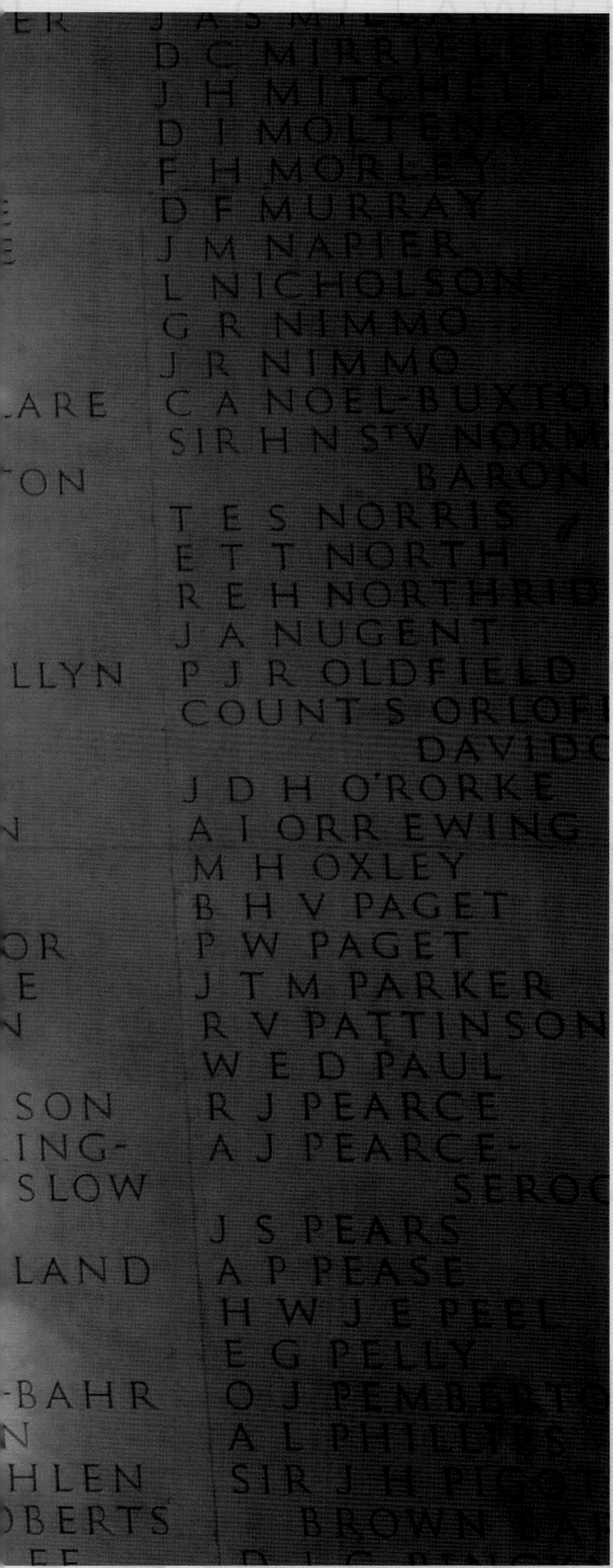

CHAPTER 5

Isaac Newton

BÉLA BOLLOBÁS *(1963),*
GORDON SQUIRES *(1956)*
AND ANSON CHEUNG *(1999)*

Isaac Newton was born in Woolsthorpe Manor in the village of Colsterworth, near Grantham, on 4 January 1643 – to Newton and his contemporaries, Christmas Day 1642 (Old Style). His father, whose family had for generations farmed a modest estate, died before Newton was born and his childhood was unhappy. At the age of 12 he went to the King's School, Grantham, where his signature can still be seen, carved on the library wall. There, under the influence of the perceptive schoolmaster Henry Stokes, his passion for learning was awakened.

When he was 17 his mother called him home to manage the family farm. His uncle and schoolmaster, recognising his talents, persuaded her to let him to go to university to study law. In June 1661 he entered Trinity, his uncle's alma mater, equipping himself with a lock for his desk, a quart bottle with ink to fill it, a notebook, a pound of candles and a chamber pot.

He entered as a sub-sizar, a student who paid his way by waiting and performing menial duties for Fellows and Fellow Commoners. In 1663 he bought a book on astrology and was surprised to find that his mathematics was not good enough to read it. So he read and, as one can see from his own copy in the Wren, noted Barrow's edition of Euclid's *Elements*, as well as studying other books on advanced mathematics, including Wallis's *Algebra*. He was awarded a scholarship in 1664 and graduated without any particular distinction in the following year.

Newton's scientific genius became evident rather suddenly when, in 1665, the Great Plague hit Cambridge and the University closed. Newton returned briefly to Woolsthorpe.

Over the next two years, he made amazing discoveries in mathematics, mechanics, optics and astronomy. As he said later, 'All this [work] was in the two plague years of 1665 and 1666, for in those days I was in the prime of my life for invention, and minded mathematics and philosophy more than at any time since.' By 'philosophy' he meant natural philosophy or what we now call science. Newton returned to Cambridge in 1667 and was elected to a Fellowship; two years later he succeeded Isaac Barrow in the Lucasian Professorship of Mathematics.

While at Woolsthorpe Newton laid the foundations of differential and integral calculus, several years before its independent discovery by Leibniz. He developed this 'method of fluxions' to unify earlier techniques for solving seemingly unrelated problems such as finding tangents, the extrema of functions, the areas under curves and the lengths of curves. He presented his findings in 1671 in *De Methodis Serierum et Fluxionum*, but published posthumously only in 1736, in an English translation by John Colson. Had Newton not delayed publication, his subsequent bitter priority argument with Leibniz would have been avoided.

At Woolsthorpe he had started experiments in optics that he continued in Cambridge. He showed that when a beam of white light passed through a glass prism it spread out into a range, or spectrum, of colours. He deduced that white light was a combination of colours, and proved the point by recombining the different colours to produce white light. Previously, it had been believed that white light was the pure quantity, and that colours were additional complicating effects. He realised that because different colours are refracted by different amounts in glass, the sharpness of an image in a lens telescope is limited. So he built a telescope with a spherical mirror instead of a lens; today's large telescopes are all of this type.

Newton's greatest achievement in physics was in the field of mechanics. Again, this began at Woolsthorpe. The starting point was what are now called Newton's laws of motion. Their central idea is that a body continues in a straight line at the same velocity unless acted on by a force. This was contrary to the ideas of the ancient Greeks – then still prevalent – that a moving body needed a continual force to keep it moving. Newton's laws have stood the

Charles Montagu, 1st Earl of Halifax, 1661–1715, by Kneller. Given by Dr Bainbrig. After six years as a Fellow of Trinity, Montagu left in 1689 to pursue a career in politics. In 1694 he steered through Parliament legislation creating the Bank of England, an archetypal central bank, which was soon helping finance William III's Continental wars. In 1695–6 Montagu arranged for his Trinity friend Isaac Newton to reissue the coinage, which had been severely clipped.

test of time; they apply in all branches of science, and although since modified by Einstein, the modifications are negligible unless the bodies are moving at speeds close to the speed of light.

Next came the law of universal gravitation. Newton later said this came to him when he saw an apple fall from a tree. He realised that the same force that made the apple fall also caused the motions of celestial bodies. The conventional wisdom was that the forces were completely different. But, crucially, how did the gravitational force between two bodies vary with their distance? Here Newton proposed the inverse square law which states that the force varies inversely as the square of the distance – for example, if the distance doubles the force drops by a factor

Statue of Isaac Newton by Roubiliac in the Ante Chapel.

of four. Using his laws of motion and the inverse square law, he proved that planetary orbits are ellipses, confirming a law Kepler had derived from astronomical observation.

Newton published his discoveries in 1687 in *Philosophiae Naturalis Principia Mathematica*, commonly known as the *Principia* and regarded as the greatest work in scientific literature. It sold for 6/- (30p), or 5/- for ready money; a copy costs rather more today. It contained not only Newton's laws of motion and his calculations of the orbits of the planets and their satellites, but also a discussion of more complicated motions like those of bodies in resisting media and of fluids in creating resistance. The *Principia* made Newton famous. While he did not write it in the language of calculus, he made extensive use of calculus in its geometrical form, so that the *Principia* has been called 'a book dense with the theory and application of the infinitesimal calculus'.

As Rouse Ball wrote, in addition to founding calculus, Newton distinctly advanced every branch of mathematics then studied: in particular, he discovered the generalised binomial theorem and the identities named after him, introduced his method in numerical analysis, proved important formulae bearing his name in the theory of finite differences, used geometry to obtain solutions of Diophantine equations and was the first to make substantial use of power series.

Newton's scientific outlook is contained in one of his most famous sayings, 'Hypotheses non fingo' (I frame no hypotheses). By 'hypothesis' he meant an axiom unsupported by observation, as in Aristotelian science. Newton's method was to state a principle or generalisation drawn from a series of observations and then compare its predictions with the results of further observations. As he said, his method was to 'derive two or three general Principles of Motion from Phænomena, and afterwards to tell how the Properties and Actions of all corporeal Things follow from those manifest Principles, though the causes of those Principles are not yet discover'd'. This is the outlook of scientists today. While they cannot tell you the cause of gravity, they can predict with great accuracy the next eclipse of the sun.

In 1689 Newton was elected Member of Parliament for the University of Cambridge. He sat for less than a year and is

Extract from the annotated first edition of Principia Mathematica, *1686.*

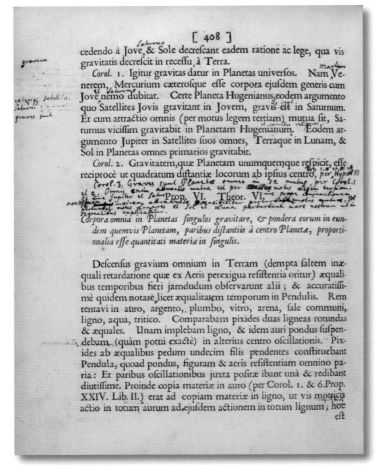

In 1696 the great Swiss mathematician Johann Bernoulli challenged all mathematicians to solve two problems. One was the brachistochrone (shortest time) problem. This asked for the shape of the curve down which a bead starting from rest and accelerated by gravity will slide, without friction, from one point to another in the least time. In January 1697 Newton returned home from the Royal Mint to find Bernoulli's letter. Working until 4am, he sent the solution that morning to Montagu, then President of the Royal Society, for anonymous publication. Bernoulli knew its author instantly, saying: 'tanquam ex ungue leonem' (we know the lion by its claw). While he did not enjoy being 'teased by foreigners about mathematical things', Newton's solution of the brachistochrone problem is commonly seen as the start of the branch of mathematics called the calculus of variations.

In 1703 Newton became President of the Royal Society, a position he held until his death. Not being an aristocratic figurehead like his predecessors, he started the practice of scientific demonstrations at meetings, and greatly increased the Society's authority.

His second major work, *Opticks: or a Treatise on the Reflexions, Refractions and Colours of Light*, written in English, was published in 1704. It deals with all his experiments in light, greatly developed since his original work with prisms, and included topics such as colour vision and the formation of rainbows.

Queen Anne visited Cambridge in 1705 and conferred a knighthood on Newton in Trinity's dining hall, a unique honour at the time for a scientist. Newton died in March 1727. His body lay in state, like that of a sovereign, in a chamber adjoining Westminster Abbey; he was buried in the Abbey itself. Typically, he had managed his own finances well and left £32,000, then a very large sum.

While Newton is still revered as one of the very best mathematicians and physicists, to dwell on his scientific and administrative work alone fails to give a true picture of his activities. He had two other passions which occupied still more of his time and energy than mathematics or physics. These were alchemy and theology. Maynard Keynes called him 'the first scientist and the last magician'. In 1669 he bought apparatus

recorded as having spoken only once – to ask an usher to close a draughty window.

Seven years later Newton moved from Cambridge to London, following his appointment as Warden, and subsequently Master, of the Mint. The coinage, represented by thin unmilled pieces of silver, was in a bad state; clipping coins was a popular fraud. Newton estimated that 20 per cent of coins in circulation were counterfeit. His friend Charles Montagu, Trinity man and founder of the Bank of England, devised a scheme of reform which Newton carried through so well that he bravely, and successfully, prosecuted 28 counterfeiters.

By the 1690s Newton had not worked on mathematics for decades but was still, by far, the world's best mathematician.

The apple tree at Trinity, which was grown from a cutting from Newton's tree at Woolsthorpe Manor.

he produced several tracts on the literal interpretation of the Bible. Later he wrote a book on the chronology of the ancient kingdoms, and another (published posthumously) on the prophecies of Daniel and St John's Apocalypse. It appears that his reading of St John's Gospel caused Newton to become an anti-trinitarian; he resisted ordination into the Anglican priesthood, normally required of Fellows of Oxbridge colleges. The terms of the Lucasian professorship, he said, prevented the holder from being active in the church. Charles II concurred and Newton was never ordained.

Newton had his weaknesses. He suffered from depression and had two nervous breakdowns. He was very sensitive on issues of priority, and could be difficult. His later years were overshadowed by quarrels with Hooke, Leibniz and others, which were not to his credit. His bitter controversy with Leibniz concerned the invention of calculus. The widely accepted view today is that both developed calculus independently, although Leibniz began to publish a full account of his methods in 1684, while Newton published very little about it until 1693, and gave his first full account only in 1704. Leibniz's 'd' notation is certainly more convenient than Newton's 'dot', and was immediately adopted by mathematicians on the Continent, England following suit only in 1820. Newton abhorred the slightest criticism; his rage against Leibniz knew no bounds. Sadly, he even used his position as President of the Royal Society to attack Leibniz. The Society appointed an 'impartial committee' to decide who invented calculus; Newton wrote its report, coming down in favour of his own claim. But he could be kind and considerate to those he thought understood his work, in particular the young men who helped to bring out successive editions of the *Principia*. His relations with women were minimal, although he was close to one of his nieces. He dropped his acquaintance with Vigani, Cambridge's first professor of Chemistry, when the latter 'told him a loose story about a nun'.

Whatever one thinks of his character, Newton was perhaps the greatest scientist the world has ever known. As Alexander Pope's epitaph has it, 'Nature and nature's laws lay hid in night; God said "Let Newton be" and all was light'.

for conducting experiments in chemistry while reading widely in alchemy, collecting and copying many manuscripts. He often experimented with mercury and it seems likely, judging by the mercury concentrations found in his hair at his death, that he suffered from mercury poisoning.

Newton was a firm Christian all his life: he saw God as the irreducible master creator and warned against using his own laws of motion and gravitation to turn the universe into a machine. 'Gravity,' he said, 'explains the motions of the planets, but it cannot explain who set the planets in motion. God governs all things and knows all that is or can be done.' From the 1690s

DOGS AND CATS

College regulations are clear: no dogs. The Senior Bursar's accounts for 1656 contain records of quite large sums expended on keeping dogs out. Byron famously brought a bear to College because he was not allowed to bring a dog. Nonetheless, the College has been home to some mythical and not-so-mythical dogs. Prince Chula Chakrabongse of Siam matriculated in 1927 and quickly became famous for his lavish lifestyle, bringing with him in his second year both a chauffeur-driven sports car and a pedigree wire-haired terrier named Tony. The Prince and Tony lodged at 32 Trinity Street, where Tony made himself useful by carrying the Prince's mortarboard for him. A monument to Tony still stands on Mitcham's Corner, paid for in 1934 by the Prince.

Precedent now established, Hugh Northcote (1958) was also allowed a dog:

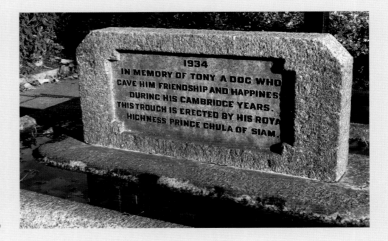

Having made friends with a Trinity man reading agriculture, I became interested in shooting. At Over and on the Wash, it was obvious that a dog was better at swimming after my quarry than I was. It was not difficult to find a gun dog in Cambridge so I could get one, but was it allowed for an undergraduate to have one? Going on the advice given to me by an old monk at my school, that you could get away with anything if you asked, I went to my Tutor to ask if I might have a dog. I was told, certainly not – a cat, yes, but not a dog. I then told my Tutor that there was a drinking trough in Chesterton Road dedicated by Prince Chula to his dog who was up at Cambridge with him. My Tutor changed his judgement saying that what was good enough for Prince Chula was good enough for me and I was granted permission.

My dog came to Hall with me most nights and I left her in the Porters' Lodge on a blanket behind the desk. I only got into trouble if I did not bring her – they loved having her. It was most unusual to be asked to look after an undergraduate's dog – they hadn't done so before in 300 years!

Above: *Monument to 'Tony', a Trinity dog, on Mitcham's Corner.*

Left: *Titan. She and her sister Ricardo were given their masculine names after being sexed by Trinity veterinary medicine students. She disappeared in 1999, while Ricardo died in 2010 at the age of 18.*

Undergraduates with dogs in lodgings were one thing, but a dog in the Master's Lodge required some discretion. Tim Ridley (1966) recalls: 'When Rab was appointed Master during my time at Trinity, Mrs Butler brought a dog with them to the Master's Lodge. I recall the Head Porter observing, "That is not a dog, Mr Ridley. College Regulations do not permit that. It is a cat."'

Certainly, Trinity will have housed generations of cats to keep rodents at bay, although whether or not Isaac Newton owned one is open to question. Newton mythology has it that he invented the cat flap in order to allow his cat to leave his rooms without disturbing the light while he conducted experiments into optics. The earliest known version of this is from an essay of 1802 which seeks to overturn the myth of Irish stupidity by citing examples of English incompetence, in this case asserting that Newton cut two holes in his door for the cat and its kitten, not realising that the kitten would follow the cat. The anecdote is revisited by J.M.F. Wright (1815), who occupied Newton's set a little over a century after Newton left Trinity:

> *He possessed himself of a cat as a companion to his dog Dido. This cat, in the natural course of events, although Newton had probably not calculated upon it, produced a kitten; when the good man, seeing at a glance, the consequences of the increase of his family, issued orders to the college carpenter to make two holes in the door; one for the cat and the other for the kitten. Whether this account be true or false, indisputably true is it that there are in the door to this day two plugged holes of the proper dimensions for the respective egresses of cat and kitten.*

The name usually attributed to Newton's dog is not Dido, but Diamond, although there is little evidence that Newton ever had a dog. Newton's younger contemporary, Humphrey Newton, who matriculated in 1685, states that Newton had no animals in College, either cat or dog. A disastrous fire, which destroyed some of Newton's work, is often attributed to the exuberance of the mythical dog and an unattended candle, although Abraham de la Pryme, writing in 1690 of such an accident in College, makes no mention of a dog in his account. As with the cat story, the tale of the dog was adopted and popularised by propagandists, in this case Newton offering to Victorian children a saintly model of forbearance in the face of the destruction of his work by his beloved dog.

Despite their prohibition from College, Trinity still lends its name to the Trinity Foot Beagles, founded in 1862 by undergraduates but amalgamated into the Trinity Foot and South Herts Beagles in 2003 and no longer formally linked to the University. One Trinity whip, Willie Pryor, took empathy with the pack to new levels in 1965 when, 'after a kill on Smithy Fen he got down amongst the hounds to sample a morsel of hare. The uninhibited carnivore emerged triumphant and satiated with the words: "It had a hot, purplish taste."' Willie Pryor later became a curate in Oxford and brought with him the cartoon (left) when proposing the toast at the Annual Gathering in 1989.

FRANKLY MY LORD, IT IS THE HOT PURPLISH TASTE I CAN'T RESIST

CHAPTER 6

Trinity's Physicists

GORDON SQUIRES *(1956)*
WITH ANSON CHEUNG *(1999)*

By common consent the four greatest physicists in history are Archimedes, Newton, Maxwell and Einstein. Two of these were at Trinity. No doubt Archimedes would have come had Henry VIII lived before him, but Einstein was a late developer and would not have been admitted with the present admission standards. Trinity, and Cambridge in general, owes its list of distinguished physicists to the development of the Senate House or Tripos examination. Undergraduates were trained in mathematical problem solving, which increased in sophistication as the centuries passed. This process cultivated a competitive community of students with the same mathematical culture, technical background and language. Dissemination of research could assume this shared basis, and it was commonplace to announce new results as Tripos questions.

The mid-19th century saw several Tripos reforms. The developments of applied mathematics in the theories of electricity and magnetism and of heat made it impossible for undergraduate coaches or supervisors to master the whole syllabus. This prompted a young Trinity Fellow, James Stuart, to offer the first intercollegiate courses and thus initiate the eventual creation of a new class of University employee: the University lecturer. There was also concern over the practical training of scientists and engineers, resulting in the formation of the Natural Sciences Tripos in 1851. However, practical instruction had to wait until 1874 for the opening of a laboratory, which was financed by the then Chancellor and a Trinity Second Wrangler and First Smith's Prizeman, William Cavendish, 7th Duke of Devonshire. The

Previous pages: *The 1897 Cavendish Laboratory research group, which include J.J. Thomson (seated, centre) and Ernest Rutherford (seated, far right).*

Below: *James Clerk Maxwell.*

first five Cavendish Professors of Experimental Physics were Trinity men. They all won Nobel Prizes except Maxwell, the first Professor, who died before the prize was instituted.

The end of the 19th century represented a watershed in physics. By that time, the phenomena that could be understood via Newton's laws were many and varied. For instance, the laws of heat or thermodynamics could be explained by the constant random motion of tiny atoms. Of everyday experience only the mystery of electricity and magnetism lay in want of explanation. Their unification was Maxwell's triumph. What remained was viewed as applied problem solving and one of the masters of this craft was Lord Rayleigh, who will be discussed later.

James Clerk Maxwell was born in Edinburgh on 13 July 1831. Unlike Newton, whose family had no scholastic tradition, he came from a family whose members were distinguished in law, science and the fine arts. Sadly, his mother, a strong influence on his early education, died in 1839. There followed an unhappy period with an unsuitable tutor who used physical punishment on the young Maxwell, treatment which may have been responsible for a later hesitation in his speech. Rescued by an aunt, he was sent to school at the prestigious Edinburgh Academy until 1847 when he went to Edinburgh University.

In 1850 he came to Cambridge and entered Peterhouse to study mathematics, but after one term he transferred to Trinity. A professor at Edinburgh University wrote a letter of recommendation to Whewell, the Master, saying: 'He is not a little uncouth in manners, but withal one of the most original young men I have ever met with and with an extraordinary aptitude for physical enquiries.' Maxwell's transfer to Trinity was not because he recognised Trinity's superiority, as we might have thought, but for the opposite reason – he thought the competition for a Fellowship at Trinity would be less severe than at Peterhouse. His assessment was confirmed when Peterhouse's Routh was Senior Wrangler in the 1854 Mathematics Tripos and Maxwell was second. However, they shared the Smith's Prize. Maxwell won a Fellowship the following year in Trinity, which he held for one year before taking the chair of natural philosophy in Marischal College, Aberdeen.

When Marischal College was amalgamated with King's College, Aberdeen, in 1860, only one professor in Natural

Philosophy was required. Maxwell was discharged, but was finally appointed at King's College, London. In the five years he spent there, he laid the foundations of his major contributions to physics, the theory of electromagnetism and the kinetic theory of gases. In 1865 he retired to work on a classical treatise in the former subject at the family home at Glenlair in Galloway.

In 1871 the Cavendish Chair in Experimental Physics was founded and Maxwell became the first holder; two others, Kelvin and Helmholtz, had turned down the chair before he was appointed. The Cavendish Laboratory was opened in 1874, and for the rest of his life Maxwell oversaw the laboratory, choosing the equipment and devising undergraduate practical classes. Maxwell died on 5 November 1879 at the same age and of the same illness – abdominal cancer – as his mother. After a preliminary funeral service in Trinity Chapel, he was buried at Parton near Glenlair.

Maxwell's first major accomplishment came soon after he graduated. In 1848 St John's College established a prize to commemorate the prediction by John Couch Adams of the existence of the planet Neptune. The 1855 topic was 'The Motion of Saturn's Rings' the examiners requiring an explanation of the stability of the rings. Maxwell submitted his essay in the following year. He showed that the rings could not be solid or liquid, for such rings would not have stable motions. Rather, they must be made up of a large number of small satellites moving independently under the gravitational forces of Saturn and the other satellites. His mathematical calculations to demonstrate the stability of this model were a tour de force. The Astronomer Royal, George Airy, commented that it was one of the most remarkable applications of mathematics to physics that he had ever seen.

Maxwell was greatly interested in colour and colour vision, and he created the science of colour measurement. He showed that any colour could be matched by a combination of three primary colours – red, green and blue – and he built instruments at Edinburgh and at Aberdeen for measuring the intensity of the three primaries to match the colour of a given sample. He tested the colour vision of several observers, and showed that colour-blind people are deficient in one of the

The world's first colour photograph, taken in 1861, by James Clerk Maxwell. It is of a tartan ribbon.

three receptors in the eye. In 1861, he took the world's first colour photograph (see above).

Another field in which Maxwell made seminal contributions was the kinetic theory of gases, in which the macroscopic properties of a gas, such as its pressure, diffusion, viscosity and thermal conductivity, may be calculated from the random motions and collisions of its molecules. When he found that a published experimental result disagreed with his calculation, he performed the experiment himself and found that the previous result was incorrect; his own calculation agreed with the theory. As the kinetic theory was in its infancy at the time, this spoke strongly in its support.

Maxwell's crowning achievement was in the theory of electromagnetism. A mass of evidence from British, French and Danish scientists in the first half of the 19th century had established the basic laws of force between stationary electric charges, and between moving charges (electric currents), and also the laws governing the magnetic effects of currents. This had culminated in Faraday's discovery of the law of induction, which says that a moving magnet generates an electric current in a nearby circuit. Faraday introduced the idea that electric charges and currents give rise to a state in space that physicists call a field. The field generated by one electrical entity acts on another entity. Maxwell adopted this view, which has proved extremely fruitful, and gave it a mathematical formulation, which Faraday had been unable to do.

Maxwell put the last piece in the jigsaw of electromagnetism in 1861 with the suggestion that a changing electric field produces a magnetic field – the counterpart of Faraday's law of induction. Thus, a changing electric field can give rise to a changing magnetic field, which, by Faraday's law, gives rise to a changing electric field, and so on, resulting in an electromagnetic wave. When he calculated the wave velocity from the theory, he found that it was the same as the measured velocity of light. He stated: *'We can scarcely avoid the inference that light consists in transverse undulations … which is the cause of electric and magnetic phenomena'* (the italics are Maxwell's). This was a revolutionary discovery. We now know that it is not only light that is propagated as an electromagnetic wave: radio waves, heat, X-rays and gamma rays are all forms of electromagnetic waves, with the same velocity but differing wavelengths. The basic laws of electromagnetism are contained in four short equations, known as Maxwell's equations.

Although we have summarised Maxwell's major discoveries, mention should also be made of a paper in 1868 entitled *On governors*, a governor here being a device for controlling the speed of a machine by using a signal fed back by the machine itself. This feedback principle is a fundamental one in the control of machines including robots, and Trinity man Norbert Wiener, inspired by Maxwell's pioneering work, called the subject 'cybernetics' from the Greek for a steersman, corrupted to the Latin derivative of 'governor'.

Maxwell was a deeply religious man with a profound social conscience. While at Trinity he came under the influence of F.D. Maurice, a theologian who thought that the Church should be involved in social questions, and at Aberdeen and in London he taught regular evening classes for working men.

A man of considerable versatility, he painted pictures for his optical models, and he composed poetry, both serious and humorous. He had an ironic, occasionally impish, sense of humour. His inaugural lecture as the Cavendish Professor was given little publicity, and few of the high University officials attended. When he gave his first undergraduate lecture, many of them came, thinking this was the inaugural lecture. They were treated to an account of the relation between the Fahrenheit and Centigrade temperature scales! It is thought that Maxwell had some part in the misunderstanding.

In contrast to Newton, Maxwell's achievements were not appreciated fully during his lifetime. As we have seen, he did not get the chair of the amalgamated colleges in Aberdeen, and he was not the first choice for the Cavendish Chair. A factor that undoubtedly contributed to this was his extreme modesty. In the Presidential address to the British Association for the Advancement of Science in 1870, Maxwell discussed electromagnetism. He first gave a polite summary of the theories of others, and then continued, 'Another theory of electricity which I prefer …'. This was how he referred to his epoch-making discoveries.

Maxwell's contributions to physics are now regarded as comparable to, and as profound as, those of Newton and Einstein. Newton said of his own work that he stood on the shoulders of giants. When Einstein was asked if he stood on the shoulders of Newton, he replied, 'No, I stand on the shoulders of Maxwell.' 'From a long view of the history of mankind,' said the Nobel Laureate, Richard Feynman, 'seen from, say, ten thousand years from now, there can be little doubt that the most significant event of the 19th century will be judged as Maxwell's discovery of the laws of electrodynamics.'

John William Strutt, 3rd Baron Rayleigh, the second Cavendish Professor, was born in 1842. He came to Trinity in 1861 and was Senior Wrangler and First Smith's Prizeman in 1865. Though he was elected to a Fellowship in 1866, he was forced by the College statutes at the time to resign it five years later when he married Evelyn Balfour, a sister of Arthur Balfour, later to be Prime Minister. On the death of his father in 1873 he became the 3rd Baron Rayleigh. Rayleigh was a very versatile physicist, but waves, both optical and acoustic, were his major field. One of his earliest achievements was, in 1870, to explain why the sky is blue. The light from the sky does not come directly from the sun, but is the sunlight that has been scattered by the molecules of air in the atmosphere. Rayleigh developed a theory of the scattering of light waves, from which he deduced that the shorter the wavelength of the light, the more it is scattered. Thus, blue light, whose wavelength is shorter than that of red light, is scattered more strongly, and this gives the sky its characteristic colour. The same theory accounts for the red colour of the sun that we see directly at sunrise and sunset. At those times, the light has further to travel through the atmosphere, so the blue light is scattered out completely from the rays from the sun and we see the residual red colour.

When Maxwell died in 1879, Rayleigh was offered the Cavendish Chair. He would not normally have accepted, as he had his own laboratory in the family home at Terling Place in Essex and would not have wanted to be diverted from his research by the administrative duties of the head of a university laboratory. However, the family income was derived from farming (the enterprise still exists), and there was an agricultural depression in England at the time. So to supplement the family income he agreed to come for a short period. After five years, the family finances having improved, he returned to Terling Place, where he did all his subsequent work. When Balfour was Prime Minister he often stayed at Terling Place, as his own home was in Scotland. While at Terling he would help Rayleigh with his experiments – not many scientists have had a Prime Minister as a laboratory assistant!

During his period at the Cavendish Laboratory, Rayleigh worked on the establishment of accurate standards for the basic electrical quantities: resistance, current, and voltage. The standards were necessary for theoretical purposes, and also commercially for the supply of electricity and the design of electrical equipment.

In 1892 Rayleigh measured the density of nitrogen produced from two different sources: one was from air in which all the oxygen had been removed, and one was chemically produced from ammonia. He found that the former was slightly, though significantly, denser than the latter. Two years later the chemist, William Ramsay, joined in the work, and together they isolated a new chemically inert gas, argon, which constitutes about 1 per cent of air. They were awarded Nobel Prizes in 1904 for the discovery – Rayleigh in physics and Ramsay in chemistry. Argon was heavier than any gas known at the time, which led some scientists to be sceptical about the discovery. Rayleigh replied that 'the anomalous properties of argon seem to brought as a kind of accusation against us. But we had the very best of intentions in the matter. The facts were too much for us, and all that we can do now is apologise for ourselves and for the gas.'

Rayleigh received many honours and occupied several high level positions during his life, including the Chancellorship of the University from 1908 until his death. In the course of his life he wrote no fewer than 446 papers, some of which were published posthumously. His name is attached to 17 laws, instruments and criteria in physics. All his work was in classical physics, that is, physics before the discovery of quantum theory in 1900 and of special relativity in 1905. Although he survived nearly two decades after those discoveries, he did no work on the new theories. His reaction was that they were not his way of thinking and he would leave them to younger physicists. He was very conservative by nature and once remarked that the only change he could think of that was for the better was the exposure of the beams in Terling church.

He died in 1919 and was buried in the family area in a quiet corner of Terling churchyard. Two years later a memorial to him was erected in Westminster Abbey. The inscription reads: 'An unerring leader in the advancement of natural knowledge.'

The next two Cavendish Professors revolutionised our thinking about atoms. The fundamental constituents of matter were called atoms from the Greek for indivisible. However, Thomson discovered the electron, and Rutherford the nucleus, giving us the modern picture of the atom. Their discoveries paved the way for all of nuclear physics, for the understanding of the chemical properties of the elements and their compounds, and for all electrical devices, such as the telephone, radio, television and computers.

When Rayleigh resigned the Cavendish Chair in 1884 the selectors met and, after a deliberation of less than a week, they offered the chair to Joseph John Thomson. Thomson, born in 1856, came from a family of modest means that had no tradition in science. His parents had intended him to be an engineer, a fitting occupation for a bright boy in Victorian days, and, at the age of 14, he was sent to Owen's College (which became the University of Manchester) to await a vacancy in a firm of locomotive makers. Two years later his father died, and as his mother could not afford the apprenticeship premium he switched from engineering to mathematics and physics. In 1876 he entered Trinity with a minor scholarship, having failed to get one the year

before. He remained there for the rest of his life. He was Second Wrangler in 1880 and submitted a dissertation for a Fellowship the same year. His tutor told him that he was wasting his time and stood no chance. He was elected.

Thomson's appointment as Cavendish Professor was surprising on two counts. First, he was only 28 years old, and second, the chair was of Experimental Physics. Thomson was primarily a mathematician, and up to that time had done little experimental work. However, the electors had made an inspired choice. Thomson's research, and his guidance of the work of others, made the Cavendish into the leading physics laboratory in the world.

Soon after his appointment, Thomson started to study the conduction of electricity through gases, which led to the discovery of the electron. At atmospheric pressure a gas is an insulator, but if the pressure is reduced for a gas in a sealed chamber and a large voltage is applied between two metal terminals inside the gas, the gas becomes conducting and a current flows. A bright glow is observed between the terminals. The effect had been observed since about 1830, and many attempts were made in European laboratories to understand the phenomenon. It was observed that rays were coming from the cathode, the negative terminal, but there was controversy as to their nature; the German physicists thought that they were some kind of electromagnetic radiation, while the British and French physicists thought that they consisted of charged particles.

In 1896 Thomson succeeded in deflecting the rays with an electric field, which showed that the charged particle model was the correct one, and the direction of the deflection showed that the charge was negative. Thomson's claim to be the discoverer of the electron rests on two key observations. First, by measuring the deflections produced by electric and magnetic fields he obtained the mass of the particle, which proved to be about 2,000 times less than the mass of a hydrogen atom, the lightest object known at the time. Second, he repeated the measurements using different gases and different cathode materials, and found that he got the same values for the mass. Thomson had discovered a universal particle – the electron. In his own words: 'We have in the cathode rays matter in a new state, a state in which the

subdivision of matter is carried very much farther than in the ordinary gaseous state; a state in which all matter is of one and the same kind; this matter being the substance from which all the chemical elements are built up.'

Thomson remained the Cavendish Professor until 1919, his tenure of 35 years being the longest so far. He was a popular and inspiring figure. Once a year, just before Christmas, the Cavendish research students held a dinner to which J.J. (as he was always known) and some of the senior members of the laboratory were invited. Lyrics were made up and sung to the popular tunes of the day.

Thomson was awarded the Nobel Prize in physics in 1906 for investigations in the conduction of electricity through gases. He was knighted in 1908, received the Order of Merit in 1908 and was

Left: *Lawrence Bragg lecturing on optics, 1933.*

Below: *Ernest Rutherford's notes on the structure of the atom.*

Thomson married Rose Paget in 1890, and they had a happy private life, with two children. His son, George, another Trinity alumnus, also received the Nobel Prize, for demonstrating the wave behaviour of the electron, thereby confirming one of the (many) strange predictions of quantum theory that an electron can behave as a wave or a particle. The father demonstrated the particle behaviour, and the son the wave! The elder Thomson died in 1940, and his ashes were buried in Westminster Abbey. 'He, more than any other man,' said Lawrence Bragg, 'was responsible for the change in outlook that distinguishes the physics of this century from that of the last.'

Ernest Rutherford, the founder of nuclear physics and one of the greatest experimental physicists of all time, was born at Spring Grove, near Nelson, on the South Island of

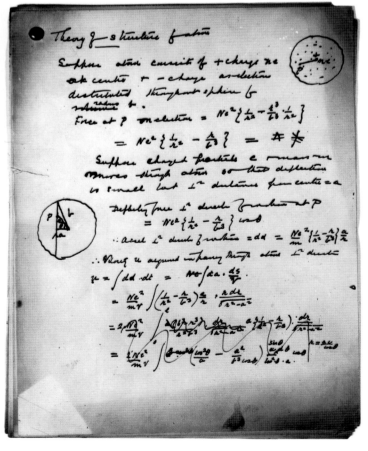

President of the Royal Society from 1915 to 1920. He became the Master of Trinity in 1919 and remained so until his death. His Mastership was a great success; he maintained cordial relations with the Fellows and took a genuine interest in the academic and sporting activities of the undergraduates. Without his foresight and casting vote, Wittgenstein would not have been elected a Fellow.

The *Manchester Guardian* (now the *Guardian*) once reported the words of a dignitary on the local council. 'There was a clever boy at school with me, little Joey Thomson, who took all the prizes. But what good has his book learning done him? Whoever hears of little Joey Thomson now?' The remarks were quoted by the chairman at a dinner at which Thomson was the guest of honour. Rising to reply, Thomson said, 'I wish you were not going to hear little Joey Thomson now.'

New Zealand on 30 August 1871. His family had no academic background. His father, who was a farmer, had emigrated from Scotland, and his mother from England. Rutherford was the fourth of 12 children. His mother was very keen on the education of her children, and Rutherford attended the local school where a single teacher taught 40 children, aged five to 14. Rutherford was deputed to teach two of his younger sisters; to ensure that they did not run away during the lesson, he tied their pigtails together. He later won scholarships to Nelson College and to the University of Christchurch.

After taking his degree he started experimenting with the effect of high-frequency electromagnetic waves on the magnetisation of iron. This led to the award of an 1851 Science Scholarship. Borrowing money for the passage, Rutherford came to Cambridge in 1895 to work with Thomson. Up till then research students had to be graduates of Cambridge, but in that year the university authorities changed the rules to admit students from outside, and the first one to come was Rutherford. On Thomson's advice he entered Trinity, and was later awarded a Coutts Trotter Studentship by the College, which still exists to help promising students.

He first worked on the transmission of radio waves, using his work in New Zealand to make a detector for the waves. He sent signals from the University Observatory to the Cavendish Laboratory, a distance of two miles, which was the world record in 1896. But after a time he changed to the study of radioactivity. Radioactivity was discovered by Henri Becquerel in Paris in 1896. He found that some photographic plates near a uranium salt had become fogged. (A British physicist had made the same observation previously, but he complained to the manufacturer of the plates and received a fresh supply.) Pierre and Marie Curie entered the field and found that thorium and their newly discovered radium had the same effect on photographic plates. They deduced that the substances were giving off rays, but the nature of the rays and the underlying processes were a mystery.

In 1898 Rutherford was appointed Professor of Physics at the University of McGill in Montreal. In his first six years there he elucidated the basic features of radioactivity in a series of incisive experiments. He first showed that the emitted rays were of three types, of different penetrating powers, which, not knowing their nature, he called alpha, beta and gamma rays, alpha rays being the least penetrating, and gamma the most. He then developed an electrical method for measuring the amount of radioactivity which was more accurate than the fogging of photographic plates.

He was joined by Frederick Soddy, a young chemist from Oxford in 1901. They showed that when a radioactive atom decays it changes to an atom of a different chemical element. This was in flat contradiction to the view held at the time that such a change, known as transmutation, was an impossible dream of the alchemists. Rutherford and Soddy called the decay a 'sub-atomic chemical change', deliberately avoiding the word 'transmutation' with its alchemist associations.

Rutherford later showed that an alpha particle is a helium nucleus, a beta particle is an electron, and a gamma ray is a very short-wavelength electromagnetic wave, and he showed how the change in the atom on radioactive decay was related to the particle emitted. He was awarded the Nobel Prize in chemistry in 1908 for his work. In his speech at Stockholm he said that he had dealt with many transformations, but the quickest he had met with was his own transformation in one moment from a physicist to a chemist.

After moving to the University of Manchester in 1907, he made two further major discoveries. In 1909 he suggested that two of the workers in the laboratory should measure the scattering of alpha particles from gold foils, expecting that the particles would be deviated only by small amounts, but in fact they were scattered through large angles, some even bouncing backwards. Rutherford said this was an incredible result. 'It was as if you fired a 15-inch shell at a sheet of tissue paper and it came back and hit you.' A year later he hit on the explanation: the atom must have a dense region from which the alpha particle is scattered backwards in a single collision. The model of the nuclear atom was born. Rutherford's model, now the established one, is that an atom is like a miniature solar system, with a small heavy nucleus at its centre around which the electrons circulate like planets. His second discovery, made in 1919, was that an alpha particle that struck an atomic nucleus could cause it to disintegrate and give rise to a different nucleus. These two discoveries marked the beginning of nuclear physics.

In the same year he came back to Cambridge to succeed Thomson as Cavendish Professor, a position he held until his death in 1937. While at Cambridge he continued his experiments on nuclear disintegration, finding more and more examples of the phenomenon. However, his main achievement was to direct the research of workers in the laboratory, who made important advances in nuclear physics that led to several Nobel Prizes. Sir James Chadwick discovered the neutron in 1932, a particle predicted by Rutherford 12 years before, and Francis Aston (Trinity Nobel laureate 1922), Lord (Patrick) Blackett, Sir John Cockcroft and Ernest Walton and C.T.R. Wilson built novel instruments and machines for nuclear research.

Rutherford married Mary Newton in 1900, travelling from Montreal to New Zealand for the wedding. They had been engaged for six years and had waited until he could support a family. They had one daughter. Rutherford was a big, burly man with a loud voice, which he was sometimes requested to moderate in the presence of sensitive equipment. A colleague, Andrade, wrote that 'he was quite without affectation, self-consciousness, or pretentiousness of any kind. He was essentially kindly, but he was quite outspoken.'

There are many anecdotes about him. When he was at Montreal, a colleague once asked him how it was he was always riding the crest of the wave. 'Well, I made the wave, didn't I?' replied Rutherford. At Manchester a young woman had an accident with a bottle of sulphur dioxide which left her unconscious. When Rutherford heard of the incident he summoned her to his office and said, 'What's this I hear? You might have killed yourself.' 'Well, if I had, nobody would have cared,' was the sulky reply. 'I daresay not,' said Rutherford, 'but I don't have the time to attend an inquest.' On another occasion, he and a colleague, Oliphant, were conducting a PhD oral. Oliphant asked a question to which the candidate replied that he didn't know. 'And neither would you, Oliphant, if you hadn't looked it up half an hour ago,' said Rutherford.

Rutherford was ennobled in 1931, taking the title Baron Rutherford of Nelson. He died prematurely on 19 October 1937.

There was a feeling of great loss, not only among scientists but throughout the world. The *New York Times* wrote: 'It is given to few men to achieve immortality, still less to achieve Olympian rank, during their lifetime. Lord Rutherford achieved both.' His ashes were buried in Westminster Abbey, London, near the tomb of Isaac Newton.

In 1912 Max von Laue at the University of Munich had the idea that by scattering X-rays from a crystal one could deduce the structure of the crystal, that is, the internal arrangement of the atoms and the distances between them, neither of which was known at the time. The phenomenon that makes this deduction possible is known as diffraction. Each atom in the crystal scatters the X-ray waves, and in certain directions the scattered waves are in phase, that is to say, their crests and their troughs coincide. In those directions there is a diffracted ray. In all other directions the individual beams cancel each other out. From the directions of the diffracted rays and the wavelength of the X-rays, the structure of the crystal may be deduced. The experiment was tried at Munich on a crystal of zinc sulphide (in secret because the head of the department had previously refused his consent on the grounds that it would not work) and von Laue's intuition was confirmed: diffracted X-ray spots were observed on a photographic plate behind the crystal. This work provided the seed that blossomed into the new field of X-ray crystallography and gave us the structures of materials. It was now possible to start to explain the chemical and biological functions of ensembles of atoms. The pioneers of this quest to observe how atoms arranged themselves in real materials were Henry and Lawrence Bragg, who were father and son, and both Trinity men.

Lawrence Bragg shared the Nobel Prize for physics with his father in 1915 for their work on the determination of crystal structures by means of X-rays. Bragg was only 25 years old at the time. He is the youngest person to be awarded the prize, beating the next youngest by five years. He was chosen to succeed Rutherford as the Cavendish Professor in 1938.

Bragg was born in Adelaide on 31 March 1890, his father being the professor of mathematics and physics at the university there. He attended various local schools until 1905, when he entered the university to read mathematics and physics,

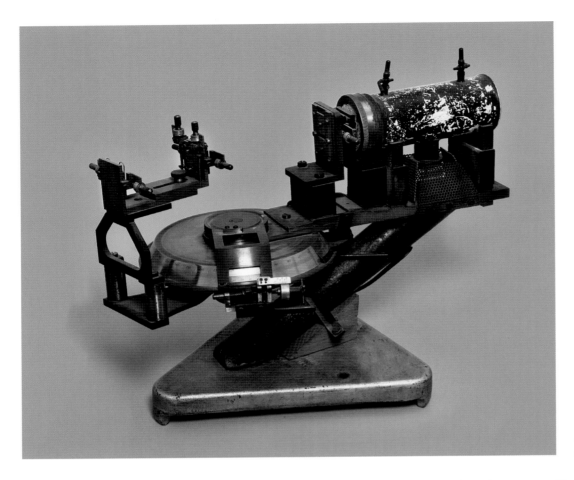

Bragg's spectrometer, in the Cavendish Laboratory Museum.

graduating in 1908. He came to Trinity in 1909 and read first mathematics, and then physics in the Natural Sciences Tripos, in which he obtained a first in 1911.

The paper announcing von Laue's diffraction experiments reached England in the summer of 1912. Bragg, who was in Cambridge doing some routine research in the Cavendish Laboratory, joined his father at Leeds. His father was now a professor there, the family having returned from Australia in 1910. The two of them were greatly excited by the news. They examined the paper, and Bragg found that there was a mistake in von Laue's analysis. The structure he had calculated for the crystal was not correct, and to account for the measurements he had made the unlikely assumption that the X-rays were of five different wavelengths. Bragg repeated the analysis for the correct structure, and the results were consistent with a single wavelength.

On his return to Cambridge he had an even greater success. While walking along the Backs one day, he realised that the diffracted X-ray beam could be regarded as the mirror reflection of the incident beam, with a plane of atoms in the crystal acting as the mirror. This result, coupled with a simple equation relating the parameters of the experiment, is known as Bragg's law. It has been of immense value in X-ray crystallography.

There followed two years of hectic activity in which the father and son determined the structures of many materials, including the alkali halides and diamond. The father built an X-ray spectrometer, an accurate instrument for doing the measurements, and the son did most of the calculations. One of the simplest structures was that of common salt, in which the atoms are arranged in a three-dimensional lattice of alternate sodium and chlorine atoms. The structure was not immediately accepted by all scientists, especially chemists, the stumbling block being the absence of a molecule of a sodium atom monogamously linked to a chlorine atom. As late as 1927, a retired chemistry professor at Imperial College writing in *Nature* said, 'It is more than repugnant to common sense … it is not chemical cricket' – strong words for an Englishman.

The Nobel Prize in physics was awarded to von Laue in 1914 for the discovery of X-ray diffraction, and the two Braggs shared the prize in the following year. The latter was a unique event; there have been other cases of a father and son receiving the prize, and one of mother and daughter, but in none of those cases was the award for collaborative work.

During the First World War, Bragg was involved in sound ranging, a method of locating enemy guns by measuring the times of the arrival of the reports at different places. He was in the front line, and although he did not take part in actual fighting, the work was dangerous and he was awarded the Military Cross. Between the wars Bragg was a professor at Manchester University and determined the structures of more complicated crystals, such as silicate minerals.

In 1938, he was appointed to the Cavendish Chair. His tenure of the chair, like that of Rutherford's, was marked not by original research of his own, but by the stimulus and inspiration he gave to others. The subject was the determination of the structures of biologically important molecules. These present far greater difficulties than the structures previously solved, thanks to the very large numbers of atoms in the molecule and the complexity of their arrangement. On Bragg's initiative, the Medical Research Council set up a Research Unit in the Cavendish Laboratory to promote the work, which had far-reaching consequences. Max Perutz solved the structure of haemoglobin and Trinity alumnus John Kendrew that of myoglobin. The climax of the Cavendish work came in 1953 when Crick and Watson obtained the structure of DNA, a turning point in biology. The MRC unit subsequently moved out of the Cavendish Laboratory, becoming the Laboratory of Molecular Biology, and maintained its brilliant record, summarised by the title of John Finch's history *A Nobel Fellow On Every Floor*.

Bragg also had the foresight to support the beginnings of Cambridge radio astronomy which had 'intriguing problems in optics'. This later allowed the group of another Trinity man, Martin Ryle (Nobel Prize 1974), to discover quasars, which are cosmic objects of high luminosity and are some of the most distant known objects in the universe.

Bragg retired from the Cavendish Chair in 1954 to become the Resident Professor of the Royal Institution. The Institution was in some disarray at the time, but Bragg, by his tact and enterprise, managed to put it on a sound footing. He became the director, a newly created post, in 1966. He finally retired the following year.

Bragg married Alice Hopkinson in 1921. They had a very happy marriage with four children. Bragg was a devoted and inventive father. He built a model railway for the children, and a shadow theatre to illustrate Winnie the Pooh stories. He was

rather shy, and everyday administration was not to his taste. When he was the Cavendish Professor he was ably assisted in this side of the job by a radio astronomer in the department, Jack Ratcliffe, who accompanied him at university committee meetings, opening his remarks with 'We think, don't we, Professor …'.

Among Bragg's many awards were prestigious medals from the Royal Society. He was knighted in 1941. He died on 1 July 1971, respected and revered as the father of X-ray crystallography.

The final gallery of Trinity physicists have studied matter at the extremes. Instead of just three states of matter – solids, liquids

Eric Gill's Crocodile on the side of the Mond Building, once part of the Cavendish Laboratory. Crocodile was Kapitza's nickname for Rutherford.

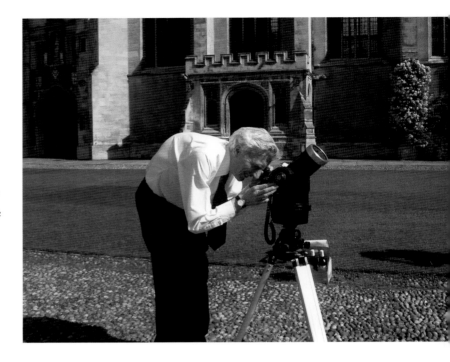

The Astronomer Royal observing the transit of Venus in Great Court, 8 June 2004.

and gases – there are in fact myriad exotic states at high and low temperatures and pressures. These states cannot be explained by classical intuition, but instead require models consistent with the principles of quantum mechanics.

In 1921 Pyotr Kapitsa (1894–1984) was a member of a delegation from the Soviet Union studying European physics laboratories. When the committee came to Cambridge he jumped ship and persuaded Rutherford to allow him to stay and work in the Cavendish Laboratory. His research in magnetism and low-temperature physics was so successful that a special laboratory, the Mond, was built for him in 1933.

In the following year he visited the Soviet Union as he had done many times before, despite repeated warnings that it was unsafe. This was a visit too far. He had claimed, incorrectly as it turned out, that his work would revolutionise the production of electricity. Unfortunately for him, the Soviet authorities, who were trying to modernise Russia with the emphasis on electrification, took him at his word and he was not allowed to leave. Rutherford, with characteristic generosity, sent his Cambridge equipment to him so that he could continue his work. When he was awarded the 1978 Nobel Prize for his work in low-temperature physics, he remarked that it was 30 years since he had done the experiments, which was a coded message to the Nobel committee that he should have received the prize earlier.

Kapitsa's major discovery was the superfluidity of liquid helium. When helium is cooled sufficiently it enters a state in which it can flow without resistance. It can pass through any pores in its container. Even more strangely, if a superfluid sits in an open container, it may flow up the sides and drip off the bottom! Not only do certain liquids exhibit weird behaviour, it is possible for electrons to form a superfluid. In doing so, the host material becomes a superconductor because current can flow without resistance. While still a graduate student, Brian Josephson (1940–) predicted the possibility for super-currents to pass between an insulator separating two superconductors. This current is extremely sensitive to external magnetic fields, which makes Josephson junctions perfect magnetic field detectors.

R.H. Fowler (1889–1944) studied at Winchester College before winning a scholarship to Trinity. After the First World War, he returned to Trinity as a College lecturer in mathematics in 1920. Working on thermodynamics and statistical mechanics, Fowler advanced the understanding of electron energy states in materials, and was the first person to recognise the need for the zeroth law of thermodynamics in order to make the subject logically consistent. Together with his student Paul Dirac, Fowler discovered the type of inherently quantum mechanical electronic matter present in white dwarfs – the final phase of life for the majority of stars in our galaxy. Stars that are incapable of becoming supernovae shrink to a fraction of their former size. For instance, our Sun will contract to the size of the Earth. Gifted as a teacher, Fowler supervised 15 Fellows of the Royal Society and three Nobel Laureates. Among his other collaborators was Trinity man Sir Arthur Eddington (1882–1944) who explained Einstein's general relativity to the English-speaking world and conducted its first experimental test during the solar eclipse of 1919.

Subramanyan Chandrasekhar was born in 1910 in Lahore, then part of British India. Initially home schooled, Chandrasekhar received his BA degree at Presidency College, Chennai, before winning a government award to pursue graduate work at Trinity in 1930, where he went on to win a Prize Fellowship. En route to Cambridge, Chandrasekhar applied quantum mechanics and relativity to stellar matter, going beyond the densities considered by his supervisor Fowler. He found that stars above a certain mass, the Chandrasekhar limit, would be unstable and would ultimately collapse to form a neutron star or black hole. This and his later work on the structure and evolution of stars won him the 1983 Nobel Prize.

Coming full circle, Chandrasekhar in his final years embarked on a study of Newton's *Principia*, translating Newton's geometrical language into modern notation and thereby allowing a whole new generation to uncover its secrets. Trinity has a physics heritage indeed! But the College does not intend to rest on its laurels. Our Fellows and students are still at the forefront of discoveries in novel quantum matter, and in particle physics at the Large Hadron Collider. And once again a Trinity man heads the Cavendish. A warm and stimulating welcome awaits students who contemplate a career in a subject that has exercised some of the finest human minds.

Gordon Squires (1924–2010)

Sadly, Gordon Squires passed away during the writing of this article. Born in 1924, Gordon was a learned scholar and a courteous and kind man. In addition to being a pioneer of thermal neutron scattering, he was a dedicated teacher; his textbook on experimental physics is required reading by all undergraduates. After retiring as a University lecturer, he devoted his energies to curating the Cavendish museum. He was universally loved, and his wisdom and good humour will be missed by the many friends and students whose lives he enriched.

———— ·—•—·—— ————

WHEN I WAS ACCEPTED AT TRINITY, I DIDN'T REALISE I HAD been invited to join an institution which had housed and nurtured some of the greatest scientific minds in history. As often as this thought has occurred to me, it is still amazing. I am only one line in the matriculation book, one book among many. Nonetheless, our supervisors are always willing to believe we may be capable of brilliance, and never treat us as the cogs which we may be later in life. It seems that in science, genius can come in two forms: a flash of inspiration from which theories spiral out, or the determined grind of hard work which eventually yields the diamond. It is most often the latter which is seen in College life.

A science student's life is governed by labs, rather than the mysterious 'classes' which dictate an arts student's schedule. The throng of bicycles which descends upon Trinity Street heralds the beginning of the day and the compulsory lab. For a few crucial moments, it is as if the Tour de France has taken a drastic re-route. I have often found myself stranded on the Great Gate side of the street, unable to access my room in Blue Boar or my notes for the day. Examples papers are also an unpleasant fixture of life. It means at least three hours in isolation while pencil is applied to paper in an effort to appease a supervisor. Working under pressure is a necessary skill; most students find their productivity rising exponentially as the available time decreases.

Cambridge is a bubble which protects the intellectually gifted from the harshness of the outside world. Trinity offers an extra layer of shelter, for one need never leave its walls, except for labs and Sainsbury's. The pastoral care is remarkable. The interest which the professors, so highly regarded in their fields, take in the mundane details of a student's life is impressive and touching.

The nature of science is change and, while still remaining conservative, Trinity recognises and embraces this. My own presence here as a woman and a foreigner is a testament to this evolution. Some changes are met with a frown of nostalgia from the students, like the replacement of the handle on the small Great Court door, the abolition of Buttery cards or the appearance of the temporary kitchen, a blight on the pristine lawns. However, constancy can be found in the sandy walls of Great Court and the endless trickle of the fountain. When my thoughts turn to leaving, I feel as if Trinity is a secret world to which I have been given a key, and it is comforting to know that wherever the course of my life takes me, it will always fit the lock and let me back inside again.

Julia Attwood (2007)

IN 1958 MY GREAT CHUM GORDON MELLAR AND I WERE IN OUR second year at Trinity. We were reading engineering. A bad mistake for all, far too many afternoons at drawing-boards. A very bad mistake for me, given my zero aptitude for engineering. My hugely talented supervisor, Arthur Shercliffe, was of the same opinion. 'Eee, Malik,' he once said in exasperation. 'If you ever build a bridge, for God's sake put your name on it and I'll cross by another.' 'I will come with you, sir.' 'Will you? Then you are not as daft as I thought.'

Omar Malik (1956)

THE GREAT COURT CLOCK

A clock was first installed in Great Court 400 years ago, in 1610. It had a modest small dial. In 1726 our masterful Master Bentley had it replaced by something grander. The 1610 clock is still running in the tower of Orwell's village church. The Bentley clock mechanism was replaced a century ago, in 1910, thanks to a bequest from Lord Grimthorpe.

Only when it is stopped may one realise how frequently a clock is wont to be consulted. So it was in Trinity when the Great Court Clock was inactivated for over a month at the end of 2008 for modifications to the winding mechanism. That we have a clock to be so missed is largely due to the remarkable Trinity alumnus Edmund, 1st Baron Grimthorpe (1816–1905), sometime Edmund Beckett Denison, sometime Sir Edmund Beckett, Bart, brilliant barrister, ecclesiastical lawyer, amateur architect, innovative horologist and locksmith, multi-millionaire, controversialist and bully-at-large.

During the 1840s Edmund's interest in the improvement of clock accuracy led to the invention of his friction-reducing three-legged escapement. At the Great Exhibition of 1851 he was a well enough respected horologist to be chairman of the clock-judging committee. The new Houses of Parliament were nearing completion at this time; the Astronomer-Royal, G.B. Airy (Trinity, 1819–36) proposed performance criteria for a clock to occupy the tower. The doyen of London clockmakers, Vulliamy, decreed Airy's specified accuracy to be unobtainable. Edmund disagreed; not without a fight, he gained the task. The resultant Great Clock, with Edmund's improved double three-legged gravity escapement, was at its installation in 1859 the most accurate as well as the largest clock ever made, and since then has been the model for all good mechanical turret clocks. For the striking scheme of the Great Clock, Edmund reproduced the mechanism of the melodious 'Cambridge Quarters'. Previously

Above: *Pigeons disturbing the accuracy of the College clock.*

Right: *The mechanism of the College clock.*

little regarded, these, thanks to him, are globally familiar today, but now of course as the 'Westminster Chimes'.

Widowered and childless, Edmund spent the first five years of the new century – and the last of his long life – in the harrowing of his will. The final multi-codicilar document, probated at just over £2 million gross (in excess of £150 million today), contained a minor bequest to Trinity College for a replacement, to the Grimthorpe design, of the King's Tower clock commissioned in 1726 by Bentley. The gift was conditional, inter alia, on the construction of a new clock dial bare of numerals. To lose the familiar roman and arabic numerals of the old dial seemed, however, a step too far for all. The Senior Bursar, McLeod Innes, adroitly ensured that the projected cost of a new clock, and recasting of the bells, would leave little from the legacy. So when in 1909 the bequest was finally accepted, the 18th-century dial was saved. The old mechanism, said to be too worn for repair, was hustled off, presumably for scrap.

Graham Chinner (1972)

Is it possible for pigeons to stop the clock by sitting on the minute hand? A quick calculation of power balance can help us decide. Suppose a pigeon weighing 1kg is sitting on the minute hand at a distance of 50cm from the pivot. The hand would be rising at about 1mm/sec and would therefore require about 5mW (milliWatts) of power to lift it. The clock is driven by an 80kg weight which falls 9 metres in 7 days, equivalent to 12mW of power. It seems that there is only just enough power to lift a single pigeon. A couple of pigeons could easily stop the clock.

Three consecutive pigeon-events have occurred around 10.45am, when the minute hand is conveniently horizontal, stopping the clock for a total of 4 minutes on 8 December 2009. This was in the middle of Admissions Interview season. Already nervous candidates might have thought that their punctuality was being tested as a fiendish new admissions test!

There are other events that can only be understood when plotted on graphs. I am convinced, for instance, that a spider spinning its web around the pendulum rod caused the clock to gain 300 milliseconds overnight on 3–4 May 2009. And during this 'spider' incident a scatter plot of 'going' vs 'amplitude'

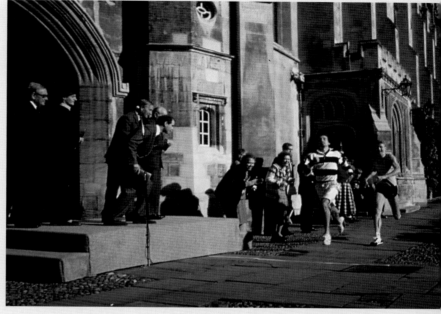

The Great Court Run in aid of Great Ormond Street Hospital, 1988. Sebastian Coe managed to beat Steve Cramm but not the chimes, which allow about 43 seconds to complete the 341 metre course. Runners are now allowed to run on the cobbles and to cut the corners, making it more likely that others will match Lord Burghley's feat of 1927. The Great Court Run is still run on the day of the Matriculation Dinner, but at midday not midnight. Photograph by John Evans.

shows a beautiful straight line with a gradient of –580ms/day for every 1mm change in the amplitude of pendulum swing. This agrees perfectly with small-amplitude pendulum theory.

Hugh Hunt, Keeper of the Clock (1990)

UP UNTIL 1995 IT WAS TRADITIONAL FOLLOWING THE MATRICULATION Dinner to have the new students race round Great Court while the clock strikes midnight. In 1995 when this took place, some half a dozen students had to be taken to Addenbrookes Hospital. One of my friends broke his arm after tripping over a dark shape which was in fact another student who had also tripped over. It turns out that a mass of drunken students running over cobbles at night whilst holding wine glasses is not such a good idea! Now the Great Court Run is done at 12 noon instead.

Richele Long (1995)

CHAPTER 7

Scenes from College Life (1930s–1950s)

Music and Chapel

When Francis Hovell-Thurlow-Cumming-Bruce came up to Trinity his identical twin brother Roualeyn was sent to Magdalene because this would make things easier 'if we fell in love with the same girl'. The precaution proved optimistic; he cannot remember meeting a single woman during his three years as an undergraduate.

Britain was in the depths of the Depression, and Marxism was fashionable. Roualeyn became 'the hottest of communists' and introduced Francis to Guy Burgess in the year above; Francis thought Burgess 'a cold fish' but liked Donald Maclean. Unable to counter the Marxist case his younger brother made at mealtimes during the vacations, Francis became a 'titular communist for a while'. He has a vivid memory of the moment he abandoned the creed; he was 'lying under a tree in the Bois de Boulogne reading a book by a Norwegian sociologist – it knocked the bottom out of Marxism. I was so relieved I didn't have to be a Communist any more'.

Coming from Shrewsbury, 'a good classics school', he was told he simply needed to 'keep his classics freshened up' to score a first – which he duly did in Part One. Roualeyn had spent his first two years making friends with influential dons like Maynard Keynes, and, according to Francis, his papers were 'an abomination' – but he got a first anyway, because, said Francis, the dons thought it wrong to award a different class to a twin.

From his rooms in Whewells Court he watched A.E. Housman and Wittgenstein 'trudging off to hall, neither with a smile on his lips'. He heard a rumour that Wittgenstein spent his time thinking

Right: Stephen Bragg's College account for the Lent term 1944. He points out that, based on this bill, annual tuition fees were then about £150, comparable after inflation to today's.

Below: In December 1939 Peter Plesch was the last man to be fined under the College rule against smoking before it was rescinded.

in a deckchair in an otherwise furniture-less room. Adopting the persona of a Christian charity worker in search of donations, he knocked on the great man's door; Wittgenstein greeted him 'with blank amazement', but Francis was able to verify the rumour. He tried Housman's lectures on 'textual criticism' but found them dull.

In his last year he moved to the grandeur of a set on K staircase in Great Court, sharing with Humphrey Whitbread of the brewing dynasty. On inspecting the College furniture Humphrey's mother declared it woefully inadequate and replaced the lot with much smarter stuff. Francis was 'paid the going rate for the job' by his parents, which meant he could hunt at home in County Durham in the winter and – on the advice of his father, another Trinity man – eat at the Pitt Club during term. He was untroubled by the charges for coming back to College late – a penny after ten, tuppence after eleven.

For Part Two he read Economics, still struggling, like many of his contemporaries, to understand the Depression. They worried about getting jobs too. Francis chose the Dominions Office on the grounds that his great-grandfather, Lord Elgin, had been 'Governor of the Two Canadas' and Viceroy of India. His twin Roualeyn was called to the Bar and became a High Court Judge.

Francis, 8th Baron Thurlow, former High Commissioner to New Zealand and Nigeria and former Governor of the Bahamas. Born 1912, matriculated 1930. These memories were recorded in conversation with the editor.

I CAME UP TO SIT FOR A HISTORY SCHOLARSHIP AT THE COLLEGE along with a friend who was sitting for another college. In those days there was little television, we certainly did not have TV at home and little in the way of colour supplements, etc. which today make Cambridge known visually all over the world. We were both grammar-school boys from the northeast and we travelled by overnight bus, climbing on to it at the old Sunderland Bus Station (long since demolished) and dismounting at Biggleswade on the Great North Road at about 5am when it was still dark. We

then hitchhiked to Cambridge by a series of milk lorries and early workers in cars. I had very little idea of Cambridge or Trinity; I imagined the University as one of a series of similar buildings, each college rather alike, an impossibly naive idea today. When we arrived at Trinity Street the dawn had broken and the clouds were slowly lifting. There we saw what seemed like medieval castles and huge cathedral-like structures, and to me the immensity of Trinity Great Court was a revelation.

Brian Rees (1948)

WHEN I CAME UP, MOST STUDENTS HAD been in the armed forces during the war. I remember feeling a sense of elation to be in a place where I could do what I wanted compared with the years before. However, I couldn't do whatever I wanted. College regulations required students to return to the College by 10pm. A straightforward rule, but it sometimes had an unexpected twist.

BYRON'S BEAR

Far left: *Byron and his bear, from the* Trinity Review *of 1984. Attributed to Lawrence.*

Left: *I staircase, Nevile's Court*

J.M.F. Wright, a mathematician and Fellow of the College, published his memoir, *Alma Mater*, in 1827. Although now considered somewhat unreliable, Wright matriculated only ten years after Byron and relates the story of the bear:

Mr Hudson (the Tutor), however, did not here leave me, but showed me a single room in a turret of the Great Court, called Merton-hall Corner, commonly styled Mutton-hall Corner by the gyps and some other learned bodies … When Lord Byron was at Trinity, he kept in rooms on this staircase, round which you might drive a coach and six, and had moreover, the use of the small Hexagonal one in the tower. His lordship used to parade the streets accompanied by an immense bear, following him like a dog, which bear had the sole use of the apartment in

the turret. Poor Bruin peeping out one day from this retreat, bestowed so ardent an embrace upon a 'small College-man' that his lordship was constrained, at the suggestion of the Tutor, to 'cut' him. So attached, however, were this singular pair, that the whole power of the Tutor was scarcely able to divide them.

J.M.F. Wright, *Alma Mater*, pp.166–7

In an article for the *Trinity Review* in 1961, Keith Walker states that Byron kept his bear in Ram Yard, Bridge Street. This may, of course, have been as a result of its eviction from College, where the turret room Wright refers to is thought to be K8. J.W. Clark, son of William Clark, one of Byron's Cambridge friends, suggests that Byron's rooms were, in fact, in Nevile's Court, possibly I1. Records of room occupancy began to be kept only in 1824.

One evening, a student friend and I were late. We stood outside the Great Gate, rang the bell, the porter let us in and we paid our penny fine. A few weeks before, my friend had been a major in the Indian Army.

Dane Gordon (1948)

WHEN I CAME UP THERE WERE STILL A CONSIDERABLE NUMBER of ex-servicemen in their early twenties in a large undergraduate population. Naturally enough there were sets or groups in College. A group of my contemporaries banded together into an informal discussion group. We met several times a week for coffee after

lunch in Hall, in either Ted Kenney's or John Cassels' rooms in Great Court or Peter Green's in Whewell's. Conversation ranged from literary wit and competitive quotation to rather more scholarly or scientific topics, hardly ever politics. The prevailing ethos was that of *The Cambridge Review*, of which Peter Green at the time and later Geoffrey Best were editors. Richard Mayne, Geoffrey Best and I were also members of the Trinity Historical Society which met in George Kitson Clark's rooms. A very fat man, he could barely squeeze himself under the steering wheel of his Austin 12, with his eyes just above bonnet level. He used to drive us on Sundays to see the wonderful churches of Norfolk

J.Grant,1951

George Kitson Clark, Reader in History and Fellow, 1922–75.

approval. He said there were too many invited for a single party and the guest list must be divided into two separate occasions. Hence invitations went out for two midday parties on consecutive days. We were on the stairs under which were all the baths for Great Court and these were commandeered and filled with ice and champagne bottles. The first party duly started, but many of those invited to the second one heard and saw what was going on and came and joined in. Subsequently many of both the first and second invitees decided to stay on for the second party, thus ensuring the first party ran on until the second one started. Eventually the uproarious occasion petered out at about 10pm on the second day.

Derek Pelly (1949)

AFTER A YEAR IN DIGS IN MALCOLM STREET, I MOVED INTO rooms in 27 Trinity Street that now form part of Angel Court. My sitting room was a favourite route for those who wanted to climb back into College after Great Gate was closed, and I would wake to hear their nocturnal movements. I never took rooms within the College because number 27 seemed to have all the advantages of both in and out, and had the atmosphere of a rather exclusive club where we could occasionally gamble on a modest scale. Other bets were won against those who did not know that an egg thrown high in the air to land on the pristine lawns of Great Court would not break if used only once. Engineers justified the activity by suggesting implausible theories about the forces involved.

The College had then, as I suppose it has now, its characters and eccentrics. There was that great historian, Kitson Clark, with his stentorian bark. Like my brother, I used to drive up to wildfowl in the Wash. On one occasion my brother, returning from an expedition, had thrown a brace of duck over the Bishop's Hostel gate before climbing back in and finding that the duck had gone. A few days later he was given wild duck for dinner by Dr Kitson Clark. The Trinity cooks produced delicious menus for those who managed the expense of hosting a dinner party in their rooms. The crème brûlée, still browned with a hot plate, was the best in the world.

Then there was Dr Simpson, the last life Fellow of Trinity, who had a huge reputation as a preacher, and a vast congregation gathered in Great St Mary's to hear what was announced as his

and Suffolk. My tutor was Outtram Evennett, a delightful and courteous man who, it was related, had dealt with a Fulbright student whom a porter had detected to have had a girl in his rooms overnight by saying: 'The incident last night has been drawn to my attention. I shall have to fine you five shillings which is the usual charge for College guests.' This shows that the kind of discipline deemed appropriate for school-leavers was already becoming more relaxed with the presence of more mature ex-servicemen. I remember the resentment generated by an unfortunate remark of Canon C.E. Raven as Vice Chancellor about the bad effect on Cambridge of 'two hundred vicious young men, mostly from the British Army of the Rhine'.

Francis West (1949)

AT THE END OF MY SECOND YEAR (1951), I WAS SHARING ROOMS in Great Court and our neighbour, Johnnie Lewis, who was going down, decided to throw a a large leaving party. We agreed that he could use our rooms too, but the party required the Master's last sermon. It was such a success that he then delivered a whole series of last sermons! This was a time of religious revival in Cambridge. Great St Mary's was packed every Sunday evening to hear the preachers that Mervyn Stockwood gathered there. Within the College two talented and very different chaplains stirred our interest. Simon Phipps, a decorated officer and friend of Princess Margaret who he entertained in his rooms in Bishop's Hostel, was president of Footlights and was later to become a bishop. Eric James, a poor boy from Bermondsey, radical and political, made a huge circle of lifelong friends and admirers.

In those days it never occurred to me that I might become an MP or later find myself taking part in Lords' debates with the Master of Trinity. At the time when Rab Butler was Master I attended a dinner of Trinity MPs, who included Willie Whitelaw and Enoch Powell. Late in the evening undergraduates were startled to witness the unlikely spectacle of those MPs setting out to run round Great Court while the clock struck 12. Not surprisingly, few of us got very far!

Nicholas Edwards (Lord Crickhowell) (1954)

WHILE I WAS IN RESIDENCE HALL HAD BENCHES AND LONG tables. It was accepted that the only practical way of getting to a vacant place on the far side of a table set against the wall was to put a foot on the nearside bench, then a foot on the table and walk as far as necessary to gain access to the desired spot and climb down there. Perhaps ill mannered but a sensible way of getting to where you wanted to sit. I'm amused to tell non-Trinity people of this memory as, without exception, they react to what to them is uncouth behaviour at its worst! A lovely contrast to the wonderful august surroundings. I was never aware of anyone putting a foot on someone's meal and all diners accepted this manoeuvre.

Graham Young (1956)

IN 1959 IN OUR FIRST SUMMER AT TRINITY MY FRIEND ANDREA Pampanini and I bought a punt. I was familiar with them and appreciated their stability; punters could change places much more safely than rowers! We paid £5 for it, and another £5 to get it delivered to Cambridge. It was much more beautiful than punts are nowadays, being mainly mahogany, with bottom planks along its length, and seat backs that could be removed to make more room to lie down. Andrea's mother had the cushions reupholstered for us, and we quickly bought a pole and a dustpan to bail out the rainwater.

We could not keep it on Trinity Backs, so it lay at the slipway between Trinity punts and Garrett Hostel Bridge. We were able to store the pole along the foot of the Trinity side of the dividing fence, padlocked to it. The cushions were more awkward, and I think we cultivated and then bribed a friend in New Court to accommodate them in exchange for using the punt.

We registered it with the River Cam Conservators and got a licence plate, and had another small brass plate engraved with its new name, *Vamp*.

Then it became a serious distraction from my work. I had never owned a boat (or a car) before and so I spent a lot of time caring for it. Some of us got into the habit of going to Adams' delicatessen on St John's Street to buy rolls, cream cheese, lettuce and fruit, and take a picnic on the river on an ordinary working day. With a bit more preparation we could take an evening picnic on the upper river with more elaborate food and wine glasses.

To reach the upper river we used the rollers by the sluice at Laundress Green, aided by sections of retired punt poles slightly longer than the width of the boat, which were used on the footpath between the bank and the formal rollers. At weekends boys who swam at the bathing place near Newnham Croft were inclined to 'bomb' punts, but a punt pole was usually enough to discourage them.

There was one occasion when friends wanted hotel accommodation for their girlfriends at a busy time and could not find any. They appealed to me and at least some of them spent the night in the punt under a bridge.

After we graduated we sold the punt through the columns of *Varsity* and both left the country. My parents lived in Cambridge and told me later that the punt had been washed away in flood water and taken as salvage by Scudamores. They had tracked the ownership to me, but the new student owners had let the registration with the Cam Conservators lapse. I hope the students did not lose their investment.

Laurie van Someren (1958)

Singing on the river, 2009.

My tutor, Harry Williams, was in the habit of giving dinner parties in his rooms, between Chapel and the Master's Lodge, to get to know his charges. His liberality with the gin and the wine ensured that he got to know us and we got to know each other. Food, wine and service were provided by the College, and Harry urged us to do the same in our own rooms.

I plucked up the courage to do so in my last year when I got the rooms of my dreams, N3 in Great Court. One would call on Mr Buck, the Clerk of the Kitchens, and discuss the menu; he would always urge one to start with the scampi frite – 'bits of cod in batter', as Harry scornfully (and wrongly) described it; then pheasant or steak with a sauce piquant – a phrase which Mr Buck had an odd way of pronouncing; then, invariably, for dessert, the crème brûlée. One could also borrow the College silver to dress up the table. Then it was off to Mr Nightingale at the Buttery to order the wine. If one was popular with Mr Nightingale some of the claret on the Fellows' wine list would miraculously become available; I remember in particular a chateau-bottled Margaux Premier Cru 1949.

On the appointed day, early in the evening, a Pole would appear bearing on his head a Georgian butler's tray laden with green baize bags containing pairs of candelabra and candlesticks. From that moment on one felt rather grand. At my dinners either Harry himself or Keith Walker, my supervisor, was usually present, so there wasn't too much baying for broken glass or falling into the river at the end of the evening.

N3 was a unique set of rooms, I believe, because the bedroom was above the first-floor main room, up a spiral stair in one of the turrets of Queen's Gate. The main room had 17th-century panelling and a built-in 18th-century pedimented bookcase in one corner; and this had a concealed door amidships leading into the windowless space of another turret. This 'secret' room was ideal for the modest stock of antiques in which I dealt as a help towards paying the buttery bills.

In those days it was possible to buy certain things from the many antiques dealers in Cambridge and sell them for a profit in London; and in London it was possible to buy fine but flawed early English china and sell it to Gabor Cossa, opposite the

Matthew and Son, grocers, was a fixture of the Trinity Street landscape opposite Great Gate for 130 years until it finally closed in 1962.

Fitzwilliam, for his discerning but straitened clients. By this time my Girtonian fiancée was at LSE and, after spending the evening with her, it was usually a question of taking the last train back to Cambridge. Climbing into Trinity with a free pair of hands presented no problems; but doing so with a box or two of 18th-century china and glass meant recruiting another Trinity man on the late train or at the Cambridge station taxi rank. I made some good friends that way because, of course, I had to reward my helpers with a glass or two of wine back at N3.

David Kenrick (1958)

It was on a Thursday evening during the Michaelmas term of 1959 – or was it the Lent term of 1960? – that this incident occurred.

I had retired early, with an essay completed and a 9am lecture to attend, when I was rudely aroused by knocking on my bedroom door and my roommate's voice crying, 'Wake up! Wake upl, the place is on fire!'

Pausing only to don my spectacles, acquire my dressing gown and pick up my wallet (why I cannot tell) I proceeded towards the nearest exit which also turned out to be the source of the excitement. At the head of the stairs I equipped myself with a fire extinguisher and descended the staircase to the landing below.

Clearly my moment of heroism had come. It was my destiny to save the College. With a cry of, 'Make way! I have a fire extinguisher,' I flung myself into the room with, on reflection, more gallantry than common sense. Not only was the smoke considerably thicker here, but it was as hot as the Devil's hearthside. Judging as best I might, I discharged the fire extinguisher in what I hoped was the correct direction and retreated considerably more rapidly than I had entered, with chest heaving and streaming eyes.

While I was beginning to appreciate that my lungs were actually still working and life extant, the Fire Brigade arrived. In a few short seconds it was all over. The fire, which had been caused by an unextinguished cigarette dropped into a sofa behind the door, was well and truly put out with the use of a plentiful supply of good Cambridgeshire water. We retired to bed, having opened all the windows.

The following morning revealed the true state of affairs. Several others before me had braved the inferno and discharged fire extinguishers in what they had, like myself, erroneously assumed to be the seat of the conflagration. In consequence the floor was many inches deep in water supplied by the Fire Brigade, together with a considerable amount of whatever liquid they put in those fire extinguishers. Water, they say, will find its own level, and this was proved true within a matter of hours. The noxious fluid percolated effortlessly through the ceiling into the Bakery Department of Matthews Grocery shop below.

The following Saturday *Varsity* carried the deathless headline, 'Tarts Ruined, Trinity Saved'

F.R.H. Elgood (1957)

Beware of the Punt

Words by Tony Firth, music by Jack Thompson, performed by them at the Trinity May Ball in June 1960:

There once was a lovely young debutante,
Lived in Pelham Crescent, South Ken,
Who, lovingly reared by her maiden aunt,
Knew not of the vices of men.
She met a young fellow from Trinity.
He took her up to the May Ball.
But her aunt said, 'Avoid the vicinity

Of the river
In case you should fall.
Beware of the punt.
Beware of the punt.
The punt is a vessel of sin.
Few girls can distinguish the back from the front
After a stiff double gin.'
The ball passed in decorous gaiety.
They danced till the dawn was at hand.
Till he, with what seemed spontaneity,
Began the campaign he had planned.
While she gazed around her ecstatically,
He doctored her large orangeade.
She followed his lead automatically –
To the brink, when a ghostly voice said:
'Beware of the punt.
Beware of the punt.
The punt's a lascivious craft.
By dawn your perceptions are certainly blunt
And you can't tell the fore from the aft.'
Too late – she has boarded the ill-fated barque.
Too late now for even a scream.
Too late – she detected just what he expected
In the dark of the swift-flowing stream.
In vain she invoked his benignity.
His looks remained savage and black.
He forced her with horrid malignity
To punt him to … Clayhythe, and back.
But as they were passing by Trinity,
Her punt pole stuck deep in the loam.
She hung for a while in infinity,
Then sang, as she sank 'neath the foam,
'Beware of the punt.
Beware of the punt.
Young ladies, take warning from me.
For a girl who goes out with a boy in a punt
Will soon lose her …
EQUILIBRIUM!'

Jack Thompson (1957)

The Chapel
Michael Banner, Dean of Chapel (2006)

The Chapel is a dominating presence in Great Court. Even those who never enter the building cannot fail to notice it lit up on a winter's evening, or to hear the strains of organ and choir reverberating over the College and the street beyond. It would be natural to wonder, however, whether the physical presence is disproportionate to the Chapel's actual significance in the College. After all, it is nearly 150 years since Matthew Arnold (Balliol, not Trinity) heard the 'melancholy, long, withdrawing roar' of the retreating sea of faith, and even the sound of the choir, no matter how winsome, provides no evidence that the tide has turned and is rushing back to shore.

Well, in the annual round of the year, a surprising number – surprising even to the clergy sometimes – do set foot in the place. At the freshers' service, on Remembrance Sunday, at the Advent Carols, on Christmas Eve and Christmas Day, on Ash Wednesday and at the regular services, especially Sunday evensong, a large number of members of the College, including many no longer in residence, plus staff and many visitors, are found in Chapel. We would find it hard to attract every week the 250-plus who came to hear Professor Amartya Sen give an address on the virtue of justice, but in the course of the year there are other peaks of similar altitude. Add to the regular events, the irregular ones (occasioned more often by misfortune than by good fortune – that is, memorial services more frequently than weddings), and the Chapel sees a good proportion of the College in the course of the year.

All that said, it would be a mistake to estimate the Chapel's significance in the College merely by reference to footfall. At the Commemoration of Benefactors, the prayer which is sanctioned for use, having listed those who have 'enriched us of their substance', and mentioned those who by 'achievement in Literature, Science, Philosophy, and the Arts' have 'brought honour' to the College, mentions also the good repute which comes to 'this House' by 'patient continuance in well-doing'. That which is not immediately noticeable may, not unnaturally, go unnoticed. But it is, of course, the 'patient continuance' of the chaplains (and indeed other members of the congregation)

The Chapel altar and altarpiece, St Michael and the Devil *by Benjamin West.*

in pastoral care which quite properly brings good repute to the Chapel; and the energy and vigour which a chaplain shows in getting to know the place is the basis for the esteem in which they are held by colleagues, staff and students alike. Trinity is a glorious institution, but not every student's experience of Trinity in particular, or Cambridge in general, is simply glorious, and the Chapel and chaplains rightly continue to take a part in supporting those who do indeed need support.

When Matthew Arnold heard that melancholy roar of the retreating sea of faith, he was, of course, standing on Dover beach. On other beaches (in Nigeria, for example, or in India, or in Louisiana for that matter) the sea of faith (though not necessarily a Christian faith) still laps the shore, and religion plays a highly significant role in shaping the thought and sensibilities of vast populations. Trinity is itself an international community, and now includes followers of many faiths as well as those with none. The Chapel properly aspires to welcome and assist all, and itself to be a place where the intellectual questions still posed to and by religion are asked and answered. What the contemporary scene suggests is not that these questions are withering away and failing to attract attention, but rather that they are receiving answers which are glib or thin. A College which includes figures with such profound yet different interests in religion as George Herbert, Ludwig Wittgenstein, Alfred Tennyson and Isaac Newton has a tradition which rather obliges it to do better than that.

⸺◦✦◦⸺

I DON'T KNOW WHO RATTED ON ME. IT MIGHT HAVE BEEN MY father or our local vicar in Windermere. But soon after I arrived at Trinity, I received a note from the chaplain, Geoffrey Beaumont, that he heard I was an altar server and he wanted to enlist my services in some of the many services we held in the Chapel in those days. Therefore, I was put on a schedule. The services were always early in the morning, of course, and Geoffrey and I were usually the only worshippers. But I did get to know him and the other members of the religious community then at Trinity. He was a great socialiser and his opening gambit to undergraduates was, 'Come and have a drink.' I had never met a clergyman like him and he became an immediate favourite of mine because

he was responsible for what many then thought a scandalous thing – putting a jazz mass into the church. I once met Lionel Gamlin there. He was the BBC producer and actor known for his programme *Lionel Gamlin Reporting*. Geoffrey also had many well-known clerical friends, including John Stott of All Souls, Langham Place. There would also be plenty of piano playing and singing. This was especially so when his replacement, Simon Phipps, arrived as they had worked together in the Footlights. Geoffrey really burnt the candle at both ends. He drank quite heavily and smoked incessantly. I once remember I arrived at the Chapel early in the morning and there he was, suffering. 'Oh! Christopher!' he said. 'I have a tremendous hangover. Can you say morning prayer for me, while I prepare for the communion?' So he stubbed out his cigarette and we went into the Chapel and I quietly said morning prayer in a corner of the Sanctuary. I also went to gatherings at the Dean's rooms, Dr Burnaby. There I met Harry Williams, the outstanding Anglican theologian. He was very bright but also good fun although Dr Burnaby was rather staid.

The statue of Mercury in Whewell's Court.

I used to row for First and Third. John Easterling was often in the same boat. Another oarsman was Rupert Hort, related to Fenton Hort, a distinguished Irish theologian and a friend of Westcott. He invited me to a meeting of the Cambridge Mission to Delhi but forgot to inform me before the meeting that he wanted me to replace him as College representative when he went down. I did not have the nerve to refuse him. My job was then to raise money from the College for the Mission. The idea was that I was to do this by asking graduates to donate their undergraduate gowns and then, next term, sell them to the freshmen. I was really too shy to do this effectively and as a result felt obliged to give ten shillings of my precious pocket money to the Mission.

Christopher Lewis (1952)

F.A. Simpson was elected to a Fellowship in 1911 and remained a Fellow of Trinity until his death in 1974 at the age of 90 (not many people knew that his given names were Frederick Arthur, and very few called him anything but 'Mr Simpson'). Alfred Newman Gilbey came up to Trinity in 1920 and was a pupil of Mr Simpson. He was ordained as a priest in 1929 and was the Roman Catholic chaplain to the University for 33 years, from 1932 until 1965. He died in 1998, aged 96. Both are now legendary figures. Indeed they were almost legendary figures when I came up to Trinity in 1955.

Most of the legends were true. It is true that Simpson was elected to his Fellowship on the strength of the first volume of his projected four-volume work on the life and times of Louis Napoleon. It was published in 1909, the year Simpson took holy orders. But when the second volume was published in 1923 Simpson was so mortified by two anonymous reviews that he abandoned the project. Thereafter he did little teaching or writing (except to newspapers, or in the Fellows' complaints book) for the rest of his long life.

He did however from time to time preach, without notes, sermons of remarkable eloquence: full of learning but also full of passion against every sort of cruelty and injustice. He had been a chaplain during the First World War, visiting military hospitals near Cambridge, and he never forgot the young men who suffered and died in the war. A constant theme of his sermons was to impress on undergraduates how fortunate they were to be at Cambridge, and how they must not waste their talents.

It is also true that Alfred Gilbey was ultra-conservative in every aspect of his life: in the practice of his religion, his devotion to the House of Stuart, his rejection of feminism and every form of modernism, his idea of what a university should be, and most obviously his dress. His obituary in the *Independent* described his everyday wear: 'shovel hat, flyless breeches, double-waisted waistcoat and frockcoat.' At times he seemed almost a caricature of himself, but none of it was ever an act. That is what he believed, and how he was. He sincerely believed that women should not be admitted to Cambridge degrees, and he resolutely refused to let Girton or Newnham women attend the chaplaincy at Fisher House. This was an absurdly misguided campaign that he could not possibly win, and eventually it led to his resignation. But Gilbey's old-fashioned ways included unfailing courtesy and patience towards the least polished and prepossessing undergraduates from the men's colleges, and great generosity. He saved the historic buildings of Fisher House from redevelopment, and over the years he must have spent a great deal of his own money on the maintenance and embellishment of the chaplaincy and on dispensing hospitality there.

As an undergraduate I often saw both men, although I was not a faithful member of Gilbey's flock, and I never had the courage to try to get beneath Simpson's forbidding exterior. When I had rooms at I2 Great Court ('et ego in Arcadia vixi') Simpson would often loom at the window in the twilight, dressed in a flat cloth cap and a scarf draped over one shoulder and with secateurs in his hand, making good what he evidently regarded as the deficiencies of the gardeners. Gow, a great classical scholar, wrote a mock memorial inscription for him which included 'collegii arbustorum mutilator indefessus' – tireless pruner of the College's shrubs.

Robert Walker (Baron Walker of Gestingthorpe) (1955)

In the early 1990s, a small stream of ordinands wound its way up Jesus Lane from Westcott House to Trinity College, where we were reading for the theology and religious studies Tripos as part of ordination training.

Trinity was my third Cambridge home. I read English as an undergraduate and graduate student at Newnham, but my then bishop wanted me to see a different Cambridge when I began ordination training. In 1993 I was among the first women to be selected for priestly ministry in the Church of England – no extended period of waiting as a deaconess or deacon. Trinity enabled me to embrace that vocation with courage and with no diminution of the commitment to academic excellence which I had developed at Newnham. The Dean, Dr Arnold Browne, made a two-year Tripos a delight: supervisions could encompass vocational and academic rigour; and extra Greek, funded by Trinity, enabled me to go from not knowing the alphabet to gaining a first in six glorious terms.

And for me, Trinity was glorious. It was funny: I matriculated in scarlet, causing first puzzlement and then jesting. It was beautiful: Great Court, the Wren Library, the Chapel are places which capture light and grace in stone. They hold in stillness something of the spirit of the Church of England, a balancing of opposing forces which, at its best, is glorious. It was peaceful. The architectural space of Great Court lifts the soul in a manner analogous to the finest churches and cathedrals of the land. It was bracing, pushing us always to do and give and be our best, with a commitment to human flourishing which set aside gender or age or ethnicity and sought only excellence. To me, Trinity was a kind place, generous and welcoming. Annual cheques would arrive in Westcott from a Trinity bequest for those reading for holy orders at Trinity who already had an Oxbridge degree. The then Master attended my first sermon in Great St Mary's and said to me afterwards, 'Quite something, starting here; couldn't you have begun smaller – perhaps the College Chapel?' And I thought, but did not say, that the combined learning of those assembled for evensong really did not make it a smaller or an easier first billet.

Trinity could be a scary place: brighter people you will not meet. But the challenges and demands it offered were exhilarating. The theological conundrums of my supervisions are still with me as I try to pass on something of Trinity's commitment to the life of the mind in my own teaching of the newly ordained and of parishioners. The place of women in the Church of England is still something which causes controversy, even consternation. But Trinity was part of what taught me that anything is possible, that prejudice and unexamined assumptions are never acceptable, that a living tradition does not value the tradition over the living and that what is not done because it is painful or difficult is almost certainly what should be done.

Jane Steen (1993)

Trinity College Choir:
A History and Reminiscence
Nicholas Yates, Chairman of the Trinity College
Choir Association and choral scholar (1991)
I did not make the best first impression. The alarm clock went off 15 minutes after my first Sunday morning service had started. It had been a punishing freshers week and I was clearly not yet ready for such rigours. There was no opportunity merely to slip in to the Chapel unnoticed. I had missed the rehearsal and the doors into the Chapel under the organ were firmly shut. I therefore sat next to Tennyson in the ante-chapel until the service finished in order to apologise to the then Organist and Director of Music, Richard Marlow. He was much kinder about this appalling start than I had expected and in retrospect I may even have caught the slight flicker of humour in his eye while I made my excuses. Happily, this faux pas was quickly forgotten and my time in the choir as a tenor, and indeed at Trinity, was hugely enjoyable and rewarding.

The choir, 2007.

One of the most vivid memories I have of my time at Trinity, or at least the ones that are likely to make it into this book, is of the reverence I had for the importance of Trinity as an academic institution and for all those illustrious members of College who had gone before. I found it difficult to comprehend that, somehow and albeit to a very small extent, I had been given, by Richard Marlow, the opportunity to partake in that and to sing in one of the best choirs in the world.

Trinity's choral associations date back to the founding of King's Hall by Edward II in 1317, from which time, Chapel Royal choristers, on leaving the Court, customarily entered King's Hall to continue their academic studies, alongside other undergraduates training for service in the royal administration.

The formation of the medieval chapel choir remains obscure, but the choral foundation which Mary Tudor established in 1553 (ten choristers, six lay-clerks, four priests, an organist and a schoolmaster) survived for over 300 years. Among the musicians associated with the choir during this time were the Tudor composers Thomas Preston, Robert Whyte and John Hilton and the organists Robert Ramsay and Thomas Walmisley. Although Walmisley's setting of the Magnificat and Nunc Dimittis in D

minor has always been somewhere near the top of the Church of England's choral classics chart, the extraordinary beauty of Robert Whyte's music, composed in the middle of the 16th century, has only recently been brought to the fore.

By way of an aside, I am told that in 1883 the requirements for admission to the choir stipulated not only 'prepared solos and sight-reading', but the translation of passages from Virgil and questions on Greek and Latin grammar. Candidates were also set an examination involving algebra, quadratic equations and Euclid Books 1, 2 and 3! For me, this is somewhat reminiscent of the New Testament Greek that I had to learn, and take an exam in, during my Part I in Theology. To say it was not my best subject is to put it euphemistically. However, my then director of studies John Bowker, whom I hold in the highest esteem, was completely undisturbed. His only concern at the time was, during supervisions on modern theology, to discuss the meanings of death and to impress upon me that he was almost certainly wrong about everything. I took heart from this.

Just before the turn of the 20th century, Charles Villiers Stanford was the organist and the legendary Ralph Vaughan Williams graduated from Trinity. Stanford left an indelible

mark on English choral music. The settings he composed for Evensong, together with his anthems, arguably form the backbone of the Anglican choral tradition.

Not long after the turn of the 20th century the College choir school closed down. Thereafter, a choir of boy trebles (holding scholarships at a local grammar school), lay-clerks (some of whom shared their duties with the choirs of King's and St John's Colleges) and students continued the regular pattern of choral services until the 1950s. This traditionally constituted body then gave way to a choir of undergraduate tenors and basses during Raymond Leppard's tenure as Director of Music (1957–68).

In 1968 Richard Marlow became Organist and Director of Music and, after the admission of women undergraduates in 1978, formed the current mixed choir in 1982. During the late 1980s and early 1990s the choir grew to become one of the finest and most able mixed choirs in the world. Richard conducted almost 50 recordings and undertook about the same number of foreign tours with the choir.

During that time, while John Bowker was Dean of Chapel, the choir also performed a number of sequences of music and readings. John would write sublime devotional texts to fit around the music that Richard was doing with the choir that term. These were compelling and deeply moving collaborations and ones which I was able to persuade John to replicate in Trinity some years later with a choir of ex-Trinity choral scholars, which I and another of my contemporaries set up in the late 90s called VOCE, Voice of Cambridge Ensemble.

It is no understatement to say that the choir of undergraduate men and women during the 1980s and early 1990s stood at the forefront of what can certainly be seen in retrospect as a long overdue movement for change: a move towards inclusivity, to correct the historical norm that viewed sacred choral music as merely a male preserve. Subconsciously, the choir encouraged others elsewhere to tread on the same sacred eggshells. For example, in 1991 Salisbury became the first English cathedral to form a separate and independent foundation for girl choristers (the same year in which the 900th anniversary of the founding of the very first boys' choir was celebrated there). Since then a great many others have followed suit, and the inclusion of women

into cloistered choirs has, except in a few bastions of tradition, become the norm.

This is not the arena to enter into a debate about the pros and cons of boys voices and women's voices. However, it was interesting to note the not infrequent letters that Richard Marlow received after his early BBC broadcasts praising him on the standard of the 'boys' voices.

During this time the choir spawned a number of ensembles of ex-Trinity choral scholars. One is mentioned above, but they also included the professional ensembles of Trinity Baroque and Henry's Eight. The former is made up of men and women, while the latter set out to sing repertoire written mainly for men. Indeed, that eight-man ensemble, which was a reincarnation of the male choral scholar close harmony group, The Trinmen, recorded a CD of choral music by the Trinity organist, Robert Whyte. I was fortunate enough to sing in The Trinmen for a couple of years, during which we toured independently around some of Trinity's Livings in the north of England and further afield to Germany. Those were indeed halcyon days, although I am not sure that our hosts will necessarily remember it in the same way.

In 2006, after 38 years at the helm, Richard Marlow retired as Organist and Director of Music. In his leaving speech given at the end of a very hot dinner held for him in Trinity to celebrate all he had done, and to launch the Choir Association (TCCA), he said, with his usual dry sense of humour, the following: 'Somewhat fortuitously, I became a Fellow in my late twenties and, through laziness, lack of worldly ambition and an ever-growing affection for Trinity, I have remained put since then, becoming the longest-serving Organist and Director of Music in the history of the College.'

Through his inclusion of women in the pews of his choir, Richard has, perhaps more than anyone else, whether consciously or not, shaped the course of choral music in the United Kingdom and at the same time propelled the Chapel choir onto the world stage where it firmly remains.

In September 2006 Stephen Layton took over the baton and has built further on all that has gone before, providing opportunities for the choir to work with some of the best orchestras and ensembles in the country and further afield.

Singing from the Towers, 2010.

AN IMPORTANT DATE IN THE COLLEGE'S MUSICAL CALENDAR IS the Singing from the Towers to celebrate Trinity Sunday. I would like to claim my tiny footnote in history: the Singing from the Towers was my baby.

I grew up in Cambridge (my father had been chaplain of Selwyn) so I had a love for local traditions anyway. When I went up to read Classics in 1970 I sang in the choir, which was only tenors and basses in those days. At that time the judge still held assizes in Cambridge, and it was while I was up, in 1972, that the civil jurisdiction of assizes was transferred to the High Court, and the criminal jurisdiction to the Crown Court. The judge had stayed in Great Court, in A staircase I think, and his arrival used to be welcomed by a trumpeter. I loved this, and when it all stopped I wrote to the College Council lamenting the fact that trumpets were no longer to be heard in Great Court, and suggesting (on the analogy of Magdalen, Oxford, singing up their tower every Ascension Day) that maybe in Trinity we could divide the choir up between the Great Gate and the King Edward Tower and sing antiphonally, with a few brass on the Queen's Gate. To my amazement the College said yes. I put it to Dr Richard Marlow, who enthusiastically agreed. We then had to find somewhere to rehearse so as to practise the huge time lag between the Decani and Cantoris sections of the choir, something that had never been done before at such a distance. I therefore suggested the Fellows' Garden, where I paced out the equivalent distance and Richard brought the choir over. The rehearsal was a success, and so was the first 'Great Court Concert' as we called it in those days – and it has continued every year since. I suspect that the large number of tourists who hear it think that it has been going since medieval times!

Andrew Mackay (1970)

Music at Trinity
Rosalyn Hindmarch (2004)

A musical tour of Trinity commences naturally in the Chapel, in which the mixed-voice College choir sings regular services and concerts. On Sundays, Tuesdays and Thursdays, members of College and visitors hear an extensive range of choral repertoire during services, from early Renaissance polyphony

to contemporary choral music from around the world. Trinity's fine Metzler organ is a dominant presence in the Chapel, and the instrument is used to great effect when accompanying the choir in sacred repertoire, as well as for solo playing. Music written by the many composers connected with Trinity plays an important role in Chapel worship; many choral scholars will have fond memories of singing Stanford's *Beati quorum via* in the choir and chapel for which it was written. The same can be said of the *Advent Responsory* by the former Director of Music, Richard Marlow, which provides a highly effective opening to the Advent Carol Service each year, sung in darkness before the Chapel gradually fills with light from the hundreds of candles held by the congregation.

The Choir spends about ten hours per week singing in rehearsals and services, which is a significant commitment for its 30 undergraduates. Nonetheless, the College choir system is unique in the opportunity it provides to work within the same group of singers for a year to produce music-making of an exceptionally high standard. Many Trinity choral and organ scholars go on to professional careers in music themselves; the training they receive in the choir is invaluable to this end.

Services and concerts by the College choir are by no means the only events that take place in Trinity Chapel. The Trinity College Music Society (TCMS) currently runs around 25 concerts a term, many of which use the Chapel as a performance space. These range from solo and chamber recitals to orchestral and choral concerts, usually organised and conducted by students from Trinity or other colleges. TCMS runs a non-audition choir, the Trinity Singers, which performs large-scale choral works, and a non-audition orchestra, the Trinity Players.

Moving around Great Court, one comes to another important performance space, the Master's Lodge. The upstairs drawing room is used frequently for concerts; for many undergraduate musicians it marks the beginning and end of their Trinity careers as the venue for the Freshers' and Leavers' Concerts. Occasionally other TCMS concerts take place here, such as a recent performance of Richard Strauss's melodrama for narrator and piano, *Enoch Arden*, in which Stephen Fry recited Tennyson's poem. In the past few years the Master's Lodge has hosted a series of concerts given by professional soloists and ensembles, owing to the generous support of Dr Ralph Kohn and The Kohn Foundation, offering Fellows and students the opportunity to hear first-rate concerts free of charge.

On the Friday of May Week each year the Hall is transformed: tables and benches are removed and replaced with a stage, lighting, scenery and hundreds of chairs in preparation for the May Week Concert. This highlight of the TCMS calendar has taken place for over a century, following a similar format for much of this time, so that the first half comprises more serious choral or orchestral items, while the second half is devoted to an operetta. The operetta is a light-hearted affair, with a libretto by Trinity students which inevitably includes familiar tropes from College life combined with a degree of poetic licence – a mathematician looking for love, a bedder frustrated by the untidiness of students on her staircase or the appointment of a swan as the Dean of College.

The interval of the May Week Concert includes dinner in the cloister underneath the Wren Library, which recently provided an enchanting setting for a production of Benjamin Britten's opera *The Turn of the Screw*. This was the imaginative idea of three Trinity undergraduates, who directed and produced the opera, ensuring that Britten's setting of Henry James' haunting story was enhanced by the gradual fading of daylight during the performance. This is not the first time that Nevile's Court has been the venue for a memorable musical occasion: in June 1923, a ballet, *Old King Cole*, by an eminent alumnus, Ralph Vaughan Williams, received its premiere here. In April 1972 the inaugural Wren Library Concert took place and included concerti grossi by J.S. Bach and Handel and a Bach motet, *Jesu meine Freude*. An Easter Term concert in the Wren is now an annual fixture.

On Trinity Sunday, as well as singing from the towers, the choir holds a concert from a flotilla of punts moored on the River Cam by Scholars' Lawn. A thousand-strong audience gathers on the riverbank to hear a concert of madrigals, folk-songs and close-harmony arrangements. As dusk gives way to darkness, the evening's entertainment concludes with the traditional singing of John Wilbye's *Draw on, sweet night*, as the choir is punted down the river and out of sight. An unfortunate incident in 1999 when some of the punts sank during this complicated manoeuvre has become somewhat legendary: copies of music rescued from the river which bear the signs of waterlogging are still present in the choir library.

Trinity's musical life frequently reaches spaces far outside Cambridge. The TCMS minutes from 1934 record the 'unqualified success' of a tour by the College's Madrigal Club to Holland, followed by a humorous reference to the College orchestra having toured as far as Sawston and Trumpington! More recently, the College choir has travelled far to bring Trinity's musical tradition to a wider audience, with concerts around the UK and tours to India, Peru, Canada, the USA and Australia, to name just a few. In addition, the Trinity sound is available through the many recordings produced by the choir in the past few decades.

Simon Phipps in his rooms at Trinity.

The Seven Deadly Sins

What can one do that's the least bit new
And hasn't been done before?
Wouldn't it be nice to discover a vice
That isn't just a terrible bore.

I long to break out and make a sortie
Into the world and go wildly naughty.
I've tried them singly and mixed up in medley,
But those seven old sins are absolutely deadly.

Can anyone think of an original sin,
Won't somebody tell me how to begin?
Seven deadly sins may have tickled Adam
But by 1951 I kind of feel we've 'ad 'em.

If only the serpent and Eve
Had had something more amusing up their sleeve.
They might have had a go at the things we're needing,
If they hadn't been so busy weeding in the Garden of Eden.

There must be one or two more,
That no one has experimented with before.
So in spite of Eve and Adam we might even add them
To the recognised list of sins that exist.

Anger and avarice have both been tried,
So have gluttony, sloth and pride,
That only leaves us envy and lust
There must be something more amusing, really there must.

So if anyone thinks of an original sin,
Won't somebody tell me how to begin.
Something with a thrill that's gay and gorgeous,
Never even contemplated by the Borgias.
Well, I suppose one could be good!

Derek Pelly (1949)

There is a well-known quotation, sometimes attributed to Elvis Costello: 'Writing about music is like dancing about architecture – it's a really stupid thing to want to do.' An account of music at Trinity can never do justice to the sheer exuberance of hearing the choir sing Stanford's *Coelos Ascendit Hodie* from the Towers, or a spine-tingling moment at the end of Messiaen's *Quatuor pour la fin du temps* during a candlelit concert in the Chapel. Nevertheless, in writing about music at Trinity, a dance around the College's glorious architecture may go some way towards capturing and understanding its unique musical life.

WHILE AN UNDERGRADUATE, SIMON PHIPPS WROTE THE attached ditty on the Seven Deadly Sins, which Geoffrey Beaumont, then College chaplain, set to music. I suggest the sixth verse is the best – it has helped me remember what the sins are.

Geoffrey Beaumont's rooms in Bishop's Hostel were regularly frequented of an evening by the likes of Simon, Julian Slade (I was a stagehand for his *Bang Goes the Meringue*) and the later hymn writer Patrick Appleford, making it full of merriment and music. In my last year I was Geoffrey's neighbour and it was often my job to call a halt so that he could get some sleep before having to be up to take early communion in Chapel. Invariably on his return all he wanted was a first gin and tonic of the day and I got his breakfast that had been brought over for him. It is said he set the record in influencing the numbers seeking ordination.

TRINITY IN CAMBERWELL: 125 NOT OUT!

On 2 March 2 1885 a letter signed by 65 junior and senior members of Trinity College was sent to all members of College: 'It is proposed to establish a Mission in some poor part of London, to be maintained and carried on by members of this College … The need to work among the poor is great … it will be of great advantage to the College as a whole that it should be united in a good work peculiarly its own, which members of the College may not only support by subscriptions, but visit and take some part in.'

The poor and densely populated parish of St George's Camberwell was chosen as the location of the Mission, to the delight of the Bishop of Rochester: 'The news about Trinity comes like a bottle of port wine to a weak man.' By 1886 a Trinity man, Rev. Norman Campbell, was established as Vicar of St George's and Warden of the Mission. A team of ex-Trinity clergymen took up residence, and premises for the Mission were rented in Albany Road. In 1893 the Master, Montagu Butler, spoke of 'bringing the

young men of Trinity face to face, heart to heart, with the poorer classes of London'. An appeal raised £13,000 for a new Mission building in New Church Road in 1895. The Mission's cultural, social and religious work in the parish flourished, including day schools, a hospital for the poor, Bible classes, Sunday schools, women's guilds; clubs for working men, lads and girls providing for sport, music, art and crafts; a girls' centre, church lads' brigade, scout troop, choirs, a temperance society, and even soup kitchens for the direct relief of poverty.

The Mission faced the two great social problems of housing and unemployment in Camberwell in the 1920s and 1930s, and its vital work continued despite occasional financial problems. There were two large boys' clubs, a young men's club, an institute for girls and women, scouts, cubs, guides and brownies. Patrick Duff, Trinity Fellow and later Vice Master, organised camping for boys in the summer.

Opposite: *The Boys' Club on a trip to Trinity College, 1923.*

Below: *From Boyhood to Manhood Foundation visit to Trinity, 2009.*

The local population has changed radically. The older poor white working families of the London dock era are gone. The parish and its school are now full of young Nigerian immigrant families and their children. In neighbouring Peckham there are shootings and knife crime, but Camberwell itself remains largely peaceful.

After 125 years the work at the heart of the community goes on. However, our 'new' building is now nearly 30 years old, and beginning to show its age. Indoors we urgently need a completely new kitchen, while the outdoor play area for the kindergarten is worn out.

(We thank Dr Lawrence Goldman of St Peter's College Oxford (Trinity Research Fellow in History 1985) for permission to quote from his book Trinity in Camberwell: A History of Trinity College Mission in Camberwell 1885–1985.*)*

Andrew McLachlan (1953) and Duncan Rodgers

The Second World War devastated Camberwell. Bombing reduced much of the area to rubble, and destroyed the patterns of social life built up over decades. Only 400 of Camberwell's 40,000 houses survived the war undamaged.

Between 1950 and 1970 there was clearance, demolition and rebuilding, the old generation being displaced and the old terraces replaced by new estates and blocks of flats. Five vast new and impersonal council estates replaced the Victorian terraced housing, leading to further social problems for the Mission to tackle. Remarkably, 25 years later, these were to be demolished in their turn and replaced with social housing on a more human scale.

It was in 1966 that a new project began: the Trinity College Centre Holiday Scheme provides summer activities for Camberwell children, still going strong more than 40 years later (and still evoking fond memories for many past Trinity volunteers).

In the 1970s the Greater London Council created the large new Burgess Park in South London, and demolished the Mission buildings to make room for it. The work of the Mission was continued in a new centre built next to St George's School. Using the compensation money, funds raised by members of the College, and contributions from parish and diocese, the current buildings were erected, containing two halls, extra rooms and a parish church leading off the main hall.

It has been an exciting time for Trinity undergraduates involved in Camberwell. A successful revival of the December Week in 2007 led to the formation of a society in 2008 whose purpose was to strengthen the links between Trinity and Camberwell, particularly at the undergraduate level. This has provided a presence for 'Trinity in Camberwell' among the student community and has given a structure to allow students to engage in the wider work of the charity; we currently have a small core of committed members and a wider group of 50 interested students.

In 2008–9, working with the College chaplains and Nicholas Elder, we organised regular trips to the Trinity College Centre to help with mentoring on the From Boyhood to Manhood Foundation. This was beneficial to everyone. Trinity students had the chance to temporarily step outside the Cambridge environment and learn at first hand about what life for some people in Camberwell is like, as well as improving their indoor footballing expertise! Helping the boys with core English and maths skills was a great help to the staff in simply providing greater numbers of people to do teaching – and also gave us all a great insight into the frustrations of teaching!

Stuart Robertson (Secretary, Trinity in Camberwell Undergraduate Society 2009–10)

CHAPTER 8

Trinity's Money

Financial Chiaroscuro

Robert Neild (1943)

When recently I set about writing the financial history of the College, exploring when and how we became rich, the College archivists led me to financial records which go back to the foundation, which are almost complete and had scarcely been touched before.

From this untapped mine of information, I found that the College was made very rich by Henry VIII. Since his endowment consisted mostly of agricultural land that the College was forbidden to sell, it prospered, like other landowners as farming methods were improved in the 18th and early 19th century; and suffered severely from the deep agricultural depression that lasted from the 1870s to the 1940s. Then, having been freed to invest as we liked, we were made richer than ever by brilliant real estate development and investment in equities in the second half of the 20th century. I described what lay behind these developments – the influence of economic and political developments, and the influence of some conspicuous persons, notably good and bad Bursars and good and bad Masters, and odd donors: characters which in my ageing memory resemble the Good Kings and Bad Kings of *1066 and All That*.

Most of the increase in the College's income in the past 50 years came from the development of two parcels of College land: an estate at Trimley on the Suffolk coast that was bought as a sound agricultural investment in 1933 and some poor farmland on the outskirts of Cambridge that came to us from King's Hall,

Top: *Trinity Science Park.*

Above: *Sir John Bradfield and the Master, Sir Michael Atiyah, on a site visit to Felixstowe in 1984.*

one of the two colleges which, with all its assets, was absorbed into Trinity at the foundation. On the Trimley estate now stands the greater part of the port of Felixstowe, the biggest container port in Britain. On the derelict farm stands the Cambridge Science Park, created by the College. The rents from these two properties account for half the College's gross endowment income of approximately £40 million, with the Science Park now yielding rather more than Trimley. Both are the fruits of the extraordinary energy and skill of John Bradfield, our Senior Bursar from 1956 to 1992.

Remarkable in the expenditure accounts is the evidence of the uninhibited greed of the Master and Fellows in the

18th century, that age of decadence, when they pocketed the College's rising rental income, quarrelled over it and failed to improve the stipends of the scholars, let alone expand the College. It was the general practice of colleges that the dons divided among themselves income in excess of what they were required by statute to spend on running the college, with the result that they had a strong incentive to be mean and to avoid any increase in the numbers of Fellows or scholars. The practice seems to have started at All Souls College, Oxford, in the late 16th century. At rich Trinity the results became exceptionally gross. The opportunities for the dons to feather their nests must have been like those recently enjoyed by bankers. How different is the lot of the dons today when their pay is linked to the mean pay scales set by the government for all the institutions it now calls universities, and the College gives away much of its income to support research and teaching in other colleges and in departments of the University.

I wrote all this up in *Riches and Responsibility: the Financial History of Trinity College Cambridge*, which was published in 2008. I omitted, reluctantly, some curious items in the College archives, feeling they were too frivolous or insufficiently relevant to my theme. I am glad to have this opportunity to write about them.

Bentley's campaign against feasts

In the archives I came across new evidence of the greed in the 18th century of the Fellows and of Bentley, our notorious Master from 1700 to 1742 with whom the Fellows fought. In a rough, rather illegible manuscript of six pages are figures

TITBITS

The following titbits, mostly found under the heading 'Extraordinaries' in the expenditure accounts, give glimpses of early College life. They caught the eye of Amy Binner, who assisted me by putting the Senior Bursar's accounts from 1547 to today (without these details) into a computer:

1576 To Mr Anen to pay the scavenger for making clean the streets.. 9s 2d

For 18 of parchment to write the statutes in......... 6s 6d

1604 A key for the great lock in the Treasure House 7d

To labourers for removing chests into the Treasure House 8d

1614 For perfume for the Hall and Chappell at the King's being here......................................16d

1640 To two Bohemian exiles £1 10s
[Sweden invaded Bohemia early in 1639.]

1643 Spent by the cook in a journey to look for the plate...£2 5s
[Trinity, with other colleges, attempted to send its plate to the King at York, but Cromwell somewhere intercepted it.]

To Mr Gregory a minister driven out of Ireland and imprisoned at London 2s 6d
[Protestants were being persecuted in Ireland.]

1644 To two Irish boys and an Irish woman 1s 6d

To two Irish women with their children 2s

1645 To Robin a poor college boy.. 4s

Towards the redeeming of Talbot a poor townsman out of prison 5s

1651 To a German Dr converted from Popery.................. £6

For scouting upon the Scots £2 3s

For two cases of pistolls to scout withal and for scouting £6
[Charles II gathered a Scots-Royalist army in Scotland, marched South and was defeated by Cromwell at Worcester in September 1651. Who Trinity paid to do what, we do not know.]

1656 To the porter for keeping out dogs...................... 6s 8d

To the porter for keeping dogs out of chapel........ 6s 8d

1657 To Old Goodwife Smyth in her sickness and for burying her... 5s

1703 To the widow Killingworth for blowing the organ .. 10s

1706 To the mole catcher for catching 8 moles and spreading ye mole hills in the squares beyond the Great Bridge 2s 8d

To the swanherd for feeding five swans................. £1 5s
[A regular prelude in this period to a 'five swan pye' dinner in early February that is recorded erratically by the Steward, sometimes with the addition of '& geese', up to 1745. Beyond that I have not looked.]

One can see that charitable gifts to poor persons connected with the College began early on, and that the College responded flexibly to the changing religious-cum-political tides of the 17th century – helping refugees, paying for 'scouting', which presumably means spying, and seeking the College silver when, destined for the King, it went astray into the hands of Cromwell.

for 1705 of the amount spent on Fellows' food and drink by Trinity and 15 other colleges, accompanied by proposals that Trinity should make draconian cuts in spending on feasts and also cut other items. These rare data are fascinating, and so are the proposals. Upon examination of the contents, surrounding documents and handwriting it seems certain that the paper is the work of Bentley and is evidence of how tactlessly he attempted, early on in his long war with the Fellows, to curb their behaviour at a time when he was already enraging them by his abuse of power and his self-indulgence in spending on the Master's Lodge.

Regrettably for social historians, Bentley's figures do not look altogether reliable and are partly impenetrable. In particular, his figures usually state how many shillings or pennies were allowed per 'mess', which one would expect to mean so much per portion (the amount allowed for one Fellow at one meal), but in some cases that clearly is not the meaning. All the same, I would not dispute the impression he gives that in this era of decadence Trinity was more extravagant than any other college. Its income in 1705 was £6,369, twice that of King's, the next richest with £3,009 a year; and far greater than that of most other colleges.

BENTLEY

Richard Bentley, Master 1700–42.

The figures show that on ordinary days Trinity and King's were lavish in their provision of Fellows' commons, meaning victuals (principally bread, beer, meat and fish) provided for common consumption, and spent nearly three times as much per Fellow as the two thriftiest colleges, Corpus and Trinity Hall. On top of that – and this is confirmed in the Steward's accounts – each Fellow of Trinity was allowed almost as much again for free sizings, meaning extras that normally were ordered and paid for by those who could afford them, including undergraduates. Similarly, King's expenditure accounts indicate that their Fellows were probably provided with extras at College expense.

As for feasts, then called 'festivals', Trinity, according to Bentley's figures, in 1705 allowed about three times as much per Fellow per feast as King's (and six times as much as most of the poorer colleges); and it also had more feasts than any other college. The expenditure accounts of the two colleges for 1705 tell of a lesser difference: at Trinity 13 feasts at an average total cost per feast of £34; at King's 11 feasts at an average cost of £16. The numbers attending were probably much the same.

We do not know what food was served at these feasts, but culinary customs may not have changed much since Tudor times. A little later, in 1535, when Dr Leigh, one of the commissioners appointed to impose the king's new religion, was sent to enforce the abolition of canon law and the introduction of humanistic studies at Cambridge, he stayed at King's Hall, where in nine days he ran up a bill of nearly five pounds for 'beef, mutton and veal, capons, conies, mallards, chickens, larks and pigeons, pike, oysters, ling, salt salmon, plaice, whiting, tench, eels, perch and roach, warden pears and apples, eggs, butter and cream, various spices, bread, wine, three barrels of ale and more drawn from store, and *ypocras*, a cordial drink made of wine flavoured with spices' (see Alan B. Cobban, *The King's Hall within the University of Cambridge in the Later Middle Ages*, Cambridge, 1969). One must suppose that these copious supplies were provided for the pleasure of the Cambridge men with whom Leigh was dealing, as well as himself. Noted for his avarice and brutality but knighted in 1544, he hanged his cook when putting down an uprising in Lincolnshire in 1536.

In January 1706, when Bentley can only just have written his paper containing figures for 1705, he and the eight senior Fellows who together ruled the College ordered that the amount per head allowed for feasts be reduced right down to the level typical of the poorer colleges, with more allowed for Trinity Sunday. The number of feasts was not reduced, but a further blow to the Fellows was that they were in future to pay for their guests.

It is not surprising that Bentley, who dominated the Seniors by intimidation, managed to push through this swingeing cut in the allowances for feasting. Even so, he showed some caution. The minute in the Conclusion Book, written and signed by him, ends with a 'memorandum' that the allowance 'may be altered by the Master and Seniors, if upon experiment it be found too little'. Moreover, although Bentley proposed in his paper that free sizings for Fellows be abolished and that his share of the dividend be increased, neither measure was introduced. The increase in the dividend he proposed for himself at this time was nothing compared with the fivefold increase he proposed four years later.

That proposal was so outrageous that it was stopped by the Seniors and served only to aggravate Bentley's war with the Fellows, during which they twice, after long legal proceedings, won rulings for his removal from office which he, miraculously, managed to defy.

As to what happened to feasts, there is evidence that on this front, as on others, the war between Bentley and the Fellows went to and fro. After the cut ordered on his initiative in January 1706, expenditure per feast was reduced to about half its former level, but by 1720 it had crept up again almost to the 1705 level and the number of feasts had been increased; after 1720 there was a second squeeze followed by a more modest recovery and another squeeze. This was not a period of marked inflation. The final result was that expenditure on feasts had been significantly reduced but it is likely that it was still higher than at any other college.

Average cost of feasts at Trinity

	£
1705	34
1707	18
1720	28
1723	20
1737	24
1741	22

Greed and defiance of their tyrannical Master on the part of Fellows no doubt explain the upward pressure behind the figures. The downward dents are the result of deterrent measures. In 1722 the Master and Seniors ruled that any spending in excess of the 1705 allowances be docked from the Fellows' weekly allowances for free sizings; and in 1738 that any excess be charged to the account of the steward or cook according to which of them 'was the offending agent'. These measures were surely initiated by Bentley who was Master all this time. He died in the Master's Lodge only in 1742, having entered it in 1700.

James Henry Monk, the author of *The Life of Richard Bentley, D.D.* (London, 1833), observes that 'in controlling the expenses of the College festivals, Dr Bentley suffered his zeal for economy to impair the character of the hospitality which had always

distinguished that noble foundation … the society, mortified at the abolition of what they regarded as one of their glories, gave a harsh interpretation to the measure, and considered it as a paltry saving of money, to be devoted to the expenses of the Master's Private establishment'. Monk, who did not immerse himself in the financial records, will not have seen that the Fellows fought back with some success to preserve the tradition of rich feasting.

The regime of bread, beer, meat and fish for commons and elaborate meals for special occasions seems to have been common for a long time at colleges, and more generally in England. A scholarly American playboy who spent several years at Trinity in the 1840s wrote that he was surprised by the lack of variety of food in England, 'by the eternal steak, chops and potatoes, and big joints everywhere', though in the company of BAs at Trinity he would on festive occasions enjoy 'a recherché dinner'. And a guest at the Commemoration Feast in 1827 remembered, perhaps hazily, enjoying 'Turtle and all other fishy delicacies, haunches and pasties of venison, a baron of beef, and all sorts of other such specimens of baronial hospitality; tarts and pufferies garnished and decorated with all the devices of cookship'.

From farming to freight: a Bursar's tale
Extracted from a speech given by Sir John Bradfield at a High Table Dinner in October 2005 to mark his 80th birthday. The full text may be found in the Annual Record for 2005.

My five years as Junior Bursar began with a massive refurbishment of the Master's Lodge, where nothing had been done for decades – owing to wartime difficulties and financial stringency in the 1930s. Most exciting was strengthening the floor of the Large Drawing Room, where the ancient floor beams might have given way when a big party assembled. The superb Sheffield consulting engineer, H.C. Husband, had a marvellously simple approach. He lined up our engineering students in increasing numbers over each beam in turn, and measured the somewhat frightening deflections of each beam in the Dining Room ceiling below as the load above increased. A health and safety inspector would have had a fit. But all was well. Husband designed a simple solution on the spot – with a suitable steel beam on each side of each old oak beam, screened by the elegant oak-faced casing which

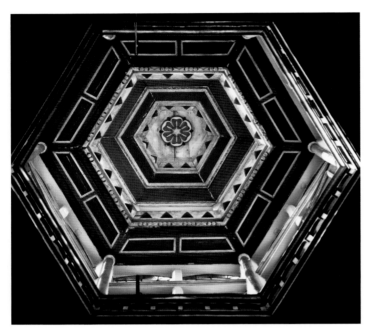

you see in the ceiling of the Dining Room today. Later his team designed Angel Court; he was also responsible for a big kitchen reconstruction and a massive installation of central heating and hot water throughout the old College, and he cross-tied the bridge to help withstand modern traffic.

The final stages of my time as Junior Bursar were marked by two notable events. First, a sad failure to get a fine residential building on the Brewhouse. Second, major refurbishment of the Hall in honour of a royal visit. Nothing much had been done there for a century. Gilding and paint were grimy and chipped. The splendid Jacobean oak panelling at each end was extensively cracked and long before had been thickly painted with brown paint over white and grained to look like the genuine oak beneath (which it didn't). We dismantled the panelling, removing every last bit of moulding, stripped the paint, repaired, reassembled, and restored a warm glow with careful waxing. For repairs we bought cheap oak tables in junk shops to get seasoned timber, none being

Above left: The Tudor rose in the centre of the cupola in Hall, and (left) scaffolding in Hall for renovations in 2001.

Tressilian Nicholas planting a tree in the Fellows Garden with young family members at his 100th birthday celebration in 1988.

available from merchants then. We had tremendous fun with the Royal Arms, where we coated the unicorn with palladium, which I knew from electron microscopy was much cheaper than the usual platinum. The lofty cupola in the roof was so decrepit and faded (beneath the congealed grime, dead flies and bird droppings) that we had to invent a new decoration scheme – with a splendid one-foot-diameter vermilion and gilt Tudor rose in the centre looking down into the Hall, plus much supporting colour. The whole work cost about £7,500 (or roughly £200,000 at today's building prices – modest for such extensive skilled work).

Shortly after this exciting exercise, Tress Nicholas – the Senior Bursar and former teaching Fellow in Geology, who was about to retire as Bursar at 67, though he survived to 101 – asked me one day in the Parlour if I thought I could do his job. After a week of pondering I decided I would like to try, and was duly appointed in 1956 on the recommendation of a committee of Harry Hollond, Patrick Duff, Charles Oatley and Tress himself (there were no inhibitions then about including the incumbent in the committee, because he knew much more about the job than anyone else and cared deeply and without self-interest for the welfare of the College).

There was the slight difficulty that I knew virtually nothing about investment in property or securities. But a Trinity contemporary and lifelong friend, Peter Brackfield, kindly invited me to spend a month in his family's investment bank, Singer and Friedlander. I did so and learned a lot. I read a lot too, and learned in a practical way by investing small sums of my own modest savings – nothing sharpens the mind better than losing one's own money. On the property side I formed close friendships with the College's excellent agents – and got the best out of them that way. I felt at home in agriculture as my family on both sides had been farmers. I scanned the *Farmers' Weekly* and the *Estates Gazette* to follow rural and urban prices and look for bargains. I well remember spotting the advertisement of our Ashford (Kent) farm in 1967, and sitting in my car there wondering how much to pay for it as a reasonable long-term portfolio addition. Bidwells got it at the auction the following week for a little under our limit, and it proved an excellent investment. We established really friendly long-term relations with the farm tenants; the

husband suffered badly from MS, so we replaced the awkward small farmhouse with a spacious new bungalow. Later his devoted wife drove him to a farm dinner at Trinity in their van fitted with lifting gear, and they really enjoyed themselves, because the other farmers rallied superbly to help in College.

In College the most important success – due to some lucky breaks and much hard work – was increasing external revenue (the income from our main capital fund) by over 75 times in money terms and over six times in real terms, i.e. adjusted for inflation (still modest compared with Trinity's needs in terms of academic excellence, buildings etc., combined with the needs of those we would like to help). Total return (i.e. capital growth and net income combined) averaged in money terms about 16½ per cent a year for 36 years (which contained several stock exchange and property setbacks) and would have been slightly more on the customary basis of all net income being reinvested instead of spent. So we could comfortably look the likes of Harvard and Yale in the eye, despite their well-publicised achievements.

I have left till last the two projects which have pleased me most, but also stretched me most – the Cambridge Science

Park and Felixstowe. Most of the Science Park land on Milton Road was given to King's Hall in the 1440s and passed to us in Henry VIII's 1546 collegiate merger of King's Hall and Michaelhouse to form Trinity. It remained a simple farm on the outskirts of Cambridge for some 500 years and then became a tank marshalling yard in the 1939–45 war, after which it was left derelict. In the 1960s Harold Wilson urged all universities to think more about their links with industry in the light of the white-hot technological revolution. In October 1969 a University committee, including our own much-loved Charles Oatley, recommended a moderate growth of high-tech industry in Cambridge. I thought about it in the Christmas vacation when we had got the audit out of the way, discussed it with Charles and others, and recommended to the Council at their first meeting in January 1970 that we should try to develop a Science Park on the Milton Road land. They agreed – and we were in business. From the date of publication of the University report, it had taken Trinity about 12 weeks (including a Christmas vacation) to decide to create the first Science Park in England, which was much visited and much copied – locally, nationally and internationally. The factors that enabled us to move quickly were, I think, that we had the land, we had the money, we understood the arrangements as regards development, University liaison, etc., and finally we were not too committee-ridden. By contrast it took two years to get the necessary consents from local and central government.

With help from numerous Fellows we worked hard on University liaison for tenants – e.g. library access and apparatus loans (on proper payment, of course), plus talks on current University research. We subsidised joint research schemes between Science Park companies and University labs; they don't produce Nobel Prizes, but they do produce invaluable human contacts, which is what it's all about.

Enthusiastic Fellows have included not only scientists but also that powerful character Jack Hamson, Professor of Comparative Law. He became so enamoured of the Science Park that, entirely without my knowledge, he persuaded the tenants and Trinity to offer to share the cost of a portrait of me.

Nowadays there are 60 or 70 tenants, big and small. There's an increasing amount of biotechnology, together with pharmaceuticals, a wide range of software (including financial and geographical systems), some hardware, fascinating other semiconductor applications, scientific instruments, contract research, the Royal Society of Chemistry, patent agents and venture capitalists. At least two highly relevant University sub-departments (microelectronics and photonics) have been located there for a time. You can read about it in the admirable magazine so I'll leave it at that – except just to say how the Science Park got its hump, a little-known story.

A fine Canadian architect produced the big and beautiful Napp Pharmaceuticals building beside the A14. We were assured that its sloping glass sides would not produce problems. But in

fact on certain days they reflected the sun into a nearby unit, the tenant of which threatened to sue Napp in 1983. I became very worried about potential damage to the Park's reputation. We brought great pressure to bear on Napp, and after protracted negotiation they shielded the other tenant by building a small hill beside one of the three small lakes and covering the hill with trees. So that's how the Park got its wooded hump, a very welcome feature in a flat 100-acre site.

Turning to Felixstowe, our property there was shrewdly bought in 1933 by my predecessor, Tress Nicholas, as a reasonable agricultural estate with some housing land potential. The adjacent small port at the mouth of the River Orwell was semi-derelict then and of no account in the purchase. The 1½-mile river frontage was a nuisance because we had to repair the river wall. There followed modest land sales for good residential schemes, particularly in the 1950s and 1960s, and we greatly improved the farming. But the real bonanza was in the proximity of the port, which came alive again when it was bought in the 1950s by a tough Norfolk grain trader, Gordon Parker. He felt overcharged for exporting his grain through King's Lynn and Yarmouth and swore he'd have his own port. The place became much more efficient than its competitors. It expanded far beyond grain into bulk liquid storage, a brisk roll-on roll-off lorry trade, busy passenger ferries and ultimately and most importantly into more and more container berths. It is of course smaller than Rotterdam and the big Far East and American ports, but on our land, surrounding the original dock area, we have produced lots of roads, a railway, other services, warehouses and open-air storage, where there had been only marshes and mud tracks before, and Felixstowe has become Britain's biggest container port, stretching about a mile along our river frontage with some

Left: *The Great Freeze of 1963. Robert Robson is pictured on the bank in front of the Wren Library, supervising the sons of the Junior Bursar, Richard Glauert, who took the photograph.*

Below: *Menu for the luncheon to celebrate the opening of the Science Park, with caricatures drawn by Otto Frisch.*

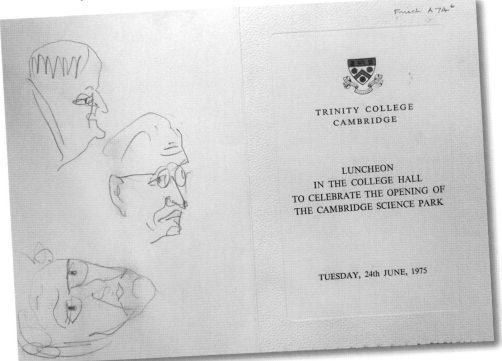

TRINITY COLLEGE
CAMBRIDGE

LUNCHEON
IN THE COLLEGE HALL
TO CELEBRATE THE OPENING OF
THE CAMBRIDGE SCIENCE PARK

TUESDAY, 24th JUNE, 1975

The Sir John Bradfield Viewing Area and Trinity I dock at Felixstowe.

20 huge container cranes hovering like giant locusts over the big ships of many nations, which come there from far and wide.

All very exciting. But much the most exciting moment was when (under a Labour government) an attempt was made in 1976 virtually to nationalise the port. Gordon Parker was always short of money for its development. He was persuaded to sell to Associated British Ports (a semi-state body owning 19 ports such as Hull, London and Southampton, which resented Felixstowe's competition – they were bureaucratic and much hindered by the dock labour scheme). But this sale needed a private act of Parliament. We hated the proposal. But one of the chief port users, European Ferries, hated it even more, fearing, like us, that Felixstowe would become inefficient and expensive. Their outstanding young Chairman, Keith Wickenden, declared total opposition. We backed him strongly, and so did the port's trade union (which feared their good pay and conditions would suffer if the sale went through).

Keith, the three Union shop stewards (with whom we were soon on Christian-name terms), Christopher Buxton (the dynamic Bidwell partner involved) and I all gave evidence to the Commons Committee against the Bill. We were each mauled by the Associated British Ports barrister. The Committee, having a Labour majority, recommended that the Bill should proceed, and it was duly passed in the Commons (though several Members, including some Trinity MPs, spoke cogently against). The same team on our side did battle in the Lords Committee. But they too recommended the Bill, though only by one vote, and it was due for Third Reading in the Lords, the final stage. Christopher Buxton of Bidwells and I felt we must pull out all the stops. We worked through the whole of one night and most of the next day writing to every Conservative and Liberal Member of the House of Lords seeking support. A few days later the Third Reading debate took place. There were numerous speakers for the Bill and numerous on our side against, the latter including Lord Cross (Law Lord and Honorary Fellow) and Rab Butler, Master, both declaring interests of course. The tense debate ended. The House divided. We held our breath. It seemed an age before the vote was counted and then announced in the Chamber. To our amazement and delight the Bill had been defeated by 147 votes

to 71 (a 2:1 majority). We were told that only twice before in the history of Parliament had a Private Bill been defeated on Third Reading in the Lords in this way – at the 59th minute of the eleventh hour as it were. We had saved the port from what would undoubtedly have been a slide into bureaucracy and mediocrity.

We had a great dinner in Hall to celebrate. European Ferries bought the port. It flourished even more. Keith Wickenden became an MP and an even closer friend and gave me one of the most precious books I possess, a richly bound copy of all the Hansards of the Parliamentary debates with a special goodwill message on the flyleaf.

But shortly after that disaster struck. Keith, who was always a bit of a daredevil, crashed his small aeroplane and was killed at once. It was a tragic loss to Felixstowe. The port passed through various hands, and was ultimately acquired by its present owners, Hutchison Whampoa, the major Hong Kong ports and other infrastructure company of Mr Li Ka-shing, believed to be the richest man in China. He is using the big Hutchison income to support massive expenditure on introducing 3G mobile phones into the UK, Italy and other places. So watch this space. Dickens could have made a splendid best-seller out of it all.

I'm glad to say our relations with the port remained good through all these changes and continue so today. The port named its latest major extensions Trinity 1, Trinity 2 and Trinity 3; and entirely unknown to us until afterwards they named after me a fine viewing point near the river mouth where the public can watch world shipping coming or going, and see the yachts sailing by.

The Senior Bursar's view today
Rory Landman (2006)

The generosity of benefactors and diligence of past bursars have left the College in a strong financial position. And of course Trinity's material capital is vastly enlarged by the goodwill of its alumni and by its members' long history of outstanding achievement, not only in academic research but in all the different spheres of life.

The policy of Trinity's Senior Bursars has always been to preserve the College's capital while spending its income. Our investment policy aims to increase Trinity's disposable income in real terms.

The College's investment portfolio, therefore, is a mixture of high-quality property in the United Kingdom and equities selected from around the world. This means that we try to take a long-term view of the prospects of the first while seizing sometimes shorter term opportunities with the other. Our property portfolio, moreover, provides about three-quarters of our income. It is directly held and managed with a variety of strategies that take account of the prospects in different areas of the UK economy. Thanks to the historical depth of some of our holdings and their economic variety we are able to take a much longer view of potential investment returns than a commercial property company and therefore take opportunities that may not commend themselves to those with shorter horizons. We own our agricultural land for strategic and development reasons; we value shops for their low depreciation rates and real rental growth; our Science Park and Felixstowe portfolios grow with particular attention to the future needs of our tenants; we also look for opportunities to diversify our ground rent portfolio. We acquired our most notable estate, in Leeds, in 2000. This strategy also determined our purchase of the site of the O2 Arena in 2009; we are also buying brownfield sites that have good-quality tenants and potential for development on a timescale of ten years or more.

We expect our global equity portfolio to provide growing dividends in real, sterling terms over the long term. Trinity's investments are partially financed by a long-term loan at fixed interest, repayable in 2057. This loan amounts to about 10 per cent of the College's net assets.

However unusual our time horizon may be, our sources of income are themselves not immune to general trends. They are therefore under pressure at the time of writing. Dividends, rents and interest rates are all falling. Trinity's combined focus on good-quality properties at home and overseas equities has provided us with some cushion. Nevertheless, the downward trend in income looks likely to last for the next few years at least. Yet all our costs are also being pushed higher by government action, whether through increased indirect taxation or expanding bureaucracy.

This scissor effect of falling income and rising costs is all the more serious when we consider our growing responsibility to use Trinity's resources to assist not only our own students but also the wider University. We are particularly concerned that what we assume will be the inexorable rises in student fees towards their real cost will lead to much higher demands on our income in order to continue our needs-blind access policy.

The College makes substantial donations, amounting to nearly one-third of our income, to support students, college teaching and research around the University. Nor are these grants discretionary, a tap we could turn off if we wished. The needs they meet are essentials, not frills. Our substantial support for the Cambridge Trusts and the Isaac Newton Trust is especially important. The former bring in graduate students from around the world, while the latter is responsible for bursaries in all the University's colleges, as well as for new research initiatives across all its faculties and departments.

Trinity is fully aware that the fortunes of the University and the College are inextricably intertwined. Despite the current financial pressures, we are still able to reinforce that relationship. We are doing all we can to accelerate that virtuous circle by which academic excellence feeds on itself across the collegiate University of Cambridge as a whole. Nonetheless, Trinity will need all its great resources and more if it is to help future generations to continue to build on the achievements of the past.

Below: *Henry being replaced in Hall in 2002 after the renovations.*

Opposite: *The annual gathering, September 2009.*

IT IS EASY TO BE DAZZLED BY TRINITY'S STATURE AND achievements and to forget that the College is fundamentally dependent on the standing of the University. In recent years, when universities have been ranked, either within the UK or worldwide, Cambridge has regularly been among the top three, and frequently number one. The colleges and the collegiate system play an important part in this success but it depends, primarily, on the achievements of the University's departments, subject by subject. Were departmental performance to drop below that of other universities, Cambridge's ranking would suffer. The colleges could not, on their own, prevent this and their status would decline.

Since many universities seek to improve their performance and ranking, there is no room for complacency. Overseas competition is strong, notably from leading institutions in the United States such as Harvard and Princeton, but also increasingly from universities in China and India. Accumulated wealth, based on strong fund-raising over many years, has made the major American universities very formidable competitors. In developing countries, ambitious governments are willing to consider large-scale investment in higher education. If it is to retain its ranking, Cambridge must endeavour to stay ahead of competitors at home and abroad. Trinity has recognized that, to maintain its own position, it must do all it can to help and support the University in this ambition.

There are two main ways in which Trinity can give support: through people and with money. It is the staff across the University who, by their efforts and achievements, create what can conveniently be called 'academic excellence'. Trinity can help to maintain this excellence by ensuring that, when Fellows are appointed, they are of the highest quality in their subjects; similarly, graduate students who are enrolled should be of a very high standard. However, if the highest quality staff are to be secured, it is also essential that buildings, facilities, resources for research projects, salaries and living conditions are good enough to attract and retain them – and, where relevant, to attract their spouses or partners. All this inevitably requires substantial investment, not only to see that Trinity maintains high standards in its own buildings and facilities, but also for the College to help the wider University to create these conditions.

In considering financial strength, endowments are important. These are capital, of which the earnings may be designated in perpetuity to fund, for example, a professorship, a readership, or some other important and continuing need. Earnings from an endowment which is not so tied can be used to provide funds as new needs arise. Trinity has accumulated wealth through the generosity of benefactors and the shrewd way its finances have been managed by a succession of Senior Bursars. This wealth is an endowment; its earnings provide the money for Trinity's own needs and for the various ways in which it already supports the University. Even though Trinity has this substantial endowment, more money will be needed if support for the University is to be

Below: Martin Rees, Master, entertaining alumni in the Wren Undercroft at the Annual Buffet Luncheon, held every September.

increased. This will require a vigorous and sustained fund-raising campaign, supported by the Fellowship and the alumni.

The University is well aware of its need for more income. It marked its 800th anniversary with a major campaign to raise £1 billion, a total that includes new funds raised by Trinity and the other colleges. Beyond the anniversary campaign, further substantial fund-raising will need to continue into the future.

Trinity has recognised for many years that, when it has income greater than it requires, money should be used to help the collegiate University. One good example is Trinity's provision of half the initial funding for Darwin College, which was founded specifically to increase the number of Cambridge's graduate students. Similarly, in 1988 Trinity set up the Isaac Newton Trust as a channel through which financial help to the colleges or University departments could flow. The Trust had a considerable measure of independence in deciding how the money allocated to it by Trinity, or from other donations, should be used. A number of trustees were from other colleges and, for the first 11 years, meetings were chaired by a non-resident Trinity alumnus.

Since its inception, the Trust has helped a wide variety of projects. A notable early development was the bursary scheme to help undergraduates from less-well-off families. This was based on Trinity money and applied to all colleges, who contributed, or were assisted, according to their means. It has since developed further, to give greater help to a larger number of students. It has become the Cambridge Bursary Scheme, funded primarily by the University, in part by Trinity and other colleges, and in part by private donations. The Scheme is run for the University by the Isaac Newton Trust.

Another important initiative by the Trust has been to help post-doctoral or early career research. It has enabled very worthwhile projects to get started that otherwise would not have got going or would have been greatly delayed. In parallel with the Isaac Newton Trust, Trinity has sponsored other trusts designed to bring more overseas students to Cambridge, namely, the Commonwealth Trust, the European Trust, the Overseas Trust and the Malaysian Trust.

In summary, Trinity has a wonderful history of academic excellence within a highly successful University. To ensure that this achievement continues, Trinity must aim for the highest academic standards. It must also continue to use part of its income to support the wider University, including other colleges, as well as meeting its own needs. Spending by other leading universities is likely to grow, which means that Cambridge, to keep up, is likely to need substantially more financial help. It would be a tragedy if the challenge were not met and the University's standing started to slip. To counter this possibility, Trinity must be the college that takes the lead in giving substantial and steadily increasing financial support to the University.

Robin Ibbs (1944)

IT IS 30 YEARS SINCE I LEFT TRINITY. THE COLLEGE, AND THE university, were being transformed, gradually but very positively, by the admission of women. The Footlights' smokers, often held in Trinity, were at a high, with Fry, Thompson, Laurie, Bathurst et al. Trinity's film club seems, in memory, to have been playing the *Man with No Name* series in a loop. The bar was overflowing with good company. The English faculty, which I watched from a distance, was having a mental breakdown over 'structuralism'. But, looking back, terrific and life-changing as all that was, it is not what matters most to me about College life.

What Trinity gave me, I realise, was a thread, ever so tenuous, to the mental life of the past. This wasn't especially on account of seeing an ancient Littlewood – I think it was him – walk across the College lawns, remarkable though that was. Nor was it the statues of the great but intimidating figures from the College's past that line the ante-chapel. It was really down to being taught philosophy for a few terms by Casimir Lewy, after the College and university had kindly allowed me to stay on for a fourth year. And Lewy, an émigré Pole with a shock of white hair and a quavering but bold voice, had been taught by Wittgenstein! I guess he was probably not as favoured a pupil as Elizabeth Anscombe, but I only attended her lectures and some graduate seminars, whereas, with Lewy, it was one-on-one – a patient and kindly dissection of my weekly essay. And he sometimes made it feel like that in lectures too; on one occasion standing in front of me, banging my desk as he made some important point about Wisdom or Straaaawson (always a very long a) – with passion. The passion lit me up. Here was a man who had sat with some of the 20th-century's greatest thinkers, still cared desperately about the issues, and actually took an interest in my studies.

When I left I asked Lewy for advice on how I could sustain my interest in philosophy. He encouraged me to joint the Aristotelian society, which I did.

The same year Rorty's *Philosophy and the Mirror of Nature* came out. I devoured it, alongside bits and pieces of the later Wittgenstein. The issues have been abiding interests, which I owe very largely to a great teacher. I doubt Lewy would have altogether approved, although I did also work through his own *Meaning and Modality*.

Lewy helped me to see what was so special about the Oxbridge system of tutoring. And by exposing me to the precision and care needed in his own field – philosophical logic – he even helped me greatly in my job!

Paul Tucker
Deputy Governor, Bank of England (1976)

COLLEGE SILVER

With its roots in two of the earliest college foundations of medieval Cambridge, it is interesting that Trinity possesses no silver older than the 17th century. Indeed, the College has in its collection only four items to have survived the Civil War, when, in common with many other colleges, Trinity sent large amounts of plate to Charles I to be sold or melted down to pay his soldiers. Two silver-gilt Chapel flagons, dating from 1607, are the College's oldest pieces of silver; they were given by the sons of the 3rd Duke of Lennox, whose fervent support for Charles I saved the flagons from the melting pot. Another precious survival is the Nevile Cup, which was a gift to the College from its Master, Thomas Nevile, in the year of his death, 1615. Noblemen and fellow commoners were expected to present plate to the

High Table or to give a sum of money to buy plate. One of these was the Duke of Buckingham, Chancellor of the University from 1671 to 1674, who visited the College in 1671 with Charles II and ordered the College to buy a piece of plate costing £102 7s (approximately £14,000 today) to commemorate the occasion. The resulting basin and ewer form the largest and one of the most valuable pieces of plate in the collection. Fortunately, the Buckingham ewer and dish escaped the attentions of Richard Kidman and William Grimshaw. This pair of burglars, one a clockmaker and one a chimney sweep, wreaked havoc on the silver safes of King's, St Catharine's, Emmanuel, Caius and Trinity between 1796 and 1799, when they were finally caught; Grimshaw was executed and Kidman transported to Botany Bay. Among

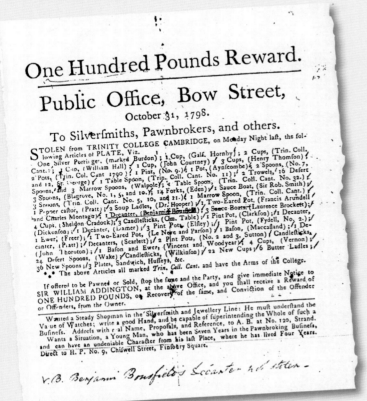

Above: *Newspaper advertisement soliciting information after the silver theft of 1798.*

Right and opposite: *The Nevile Cup and the Buckingham plate.*

large numbers of other items from Trinity, Kidman made off with a pre-Civil War piece known as John Clarkson's Pot. Nonetheless, the collection of plate remains considerable, comprising well over 500 items or sets of items and a large quantity of table silver. The Huguenot craftsmen who arrived in the late 17th century are represented, as are the great candlestick-makers of the 18th century, such as William and James Gould, William Cafe, Ebenezer Coker and John Carter, who made the pair of large altar candlesticks given for the Chapel in 1773. There is a splendid array of tankards, cups, ale mugs, coffee pots, punch bowls and plates, reflecting the changing habits and tastes of four centuries. The tradition of giving plate, now more usually as bequests, has continued with some interesting 20th-century gifts, including a beaker and cover engraved with a representation of the hospital set up in Nevile's Court to treat the war wounded in 1914, given by the medical officers of the 1st Eastern General Hospital.

CHAPTER 9

The Humanities

RICHARD SERJEANTSON *(1993)*

Trinity, the College of Isaac Newton, has since the 18th century cultivated itself as above all a house of science. In the modern era the presence on the Fellowship of such figures as James Clerk Maxwell, Lord Rayleigh and J.J. Thomson (to mention only physicists) more than vindicates that perception. But Trinity has also been, and remains, a place where the humanities – and more recently also the social sciences – are encouraged, studied and taught. Newton was a contemporary of the difficult but brilliant Richard Bentley (Master, 1700–42), a figure to whom English classicists still look back as one of the greatest in their discipline. And a part of Trinity has always been as conscious of Bentley's shadow as of Newton's: in the later 18th century Richard Porson was compared to him; in the early 19th, Porson's successor as Regius Professor of Greek, J.H. Monk (Fellow, 1805–22), wrote a biography of Bentley that has still not been superseded; and in the 20th century A.E. Housman (Fellow, 1910–36) bore comparison (against his wishes) with Bentley the Master. Yet just as Trinity's scientific side offers more than the legacy of Newton, so the humanities have developed beyond the classical languages of Latin and Greek. By the later 19th century the humanities at Trinity were beginning to enlarge their scope. I want in this short essay to say something about how that happened, and about some of the directions in which the study of the humanities at Trinity has gone since 1875, when reforms removed the obligation of celibacy from Fellows – thereby permitting humanistic scholarship to be pursued as a career, as well as a vocation – and when new subjects and new Triposes began to emerge in the University.

Previous pages: *Statue of Alfred, Lord Tennyson in the ante-chapel by Thomas Thorneycroft.*

Below: *Instructions to referees regarding the Fellowship election of 1950.*

The story of the humanities at Trinity in the modern age deserves to be told at greater length than is possible here, but there is a means of getting quickly to the heart of it – or at least (since we are not here concerned with physiology) to one of its hearts. That way is the Fellowship Election. In every year of the modern era, except during parts of the First and Second World Wars, when it was temporarily suspended, Trinity has held, as the Statutes require, an Annual Election of Fellows. The Master and a board of Electors ascertain (in the words of the 1877 Statutes) 'The intellectual qualifications of the candidates and their proficiency in any branch or branches of the University studies', and 'choose in each case that candidate … whom they shall deem to be most fit to be a Fellow of the College as a place of education, religion, learning and research'. Such Fellows are thus chosen with no regard to teaching need, or the balance of subjects within the College, or any criterion other than academic merit. Like Isaac Newton, who was himself chosen in an Election of 1667, they receive a modest stipend, room and board, and virtually no prescribed duties. Yet, as Lord Macaulay (elected 1824) wrote in his Report on the Indian Civil Service of 1854: 'It is notorious that the examinations for Trinity Fellowships have, directly and indirectly, done much to give a direction to the studies of Cambridge.' Now characteristically in the latter stages of their PhD, successful candidates become Fellows for four years, with no obligations other than to pursue research or, in certain cases, to study for a profession. (Fellows who abandon the life of the mind for the lure of lucre these days tend to go into banking at least as often as law or medicine.) Until very recently, Fellowships in the Annual Election were open only to existing members of Trinity. Most, therefore, were in the College at the moment when the Electors assembled in the Chapel and intoned 'electus' after the name of each successful candidate was read out. In a giddy moment of elevation they were raised from being merely *in statu pupilari* to becoming a Fellow of the College, no longer under the sway of their Tutor but rather of the Vice Master. They might now walk on the grass, borrow rare books from the Wren Library, and (as G.H. Hardy, elected 1900, recalls so ardently desiring in his memoir *A Mathematician's Apology*) drink port and eat walnuts in the Combination Room.

TRINITY COLLEGE FELLOWSHIP ELECTION REFEREES' REPORTS

In accordance with the Statutes of the College, it is the duty of the electors to ascertain the intellectual qualifications of the candidates and their proficiency in any branch or branches of University studies, and to choose in each case that candidate whom they deem to be most fit to be a Fellow of the College as a place of education, religion, learning and research.

It is the function of a Referee to assist the Electors in estimating the merit of the thesis or theses submitted by the candidate, and it is important that he should state in some detail the reasons for his judgement. Since however each candidate is required to submit to the Electors a non-technical account of his thesis, it is unnecessary for the Referee to supply a detailed summary of its contents.

A Fellowship thesis may, in some cases, be submitted fairly soon after the commencement of a candidate's research. It may, therefore, give an account of work which is not necessarily complete, and may in various ways differ from a thesis for a junior doctorate, which is submitted at the end of a comparatively long period of research. In awarding a Fellowship the Electors may attach importance not only to the actual achievement of the candidate but also to the promise shown by his work. It is therefore helpful if the Referee can give an estimate of such promise as well as an assessment of the achievement.

Since as a rule more candidates merit election than can be elected, it is most helpful to the Electors to be informed if a thesis is not of a standard which would entitle its author to a Fellowship even if one were available. It is usually found that a referee can adequately express his views in not more than two or three pages of typescript.

The nature of the Annual Election of Fellows, which has a sacred status within the College, has nonetheless changed over the years. A competition that began after the founding of the College in 1546 as the principal mechanism for acquiring new Fellows has now become a strictly temporary (albeit prestigious) position. Until the earlier 20th century such Fellows were called 'Title (α)'; they are now 'Title A' (beside classicists, only mathematicians now think in Greek). Originally such Fellows were required by Statute to enter holy orders within seven years of taking their MA; when the clerical obligation was removed the tenure became six years, then five; now the duration of their reward – for it is still by some also called the 'Prize Fellowship' competition – is four years. In the earlier part of our period candidates for the Trinity Prize Fellowship – as those at All Souls College, Oxford, still are – were invited to compete, rather than

A.E. Housman by Henry Lamb.

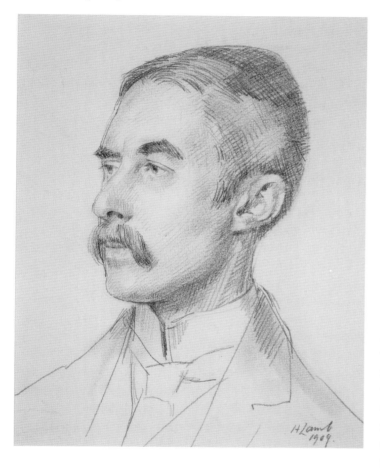

Election that 'the Dissertations of our Candidates have acquired a constantly increasing importance'. 'For many months,' he went on, 'they give a definite direction to each man's reading, thought and energies.' The idea that such a dissertation might be written in a matter of months may provoke hollow laughter among modern PhD students, for whom a Fellowship dissertation usually represents three years' work. But even before the PhD became a necessary passport to the academic profession, which in Cambridge was not until after the Second World War, the dissertation was the principal means for young scholars to obtain a Fellowship at Trinity. These dissertations – which are now kept in the locked 'cage' in the deep library basement that was dug out beneath the Master's drive in the mid-1980s – offer a mirror of the study of the humanities at Trinity.

Until the 1930s, however, Trinity did not systematically retain these Fellowship dissertations – understandably enough, perhaps, in an age when many were handwritten and probably existed in only one copy. (In the era of the typewriter and now of the word-processor a copy of each successful candidate's dissertation is retained as a matter of course.) There are some from before this date, but they are copies that have found their way to the College long after the moment of election. One of the earliest, for instance, is a set of handwritten observations on the Roman satirical poet Martial written by J.D. Duff, who was elected under Title (a) in 1883, and remained a Fellow until his death in 1940, a good classicist who also translated Russian literature. The College would probably not have possessed his dissertation at all had it not been that Duff's son Patrick became a Fellow in his turn, and presented his father's dissertation to the library. Another dissertation, which proudly displays the inscription 'The Dissertation on which I won my Fellowship', circulated for many years among the author's pupils and colleagues before finally arriving in the Library.

The subjects of these dissertations are various, and the majority are in mathematics or the natural sciences, and not in the humanities at all. But in the 19th and earlier 20th centuries the subject that in most years saw a candidate elected was still classics. The literature of ancient Greece and Rome, however, encompasses several spheres, principally poetry, history and philosophy; and

choosing to apply. Moreover, until 1938 candidates also had to sit an examination for their Fellowship, with compulsory papers in English and Philosophy. And the first time that 'electa', rather than 'electus', was pronounced for a female Title A Fellow was as recently as 1980, four years after women graduate students were first admitted to the College; the field of the successful candidate, whose subsequent flourishing career in the United States includes a so-called 'genius grant' from the Macarthur Foundation, was south Asian history.

Since the 1870s, however, one aspect of the competition has remained constant: candidates for a Fellowship have made their case for election by means of an original dissertation they have written. In 1904 the then Master, Montagu Butler, remarked in one of the periodic debates over the nature of the Fellowship

Fellowships at Trinity were awarded for work in each of these areas. Philosophy, however, seems to have been particularly dominant, and several Fellowships were awarded for work in that field, usually on either Plato or Aristotle. This probably owed a good deal to the stimulus of Henry Jackson, a prominent Trinity presence since his own election in 1861, whose scholarship helped to establish the view that the later Plato had modified his earlier theory of ideas. Jackson had a powerful impact on the College and on the University, beginning with his establishment of the modern supervision system for Trinity classicists, and culminating in his election to the Regius Chair of Greek in 1908, together with his appointment to that peculiarly Trinity honour, the Order of Merit. He was also famously sociable, often entertaining guests after dinner in his rooms in G2 Nevile's Court.

One of Jackson's protégés was an ancient philosopher of the next generation, F.M. Cornford (elected 1899). Cornford achieved his ambition of winning a Fellowship with a neatly handwritten dissertation on Aristotle's *Nicomachean Ethics*. His later approach to Greek philosophy was historical, with interests in its mythology and its science, but it is notable that his Fellowship dissertation announces its goal as being 'to adopt a method not so much historical as philosophical, and to introduce order instead of reproducing disorder'. The impact of Hegel – then more associated with Oxford than with Cambridge – is also apparent in this apprentice-piece. Beyond the world of ancient philosophy Cornford is best known for a book which must owe something to his experience of Trinity: the satirical *Microcosmographia Academica* (1908), with its celebrated accounts of how to hold up any decision, including the Doctrine of Unripeness of Time, the Principle of the Wedge and the Principle of the Dangerous Precedent. Still in print, it can still be read with profit by the aspiring academic politician.

The poetry of the ancient world also had a prominent position in classical studies at Trinity. Its study was pursued throughout much of the 20th century by two scholars who were also tutors to several generations of undergraduates and formidable College figures: A.S.F. Gow (elected 1911; d.1978), who studied Hellenistic poetry, most notably Theocritus; and Harry Sandbach (elected 1927; d.1991), an expert on Menander.

Gow was a close friend of the man who is perhaps Trinity's best-known classical Fellow, A.E. Housman. Housman, who had failed 'Greats' at Oxford, became a Fellow of Trinity upon his appointment to the chair of Latin in 1910. His remarkable scholarly talents lay in the same sphere as those of Bentley and Porson: textual criticism. But Housman was also the author of the poems in *A Shropshire Lad* (1896), and the disjunction between the lyrical expression of his verse and the remorseless technical exactness of his scholarship has often been noted, not least by the dramatist Tom Stoppard in his play about Housman, *The Invention of Love* (1997). (Other Fellows of Trinity have been revivified in drama: there are plays about Newton, of course, but also a radio play about the eccentric historian F.A. Simpson, known as 'Snipper' for his habit of compulsively pruning the College greenery; *A Disappearing Number* is about Hardy and Ramanujan; and Derek Jarman made a film about Wittgenstein.)

Ancient history in its turn is represented by the early studies of another classicist: J. Enoch Powell (elected 1934). Powell's Fellowship dissertation, 'The Moral and Political Ideas of Thucydides', written at the age of 22, is among his other manuscripts in the archives of the Wren Library. It is said that as a Freshman he refused tea with the Master because he was too busy, and that as a Fellow he had double-glazing installed in his rooms because the dawn chorus disturbed his work. Powell's great ambition as a young Fellow was to obtain a professorial chair at an age younger than his hero Friedrich Nietzsche, an ambition he almost realised when at 25 he was appointed to the chair in Greek at the University of Sydney. Powell attained office, and also notoriety, in the sphere of politics; but at Trinity it is as a scholar that he is remembered. Undergraduates at the College still benefit from two funds Powell endowed: one for 'original English verse on a serious subject' (there was already a light verse prize), the other for the purchase of books on Thucydides for the Library.

It is a striking phenomenon, however, that by no means all the Fellows elected for their work in classics remained in that field for the duration of their scholarly careers. One of the most notable of these was J.G. Frazer, who was elected in 1879 with a dissertation on Plato's theory of ideas, but who went on to write *The Golden Bough* (1890–1915) and become a founding figure

Right:
*W.G. Runciman,
President of the
British Academy
2001–5 and
Fellow since
1971.*

Far right: *John
McTaggart by
Roger Fry.*

in the new discipline of social anthropology. A hundred years later the interests of another Title A Fellow would turn from Plato's later epistemology towards sociology and social theory – subjects not otherwise prominent in the Annual Election. W.G. Runciman (elected 1959) would later return to Trinity as a Senior Research Fellow in 1972 and serve as President of the British Academy (2001–5). One of Runciman's contemporaries would similarly use his Title A Fellowship to enlarge his interests in economics away from mathematics and towards philosophy, a development that would ultimately lead Amartya Sen (elected 1957; Master 1998–2004) to a Nobel Prize.

Classics, in the later 19th century, was one of the two principal humanistic subjects in which Fellowships were awarded. The other was the newer but nonetheless important field of moral sciences. The most immediate descendant of this subject – now only preserved in Cambridge by the club of that name – is philosophy. In its heyday the discipline included not only economics but also history and even law, all subjects that split off from it in the late 19th century to form their own Triposes. The presiding spirit, in Trinity and in Cambridge, over the study of the moral sciences was Henry Sidgwick (elected 1859), whose publications in ethics and politics, by contrast with Oxford Hegelianism, constituted a development of the utilitarian tradition.

Sidgwick also a left a different mark on Cambridge's intellectual life: he was, together with the classicist F.W.H. Myers (elected 1865), the founder of the Society for Psychical Research, a body that sought to put the investigation of paranormal phenomena on a scientifically verifiable footing. In Sidgwick's case this interest arose out of his troubled relationship with the Anglican Christianity to which he had to subscribe upon becoming a Fellow. (J.M. Keynes later wrote of Sidgwick: 'He never did anything but wonder whether Christianity was true and prove that it wasn't and hope that it was.') The Society and its search for psychical phenomena remained significant at Trinity into the 1940s. One of its most prominent continuators was C.D. Broad (elected 1911; d.1971), who lived long enough to encourage the studies of philosophers still working in the College. To this day Trinity has to find scientifically respectable ways to spend the income of the richly endowed Perrott-

Warwick Fund, bequeathed in 1937 'absolutely for the purpose of psychical research'.

Like others of his generation at Trinity, Broad was taught by the idealist philosopher John McTaggart (elected in 1891 for a dissertation on Hegel's *Logic*). McTaggart, who had been taught by Sidgwick in his turn, also has the honour of having interested the young Bertrand Russell (elected 1895) in philosophy. As a contributor to the humanities at Trinity, Russell cuts a slightly unusual figure, since his undergraduate studies were in mathematics and his dissertation was on the philosophy of geometry. Russell was sacked from Trinity in 1916 upon his conviction for opposing conscription; his former teacher McTaggart, an intense patriot, was one of his principal prosecutors. But Russell ultimately returned to Trinity in 1944 as a Senior Research Fellow, just as he published a book that is unquestionably humanistic, which helped him to extensive royalties and, in 1950, a Nobel Prize for Literature, his *History of Western Philosophy* (1945), a book that has never ceased to inspire interest in its subject. Russell's closest friendship at Trinity was with the philosopher G.E. Moore (elected 1898), but in the history of philosophy his name will always be paired with that of Ludwig Wittgenstein. Wittgenstein was succeeded in his chair of philosophy by his own nominee and later literary executor, the 32-year-old Georg Henrik von Wright, whom Trinity made an Honorary Fellow in 1983, long after he had returned to his native Finland.

Philosophy was not the only offspring of the moral sciences in post-reform Cambridge. Law and history are others, and this genealogy became apparent in the career of the author of one of the earliest Fellowship dissertations now in the College Library. When Frederic William Maitland competed for a Fellowship in 1875 he went to the trouble (and the expense) of having his moral sciences dissertation – *A historical sketch of liberty and equality as ideals of English political philosophy from the time of Hobbes to the time of Coleridge* – privately printed. This is one reason why it is now shelved not in the archives among the others, but in the student collection in the Lower Library. The other reason is that Trinity failed to elect to a Fellowship a figure who came to be regarded in his own lifetime, and subsequently, as the most brilliant historian of his age. After studying desultorily for the Bar, Maitland

came into his own as an immensely resourceful, industrious and philosophically minded historian of medieval English law, one to whom not only legal but also more general historians look back with respect and sometimes awe. Maitland later became Downing Professor of the Laws of England with a Fellowship at Sir George Downing's college, but Trinity rectified its earlier oversight with an Honorary Fellowship awarded in 1902.

A consequence of Maitland's association with his undergraduate College is that one of the most prestigious prizes an undergraduate lawyer or historian at Trinity can win is the Maitland Prize for Constitutional History – the reward for which is not the usual money, or even silver, but rather a slim pamphlet containing the memorial address Harry Hollond delivered to Maitland's own Selden Society in 1953. It is perhaps in the nature of the profession of academic law – the only subject taught at Trinity whose Fellows are not expected to possess a PhD – that Title A Fellows in the field have been extremely rare. When Hollond himself became a Fellow in 1909 he was, as he put it, 'the only Fellow who has been elected for alleged proficiency in law'. Good jurist that he was, he knew the wording of the Statutes.

Maitland straddles the fields of both law and history, but in the late 19th century history emerged as a Tripos in its own right and also as a fitting subject for a Fellowship dissertation.

Opposite: *Lord Acton.*

Right: The Cambridge Modern
History, *edited by Lord Acton.*

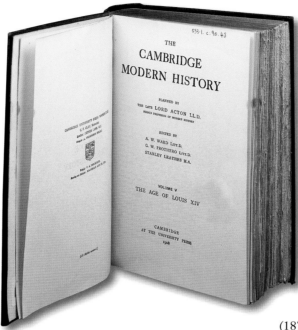

A copy of one of these, by Reginald Vere Laurence (elected 1901), is to be found in the Library. For this impressive study of *The Early Stuarts and the Papacy* the man Acton described as his 'special pupil' won not only a Prize Fellowship but also in due course a lectureship in history at Trinity, where he remained (to teach, among others, the future George VI) until his death in 1934. No doubt weighed down by his pedagogic duties Laurence, regrettably, seems to have published almost nothing. Perhaps a Fellowship at Trinity was the summit of his ambitions, or perhaps he spent too much time on the Fellows' Bowling Green, where his 'woods' are still in use.

It would be unfair to suppose that Laurence was encouraged in his abstinence by the man who first suggested the subject of his dissertation to him, the Catholic politician and historian Lord Acton (1834–1902). Acton lived in rooms in Trinity after his appointment to the Regius Professorship of Modern History in 1895. His life's work, which he never completed, was a grand *History of liberty*, and perhaps his most lasting bequest to the historical profession has been the magnificent collection of books he amassed in pursuit of this subject that are now in the University Library. Acton's collected writings in fact amount to four posthumous volumes; Laurence's only appearance in the library catalogue of Trinity is as the editor of these.

An indication of the state of history at Trinity is offered by another celebrated project of Acton's: *The Cambridge Modern History* (1902–12), of which he was general editor until his death. In a famous plan for that work that he submitted to the Syndics of Cambridge University Press in 1896 Acton desired that nobody should be able to tell, 'without examining the list of authors, where the Bishop of Oxford laid down the pen, and whether Fairbairn or Gasquet … took it up'. If one does examine the list of authors it becomes apparent that several Trinity scholars are among them – even R.V. Laurence, who wrote the chapter on the Council of Trent. The most prominent is Acton's co-editor, Stanley (later Sir Stanley) Leathes, who had been elected to a Fellowship in 1886 and taught history at Trinity until 1903, when he left to become a civil servant. Another is the Rev. William Cunningham, who failed to win a Fellowship with a dissertation on *The Influence of Descartes on Metaphysical Speculation in England* (1876), but who subsequently became a chaplain of Trinity and later still (in 1891) a Fellow and lecturer in History. Notwithstanding Cunningham's philosophical interests, it was as a founder of the study of economic history – still an important component of the Historical Tripos at Cambridge – that he is remembered and that was recognised by his election to the Presidency of the Royal Historical Society in 1910. A further Trinity contributor to Acton's history, with a chapter on the Classical Renaissance, was Sir Richard Claverhouse Jebb (elected 1864; OM 1905), otherwise much more prominent as a scholar of Greek poetry and drama than as a Renaissance historian.

Fifty short years after the publication of *The Cambridge Modern History*, the University Press brought out a *New Cambridge Modern History* to supersede it. The General Introduction (1957) to these volumes, critical of Acton's desire for permanence in historical interpretation, was written by someone who had also been a Fellow of Trinity during his tenure of the Regius Professorship of Modern History (1943–7), Sir George (G.N.) Clark. This was the period at which one of the best-selling historians in England was Master: G.M. Trevelyan, who had first been elected in 1898 for a dissertation on Wycliffe and who returned as Clark's predecessor as Regius Professor in 1927.

Trevelyan's many books sold in their hundreds of thousands, and the Fellows liked him too, extending his Mastership to the age of 75. He was even elected (as so many Masters of Trinity have been, although not usually historians) a Fellow of the Royal Society. Trevelyan is not much read now, nor much studied by scholars, but one Trinity historian of the next decade does still appear on reading lists: E.H. Carr, a pioneering historian of Soviet Russia, and author of *What is History?* (1961) – still a *vade mecum* for A level pupils. Carr had been an undergraduate at Trinity – he was another historian who began as a classicist – and returned later in life as a Senior Research Fellow (1955–82).

Neither G.N. Clark nor Carr seem, for all their external distinction, to have left much of a mark on the College, either personally or intellectually. Two historians who did both came up through the ranks of the Annual Election. One was George Kitson Clark, whose II.2 in Part I of the Historical Tripos was not a bar to his subsequently taking a Prize Fellowship for a dissertation on Sir Robert Peel in 1922. He went on to teach generations of Trinity historians and is still occasionally remembered at the High Table of the College where he lived and died (in 1975). Another was admitted as an undergraduate by 'Kitson' and achieved election to the Fellowship in 1949 with a dissertation on the history of colonial West Africa. J.A. ('Jack') Gallagher went on to dominate the historiography, and also its teaching in Cambridge, of what until very recently was known in the history Faculty as 'extra-European' history. Described in one memoir as a kind of academic Tammany Hall boss, Gallagher was an inspiring figure for both African and Indian historians in the College and elsewhere in the University, as well as a splendidly hospitable Vice Master until his death in 1980. Of this generation of Trinity historians too, although not a Prize Fellow, was the Austrian refugee Walter Ullmann, an idiosyncratic and intellectually powerful historian of medieval politics and ideas. Ullmann taught many research students, at least one of whom (Michael Wilks) was elected to a Fellowship in 1957. Another student recalls the experience of being supervised by Ullmann as a miserable one – until he realised he could shout back, at which point relations improved greatly.

An early election to a Title A Fellowship in modern and medieval languages was Dennis Green (1949) for a dissertation

in the field that would hold his scholarly attention for the rest of his long career in the College, medieval German literature. Green's Fellowship dissertation is distinguished from almost all others of the time in two ways: determined, after his own wartime service in tanks, to pursue research in *Germanistik*, Green had to go to Basle to obtain his DPhil, since the German universities were not then in a position to take students. His Fellowship dissertation is accordingly his Basle DPhil, printed in gothic German. As Cambridge's first Professor of Modern Languages he was also head for many years of the Department of Other Languages (which did not include German). Green's colleague over this time, both in his Faculty and in the College,

E.H. Carr, Senior Research Fellow 1955–82.

was Ralph (R.A.) Leigh, who was elected as a teaching Fellow in 1952 and whose scholarly immortality is ensured by his sole editorship (until his death in 1987) of the *Correspondance complète de Jean-Jacques Rousseau*, published in a mere 53 volumes between 1965 and 1998.

One subject that is now prominent among the study of the humanities at Trinity only came into its own in the College after the Second World War, somewhat later than it had established itself in the University at large: English literature. The earliest Prize Fellow elected in the subject (in 1944) seems to have been the Indian scholar Balachandra Rajan, whose *Paradise Lost and the Seventeenth Century Reader* (1947) influenced William Empson. The first teaching Fellow to be appointed in English (in 1950) was Theodore Redpath, who had read English at St Catharine's but whose PhD had been on Bertrand Russell's favourite philosopher, Leibniz; perhaps this smoothed his appointment to Trinity. Redpath's literary interests were wide, but his interest in philosophy was commemorated in his last book, a memoir of studying under Wittgenstein. Now English has as many teaching Fellows as any other humanities subject in the College, and the longest-standing female Fellow is a distinguished retired professor in the subject.

Yet well before the English Tripos was conceived members of Trinity had made significant contributions to scholarship in English literature. The works of Francis Bacon, a Trinity man, were edited in a monumental edition (1857–61) by three Trinity men: Douglas Heath (elected 1832), Robert Leslie Ellis (elected 1840) and the best of these, James Spedding (Honorary Fellow, 1872), who also published an unsurpassed *Life* of Bacon in seven volumes (1861–74), a feat unjustly satirised in Anthony Trollope's novel *Ralph the Heir* (1872). William Aldis Wright (1831–1914), who was Librarian and Senior Bursar before he became Vice Master (and whom Bertrand Russell later described, for different reasons, as a 'force of evil'), published editions of Shakespeare, Milton and his friend Edward Fitzgerald, as well as Bacon. Russell was right to consider him wicked: he wrote on the books in his charge in the Wren.

As Aldis Wright's first appointment suggests, Trinity is unusual among Oxford and Cambridge colleges in having had,

since Sir Edward Stanhope endowed the post in his will in 1607, a dedicated Librarian. In the modern period this has been a position that has played a significant role in advancing the study of the humanities in the College, for it has been held by a number of distinguished bibliographers and historians of libraries and printing, more than one of whom has become a Fellow of the British Academy. For a good part of the 20th century (1925–58, 1966–7) the Librarian was H.M. Adams, author of a bibliography of 16th-century books in Cambridge libraries that has been found useful throughout the world. Others were C.R. Dodwell (1958–66), who went on to become a distinguished historian of medieval art at Manchester, and Philip Gaskell (1967–86), whose *New Introduction to Bibliography* (1972, 1985) is the indispensable companion in the field. At least one Title A Fellow, too, has been elected for his work in historical bibliography. Ultimately the most important of all these Trinity Librarians was Walter Wilson Greg, who held the position (though not a Fellowship) between 1907 and 1913. The founder, with his Trinity contemporary R.B. McKerrow (1872–1940) of the rigorously analytical 'New Bibliography', Greg was knighted in 1950 for his services to the study of English literature; his ideas still guide editors of early printed books. Two members of Trinity, both classicists, were University Librarians in our period: Francis Jenkinson (University Librarian 1889–1923) and his successor Alwyn Faber Scholfield (1923–49).

In the 20th century the majority of Fellows chosen in the Annual Election were mathematicians or natural scientists. This ratio is also reflected in the fields of those whom the monarch, advised by the Prime Minister, whose Patronage Secretary in turn took soundings from the Fellowship, chose to be Master. The demise of classics as the dominant humanistic discipline has only accentuated this tendency towards the sciences. But Trinity has always been big enough to encompass all, or most, of the disciplines taught in the University, and so the humanistic muses cannot really complain of neglect. (The Fellowship now contains an art historian, although still no geographer.) Trinity has also, let it be said, been grand enough to attract those who bring distinction to it when they arrive, rather than having to nurture all its talent itself. Few new professors taking up a chair

Right: *G.E. Moore, Professor of Mental Philosophy and Logic from 1925 to 1939 and one of the founders of the analytical tradition in philosophy.*

Right: *G.E. Moore, Professor of Mental Philosophy and Logic from 1925 to 1939 and one of the founders of the analytical tradition in philosophy.*

Opposite: *Wittgenstein, a portrait from memory by Joan Bevan.*

in the University have declined Trinity's siren call when it comes – although more recently several have subsequently left it again to go to Harvard.

Humanistic scholarship does not lend itself to the emergence of figures on so heroic a scale as Newton. No single intellect can dominate all its mansions. Of those who inhabited Trinity in the 20th century perhaps Wittgenstein comes closest to Newton in his capacity to create new realms of thought and to inspire generations of followers. But beyond the abstractions of analytical philosophy, humanistic scholarship by its very nature has as its object of inquiry the past life of human culture. And this past is a *mare magnum*, a great sea of knowledge that does not easily lend itself to reductive explanations. Talents may blossom extravagantly, and powerful personalities may come to dominate particular fields; but their sway passes, and ultimately even their own pupils betray them, by raising different questions and looking in other directions. Nor (with the possible exception of south Asian history) are there really defined traditions of inquiry in the humanities at Trinity of the kind that might be said to exist in fluid mechanics, or pure mathematics. Perhaps scholars in the humanities are too individualistic – or too indolent – to reproduce themselves.

In 1904 there were heated debates in the College over whether all candidates for a Fellowship should continue to take a compulsory general paper in philosophy. (It was eventually abolished in 1938.) At the beginning of the 21st century the debates were over opening up the Fellowship competition and extending its eligibility criteria. Now the Annual Election of Fellows is open to candidates from throughout the world, and also to those who may have spent more time on their research than the strict three years since graduation that has been insisted upon since well before the PhD degree arrived from Germany. Nor in future will the competition take place at the beginning of the Michaelmas term, but rather in the thick of the global post-doc season, three months later. No doubt these changes will alter the character of the humanities at Trinity. But it will be for the historians of a century hence to determine which of our modern humanistic disciplines will thrive, and which will go the way of the moral sciences.

Wittgenstein at Trinity
Simon Blackburn (1962)

The 22-year-old Austrian Ludwig Wittgenstein arrived in Trinity in the autumn of 1911, in order to study the philosophy of mathematics with Russell. From the beginning he was a celebrity, dazzling and annoying people in about equal measure. But by July 1912 Russell told Wittgenstein's surprised sister Hermine that 'we expect the next big step in philosophy to be taken by your brother', and many people would say he was right.

Wittgenstein was a star. Everyone who knew him felt the shock of his extraordinary personality, and many wrote memoirs and accounts of their experience. In Trinity C.D. Broad spoke waspishly of the younger generation of philosophers 'gambolling to the highly syncopated pipings of Herr Wittgenstein's flute', but he also said, when Moore retired in 1939, that to refuse Wittgenstein the professorship would be like refusing Einstein a chair of physics. My own revered

supervisor, Casimir Lewy, who had attended his legendary classes in Whewell's Court in the 1930s and 1940s, remained sceptical of much of what Wittgenstein wrote and generally warned his pupils against being seduced by it. Yet he once told me: 'When Wittgenstein died I, Lewy, had a dream. And the content of this dream was: Wittgenstein cannot possibly be dead!' He waited for this to sink in, and when I showed a suitable surprise continued with his mischievous cackle, 'and, you know, I thought this cast considerable light on the phenomenon of the resurrection'. The comparison had been made before. Wittgenstein fought for the Austrians in the First World War, and was only lured back to Cambridge in 1929, by the brilliant young philosopher and economist, Frank Ramsey, a Trinity undergraduate but Fellow of King's. After meeting Wittgenstein at Cambridge station, Keynes wrote to his wife, 'Well, God has arrived. I met him on the 5.15 train.'

Gods can be unpredictable and terrifying, and it was no bed of roses being close to Wittgenstein. On returning from holiday with him in Norway in 1914 another Trinity philosopher, G.E. Moore, had to write to him explaining the regulations governing submitting some work for a BA degree, to which Wittgenstein replied, 'If I'm not worth your making an exception for me *even in some* STUPID *details* then I may as well go to Hell directly; and if I *am* worth it and you don't do it then – by God – you might go there.' Not a very British attitude to university regulations, although we might be better if it were. But Moore later became a central friend when Wittgenstein returned to Cambridge 15 years later: many people remained loyal to Wittgenstein because they knew that if he was hard on his friends, he was even harder on himself. Moore was also one of the examiners for his doctorate. Famously, Wittgenstein submitted his book the *Tractatus Logico-Philosophicus* for the degree, leading Moore to make the deathless verdict: 'I myself consider that this is a work of genius; but, even if I am completely mistaken and it is nothing of the sort, it is well above the standard required for the PhD degree.'

Wittgenstein's closest friend among the Fellows of Trinity was probably the Italian economist Piero Sraffa, whom he acknowledges as an important influence on his later work. Their conversations appear to have been intense, and legend has it that it was one of Sraffa's contemptuous Neapolitan gestures that alerted Wittgenstein to uses of language that are not confined to mirroring facts. Wittgenstein however also said that talking to Sraffa was like 'trying *hard* to fill a barrel which has no bottom', which suggests a rather one-sided conception of conversation.

The difficulty of Wittgenstein's writing does not lie on the page – he wrote beautifully – but in seeing the point of what lies on the page. We are accustomed to ask what problem is this trying to solve? What is the argument? What theory is being advanced? yet such questions get no answer, or seem curiously out of place. Wittgenstein indeed denies that he is solving problems, advancing arguments or constructing theories. Often what he does is more like telling stories or parables. He thought that philosophy should be a 'battle against the bewitchment of our intelligence by means of language', a kind of therapy that eventually frees the trapped fly from the fly-bottle. This can provoke the contemptuous view that 'it is all about words', or tut-tutting that the once-glorious position of philosophy as the queen of the sciences has degenerated into some kind of irrelevant verbal play. This seems to have been the attitude that Popper brought to his celebrated confrontation in the 'unusually charged' meeting of the moral sciences club at which a poker may, or may not, have been brandished. But it is a mistake. Insofar as we misunderstand our own words, we misunderstand our own activities with words and the world that we describe with them. Wittgenstein's previous work had been in physics and engineering, and his model was the work of the physicist Heinrich Hertz on the foundations of classical mechanics. Hertz held that when mechanics was formulated properly the puzzles and contradictions that plagued its notions of force and energy 'will not have been answered. But our minds, no longer vexed, will cease to ask illegitimate questions.' This was Wittgenstein's constant hope for his philosophy. In Hertz's view, achieving a perspicuous representation of mechanics is not a 'mere' matter of symbolism, but is the same thing as becoming finally clear about notions such as force and energy. And it may still be said to be an activity that is the queen of the sciences, in the sense that reflection on assumptions and methods is sovereign over thoughtless deployment of them.

Wittgenstein died in 1951. His last words were 'Tell them I have had a wonderful life.' On this one of his students, Norman Malcolm, comments: 'When I think of his profound pessimism, the intensity of his mental and moral suffering, the relentless way in which he drove his intellect, his need for love together with the harshness that repelled love, I am inclined to believe that his life was fiercely unhappy. Yet at the end he himself exclaimed that it had been "wonderful". To me this seems a mysterious and strangely moving utterance.'

God and A.E. Housman
Angela Leighton (2006)
From an address given in Chapel on 8 October, 2009:
'God and Some Fellows of Trinity' – the title of this term's addresses has the ring of 'chips with everything'. 'God' is on the menu and today, it's 'God and Housman'. But as you might guess, it's an uncomfortable pairing and not one Housman would have relished. Indeed, he would have found it laughable to be the subject of an address in Chapel, if laughing were much in his nature. Notoriously acid, suspicious, disinclined to common niceties – as when he refused to let Wittgenstein, his neighbour in Whewell 's Court, use his newly installed lavatory in a moment of need – Housman, on the whole, is not an edifying character. But then, he's an intellectual. 'God and' is not quite his scene.

He came to Trinity in his fifties. 'I shall, I hope, be a member of the Wine and the Garden Committees,' he declared. Certainly, by this time he was an expert cook, and judging by his many entries in the kitchen suggestions book, the food at Trinity was a trial to him. 'The salmon today was tasteless, and the lamb was both tastless and tough,' he grumbled. (His entries often fall into nice metrical patterns.) 'We have a great number of unattractive sweets at dinner – why not cheesecake sometimes for a change?' he suggested. (Thanks to Kevin Gray for directing me to the kitchen suggestions book.) The story that Housman introduced crème brûlée to Trinity high table is almost certainly incorrect, although hardly

out of keeping. If not sweetness of manner, he had at least a sweetness of tooth.

His reviews and lectures, however, are waspish in the extreme. His inaugural lecture, which is an excoriation of the newish discipline of literary criticism and a defence of textual criticism in its driest form, depends on such statements as the following:

Men hate to feel insecure; and a sense of security depends much less on the correctness of our opinions than on the firmness with which we hold them; so that by excluding intelligence we can often exclude discomfort. The first thing wanted is a canon of orthodoxy, and the next thing is a pope.

Against orthodoxies, popes and literary aesthetics, he pitted his own caustic intelligence. Here he is, reviling the temptations of lazy thinking and easy appreciation:

If therefore you like to go out on a clear night and lift up your eyes to the stars … and repeat, as your choice may determine, the poetry which they have evoked from Homer or David, from Milton or Leopardi – do so by all means. But don't call it astronomy.

Astronomy, he then quotes, is to be found in the third book of Newton's *Principia*: 'Let S represent the sun, T the earth, P the moon, CADB the moon's orbit. In SP take SK equal to ST; and let SL be to SK in the duplicate proportion to SK to SP.' After a paragraph of this, he concludes: 'That is how scholars should write about literature.' It is hard at this point to know how much tongue is in his cheek. Rhetorically at least, star-gazing with Milton and Leopardi (a self-consciously idiosyncratic duo) must beat 'In SP take SK'. Like Newton, who kept his scientific method quite separate from his more bizarre justifications of faith, Housman kept his classical textual studies quite separate from poetry. Asked once to explain the nature of poetry, he snapped back: 'I could no more define poetry than a terrier can define a rat.' Rats are not for definitions; they are for killing. In a sense, both Newton and Housman are reminders that the same mind can think, quite inconsistently and surprisingly, in two different languages.

In Trinity, this shy, ferocious man found a congenially protective space in which to compose his 'savage footnotes' and wistful, reticent poems. That reticence became legendary. At one college dinner he and J.M. Barrie exchanged not a word. Barrie then wrote to apologise for being so shy: Housman replied in exactly the same words, but with his own name, pointedly, correctly spelt. He turned down honours and invitations, including an invitation to give the Clark lectures, and when he died his large stock of pornographic literature, acquired on various trips to Paris, was donated to the University Library – an archive, one hopes, benefiting future generations of PhD students. One reviewer rather cruelly summed up the subject matter of Housman's poetry: 'Life's a curse, love's a blight. God's a blaggard, cherry blossom is quite nice.' Yet this rather sour, donnish character, and meticulous Latin scholar, was also to become, on the strength of two slim volumes and a sheaf of unpublished work, one of the great minor poets in the English tradition.

So what is to be said about Housman's atheism, or even, perhaps, about our own? I suggest that part of what blocks our thinking on this subject is the very abstract noun itself. The trouble with abstract nouns, though beloved of philosophers and theologians, is that they fix things in the singular. Atheism, like belief, quickly becomes a badge of communal identity, the flag of a set of assumptions, which leave nothing more to say. But Housman did have more to say, and he said it in that other language, of poetry:

If in that Syrian garden, ages slain,
You sleep, and know not you are dead in vain,
Nor even in dreams behold how dark and bright
Ascends in smoke and fire by day and night
The hate you died to quench and could but fan,
Sleep well and see no morning, son of man.
But if, the grave rent and the stone rolled by,
At the right hand of majesty on high
You sit, and sitting so remember yet
Your tears, your agony and bloody sweat,
Your cross and passion and the life you gave,
Bow hither out of heaven and see and save.

Dr Hubert Middleton allowed me to practise on the piano in his room in Whewell's Court. One afternoon while playing scales the door opened and an irate Wittgenstein appeared tearing his hair out, tormented by my noise. Being an English student I knew little about philosophy or philosophers though I knew he was some odd character who happened to be at Trinity. To pacify him on the moment I asked him if he would like to come to tea. I lived at 64 Chesterton Road opposite the footbridge and Jesus Green. Surprisingly, he agreed, so on one summer's afternoon he arrived in his old raincoat, and immediately enjoyed the home-made rock buns my mother used to post with the clean washing. I remember Wittgenstein talked a bit about Vienna. I heard for the first time about Mahler, but he seemed to like Bruckner better and said I should listen to his symphonies. By chance I mentioned English lectures and English philosophers. Quickly he brushed the subject aside and said he preferred we talk about the countryside and nature. After tea we walked together on Jesus Green. He said goodbye in a friendly way. Soon it was the end of term and although I invited him, we never had tea together again.

Peter Burton (1944)

While I was an undergraduate, my tutor Outram Evennett told me about an encounter he had had with Wittgenstein soon after being appointed tutor. Meeting Wittgenstein outside the Great Gate and feeling he should say something to the great man, Evennett said, 'Professor Wittgenstein, I understand that my tutorial pupil, Mr Jones, is a student of yours. What do you think of him?'

There was a long silence while Wittgenstein examined the cobbles. Finally he looked up and said, 'What do I think of him? I am afraid I do not know what that means.'

Sir Peter Lachmann (1950)

There is a corner of the Trinity Library where the story of the College is forever being invented. Late on a summer day, with the window closest the river pushed open, you can sit and listen to this story as it is told, when the Backs are splashed with sunset and the last punt carries a couple downriver. I worked at

extraordinary number pass the litmus test of fame, their legacy surviving in only a surname: Bacon, Herbert, Marvell, Dryden, Macaulay, Tennyson, Thackeray, Wittgenstein and Nabokov.

But what does this list mean? The arts ask about the meaning of colours and words and events, and how these shift with time. It is inevitable that an arts student, surrounded by so much splendour, should wonder what effect it is having. We look for a lesson in the stained glass and scripted flagstones, and ask what, if anything, we might give back? This is a pleasing theme on the more constant existential crisis: what is the point of studying art, history, literature, language and music?

There is perhaps an answer in the character of the arts student. Two qualities seem most prevalent here: a tendency towards stereotype during one's Cambridge career, and a tendency towards nostalgia when it has passed. Arts students, both current and long graduated, seem to delight in languid and hazy anecdotes. Over time our own pasts begin to seep with the sepia shades of champagne and longing, like photographs of ever lazier days in ever more beautiful scenery. However, these characteristics are more than an indulgence, and deserve to be defended.

Bertrand Russell said, 'I think that there is far too much work done in the world, that immense harm is caused by the belief that work is virtuous.' It is perhaps surprising, then, that Russell occupies a place on the list for both the arts and science alumni A-teams. However, such excuses give the arts student a certain reputation, one which we do everything in our power to further: reading in odd corners of the College, at odd times of the day; going to lunch in pyjamas and going to breakfast in black tie; behaving at best negligently, and at worst abusively, towards our diaries.

During Finals, between eavesdropping on passing punts, I spent many hours pacing round the Paddocks under the notion that ideas take time to digest. But it was a relief to know that Russell had whiled away a great many more hours walking rounds of the garden and wrestling with the ontological argument. The limitless nature of the syllabus for arts subjects is both thrilling and daunting. Both emotions are measured in self-discipline, but for many of us such discipline has to be learned. This is perhaps the most important lesson that university has to offer.

Guy Stagg (2006)

that desk through May, distracting myself with the voices of passing tour guides, listening to their fantastic histories and exaggerated roll-calls of celebrity alumni floating over Scholars' Lawn.

On the way back from reveries in the Library, any undergraduate can stop at the Chapel. In the first hall a more reliable list of alumni is written in marble. In the arts alone an

The cartoon inspired by the disgruntled Blackpool councillor.

THE UNIVERSITY AS A WHOLE AND TRINITY IN PARTICULAR WERE a revelation to me when I came up in October 1953. There was a sense of freedom which I had never known before. It was unimaginably different from my school days at Eton, which I had not enjoyed. Nobody at Trinity minded that I was useless at games. It was much easier to make friends. I didn't have to turn up for lectures if I didn't want to. I could drink – the standard drink in my group was Amontillado sherry. I joined the Magpie and Stump. I was invited to join the Lake Hunt, which introduced me to the Lake District and years of energetic pleasure. The long vacations provided opportunities for travel. In the summer of 1954 I joined three friends (two of them, Stephen Egerton and Mark Roskill, colleagues at Trinity) in a trip through Yugoslavia to Greece and back in an old Sainsbury's van – in those days quite an adventure.

I read law. The syllabus for the first year of the Tripos was frankly a waste of time, since the Tripos was designed to suit students who had done Part I of another Tripos and only did Part II law. However, I was fortunate to have Eli Lauterpacht as my Director of Studies for the first year and Bill Wade for the second and third. From 1959 to 1964 I was a 'sub-lector' – one of the young lawyers who used to come up from London on Friday afternoon to conduct supervisions. In the bitterly cold but sunny winter of 1963 I would take my skates up to Cambridge. I finished my supervisions at Saturday lunchtime and in the afternoon skated up the frozen Cam to Grantchester. Skating back into an icy north wind was quite a challenge.

A major improvement since I was an undergraduate is that Trinity has added many more rooms and has eliminated the need for undergraduates to spend a year in a lodging house. The rooms are also much warmer and a good deal more comfortable. When I was up, an alderman from Blackpool complained to the media that when he had come to a local government conference in Trinity, the accommodation he had been given was not fit for pigs. I moved a vote in the Magpie and Stump that the accommodation was not fit for pigs, aldermen or undergraduates. The result was a vote that the accommodation was fit for aldermen but not fit for pigs or undergraduates.

William Goodhart
(Baron Goodhart of Youlbury) (1953)

IT SEEMS TO BE ALMOST COMPULSORY THAT WHEN AUTHORS have their work adapted for television, they should make a little cameo appearance on screen: and so, when the BBC mounted a version of my novel *The Rotters' Club* a few years ago, I was duly sent down to the costume department for a fitting. The novel is set in a direct-grant school in the 1970s, and it was decided that I should portray a geography teacher. I was handed a suitable pair of flared trousers, told (rather gallingly) that there was nothing I needed to do with my hair (since it 'already looked like something from the 1970s') and then fitted with a threadbare check jacket with hilariously wide lapels. I put it on, looked at myself in the mirror, and suddenly had an overpowering sense of déjà vu: I was dressed exactly as I'd been dressed for my interview at Trinity College, back in the autumn of 1979.

It amazes me, to be honest, that this interview didn't scupper my chances of getting into Trinity altogether. Quite apart from my appalling dress sense, there was my general air of tongue-tied, provincial nervousness, paradoxically combined with a certain quirky self-assurance which determined, for instance, that when asked by my interviewer to name my favourite poet (a question which clearly required an answer such as Milton, Wordsworth or Auden) I told him, preposterously, that it was e.e. cummings.

But that was the sort of person I was when I arrived at Cambridge, having just turned 19: slightly full of myself (perhaps a prerequisite for going to Trinity at all) and yet at the same time inexperienced, diffident and narrowly educated. In retrospect, I don't envy any of the teaching staff their task of knocking me into shape, and have to concede that – given the material they had to work with – they did a more than admirable job.

When applying to Trinity, I was cautioned against it by one of the teachers at my school (King Edward's in Birmingham), who told me that the intake was too large and I might 'get lost' there. This was precisely what tipped me in Trinity's favour. 'Getting lost' was very much what I wanted to do. Still locked into an adolescent mindset, I asked of my Cambridge education nothing more than that I should be allowed to hide in my room for three years – writing, of course, and writing novels rather than essays. And that, essentially, is what I proceeded to do. It would be unseemly to complain now that nobody at Trinity seemed to notice that I was there, since I did my level best to make myself invisible.

Inaudible, too. Asked to read a poem aloud one day during a practical criticism supervision, I explained to my supervisor that I didn't like reading poetry aloud: to which his sensible response was, 'Then you should be doing another subject, really, shouldn't you? Perhaps – ' (and then a finely judged pause, to allow the hatchet blow to sink with full force) ' – perhaps *Land Economy*.' It's the kind of put-down you remember for years afterwards, although I was soon to find out that the supervisor in question had plentiful reserves of generosity lying not far beneath his caustic carapace. In which respect, perhaps – scary on the outside, warm and hospitable within – he somehow typified the College itself.

Most of my memories of Trinity are positive, in fact, although they are also complicated, and sometimes unsettling. I haven't been back to Cambridge often since graduating. The last time was a couple of years ago, when I was invited back for the 2008 Commemoration Feast, and soon found myself gobsmacked by the wisdom and self-confidence of the impossibly youthful undergraduates all around me. Early the next morning I walked into New Court, and tiptoed up the staircase upon which, in my third year, I had shared a set of rooms overlooking the river. For a few minutes I stood on the stone landing by the first-floor window, but soon found myself shivering: spooked by the presence of so many ghosts, not least the ghost of the clueless 19-year-old for whom, almost 30 years earlier, the future must have seemed as clear and as wide with possibilities as that unchanging view over the Backs.

Jonathan Coe (1980)

WE HADN'T SO MUCH AS BEEN ELECTED AS JOINT PRESIDENTS OF the Trinity History Society. Rather, my friend Emily Charkin and I had slipped into the role abandoned by the previous incumbent while he belatedly concentrated on his exams. But our lack of electoral legitimacy didn't prevent us enthusiastically planning a series of events.

During a planning session in Aunty's Tea Rooms, the name Alan Clark emerged. He was enjoying a fresh bout of notoriety, with the publication of his diaries. Aware that he also considered himself to be a historian, a handwritten note was despatched. We were thrilled when he replied accepting our offer of dinner and travel costs, and announced he'd speak on 'Why we should have made peace with Hitler in 1941'. The publicity campaign began immediately, consisting partly of printing posters and sticking them around the University and partly, as the day approached, of threatening our friends and acquaintances.

The evening came and the turnout exceeded our dreams. Students and a good sprinkling of Fellows crammed in and had to sit on floors and windowsills – both curious and appalled – as the talk proceeded. At the dinner in Hall, Emily and I were amazed to find Clark a shadow of the raconteur and bon viveur we were expecting. What must have been nerves reduced his appetite to almost nothing and ensured he drank none of the wine on which we'd spent the princely student sum of £5.50. We also later admitted to a little disappointment at the complete lack of flirting.

But once in the room, he came alive. Passionate and articulate, he spoke without notes, perching on a desk. Even the most curmudgeonly Fellows seemed to have a grudging respect for the presentation and the belief with which he offered his thesis. Looking back, it was a fine example of the curiosity and tolerance and humour I found in Trinity – and the sense that you could have an idea and make it happen, even if it involves bribing or cajoling your peers.

The cautionary tale came with the bill, on headed notepaper, from the Hon. Alan Clark. The cost of propelling his grand, vintage sports car all the way from Saltwood Castle in Kent came to a sum far in excess of the paltry figure in the History Society's bank account. Emily and I never did make it in business.

Theodora Fairley (1992)

CHAPTER 10

Built Trinity: The Last 50 Years

BOYD HILTON *(1974)*

Trinity built very little during the first half of the 20th century, merely the neo-Palladian Nevile's Court elevation of the Essex Building (E. Maufe, 1936) and Bevan Hostel in Green Street (I. Forbes, 1949). A grandiose plan by Sir Herbert Baker in the 1920s for a huge neo-neoclassical building along the whole of the western side of the Paddocks was (thankfully) abandoned on financial grounds. In the early 1950s a residential scheme by Powell and Moya for the Brewhouse site on the Backs was supported by a narrow majority of the Governing Body, but was abandoned in the face of a vociferous minority. (Watch that space.) The first significant development was the creation of Angel Court (H.C. Husband, 1957–9) on the site of an old pub and its surrounding alleyways behind the Bursary Range of Great Court. It is described on the 'Cambridge 2000' website as 'one of the most bland and least favoured buildings in the College', but there was ingenuity in its construction, and by retaining the shops and their frontages on Trinity Street it signifies as an early example of what became known as 'façadism', a very much better solution in the Cambridge context than wholesale demolition and rebuild.

At the time Angel Court was completed Trinity had just under 100 Fellows and a little over 750 junior members. By 2000 there were almost 160 Fellows and more than 1,000 students. This surge necessitated a building boom to match any in the College's previous history.

First up was the Wolfson Building (Michael Powers for Architects' Co-Partnership, 1968–72), Trinity's one uncompromisingly modernist building, which was squeezed

onto an awkwardly narrow site south of Whewell's Court. It was originally envisaged as two identical blocks, designed like ziggurats both in plan and elevation, but these were brought together during the course of development so as to form a single structure. It looks a little like an ocean liner floating at first-floor level above a sea of blue engineering bricks, the so-called podium, beneath which lie Heffers Bookshop on Trinity Street and Sainsbury's on Sidney Street. The Wolfson Building creates a striking silhouette, such as might look very well in a campus university, but it seems somewhat incongruous in the centre of Cambridge. It may seem like a backhanded compliment to say so, but the architects' greatest triumph is to have created such a huge and uncompromising development – home to 90 students on five levels – in such a way as to be entirely invisible from the three surrounding streets. Forty years later, denizens of Cambridge visiting this part of Trinity for the first time are often amazed to discover that it exists. In 2006 5th Studio Architects gave Wolfson Court a thorough makeover internally, including the

provision of additional en suite facilities as well as new fittings, new joinery, a warmer yet bolder colour scheme and improved lighting. Their most striking intervention was to insert two tall glass-fronted seminar rooms into the apices of what had hitherto been triangular voids of harsh engineering brick on each of the north and south faces. It has had the effect of humanising those Eiger-like elevations, while at the same time seeming to be entirely in keeping with the spirit of the original.

The stark hulk of the Wolfson Building posed a formidable challenge when the time came to move further south on to the site of the venerable Blue Boar coaching house. The brief stipulated that the podium referred to earlier should be extended to cover the remainder of the site bounded by Trinity and Green Streets, allowing for commercial premises below and new residential staircases above. The result is Blue Boar Court (MacCormac, Jamieson, Prichard & Wright, 1985–90), which mixes Ancaster and Clipsham stone with yellow brick. Richard MacCormac's genius was to realise that there was just sufficient

Previous pages: *Burrell's Field.*

Opposite: *David Oates and the Master, Lord Adrian, showing the Queen Mother finds made during the construction of Angel Court. She officially opened Angel Court in June 1960.*

Left: *Blue Boar Court.*

space in which to fit a whole new court, surrounded by a series of medieval-looking alleyways and mini-courts between it and the backs of the street houses. Most of the building rises two storeys above the podium, but there are turrets in the south- and north-west corners and a tower over Gifford Place, which gives vehicular access from Green Street to the retail apartments below. Much of the inside of the court is dominated by a horizontal band of lead-coated steel windows at first-floor level. From it are suspended pairs of large oriels interspersed with staircase entrances that are slightly set back and topped by bullseye windows. The court itself somewhat resembles an Italian piazza, and the effect is compounded by a campanile-style

structure at the east end. This marks the entrance to a shallow staircase that leads to a little cloister, and then on to the 150-seat Winstanley Lecture Theatre by the same architects. This is a lightweight structure, perched on the pre-existing columns holding up the ceiling of Sainsbury's below, suspended a metre or so above the podium, and hedged in by planting; it has a strong Japanese feel.

Two other developments on the main site were contributed by Ian Simpson Architects. The first, in 1997–8, saw the conversion of the Old Lecture Theatre into facilities for junior members. On the ground floor Trinity at last acquired a bar of a suitable size for its numbers (some 21 by 7.25 metres), while

Above: *Looking out of the Wolfson Building.*

Left: *View from the glass-fronted seminar room, added to the Wolfson Building in 2006 by 5th Studio Architects.*

two storeys of glass and steel common rooms above form a building within the shell of the original 1830s building, with the second floor set back from the perpendicular windows at either end to create exciting spaces 5.25 metres high. Ian Simpson's second intervention (2003–4, job architect Charles McKeith) is a sensitive westward extension of the Fellows' Parlour on Great Court in a modern style with much glass and a large exposed expanse of early 17th-century rough stone, the north-facing exterior elevation of Nevile's Court.

It is a glamorous thing to design buildings, of course, but equally important to maintain and repair them. Since 1972 there has been a continual programme of preventative repair

and conservation led consecutively by Peter Locke and Mark Wilkinson of Donald Insall Associates, and monitored in-house by Mr Adrian Biggs, Deputy Clerk of Works. There is inevitably some resemblance to the Forth Bridge in all this. Thus New Court, having been thoroughly modernised in the late 1970s, is now facing further extensive attention, not because of any inadequacy first time round but because of ever-shifting legislation with regard to multiple room occupancy, health and safety, and not least the need for environmentally greener buildings.

Trinity still has a number of hostels in central Cambridge and a few in the suburbs, but rising numbers and increasing student demand for 'living in' has forced the College to move beyond the main site and to colonise the area known as Burrell's Field. This was a large area beyond the Fellows' Garden and was on two levels, with the Bin Brook and its flood plain to the east followed by an escarpment and four suburban villas and their gardens further west – three Queen Anne-style houses

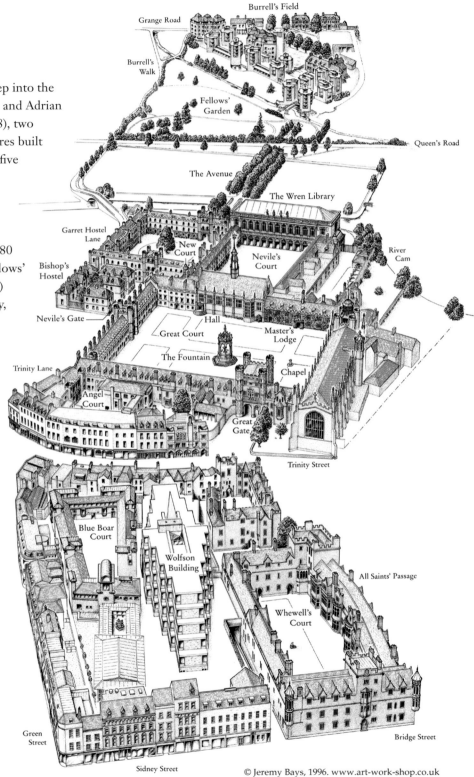

on Grange Road and an Arts and Crafts dwelling deep into the site. The first move came with the erection of Butler and Adrian Houses (David Roberts and Geoffrey Clarke, 1977–8), two hefty red-brick and red-tiled echelon-shaped structures built across the escarpment, four storeys to westward and five to the east. It was originally intended to disperse matching blocks across the whole of the site, but David Roberts died shortly afterwards and so in 1991, following a competition, the College turned again to Richard MacCormac of MJP Architects for 80 en suite residential sets plus common rooms and Fellows' accommodation. His very different solution (1992–5) was to develop the western part of the site intensively, with 12 new pavilions two, three and four storeys high. These form a series of cuboids built of buff coloured brickwork, from three sides of which huge triangular window frames of lead-coated steel protrude.

The effect is of a series of metal and glass boxes inserted diagonally into brick boxes, and tightened into place by high-level belvederes that seem to function as screw lids. These pavilions are hard up against – and form a geometric relationship with – the existing buildings, two of which were extended by the addition of common rooms. This had the advantage of maximising the area of wild meadowland either side of Bin Brook, from which the cluster of towers really does have the appearance (an appearance so often touted by architects, but rarely achieved, especially in Cambridge) of a Tuscan hill town. The effect is made more dramatic still by the creation of a second escarpment, in this case artificial and made of brick, from which the 'town' rises like a fortress. (In the original plans this edge was to have been marked by a moat, which for financial reasons was scaled down to a pond, but the juxtaposition of grass and masonry is sufficiently dramatic, even without the water.) In Richard MacCormac's words:

Burrell's Field.

'Architecturally this escarpment is interpreted as a retained terrace, parallel with the brook, defining a plateau of buildings, some of which emerge out of the wall of the terrace itself, like the towers of a walled town.'

Burrell's Field fits into an extraordinary pattern of achievement by the same architects at Worcester, Wadham, Balliol and St John's Colleges in Oxford and at Fitzwilliam in Cambridge. It is regarded by many good judges as Trinity's best building since the Wren, and as the finest Cambridge development since the war. It is also very much a building within a landscape. Again in the architect's words, this is 'garden architecture with walls, colonnades, pergolas', 'a variety of tightly organised spaces' and axial vistas contrasting with the 'open landscape outside'. 'In the spirit of the 18th-century English landscape tradition, the scheme is intended to be discovered through foliage, rather than immediately understood.' Those words were promissory, but they have been vindicated over nearly two decades, as every year brings greater intensity to the relationship between built form and nature. Approaching the development from the Fellows' Garden, one notes how much of the masonry facing the wild meadow is now covered in creeper. One enters via a bridge over the brook and between the first two pavilions, still very much aware of the greenery without. But once fully inside, one finds the interior brick faces almost entirely clean-shaven. Instead the pavilions and walkways are separated by planting of a more formal type. Further west still, where once were suburban back gardens, there is the effect of open parkland, an impression enhanced by the magnificent avenue of lime trees. The entire area, from Queen's Road to Grange Road, can only be described as enchanting.

CHAPTER 11

Scenes From College Life (1960s–1970s)

Sport and Drama

Well before I was ten I had a fascination with Cambridge. My family had no connection with the University, but my father was determined that his sons should have the chance – a chance that was never open to him.

Believe it or not, what really captured my imagination about Cambridge was a set of cigarette cards which included aerial photographs, in colour, of the colleges. Then there was the boat race: in the playground of Merton Sacred Heart Primary School we were fiercely divided between Oxford and Cambridge.

I heard about the attractions of Trinity from two schoolfriends at Wimbledon College: Anthony Eisinger, who was already up, reading natural sciences, and John Ashby, a fellow member of the classical sixth. Ashby, who was clearly better organised than I, had already applied and got a place. I duly applied and was granted an interview with Alan Ker, the Classics don. My long-felt appreciation of the good-heartedness of Trinity was born when Alan Ker was most understanding about my late arrival for the interview: in a mad fit of teenage daring, and because I was trying to save money, I had chosen to hitchhike from London to Cambridge, and it had taken longer than hoped. This was not the chosen method of transport for the 40 or so Etonians who went up in my year.

Which brings me to another embarrassing memory of late arrival at Trinity. When I went up in 1960, Alan Ker looked up from my file and said: 'Keegan, why didn't you come up last year? We offered you a place in 1957, and our policy was for people to do their National Service first: didn't yours end in 1959?'

Previous pages: *The new rooms in Angel Court, 1960.*

Left: *Tutors Alan Ker and Mark Pryor in the Fellow's Parlour, 1964.*

Below: *Theo Redpath.*

'But your letter offered me a place in 1960,' I replied.

'Goodness, you should have got in touch. You could have come up last year.'

Well it was a deferential society in those days. I had considered myself so fortunate to have got a place that I did not dare to ring up and question the date. I can see Alan Ker now, blinking in sympathy. In fact, looking back, I have no regrets. I spent the year 1959–60 teaching in Sussex and Switzerland – a kind of 'gap year' that is now so common.

However, the effect on me of a total of three gap years – two in the army and that year teaching – was that I could no longer face Greek or Latin translation. Alan Ker was most understanding about my switch to the economics Tripos, and it was as a result of being a year late, and that switch, that I made a lifelong close friend, Jonathan Agnew, with whom I shared supervisions for a while.

That switch also had an influence on my career. Not only did the economics Tripos point me in the direction of financial journalism – first the *Financial Times*; later the *Observer*, with a stint at what was then the *Daily Mail and News Chronicle* – but that brief period of sharing supervisions with Jonathan Agnew (he later switched to moral sciences) led to our taking over *The Trinity News Sheet*. The *News Sheet* contained some news but an awful lot of scurrilous gossip: no report was 'fact-checked' if

there was a danger that we might have to sacrifice what we, at least, thought was a good pun. And after one item in which we chanced our arm I narrowly avoided physical assault. Those were days of curfews and climbing in after midnight. Reports that a lot of alcohol swims around university towns these days bring to mind the phrase 'It was ever thus'.

But back to Alan Ker, my understanding moral tutor from 1960 to 1963. When I was in danger of punishment for what the police would no doubt call 'an alcohol-related incident', Mr Ker (I should never have dreamed of calling him 'Alan') said to me: 'Keegan, you are not the sort of person who would behave like that, are you?' That deceptively simple 'num' question made a lifelong impression on me and my dealings with others.

William Keegan (1960)

At my interview in the Senate House Theo Redpath asked my advice as to whether he should get married. He was perhaps aged 50 – his subject was Shakespeare. Not being an expert on the subject of marriage, I was happy for my mother, who was with me, to field the question. I think she must have been positive as he did marry and had two children.

At the beginning of each term, he would summon his pupils and mention two subjects: first, if we should become depressed we should seek his help; second, if we had a party we must take care not to leave the bottles outside the bottom of the staircase lest the press see them.

He gave me a 'scholarship' in that he arranged for me in a long vacation to teach a young aristocrat A level mathematics for four weeks on a beautiful estate in the south of France.

Francis Hambly (1963)

THE BIG FREEZE BEGAN ON BOXING DAY 1962 SO THAT BY THE time undergrads returned around 15–16 January the College was well frozen up with no running water. My first night back in K9 Great Court I used water from a jug to clean my teeth and fill a hot-water bottle, and piling every coat and my dressing gown on the bed, I turned in. The next morning I cut my gums quite badly as the water on the toothbrush had frozen (I've always dried my toothbrush since!), but the real shock came the next evening when I retrieved my hot-water bottle from the bed: it was frozen solid and had to be thawed out in front of the gas fire. So the only thing keeping it liquid the previous night was my body heat! I suppose the bedroom was around minus 5 to 10 degrees C for weeks.

The other great memory was the brief but spectacular effect of the thaw when relatively mild, damp air one Saturday morning, in early March, turned all the stone buildings white with frost for two or three hours. Cambridge can never have looked more beautiful.

Colin Snowdon (1959)

THINGS CHANGED IN 1963. TRINITY TUTOR DR REDPATH HAD made his annual talent-spotting visit to Varndean Grammar School but, when he was given the usual shortlist of young scientists for consideration, he enquired whether the school could also suggest any promising arts specialists. I was among a small group of guinea pigs taking part in the school's first Russian course. In those Cold War days, the saying doing the rounds was 'The optimists are learning Russian; the pessimists are learning Chinese.'

So it was that one Saturday morning I found myself stepping off the train in a city I had never visited before wondering how far it was to the campus. Dr Redpath was not the crusty old academic I had expected. He greeted me rather shyly with a welcome glass of sherry and as we sat down in comfortable

The Fountain during the Great Freeze of 1963.

armchairs he asked me if I was related to the great mathematician Henry Dudeney. I had to confess that I had never even heard of him and wondered whether my answer had ruined my chances of a place at Trinity even before I had taken my first sip of sherry. About ten minutes later I found myself rambling on about the relative merits of Boulting Brothers' comedies and the *Carry On* series when Dr Redpath interrrupted me: 'Your French is very good, but your Russian could be better. If I were to offer you a place – which I do – would you be prepared to attend a preliminary Russian course in Cambridge?'

I was stunned. Had he just offered me a place at Trinity or was this merely an invitation to a Russian course outside the College? No, 'Which I do' means a place at Trinity even if I do not agree to the course. I stammered out a reply, but Dr Redpath was already on the phone to Professor Hill of the Slavonic Department and everything was arranged in a few seconds.

'My name's Kenneth,' I said. 'Oh, bad luck,' he replied. 'So's mine.'

The scene was again C2 Nevile's Court, Dr Redpath's rooms, where this brace of Kenneths formed part of a gathering of freshly matriculated undergraduates. We were all quaffing excellent mulled wine with enthusiasm. All except this other Kenneth who had insisted on milk.

'Isn't Kenneth an awful name?' he said, 'I'm thinking of changing it when I become famous.'

'You could always shorten it to Ken,' I suggested.

'Oh no, that's even worse than Kenneth,' he spluttered into his milk. 'Kenny perhaps, but it's more likely I'll change my name completely.' He then treated me to a résumé of his many achievements to date and predictions for the next few years of his glittering career in and beyond Trinity. Not a moment too soon, Dr Redpath rescued me and I met other guests who had been subjected to the same stories and moved away at the earliest opportunity.

Several months later, I was in my parents' flat in Brighton one Saturday teatime in July 1965. We were watching a popular weekly programme on the BBC called *Juke Box Jury* in which David Jacobs asked a panel of celebrities to vote whether a selection of newly released singles would be 'hits' or 'misses'. Sometimes, without the panel's knowledge, the artiste in question sat behind the screen listening to their comments, which was the case with the singer and writer of a rather unusual but very catchy ditty called *Everyone's Gone to the Moon*. I clearly remember my shock when the tall newcomer introduced as Jonathan King emerged from behind the screen. It was Kenneth from Trinity. He *had* changed his name and he *was* on his way to becoming famous. Sadly, he also became infamous, but that's another story.

Ken Dudeney (1964)

Trinity College Mission Summer Holiday Scheme, 1967.

MY FIRST ROOMS WERE IN WHEWELL'S COURT, Q STAIRCASE (now deceased). My trunk was delivered to the College by BR (now also deceased), and to my rooms by the porters. Although it was new, and locked, I had taken the precaution of wrapping it in a long, tightly knotted rope for additional security in transit. A day or two after I had arrived, I was approached by a couple of undergraduates with whom I was not acquainted. They explained that they had seen my trunk in the lodge, with its rope. They requested that I lend them the rope. I do not recall exactly what reason they gave for needing it. However, they did not tell the whole truth, because, the next day, a bicycle had been secured with a rope between a pair of the statues on the parapet of the Wren Library. I was advised that it was my rope that had been used, that I would not be getting it back and that I should not admit to knowing anything about the event. I think some sort of gentle threat was made. I was extremely fearful that the porters might recognise the source of the rope, and that my time at Trinity might end after less than one week!

Although I had not been much of a cyclist prior to coming up, I had been advised that it was useful to have a bike in Cambridge. My father had bought a bike in the early 1930s which he gave

Richard Pannett and John Fox (in the water) taking part in the underwater bicycle race organised by the Damper Club, 1969.

to me. I left the bike in the bicycle shed beneath Q staircase in the Easter vacation. I had purchased a wicker basket to fit to its handlebars. Unfortunately, when I returned to Cambridge, I found that a blackbird had built its nest in the basket. A Trinity postgraduate friend who had given up cycling for some reason lent me his bike until the eggs had hatched and the birds had flown. (*Granta* published a photo of the nest.) The birds must have been very brave and determined, because bicycles in the adjacent racks remained in daily use.

In May 1969 the Damper Club arranged an underwater bicycle race. I was not a member of the Society. A good friend of mine in Trinity (John Fox) was. The race, in the Cam at King's Backs, had been publicised, and my friend had declared himself as a competitor. With many others, I turned up to watch. Unfortunately, he was the only competitor. To ensure that there was a race, I hurried back to College to change and collect my

bike. Sadly, I came second, because my bike entered a patch of deep water, I floated off it, it tipped over and fell beneath me. The *Cambridge Evening News* published a news item, with photos.

Richard Pannett (1966)

I WAS UP AT TRINITY DURING A PERIOD OF RAPID SOCIAL change. We still had to wear gowns for dinner, but not around the city. In 1967 'guests' had to be out of College by 11pm, and were allowed entry at 7am. By 1970 the rules had changed considerably. 'Guests' (which really meant females) had to be out of College by 2am and entry was allowed at 6am. In practice, I believe the College was accepting that students' girlfriends stayed in College overnight at times. One evening on returning alone at about 11.30pm, I got chatting with one of the porters. He informed me that there were 120 or so women sleeping in College that night. They were apparently all 'regular girlfriends' so they turned a blind eye.

Clive Stubbings (1967)

Memory One: PARTICULARLY OF THAT FIRST TERM – IS THE COLD. So cold, that the condensation froze on the inside of the windows in Whewell's Court. Wind all the way from the Urals and mist from the Fens.

Memory Two: no one warned me about the sanitary arrangements – six flights of stone stairs down to the toilet and across two courtyards for a bath. However, every bedroom had a handbasin that served most purposes …

Memory Three: the porters, who could fit ten different gradations of contempt into their intonation of the word 'Sir'.

Memory Four: that other venerable College institution, the bedder. In my first year, she was a tiny woman – all of 4'10" – with a strange fixation: all the stories she told ended up with the

A pantomime horse after drinking at the fountain, March 1968.

177

Left: *The cover of the Lent issue of the* Trinity Review, *1970, designed by Antony Gormley (1968).*

Below: *Contributors to the* Trinity Review, *1973.*

protagonist having 'a crushed pelvis' and her advice always took the form, 'I wouldn't do that or you'll end up with a crushed pelvis.'

Memory Five: arriving a moment late at the Matriculation Feast and sliding into my place just as the Grace ended, only to have the (inebriated) don seated next to me begin his conversation with 'You'll roast in Hell for that'.

Memory Six: the two cultures. In my first two years, I read natural sciences, although rapidly started devoting most of my time to University politics. This was not readily compatible with dutifully following my course and I stopped bothering with the practical sessions. By the end of the first year, people were apparently prepared to pay good money to watch me taking the practical part of the exam. Essentially, I was inhabiting the wrong culture (which is why I switched to economics in my third year). This was brought home to me when I bumped into another Trinity scientist towards the end of term – I expect I was canvassing for his vote – and he told me proudly that he had taken his first evening out from studying the night before for two months (I am not sure I had spent a whole evening working all year). I asked him what he had done with this freedom and he told me smugly that he'd been to a meeting of the University Physics Society. I'm not sure that I got his vote.

Memory Seven: being immersed in the Trinity fountain on the night I was elected President of the Cambridge Union. (I remember the sudden cry of 'Harris in the fountain'. I remember being dragged there. I remember going in. Strangely, I don't remember how I got out or getting dry, although presumably I did.)

Memory Eight: as President, inviting Lord 'Rab' Butler, then the Master of Trinity, to preside over a debate in the Union Chamber to mark the fact that it was exactly 50 years since his term as President of the Union. He was clearly touched, but informed me firmly (although erroneously) that I had got the dates wrong.

Memory Nine: the eerie disappearance of people as Finals approached. In my first two years, you could guarantee that long before you had crossed Great Court you would bump into someone as keen as you were to be distracted and ready for a coffee or a drink (wine was 67p a bottle in the Buttery). By the first term of the final year you could get to the end of Kings Parade and the following term you might have to go to the University Library (excellent cheese scones in the café) before you saw anyone similarly inclined. I never did discover where they all went, although some of them seemed to get better degrees than I did …

Memory Ten: the perversity of College and University prominence. Some of the brilliant stellar figures, whom everyone assumed would continue to shine and acquire glittering prizes, have vanished without trace into obscurity. Others who seemed like nonentities at the time are now captains of industry or fully paid-up members of the great and the good. The only consolation is that some of those who were irritating pedantic nerds 40 years ago have grown up to be … irritating pedantic nerds.

Toby Harris (Baron Harris of Haringey) (1971)

IT IS WELL KNOWN THAT ACADEMIC CONVERSATION IS NOT necessarily very educational. Wittgenstein is supposed to have said that the only interesting thing he ever heard at Trinity high

The first Trinity team to win University Challenge in 1975. Winning teams went on to play a team of Fellows from their College in those days. The undergraduates lost. Twenty years later, another Trinity team swept to victory but no longer had to take on their teachers.

table was when the steward said to him, about a pudding: 'If you dig a little deeper, sir, you will find the strawberry.' But my own experience with the dons – in my case, from the perspective of an undergraduate – was better.

What I remember most happily is not what Trinity dons formally taught me, but what I learnt from them in other ways. In this, we had cause to be grateful for Trinity's wealth, because it meant that it could afford to keep bachelor or widowed dons in College rooms after they had retired. When I went up to Trinity in 1975 there were at least five dons who had been made Fellows before or during the First World War, as well as the Master, R.A. Butler, who, though actually a mere 73, seemed more venerable. I loved these living witnesses to a distant past.

Of these dons, I remember four. From my first-year rooms, G3 New Court, I could watch Professor Littlewood, a mathematician. He had no bath in his set, and he would walk across New Court in search of one, sometimes wearing only his trousers with his braces over his naked shoulders. If it rained during his slow passage, he would stand quietly under the horse-chestnut in the court. Then there was Mr Nicholas, who would live to be over 100. With his snowy-white hair and ruddy features, he was the image of one of those benevolent Victorian gentlemen who sometimes appear in Dickens. When he was fighting on the Western Front in 1916, a College message came all the way up the line with the important news that the clock in Great Court would now cease chiming at 10.30pm rather than midnight, because of the hostilities. Mr Nicholas had been the Bursar, and his pre-war investment decisions had been so successful that the College would happily have fed and housed him for a thousand years.

The other two were Dr Burnaby and Lord Adrian. Burnaby was a clergyman, thin and distinguished-looking, with a wide black hat. Thanks to the chaplain, Bob Reiss, who used to organise little suppers for those of us who wanted to debate insoluble questions like the existence of God, I met Dr Burnaby and heard him speak at length. He had the old man's habit of muddling up time, so he confused the First and Second World Wars, but his processes of reasoning were perfectly clear. He talked about the fear of death. He remembered that McTaggart, the once-famous Trinity philosopher-atheist, had faced death

with total equanimity, whereas F.A. Simpson, the history Fellow and clergyman celebrated for doing nothing but dead-heading roses for 60 years, was terrified of it.

Lord Adrian was, I am told by those who know, a great scientist. He was very small and bent, and kind. He had me to lunch and told me that he had been taught by my great-grandfather at Bart's Hospital in the Edwardian era. Suddenly, he went off to his bathroom (as an ex-Master, he was granted that luxury), and tottered back with my great-grandfather's massive history of the hospital, which he kept just above the bath.

Possibly I am romanticising, but I remember in all these men a certain modesty and politeness to the young which sometimes goes with being very intelligent and very old. It was clear, too, how much they loved the place in which they had chosen to spend most of their lives. Before the phrase was invented, they gave meaning to the concept of 'lifelong learning', and they passed on its spirit.

Rab was quite different. He did not really want to be at Trinity, because he had had his eyes on No.10 Downing Street. Unlike his ever-interested wife, Mollie, he was patently bored by us. But he did have his 'anecdotage'. Once he told me that he had been the host when Mrs Thatcher, then Leader of the Opposition, had come to speak in Cambridge, wearing a black dress. In the lecture room, he took a piece of chalk and wrote the word 'Scotland' on her breast with it. She said, not unreasonably, 'Why are you doing that?' 'A Queen of England had "Calais" written on her heart, and you should have "Scotland" written on yours,' Rab explained. This story gives me great pleasure because it is so Rab-ish in every way – not least, as his son Adam confirmed to me, that it is almost certainly untrue.

Charles Moore (1975)

I ARRIVED AT TRINITY AS THE IDEALS OF THE 1960S HAD SUNK INTO a worthy joylessness. In a moment of bravado, I had dyed a hank of my hair orange-blonde shortly before coming up. I was surprised to find my old friend Nick Coleridge asking advice about hair dye within minutes of our falling into conversation and turning crimson overnight. Before long a small group of us had decided we would launch a glossy magazine, an uneasy combination of arts review and teenage girls' weekly. We would spend days and nights in one of our rooms discussing content, style, layout, but also arcane pop lyrics and the opposite sex, as we worked our Buttery bills higher. We managed to sell the first issue of *Rampage* well enough to fund an alcoholic night out. As I look back, the greatest joy of Cambridge was the apparently endless time one had to make real friendships. To this day six of us meet up for dim sum twice a year and retell the old jokes, which seem to get funnier with each telling.

Nick Allan (1976)

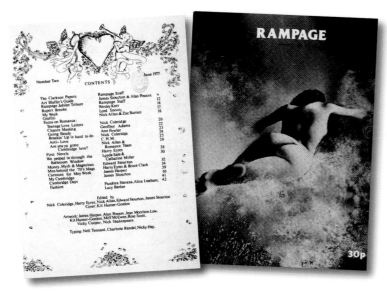

Rampage, *first and last editions, 1977–9.*

College Sport
Charlie Pearson (2005)

When Ivo goes back with the urn, the urn;
Studds, Steel, Read and Tylecote return, return.

A little-known verse of curious song lyrics adorns the face of the most coveted urn of ashes in the world, pasted on to its terracotta shell in a tiny, handwritten scrawl. The words assign three Trinity men to a place in sporting history, and they reappear perennially in one of the greatest narratives of international sport. In the summer of 1882, the England cricket team lost for the first time in a Test match to the touring Australians. Later that year, Ivo Bligh, 8th Earl of Darnley, Trinity man and Cambridge cricket captain, led England's response to the catastrophe in a mission to Australia to 'recover those ashes'. He did so with George and Charles Studd, two of a long line of Trinity brothers and fine all-round sportsmen. Bligh's intention was to tour to Australia with a team of his University chums to restore the natural sporting order, but his plan failed and the side became an All-England XI comprising eight Gentlemen and four Players. Australia were defeated 2–1 and Bligh was handed a six-inch urn containing the ashes of a cricket ball by a group of Melbourne women. The urn, which was donated to the MCC by Bligh's family after his death, would later come to symbolise the longest-running rivalry in the sport and the names of Ivo Bligh and the Studd brothers, among others, are commemorated for posterity in the mysterious verse on its side.

Not unlike the academic aspects of life at Trinity, College sport draws on a rich heritage of personalities who have their place in history at the vanguard of their fields. Cricketers seem to dominate the pantheon of those past masters, but notables from the other major sports also make appearances in the historical record. The first standardised rules of football were drawn up in the Trinity rooms of H.C. Malden in 1848, and Lord Arthur FitzGerald Kinnaird was one of the founders of the Football Association in 1863. He was also a driving force behind the first-ever soccer internationals in the early 1870s between England and Scotland and played in nine out of the first 12 FA Cup finals. In rugby, four Trinity men went on the 1891 British Lions rugby

tour to South Africa, and Charles Plumpton Wilson became possibly the only man ever to play for England at association and rugby football in 1881. Crumbling sepia photographs of men like these, with pointed moustaches, striped blazers and flannel trousers, can still be seen decorating the walls of the Field Club as testament to the days when Trinity athletes were not only leading the way in intercollege competition – as a photo of the very casual-looking Trinity rugby XV of 1897 might suggest, proudly inscribed with the team's record that season of 500 points

for and 28 against – but also leading the way in the establishment of the sports themselves.

Needless to say, some time has elapsed since Cambridge students were creating the major international sports we know today. Trinity sport now, with its spiritual home at Old Field, may not be the international powerhouse it was 120 years ago, but it is still enjoyed by hundreds of students of almost every possible degree of aptitude, amateurism and pseudo-professionalism. At times during the last ten years, however, modest sporting success

Charlotte Roach, CUSU Facilities Officer, Ospreys President and former President of the Women's Blues Committee, showing that Trinity can still nurture international athletes, here with her gold medal from the U20 European Cross Country Championships in 2007.

relative to other colleges has generated recurring concerns at Trinity's perceived inability to make its numerical advantage count in the major sports. Reports of disappointing levels of participation, low status and schoolboy organisation have been common, but as one ought to expect, a look back through decades of annual records indicates that success in College sport arrives in waves of three years as particular groups of talented individuals come and go, and the *Zeitgeist* surrounding them oscillates between eagerness and indifference. If there was a Golden Age when Trinity was in a position to dish out regular thrashings to St John's in all the major sports, it certainly hasn't been in the last half-century.

In fact, in recent years Trinity sport has been riding the crest of one of these waves. The College cricket team has challenged for Cuppers honours and re-established itself as one of the sides to beat on the Twenty20 scene. Despite the commitment troubles plaguing every sport played in exam term, Trinity cricket provides its hardcore following with enjoyable fixtures against touring sides each summer. In rugby, the College is unlikely to come close to competing against St John's and its deeply engrained rugby culture but an influx of talent has brought dividends in the league competition. Unlike other sports, football still has enough of a following to provide sufficient personnel for a competitive 2nd XI, and even a less serious third team, 'the Bruces', which regularly takes to the field, if only to revel in the comedy of its hapless performances. The hockey team, the weakest of the 'big four' for many years, is nonetheless in ascendancy and has made an impact at the 'Doxbridge' sports festival, where Trinity hockey is fast becoming something of a regular.

A panoply of sports with fewer than 11 players on a team also engages huge numbers of students. Over the years, Trinity has provided the University with some of its finest athletes and skiers (some of whom have also represented their country), tennis and badminton players, basketball and netball players, water polo and lacrosse players. Keen participation in all of the corresponding women's teams has been an obvious and welcome addition to sport in the modern era. It would be impossible in such a short space to do justice to all the many shades of sport colouring

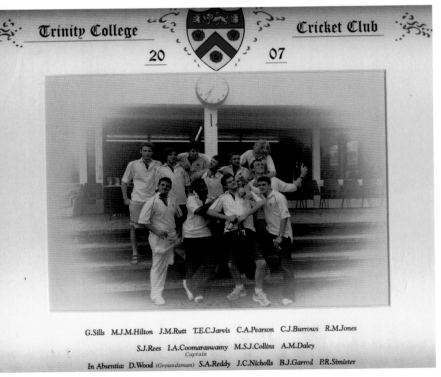

Trinity College **Cricket Club**

20   07

G.Sills   M.J.M.Hilton   J.M.Rutt   T.E.C.Jarvis   C.A.Pearson   C.J.Burrows   R.M.Jones

S.J.Rees   I.A.Coomaraswamy   M.S.J.Collins   A.M.Daley
Captain

In Absentia: D.Wood *(Groundsman)*   S.A.Reddy   J.C.Nicholls   B.J.Garrod   P.R.Simister

College life, let alone to pay homage to sporting exploits and characters of previous generations, but this brief 'state of the nation' snapshot at least gives some indication of the buoyant health of sporting activity in the College.

The First and Third Trinity Boat Club
Peter Brandt

Rowing at Trinity started in 1825 when what became the First Trinity Boat Club was established, followed closely by Second and Third Trinity Boat Clubs. Second was for scholars. It was known as Reading Trinity, but was disbanded in 1876. Third was made up of undergraduates from Eton and Westminster.

Throughout the period up to the mid-1930s the two clubs were very successful, sending winning crews to the Olympic Games and winning the Grand Challenge Cup at Henley five times and the Ladies Plate 15 times. In 1854 First Trinity won the Grand at Henley stroked by an Old Etonian. He had been made an honorary member of First for the summer.

In 1947, prompted by the Stewards of Henley, the First and Third Trinity clubs formally merged. It remains one of the most successful college boat clubs, having sent four oarsmen to Olympic Games and winning the Ladies Plate at Henley on three occasions. In 1954 the Club won the Ladies and the Visitors' on the same day, and has been Head of the River in the Mays seven times.

First and Third Ladies in their first bumps in Lent and May 1979. The captain was Amanda North and the No.7 was Joan Lewtas, now Joan Lasenby, Fellow of Trinity and keen cross-country runner.

Lents 1979

Bow: Caroline Hitch, 2. Jane Corbett, 3. Cathy Bartlett, 4. Janet Mackay, 5. Pam Nickell, 6. Claire Bollworthy, 7. Joan Lewtas, Str. Amanda North, Cox: Margaret Ainscough.

Mays 1979

Bow: Janet Mackay, 2. Claire Bollworthy, 3. Esther Giles, Str. Amanda North, Cox: Margaret Ainscough.

The May boat went Head of the River in 1964 which was Lord Adrian's last year as Master. He was awarded his first May colours, coxed a boat up to the Backs, stepped neatly ashore and attended the Bumps Supper wearing his new cap. Peter Brandt, who competed in the Helsinki Olympics and is currently the President of the Club, coached the May boat from 1963 to 1997, once coaching on horseback, as was the original practice. This created a sensation on the towpath and there was no danger of his bicycling into the river.

In 1978 the Ladies Boat Club was established and quickly became a much cherished and successful feature of Trinity rowing. Indeed, their rise was meteoric, recording four bumps and winning their oars for the first time in 1980.

One of the most memorable events in the recent history of the Boat Club took place on 25 November 2003 when Prince Charles named a coxed IV 'The Prince of Wales'. The ceremony was held under the Wren Library and was a great success. Prince Charles became a member of the Boat Club and the boat went on to win its event.

The Bumps
Dan Darley (Captain of First and Third Boat Club, 1996–7)
There were eight days each year that were approached with particularly keen anticipation, despite the nerves and anxiety. If you rowed at College, the days that really saw nerves gnawing at your stomach were not necessarily exam days, but those of the University Bumps races.

It was a consistent source of bewilderment to my non-rowing friends why I would get up early to row before lectures and spend my evenings combining supervision work with training at the boathouse. But if there was one simple reason, it was to race in the Bumps, a spectacular event that amply made up for any inconvenience or trouble that rowing might have imposed on me during each term.

Each Bumps day would begin with the surprisingly literally named 'Stomp', as the members of First and Third would gather by Great Gate to take the short walk across College, down the Avenue, through St John's College to Trinity Street and back into Great Court, by this time well woken up and looking forward to a fry-up in Hall. At the same time, the members of Lady Margaret Boat Club would walk the same route in the opposite direction, affording the opportunity for some usually good-natured skirmishes and verbal sledging before the real competition later that day.

After a good breakfast in Hall there might be Club photos taken in Great Court or Nevile's Court, and then lectures or exams for most Club members. Soon after lunch the first wave of rowers from across the University would set off to the river for the first division of the day. There would then follow a steady stream of rowers heading, somewhat solemnly, through town to the river, and later returning with cheerful smiles or deep frowns depending on their performance.

The race itself would come as something of a relief, the waiting over and the chance at last to put all of those hours of training into practice. The tension would mount again in the last minutes before your race, as first the four-minute gun sounded, then the one-minute gun, and at last the loud bang to start the race when the 18 queued crews would explode into action. Early in the day this might be a somewhat chaotic period with lots of shouting, splashing and effort perhaps not quite justified by the speed attained but always providing an entertaining spectacle and thoroughly enjoyed by all taking part. As the racing progressed each afternoon the shorts and T-shirts characteristic of the more frenzied earlier divisions would be replaced by matching all-in-one lycra outfits as the faster crews rowed up to race. By the end of the day the crowds would be out to see the 1st VIIIs racing, with the top few crews vying to finish Head of the River.

TRINITY LAKE HUNT

The historian G.M.Trevelyan (Master of Trinity 1940–51), together with Geoffrey Winthrop Young (Trinity) and Sidney McDougall (King's), founded the Lake Hunt in 1898. It enabled an invited group of Cambridge men to enjoy chasing each other, as 'hares' and 'hounds', over the fells of the Lake District, in emulation of the manhunt in Robert Louis Stevenson's *Kidnapped*, in the week following graduation each year. The Hunt split in 1901 into the Trinity Lake Hunt, organised from the College and consisting predominantly of members of Trinity, and the other Lake Hunt, organised by members of the Trevelyan family. The Trinity Hunt counts among its members a more recent Master, Andrew Huxley, and its records have been kept by two former Vice Masters, first Patrick Duff and latterly Chris Morley. The two Hunts jointly celebrated their centenary in 1998 with a hunt around the College grounds and a dinner in College, rounded off with a challenge Great Court run. In 2007 about 60 members participated in the first day of the 100th Trinity Lake Hunt at its traditional home, Seatoller House in Borrowdale. Typically about 30 members, now female as well as male, hunt each year, including seven or eight novices, these usually resident junior members of the College.

Trinity Lake Hunt, 6th July 2006. The four 'hares', Tom Rose, Richard Dewire, Ailanore Harper and Matthew Sandford, preparing to set off from Seatoller House. The 'hounds', who must wait indoors so as not to see which way the 'hares' go, set off 30 minutes later.

The boathouse has records of all the most successful First and Third crews displayed on the numerous honours boards there. These date back the best part of two centuries and include successes at Henley Royal Regatta and even the Olympics. So while we always had the slightly inevitable feeling that we were in the shadows of those who had come before, this was never more true than in the context of the Bumps, where our ambition was always constrained by our start position (which was the previous year's finishing position). To go Head of the River required not just an excellent crew, but in fact a succession of excellent crews over a number of years to be sure that a strong crew would start high enough to challenge for the headship. This continuity added to the pressure felt by competing crews – a bad result was not just a bad result for you but let down the Club's crews in following years, and wasted the hard work of previous years.

Over the last 50 years rowing participation nationally has surged with the consequence that even the best college crews are now unlikely to win at Henley, an event they used to dominate. But while the crews now have more modest targets, the Bumps remain the decisive contest for the top college crews and the highlight of the rowing calendar for everyone taking part.

Left: Neville's Nights, *a Victorian Music Hall cabaret staged in 1948 by David Price and Eric Dix.*

Below: *Trinity Revues of the early 1950s.* Beaumont's Bequests *featured two compositions by the recently departed chaplain, Geoffrey Beaumont and* Just As It Comes *was produced by his successor, Simon Phipps.*

Drama
The Trinity Revue
John Cox (1967)

Although the golden age of professional theatrical revues was in the first half of the 20th century, their legacy is still evident today in the tradition of student revues, most notably those of Cambridge Footlights.

At Trinity in the 1960s this tradition was flourishing in the annual revue of the Dryden Society held in the theatre made from the Old Lecture Rooms between Great Court and Angel Court. I was one of a group of students who responded to an open invitation to prospective scriptwriters. Those of us who turned up with our offerings not only found ourselves signed up as writers but also as performers for the production in February 1969 of *Revulution*, and subsequently a year later with *Quiet Flows the Don*. These were substantially the work of Trinity men, though women studying elsewhere in Cambridge were invited to provide contrasting female talents.

Plans for the traditional revue were therefore set in place – but both productions were to be rather unusual as one of the cast was HRH The Prince of Wales. Over many sessions we produced sketches that inevitably focused in irreverent ways upon College and Cambridge people and events as well as wider concerns. Some of those concerns unavoidably took Prince Charles away from a few rehearsals, but if he did have to attend a state banquet for President Nixon he certainly compensated with a generous provision of costumes and props from the resources of Buckingham Palace.

In 1969 it was only a matter of time before the media became aware of the involvement of Prince Charles, and in the final stages of rehearsal we came under considerable pressure to reveal to the outside world what of course had been only modestly intended for a very different audience. The Lord's Day Observance Society opportunely complained that a Sunday performance should be rescheduled – and it was. The dress rehearsal of the revue in 1970, however, involved an even stronger press interest: in attendance were three television cameras, some dozen or so photographers and the rest of the

Below: Quiet Flows the Don.

Below right: *From* Quiet Flows the Don, *left to right: John Cox, Nick Jenkins, Christian Bailey and HRH Prince of Wales.*

interviewing the latter in a well-branded shiny new dustbin. The photo was widely syndicated and it was considered extremely cutting edge for a prince to imitate a hippy in a shoulder-length wig and Dylan cap.

We enjoyed ourselves immensely and were pleased that friends and family attended – including members of the royal family. Several Fellows also deigned to attend, the Reverend Simpson staying for the entire first half of one performance to fulfil a historian's duty. Some indignantly complained at having to pay, one offering 'one of the ghastly new coins which I understand equals ten shillings'. As ever, we had very appreciative support from Lord and Lady Butler. One College member had complained to Rab about a sketch in which I had impersonated him. Rab said to me: 'I told him that some College members were offended if they *weren't* included in sketches, so he ought to be grateful.'

In addition to Prince Charles, the other cast members were Julian Fellowes, Nigel Guild, Lesley Haines, Nick Jenkins, Hywel Jones, Victoria le Fanu, Tim Landon, Freddie Markham and Ian McDougall, and the imaginative and intrepid co-producers were Christian Bailey and John Parry.

modest audience space was filled with reporters. Rumours that *Paris Match* had made an exclusive block booking of the Blue Boar Hotel may well have been true, as was the spread of a black market for tickets. A company also tried to negotiate flying in a plane full of tourists direct from Japan. One reporter did ask if we rehearsed with Prince Charles; we said that we managed it all by telepathy at a deferential remove.

Prince Charles was a great fan of Spike Milligan and so initiated the sketch where he sat in a dustbin. This was partly inspired by Milligan's 'If you've got no trousers and ragged underpants/Jump into a dustbin and dance', but it was more targeted at the dustmen who crashed about in Trinity Lane waking him before 7am. The *Cambridge Evening News* brought dustman and Prince together with producer John Parry

The 'Annual Dinner' of the Trinity Alpine Club, founded in 1912 to promote climbing on the roofs of Trinity. This dinner was held on top of Queen's Gate, Great Court in November 1912 and the menu included boiled chicken, jam sandwiches and Turkish delight.

NIGHT CLIMBING

What happened to the poet Austin Lee? I have heard nothing from him since I trod on his belly one nice dark summer's night in 1925, on my way from the Essex Building to Great Gate. Presumably he has graduated and become an abominable snowman. What other profession can there be for people who scare the serious night climber by sleeping like giant slugs in the hollows between roof and parapet?

My business that night was simple. As an official of a society called the Amalgamated Union of Presbyterians and Bodysnatchers of Great Britain and Ireland, with headquarters in Trinity, I was guiding a party who wanted to make a tour of the College. This is roof-hiking, but involves one or two pretty bits of work, and I am happy to learn from Whipplesnaith, author of *The Night Climbers of Cambridge* (Chatto & Windus, 7s 6d), that the crucial drainpipe is still as good as new, in spite of the anxiety expressed by the author of *The Roof-Climber's Guide to Trinity* over 30 years ago. *The Night Climbers of Cambridge* is not a guidebook, but it is full of good reliable information, illuminating anecdotes and brilliant flashlight photographs. It does for Cambridge what Conway's *Alps from End to End* did for the Alps, and if Whipplesnaith had no Gurkhas in his retinue, he nevertheless picked up one or two men from Pembroke.

It is important to remember, however, that Cambridge differs in some respects from the Alps. Whipplesnaith quite rightly points out that there are no drainpipes in the Alps, whereas Cambridge without drainpipes is unthinkable. The relative scarcity of snow and ice in Cambridge is another important point of difference, and

Whipplesnaith errs, I think, in not including a chapter on winter climbing. Good winter conditions are rare in Cambridge and the snow is always liable to avalanche, but for those who enjoy the beauties of nature as well as the thrill of achievement there is no finer viewpoint than the roof of Trinity Library on a frosty night.

In general, however, it is true to say that the man who has mastered drainpipe technique and can do a neat foot-and-back up and down a chimney is equal to any problem that Cambridge can set him, provided that he knows the difference between good rock and bad. Whipplesnaith's experience of this matter is invaluable, but if I may revert to my home district for the moment, I would like to add something to his warnings and say that I know of nothing more treacherous than the stucco of New Court, except probably the lower reaches of the southern Aiguille d'Arves.

But Trinity, after all, is not the whole of Cambridge. To borrow a phrase from the poet Aiken, it is like 'the vast ruin where Godhead dwells': it has some sensational climbs that are really quite easy; it has some first-rate stuff that is only perceptible to the experienced eye; it is a magnificent jungle; and it offers excellent facilities for escape from porters. But for good straightforward climbs it has little that can be compared with the Old Library, the Fitzwilliam Museum or the south face of Caius. Whipplesnaith knows all this ground as well as a Chamonix guide knows the Grépon, but his deepest affection is for King's Chapel. It is interesting to note, from his account of the 'Save Ethiopia' climb, that the old alliance between roof-climbing and extreme liberal sentiments still prevails at Cambridge.

Richard Hall (1958) and *Phil Sykes (1958)* write: *We suppose that if we now own up to embellishing the chair leg, our endeavour on a dark and stormy night, sometime in 1960–1, will go unpunished. Mr Sykes and I hesitate to be counted as 'Cambridge Night Climbers'. Our escapade was carried out at night, but the only climbing involved was the ascent of a long ladder cheekily borrowed from a nearby building site! However, we do think that the end result, while not in the first division of night climbing outcomes, was rather pleasing; as was the fact that the foramen magnum at the base of the skull was a very neat fit to the top of Henry's chair leg.*

It is seldom, however, that the serious climber allows ulterior motives to influence his action. He has no thirst for notoriety and no desire to enhance the reputation of his college or his political party by an act of exhibitionism. 'Very quiet gentlemen, sir, they never disturb us if they can help it.' The serious roof-climber eschews banners and jerries as the serious alpinist eschews pitons. These easy roads to notoriety are all very well in Oxford, and among German climbers, but they have no place in Cambridge. Whipplesnaith's moral principles – no damage to buildings, no unnecessary intrusion on residents, no personal violence to bobbies, or even to porters – shows that the sport is developing on sound lines.

Whipplesnaith is, indeed, one of the finest products of Cambridge of recent years; he has just the right mixture of dash and prudence, he keeps off the drink at the right time, he has useful friends in the Force, and he is a man of wide interests. He keeps an eye on the things of general importance and his discovery that the dome of the Fitzwilliam is an iron dummy deserves some public recognition. His interest in the folklore and anthropology of the country he explores is genuine and acute. He tells how, in the old heroic days, the Master of Pembroke was feeding with his Fellows one day when the meat course was brought in. 'With a resounding "What, hash again!" the Master brought his spoon down heavily, causing the present breach in the walls.' Of this college in general he says: 'Its stone is good, its climbs legion, and we can thoroughly recommend any night climber to pay a few visits to it. Its hospitality is lavish and sincere, and it breeds those strong, silent Englishmen who suck pipes in the Malayan jungle but do not pass exams.'

Finally, with admirable insight and good taste, Whipplesnaith makes his apology for the sport. He might have said that its moral value is incalculable; like rugger, it does this, that and the other; it strengthens something and intensifies something else; it expresses the nature of the world, the struggle between disinterested moral virtue and the purely prudential values of society, etc., etc. But instead of this he merely talks about its use in giving a nervous man a job he can do and enjoy doing.

Michael Roberts (1922)

(First published in Night and Day *(eds Graham Greene and John Marks) 4 November 1937, as a review of Whipplesnaith,* The Night Climbers of Cambridge *(1937).)*

Michael Roberts (1902–48) matriculated in 1922 as W.E. Roberts. At Trinity, where he read mathematics, he adopted the first name of Mikhail Lomonosov, the 18th-century Russian scientist and poet. By 1937, the date of the above review, he was sixth-form master at the Royal Grammar School, Newcastle upon Tyne, and had been elected to the Alpine Club. From 1941 to 1945 he worked in the BBC European Service; he then became principal of a teacher-training college in Chelsea. A selection of his writings, edited by F. Grubb (Trinity, 1951), was published in 1980.

The Dean of College wishes it to be known that, while a previous Master of the College, Lord Adrian (Trinity 1908, Nobel Prize for Neurophysiology 1932, Master 1951–65), was known for his skill in roof-climbing, to climb on College property today is not permitted and is subject to terrifying sanctions. The Dean will, however, on request, be pleased to demonstrate that perfect exercise for mind and body, demanding balletic skill and co-ordination, and no more than 12 inches above ground: The 'Nevile's Court Girdle Traverse', originally described in Geoffrey Winthrop Young's anonymously authored The Roof-Climber's Guide to Trinity *(c. 1900).*

On my arrival at the College on my first day, I found my rooms in Angel Court.

Among the mail waiting for me there was the following invitation: '*You are cordially invited to join the Trinity Goat Climbers Club. We meet every Wednesday at 4pm on the roofs of the Chapel. Access can easily be arranged through the windows of A staircase Great Court.* [I forget the exact directions.] *We look forward to welcoming you as a member.*'

Charles Bromley (1977)

CHAPTER 12

Trinity and the Biomedical Sciences

ALAN WEEDS *(1975)*

Trinity is proud to record 27 Nobel prizewinners in the sciences among its members. Eleven of these are in physiology/medicine or biological areas of chemistry and they form the majority of the College's science prizewinners since the first was awarded to A.V. Hill in 1922. Trinity was instrumental in establishing biomedical sciences in Cambridge and key roles were played by a number of our Nobel Laureates. The foundations of the Medical Research Council and the Wellcome Trust, the two principal funding bodies for biomedical research today, owe much to the vision of some of those described here.

How physiology came to Cambridge

The term 'scientist' was first used in 1833 by William Whewell. Whewell, who was successively Professor of Mineralogy and Professor of Moral Philosophy, played a major role in establishing both the natural and moral sciences Triposes in 1848, during his 25-year tenure as Master of the College. Physiology as a subject in Cambridge had its origins in 1870 with the appointment of Michael Foster as Praelector in Trinity. Foster was born in Huntingdon in 1836, eldest son of a local surgeon with strongly nonconformist views. He was educated to the age of 13 at Huntingdon Grammar School, then at University College School in London. Precluded entrance to Cambridge because of his inability to subscribe to the 39 Articles of Religion as required by the Test Act (not repealed until 1871), he entered University College at 16, graduating top in classics at 18. He then switched to medicine and won gold medals in anatomy, physiology and

Below left: *Frontispiece of* Sylva Sylvarum, *Francis Bacon, 1627.*

Below right: *Michael Foster.*

chemistry and graduated MD in 1859 at the age of 23, with T.H. Huxley ('Darwin's bulldog') as one of his examiners. Huxley continued to be a major influence on Foster's career and scientific philosophy. After a period as a ship's surgeon and in his father's practice, he accepted a teaching appointment in physiology in London in 1867 and succeeded Huxley as Fullerian Professor of Physiology at the Royal Institution in 1869. His maxim, following that of Huxley, was 'if scientific training is to yield its most eminent results, it must be practical'. At the same time Trinity created the post of Praelector in Physiology in response to pressure from Rev. Coutts Trotter, lecturer in physical science at Trinity, who had a special interest in physiology as a result of working with Helmholtz in Heidelberg. With the support of Huxley and (probably) also of the novelist George Eliot, Foster was offered the post, thereby enabling him to enter the University without compromising his nonconformist principles. Trinity provided a generous grant of £400 for equipping his laboratory – a considerable sum, equivalent to about £36,000 today, but at nearly 1 per cent of the College's external revenue in 1870, a very substantial sum. Practical classes were at the heart of his teaching, and he greatly encouraged research.

Foster's own research interests from very early on were in muscle activity, particularly the rhythmical contractions of heart muscle, but his distinction was in his teaching and scientific leadership, not his own research. His enthusiasm attracted students throughout the University: numbers increased from 22 in 1870 to 130 in 1883, when he was appointed the first Professor of Physiology in the University. Cambridge had become the destination of choice for ambitious medical students and researchers; pupils of his, including a number from Trinity, went on to become professors in physiology, pathology, chemistry, zoology and animal morphology. His *Textbook of Physiology* with its strong emphasis on experimental evidence set new standards, and he founded both the Physiological Society and the *Journal of Physiology*. Elected FRS in 1872, he served as Secretary of the Royal Society for 22 years from 1881 in succession to T.H. Huxley and was MP for London University as a Liberal Unionist for six years from 1900, speaking authoritatively on scientific matters. His advocacy was central to the establishment of the School of Agriculture in Cambridge and the Marine Biological Laboratory in Plymouth (where Hodgkin and Huxley were later to do their pioneering work on nerve conduction).

Foster served on a number of Royal Commissions dealing with medical problems and was awarded a KCB in 1899. One of these had far-reaching consequences. As Chairman of a Royal Commission appointed in 1901 to enquire into the relations of human and animal tuberculosis, he determined that the Commission should not rely on the opinion of 'experts', but conduct experimental investigations of its own. This Commission can be seen as the precursor to the Medical Research Committee established under the National Insurance Act in 1911. The Committee first met in June 1913 and Walter Morley Fletcher (Fellow and Tutor in Trinity and one of Foster's students) served as its first Secretary from 1914 until his death in 1933. Fletcher was determined that the Committee should serve the needs of the country in medical research, but equally that it should be freed from political influence. Under the Ministry of Health Act of 1919 the Committee was brought under the Privy Council to maintain its independence and incorporated by Royal Charter in 1920 under the name Medical Research Council (MRC). From the beginning, the MRC was to be in close contact with the Royal Society with the then President (Sir J.J. Thompson, Master of Trinity) having to approve membership of the Council.

The MRC today has a research budget of over £700 million per annum and is best known for the Laboratory of Molecular Biology (LMB) established in 1962, under the Chairmanship of Max Perutz and with John Kendrew (Major Scholar and later Honorary Fellow of Trinity) as Vice-Chairman. Perutz and Kendrew shared the Nobel Prize for Chemistry in 1962 for solving the three-dimensional structures of haemoglobin and myoglobin, the oxygen-transporting proteins in blood and muscle – the first proteins for which X-ray structures were determined. Later Trinity members who won Nobel Prizes at the LMB were Sir Aaron Klug in 1982 and Venkatraman Ramakrishnan in 2009, both for ultrastructural work, largely X-ray analysis of macromolecular structures, in Klug's case, viruses and in Ramakrishnan's the ribosome. It should be remembered that X-ray crystallography was first developed by Henry and Lawrence Bragg (Trinity Nobel Prize winners in Physics) and that Lawrence Bragg, as Cavendish Professor of Physics, had been instrumental in securing the support of

the MRC to set up a protein X-ray crystallographic unit at the Cavendish, under the heading of biophysics. This occurred at a time when there was no evidence that it would ever be possible to determine protein structures by this means because of their size and complexity. The unit was renamed the Unit of Molecular Biology in 1947 and became the LMB in 1962 when it moved to the Addenbrooke's site.

Foster retired from his Chair in 1903 and was succeeded by his student, John Langley (also a Fellow of Trinity). Foster's chief recreation was gardening; he produced a number of new and attractive hybrids, notably of irises, and wrote over 20 papers on horticulture over the later part of his life. He died on 28 January 1907 and at his memorial service in Trinity another of his former Trinity students, Walter Gaskell, said of him: 'There have been many greater scientific men than Foster. It is hardly too much to say that no man ever devoted himself more whole-heartedly to science, and that if science can be served by strengthening the influence and promoting the spread of the scientific spirit, few have done it better service.' One of Foster's greatest services to the University was to invite Frederick Gowland Hopkins to come to Cambridge in 1898 to develop teaching and research in the chemical aspects of physiology – to found biochemistry – and in this, too, Trinity played a critically important role.

Biochemistry in Cambridge

Hopkins ('Hoppy' as he was later affectionately known) was born in Eastbourne in 1861. According to family tradition, his great-grandfather had commanded a ship at Trafalgar. His father's death in his early infancy meant that he had a lonely childhood, but he found solace in reading Dickens before the age of ten and was later allowed limited use of his father's telescope and microscope which stimulated his scientific curiosity. The family moved to London in 1871 where he excelled in chemistry at the City of London School, but found the teaching so uninspiring that at the age of 14 he was expelled for truancy – not an auspicious start to an academic career! At 17 he was articled to a consulting chemist and for three years worked from 9am to 6pm without remuneration or formal instruction – an experience he understandably found both unsatisfactory and unpleasant.

'Hoppy' in Great Court, November 1943.

Although he was advised to go to Cambridge, with a small legacy from his grandfather he studied chemistry at the Royal School of Mines, but when the course stopped after six months he moved to University College, where his success brought him to the notice of Dr Thomas Stevenson, a distinguished forensic analyst. Stevenson offered him a five-year appointment as an assistant in 1883 while he continued working for his BSc at University College in his spare time. In 1888 he began medical studies at Guy's Hospital and was gold medallist in chemistry in his intermediate MB, qualifying in 1894 at the advanced age of 33. He was encouraged to do research and in 1893 published a method to determine the uric acid content in urine (uric acid is the causative agent of gout). From an early age he had been interested in natural history and was fascinated by the colour pigments in butterfly wings. He speculated that these might be related to uric acid, based on similarities in crystallisation and response to key chemical tests. Further purification led to the identification of compounds we now call pterins; Hopkins's interest in these substances stayed with him and his last paper,

published in 1942 in his 82nd year related their structures to his earlier work. Although his training had been unusually demanding and tortuous, his expertise as a chemical analyst, in combination with his clinical knowledge and experience in forensic medicine gave him the ideal foundation for the work on which he was about to embark.

The turning point for Hopkins and for Cambridge came in 1898 at a meeting of the Physiological Society, when Michael Foster overtook him after dinner outside Christ's College and invited him to develop teaching and research in biochemistry. Biochemistry as a subject did not exist under that name but over the next 20 years he was to establish it as a discipline not just in Cambridge but in Britain and beyond. His lectureship carried no Fellowship, and to supplement his £200 annual stipend he supervised medical students at Emmanuel College, while in addition preparing lectures for Part II courses, very challenging for someone with no previous teaching experience. In 1902 he was made Reader in Chemical Physiology with financial support from Emmanuel, but the College added to his burdens by making him Science Tutor in 1906. With all these demands, he had little time for research, but things reached a critical stage when he violently banged his head against the spiral iron staircase in the old Physiological Laboratory, which led to a breakdown and he left Cambridge for Switzerland to recover. It was while he was recuperating there that he heard that Walter Fletcher, his close collaborator and tutor at Trinity, had persuaded the College to offer him an appointment as Fellow and Praelector in Biochemistry, a post that provided sufficient income but involved no duties beyond his own research. He retained his Readership (together with an honorary Fellowship by Emmanuel) and four years later became the first Professor of Biochemistry in Cambridge, though his income was still largely derived from his Trinity Praelectorship.

Hopkins's researches provided the foundations in several areas of modern biochemistry. He had started working on proteins in London, crystallising albumins from blood serum and egg-white (published in 1898). In 1901 he identified the amino acid tryptophan, as a result of anomalous experimental results using a conventional colour test. As a clinician he had long felt that nutritional deficiency was underrated as a cause of disease, even though it was well known that an essential dietary component in citrus fruit prevented scurvy. He showed that addition of tryptophan to the maize protein zein (a protein that lacks tryptophan) promoted the lives of young rats which did not survive on zein alone. This led to the identification of other essential amino acids and intensified his search for other essential accessory factors – factors that were to become known as vitamins. Between 1906 and 1912 he carried out meticulous experiments to confirm the presence of such factors. He found that milk contains a substance that made all the difference between life and death for rats fed on a purified synthetic diet – even half a teaspoonful a day was sufficient. What marked out his experiments was their quantitative nature and the very strict protocols used, so that only one condition at a time was investigated. He identified essential fat soluble substances – vitamins A and D as we now know them. Hopkins was awarded the Nobel Prize in Medicine in 1929.

Notwithstanding the Nobel Prize, Hopkins never regarded this as his best work. Rather, he was fascinated to unravel

the metabolic changes that provide the energy for muscle contraction, what Foster had earlier called the 'steps taken by oxygen from the moment it slips from the blood to the moment when it issues united with carbon as carbon dioxide (in carbonic acid)', part of what we now call intermediary metabolism. Earlier theory supposed that the oxygen and other substances built up into a giant unstable protoplasmic molecule, ready to break down on stimulus to provide the energy for contraction and that carbon dioxide production was independent of oxygen supply. Fletcher had introduced Hopkins to muscle physiology and they collaborated on lactic acid and carbon dioxide production in frog muscle. By 1907 they had shown a clear connection between muscle contraction and lactic acid production under anaerobic conditions, work they presented in their Croonian Lecture at the Royal Society in 1915. Their collaboration was ended by Fletcher's appointment as Secretary of the MRC in 1914, and during the war Hopkins was actively engaged with the Royal Society's wartime food committee. But their joint research laid the foundation for later work on muscle, notably by A.V. Hill (Trinity Nobel Prize winner in 1922) and founding father of biophysics. (A report in 1937 had suggested the founding of 'a Cavendish Laboratory for biologists and doctors' as a memorial to Rutherford. In 1944 Hill, as Biological Secretary of the Royal Society and Member of Parliament for Cambridge University, sent a further report on the need for an Institute of Biophysics to the Secretary of the MRC. The outcome as already described was the MRC X-ray crystallographic unit.)

After the war biochemistry achieved recognition as a separate subject for Part II of the natural sciences Tripos, but the defining moment for the Department came in 1923–4 when, in response to Walter Fletcher's recommendation, the trustees of the estate of Sir William Dunn, wishing to provide for 'the relief of human suffering', endowed a special chair and provided £200,000 for an Institute for Biochemistry, opened by Lord Balfour, Chancellor of the University and Chairman of the MRC. The new building provided for considerable expansion of the Department, with sub-departments of enzyme biochemistry, the MRC nutritional science laboratory, MRC microbiological unit and a protein

Henry Hallett Dale (left) and his Nobel Prize awarded in 1936.

chemistry group, where Fred Sanger later did his pioneering work on the chemical sequence of insulin.

Inevitably Hopkins was drawn away from Cambridge – he became a member of the first Medical Research Committee in 1913, and was responsible for setting up the Biochemistry Division at the National Institute for Medical Research. Awarded the Royal Medal of the Royal Society in 1918 and the Copley Medal in 1926, he became the Society's President in 1931 and was awarded the OM in 1935, his final year as PRS.

Hopkins continued as Sir William Dunn Professor of Biochemistry until 1943, though failing health restricted his laboratory work. His direct pupils subsequently held over 100 chairs throughout the world and included some 30 Fellows in the Royal Society and four Nobel Laureates (including another Trinity student, R.L.M. Synge, whose prize was awarded for his pioneering methods in chromatography). At a personal level he was a great believer in people and a man of extraordinary charm and goodwill. Joseph Needham (for many years the Sir William Dunn Reader) assessed his outstanding intellectual characteristic as a 'deep intuitive faith in the explicability of the biochemistry of the living cell'; the relentless advance of biochemical and molecular biological research since his death in 1947 has more than vindicated this faith.

The origins of neuropharmacology

The founding father of neuropharmacology was another of Foster's students, Henry Hallett Dale. Dale also played an important role in establishing pharmacology in the MRC and guiding and directing the work of the Wellcome Trust as a major funding charity for biomedical research. Born in 1875, he entered Trinity from the Leys School, where he had been encouraged to read Foster's textbook and introduced to Part II topics in physiology (though he later wished he had been grounded more firmly in physics and maths). Graduating first class in physiology in 1897, he spent the next two years as a Coutts-Trotter student, working on neurophysiology with J.N. Langley. Having qualified in medicine at St Bartholomew's Hospital in 1902 he started research at University College London, but two years later Henry Wellcome invited him to set up a research laboratory in physiology at the Wellcome Research Laboratories. Such was Wellcome's confidence in him that he was promoted to Acting Director within 18 months and soon thereafter to the Directorship, at a salary of £1,000 per year, almost twice that of a Cambridge Professor at the time! Wellcome encouraged him to work on the pharmacology of ergot, a naturally occurring fungus of rye which was then used to stop maternal bleeding after childbirth. He isolated a number of pharmacologically active constituents from ergot, including tyramine, histamine and, in 1914, acetyl choline, the first neurotransmitter to be identified. He also identified a compound (ergotoxine) which inhibited the natural action of adrenaline – a forerunner of the modern beta-blocker drugs. This work formed the foundation of much of his later work on the physiological roles of a wide range of neurotransmitters.

With the establishment of the National Institute for Medical Research, Dale was encouraged by Hopkins to become Director of the Department of Biochemistry and Pharmacology. Reluctant at first to take the post, news that Walter Fletcher, one of his tutors at Trinity, was to become the First Secretary of the Medical Research Committee prompted his immediate acceptance and he was appointed from July 1914. Dale spent the war on medically related projects, including amoebic dysentery and 'wound shock', a condition in which men with no evidence of sepsis suffered depression of vitality and circulatory failure, often leading to death. This reminded him of the vasodilating effects of histamine in anaphylactic shock, where the heart receives too little blood due to increased permeability in blood-vessel walls. His suggestion that this might be remedied by transfusion of blood or plasma became standard treatment and saved many lives.

After the war Dale was influential in the changes of governance needed to ensure the independence of the MRC: making the MRC accountable to the Lord President of the Council rather than the Ministry of Health ensured that it had the greatest degree of liberty to develop its own policy. Although the youngest of the Divisional Directors at the National Institute, he was soon appointed Chairman of the Directors, and in 1928 Director of the Institute, a post he held until his retirement in 1942.

With the discovery of insulin in 1921, it was important to have standards by which biological activity of hormones and other substances in tissue extracts could be evaluated. Most compounds were tested on mice, but were these tests relevant to the treatment of humans? Dale was instrumental in establishing international standards for a number of hormones and drugs from what he later described as 'the chaos which threatened them'.

Dale continued his earlier research on acetyl choline. Following his isolation of acetyl choline from animal tissues in 1929, he carried out some of the finest pharmacological studies ever, research that became the 'gold standard' for the analysis of drugs. His discovery of cholinesterase in blood and tissues, the enzyme that hydrolyses acetyl choline, explained the rapid destruction of acetyl choline and hence the evanescent nature of the signal. Although the concept of cellular receptors went back to Ehrlich's much earlier work on toxins and antibodies, the idea of a chemical intermediary in nerve transmission was against the views of electrophysiologists. His discovery of the role of acetyl choline as the neuromuscular transmitter in striated muscle was regarded by some electrophysiologists as 'pharmacological interference'! At that time nerves were classified on the basis of their anatomic origin and not in any functional way. Dale coined the terms 'cholinergic' and 'adrenergic' to distinguish them on the basis of their chemical neurotransmitter, acetyl choline or a substance like adrenaline (now known to be noradrenaline). For his pioneering research on the chemical transmission of the effects of nerve impulses, he was awarded the Nobel Prize in 1936.

Dale was a great wartime President of the Royal Society from 1940 to 1945 and the first to appoint women Fellows of the Society. In 1936 he was to his surprise appointed one of five Trustees to administer the Trust set up on Sir Henry Wellcome's death. He became Chairman of the Trust in 1938 and worked unstintingly in that role until his 85th birthday in 1960, then as scientific advisor to the age of 90, though he continued to give the Trust his advice until the week before he died in 1968. He was largely responsible for its policy of grant-giving to universities and research institutes, with an income of £1.8 million in 1993. Today the Wellcome Trust provides in excess of £600 million a year to fund medical research. Knighted in 1932, Dale received many honours in his lifetime, but the award of the OM in 1944 was to him the most gratifying.

Trinity's neurophysiologists and how the nervous system works
Foster's successor as Professor of Physiology in 1903, John Langley (elected Fellow in 1877), investigated the nervous influence exerted on gland cells and did much to establish the physiology of the autonomic nervous system. His work on adrenaline in 1907 suggested the presence of a receptive

substance and presaged the later work of Dale described above. Keith Lucas (scholar in classics 1898 and Fellow in Physiology 1904) was a brilliantly inventive experimentalist and instrument designer. By the early part of the 20th century it was known that the strength of a twitch in a muscle varied with the strength of the electric shock applied to the nerve, but in 1909 using a very small frog muscle that was controlled by a nerve containing only about nine nerve fibres, he showed that this increase occurred in a stepwise manner dependent on the number of fibres present, each acting in an 'all-or none' manner. This key finding was taken further in the work of his most distinguished student, Edgar Adrian (later Lord Adrian). Lucas tragically died in a plane crash in 1916 while working in the Royal Flying Corps, and in his Nobel Lecture in 1932 Adrian wrote of him:

'I have tried to follow the lines which Keith Lucas would have developed if he had lived and am happy to think that in honouring me with the Nobel Prize you have honoured the master as well as the pupil.' Until the work of Lucas and Adrian, ideas about nerve activation were muddled, with conflicting evidence and no accepted principles.

Adrian entered Trinity as a Major Scholar in 1908. In Part I he studied five subjects, not the usual four: physics, chemistry, anatomy, physiology and botany, gaining a First in each; according to Fletcher, his tutor, he obtained 30 per cent more marks than the highest marks in recent memory! He started research with Lucas in 1911 and within two years was elected to a fesearch fellowship. With the exception of his 14 years as Master, he remained a Fellow of the College for the rest of his life. With

E.A. Adrian in Nevile's Court cloisters, 1974. Photograph by Peter Goldberg.

Sir Andrew
Huxley, Master
of Trinity from
1984 to 1990,
in immediate
succession to Sir
Alan Hodgkin,
with whom
he shared the
Nobel Prize in
Physiology or
Medicine in
1963.

sensory area devoted to touch is given to fibres from the snout. For his work in developing understanding of the sensory nervous system as a whole and how individual nerve cells function, he was awarded the Nobel Prize in Physiology in 1932. Like many physiologists, he used himself as the experimental animal: these demonstrations were used to great effect in his lectures! He devised methods to analyse the gross electrical activity of the brain, rhythms discovered by Berger: this work opened the way to electroencephalography (EEG), invaluable for the diagnosis of various kinds of neurological disorders. This work must have taken him back to those harrowing experiences of working with patients in the First World War, and in later life the brain and the mind became his dominant interests.

Excessively modest about his own research achievements, he wrote of himself: 'Looking back on my scientific work I should say that it shows no great originality but a certain amount of business instinct which lead to the selection profitable line.' His skill in dissection, his use of pioneering techniques, the breadth of the systems he studied and the highly imaginative and original nature of his work testify somewhat differently.

Adrian was President of the Royal Society from 1950 to 1955 and Master of Trinity from 1951 to 1965. His speeches as Master are still regarded as exemplars. Following the award of the OM in 1942, he was created one of the last hereditary peers as Baron Adrian of Cambridge in 1955 and attended the House regularly, speaking on issues of scientific importance. In 1957, at the age of 68, he became Vice Chancellor of the University and its Chancellor in 1968 at the age of 78, serving until after his 85th birthday, just two years before his death.

The story of Trinity's contribution to the physiology of the nervous system would not be complete without a description of the work of Adrian's most outstanding student, Alan Hodgkin, and his student, Andrew Huxley. Hodgkin entered Trinity as a scholar in 1932. Although he specialised in physiology and commenced research as a Part II student, his Director of Studies, Carl Pantin, encouraged him to learn as much mathematics and physics as possible. Following Lucas, Adrian and others, he studied nerve conduction, building (and paying for!) his own equipment, and in 1936 was elected to a

the advent of war in 1914, everything changed. Adrian completed his medical training and worked on nerve injuries and shell shock, the horrors of which were to stay with him and influence him throughout his life.

Returning to Cambridge in 1919 as college lecturer and university demonstrator he pioneered understanding of the sensory nervous system. He was very skilled at dissection and, using valve amplifiers in conjunction with capillary electrometers had fabricated, he was the first to record signals from single fibres. He analysed the action potentials (electrical signals) generated by stretch receptors in muscle or receptors responding to touch, pressure on the skin or pain (e.g. pricking the skin with a needle) and showed how different receptors differ in the way they respond to a constant stimulus. Some responses diminish rapidly, others slowly or remain almost steady. Later studies focused on other sensory systems including hearing, vision and smell. He showed that the part of the brain devoted to a particular kind of sensory organ is related to the special needs of the animal: thus the area of the brain devoted to the face and hands in man is large, while in the pig, almost all the

Gouache drawing of a squid from the Hodgkin papers, inscribed 'Plymouth Sep 1947', together with a photograph of Alan Hodgkin working on squid axons.

100mV giving an overshoot of 40–50mV – a very unexpected result. Within three weeks the work was prematurely stopped by Hitler's invasion of Poland.

Hodgkin's war work was on the development of airborne radar to detect target aircraft, using the cavity magnetron developed by John Randall. He devised a new scanning display to help separate the echoes from targets from ground echoes and later, in 1942, was in charge of research on a radar system to defend night bombers against fighter attack, whereby using a cathode ray tube, the position of the fighter could be visualised and fed directly to the range finder of the machine guns – he showed that the guns could be trained to within an accuracy of 0.5 degrees. This system was later adopted for use by anti-aircraft guns against V1 bombers.

Huxley rejoined Hodgkin in 1946 to continue their work on the overshoot. Knowing that there were differences in permeability of membranes to potassium and sodium ions, they theorised that the overshoot might be explained by uptake of sodium ions from the seawater, due to increased membrane permeability to sodium. Using crab fibres Hodgkin found that the action potential was rapidly and reversibly abolished in sodium-free solutions and its magnitude was related to the external sodium concentration. To understand the relationship between the electrical measurements and membrane conductivity, Hodgkin and Huxley designed electrodes with two fine wires inserted, one to measure the voltage and the other to deliver the current necessary to maintain the voltage using a feedback amplifier – a system that became known as a 'voltage clamp'. By varying the voltage changes under different ionic conditions in the bathing fluid, they monitored changes in conductivity of the membrane to sodium and potassium ions. The key experiments were carried out using squid axons over a few weeks in Plymouth in 1949, but the analysis and writing took two years – there were no computers and the mathematical calculations of the complex exponentials were done by Andrew Huxley using a mechanical hand calculator! Their theory – the Hodgkin–Huxley equations – suggested the existence of three processes governed by membrane potential changes: the first opened channels for sodium ions; the second, slower one, in series with the first, closed and inactivated the sodium channels; while the third opened channels

Fellowship after one year (still a record). At Adrian's suggestion, he started work on crab nerves, their much larger fibres (about 0.03mm diameter) making them easier to dissect, and was able to measure responses along the surface of the fibres. Bernstein had put forward the 'membrane theory of nerve conduction' in 1902 whereby the electrical potential changes in nerves might be explained by changes in the permeability of cell membranes to sodium and potassium ions. Hodgkin tested this by lowering the salt concentration of the seawater surrounding the fibres and found that the speed of the action potential along the nerve was reduced, reflecting the lower electrical conductivity of the solution. In 1939, using giant axons from squid (fibres up to 1mm diameter), Hodgkin and Huxley measured action potentials between the inside and outside of fibres by inserting a fine glass capillary electrode directly into the fibres. Before stimulation, the membrane potential was about 50mV negative, as expected, but when stimulated, the potential rose by nearly

Photograph of a squid nerve axon with diagram, from the Hodgkin papers.

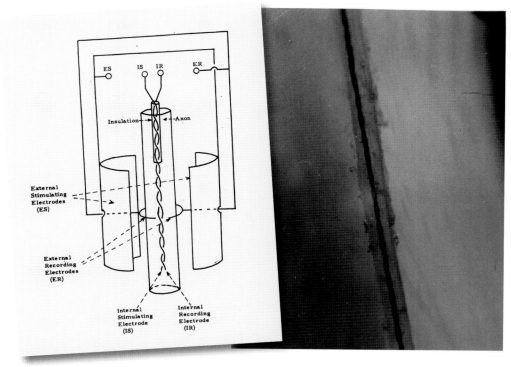

for potassium ions. Confirmation of their results came from the use of radioactive tracers to monitor the changes in ion concentrations directly. The work, published in five papers in 1952, led to their being awarded the Nobel Prize in 1963.

In 1962 Hodgkin started work on vision, measuring electrical changes induced by light flashes using eyes from horseshoe crabs. He later worked on vertebrate retina to establish the mechanisms of activation of rods and cones and particularly the role of calcium in modulating the response. In Huxley's Royal Society biography of Hodgkin, he emphasises Hodgkin's remarkable ability to recognise important problems, combined with his skills both as an experimentalist and in electronics together with his exceptional fluency in mathematics, which enabled him to tackle problems quantitatively.

Awarded the Copley medal of the Royal Society in 1965, Hodgkin served as President of the Society from 1970 to 1975. In 1972 he was made KBE and was awarded the OM the following year. He became Master of Trinity in succession to Lord Butler in 1978, the year that the College admitted women as undergraduates. Alan and Marni were greatly respected for their devotion to the College and particularly for the way they entertained junior members. He was a very modest man, with many interests outside science, notably literature, art and travel. It was tragic that as a result of an operation in 1989 to relieve pressure on the spinal cord from one of the disks in his neck, he was no longer able to walk and he had to rely on a wheelchair for the last nine years of his life. Fellows saw much less of him than they would have wished in the final years of his life.

Trinity has continued to dominate physiology in Cambridge to this day. Huxley's research on muscle contraction by interference light microscopy led to the sliding filament hypothesis (proposed independently by his unrelated namesake, Hugh Huxley, in 1954) and over the next two decades he carried out a detailed kinetic analysis of the mechanical properties of single muscle fibres to establish the way in which myosin cross-bridges produced force between the thick and thin filaments of muscle fibres to try to establish the way in which myosin cross-bridges produce force between the thick and thin filaments of muscle. Huxley served as President of the Royal Society from 1980 to 1985 and as Master of Trinity in succession to Hodgkin from 1984 to 1990. He is one of the four current Fellows who holds the Nobel Prize, two of whom are biologists, and there are two Nobel Prize winners in biological subjects among our honorary Fellows (Sir Aaron Klug and Walter Gilbert, of Harvard University). Biological sciences continue to flourish throughout the Fellowship. Twenty-three of our current 179 Fellows are biologists, 13 of whom are Fellows of the Royal Society, and the College continues to attract very bright students in biological sciences at both undergraduate and graduate levels.

At interview in the College in March 1955 I was offered a place conditional on suitable science A level grades. By the time my place was confirmed there were no rooms available in College so I had to obtain accommodation in the town. I was billetted at 35 Jesus Lane. My landlord/landlady reluctantly agreed to this, having already given the College notice that they wished to retire.

In mid-March 1956 I experienced an event that was to have a profound impact on my medical career for the rest of my life. It was not part of the structured undergraduate curriculum nor was it expected. My landlord, then in his mid-70s, suddenly one midweek afternoon developed bad chest pains, his GP was summoned and diagnosed a severe heart attack. The doctor administered an injection of morphine for his patient's pain, told us that the prognosis was poor but also that he did not feel it justified to try and find him a bed in Addenbrooke's hospital. The landlady and I sat up with him the whole evening until his groaning ceased and he slipped into an uneasy restless sleep. Finally his laboured breathing quietened and then he just drifted into unconsciousness until we realised, about 2am, he had stopped breathing and had changed colour. I had never seen death as such at close hand before but I had been dissecting human corpses for some months as part of the anatomy teaching. I was certain he had died and told my landlady so. Neither of us knew what we were supposed to do but I imagined that medical input was required. There was no telephone in the house so I hunted the streets of Cambridge until I located a working public telephone box and negotiated the technology of the day (remember buttons 'A' and 'B'?) to place a call to the doctor's number. A very sleepy voice enquired of my purpose but when I explained the circumstances the doctor was roused to wrathful wakefulness. He wasted no time in telling me in no uncertain language that my call was inappropriate and should not have happened. He had told us some hours before that this was the likely outcome and I should therefore have waited till the morning before contacting him. He had no patience with the uncertainties of an 18-year-old with no knowledge of 'correct procedure'. I have many times in my subsequent career had to be involved in a patient's terminal illness but I have always made it plain to worried relatives that if they felt they needed to contact me at such a time I would be available and would, at the very least, speak gently with them.

Anthony Peter Joseph (1955)

ACADEMIC LIFE AS A NATURAL SCIENCES UNDERGRADUATE MEANT cycling to the Old Cavendish site or to Lensfield Road for chemistry lectures. We used to say that the lecture content went from the lecturer's notes to ours without disturbing the brain of either. One day my supervision partner and I had an evening chemistry supervision in Trinity and we were asked the reasonable question: 'What did the lecturer cover in this morning's session?' Sadly neither of us could remember.

During my second year I read Anthony Sampson's book *The Anatomy of Britain* and this opened my eyes to a wider world beyond the test tube. I therefore decided to move from natural sciences to management studies. As Cambridge still rather looked down on trade (it had recently rejected the offer by Harold Wilson of a new business school in parallel to the ones established in the 1960s in London and Manchester) this subject was tucked away as Group F of the engineering Tripos. I did however learn about organisational theory and such areas as scheduling and queuing.

Eventually this decision came full circle and I was able to become the instigator of the Judge Business School.

My third year was spent in N1 Great Court with its marvellous view across to the Chapel. Social life was varied although with girls only being 10 per cent of the student population it was also somewhat limited despite the 5.10pm Friday train from Liverpool Street, which became known as the passion wagon. Dining in Hall was still a frequent requirement, with Queen Anne's motto under the Coat of Arms of *Semper Eadem* being interpreted by the undergraduates as referring to the food: Always The Same. Most weekday evenings after Hall we would have coffee or something stronger in a friend's room in Trinity. Conversation would range from sorting out the problems of the world and discussing major philosophical issues to scandal-mongering about our superiors or hearing about the latest prank. We would mix not only with other scientists and mathematicians but also with classicists who would suggest other mottoes such as *Semper Ubi Unter Ubi*: Always Where Under Where. Occasionally we would even be invited into a don's room after Hall and I especially remember one whose answer to many of the issues most perplexing us was: 'We just don't know.'

There were official Trinity occasions such as having tea with the Master, 'Rab' Butler. He was very congenial and showed us his collection of political cartoons about himself which used to adorn a staircase in the Master's Lodge. His wife Mollie told us about the surprise finding in the basement of a whole cache of family silver which had been left there by Rab's great-uncle Henry Montagu Butler who was Master from 1886 to 1918. Rab also gave me my first lesson in after-dinner speaking when he told us at our Matriculation Dinner that he had learned that such speeches 'should be like a lady's dress: short enough to be interesting but long enough to cover the essentials'.

I still return to Trinity as my son has gone back there to do his PhD with Rolls-Royce in aeronautical engineering and I serve on the Finance Committee and the Alumni Committee. It remains such a vibrant community of excellence and I always feel welcome. Although some things have changed, including the food, in its essentials it is still *Semper Eadem*.

Paul Judge (1968)

CHAPTER 13

The Wren Library

DAVID MCKITTERICK *(1986)*

The middle of the Lent term. The middle of the academic year. To the right as you enter the Library the reading room sprawls with students preoccupied with term-time demands. To the left, and a little further up the stairs, is the Wren Library, with its readers from all over the world in search of manuscripts, archives and early printed books.

It has not always been thus. The reading room was built in the 1890s, and it was extended and improved 100 years later, when a large adjacent underground bookstore was excavated. The Wren Library was finished in 1695 – about 200 years before the reading room.

Nor will it always be thus. The wiring of all parts of the Library for computer access is but one aspect of immense changes that are taking place in the delivery of knowledge, education and research, of how we manage them and how we communicate with each other. Books – past ones as well as those yet to be published – will always be necessary. They are uniquely efficient ways of organising thought, and as artefacts they are irreplaceable evidence of authors and readers alike. But they will be complemented with more ambitious developments at which we can little more than guess.

When the Wren Library was conceived, the Western world was experiencing an intellectual and material expansion greater than ever before. The Royal Society was founded in 1660, about 15 years before Isaac Barrow, as Master of Trinity, took the lead in planning a library on a scale larger than any other in Cambridge. Across most of western Europe, books were being

The Wren Library and the Backs, summer 2010.

printed at an unprecedented – and alarming – rate. In England, the Civil War had been a sharp reminder of the fragility of libraries and of how important it was to ensure the survival of the country's memory. Many members of the University had lost their livelihoods. Some had fled abroad. Those who returned brought back with them ideas and memories that influenced both ways of thought and ways of living.

For the University as a whole, the late 17th century was a time of hope. With the king restored to the throne in 1660, it began to take stock. As so often, confidence was reflected first in suggestions for new buildings. But there was a world of difference between bright ideas, even for much-needed developments, and their implementation. The story of the origin of the Wren Library has been printed before, and it bears repeating here, from the account left by the biographer of John North, who succeeded Isaac Barrow as Master of the College in 1677.

The Tradition of this Undertaking runs thus. They say that Dr. Barrow pressed the Heads of the University to build a Theatre; it being a Profanation and Scandal that the Speeches should be had in the University Church, and that also be deformed with Scaffolds, and defiled with rude Crouds and Outcries. This Matter was formally considered at a Council of the Heads; and Arguments of Difficulty, and want of Supplies went strong against it. Dr. Barrow assured them that if they made a sorry Building, they might fail of Contributions; but if they made it very magnificent and stately, and, at least exceeding that at Oxford, all Gentlemen, of their Interest, would generously contribute; it being what they desired, and little less than required of them; and Money would not be wanted as the Building went up, and occasion called for it. But sage Caution prevailed, and the Matter, at that Time, was wholly laid aside. Dr. Barrow was piqued at this Pusillanimity, and declared that he would go straight to his College, and lay out the Foundations of a Building to enlarge his back Court, and close it with a stately Library, which would be more magnificent and costly than what he had proposed to them, and doubted not but, upon the Interest of his College, in a short Time, to bring it to Perfection. And he was as good as his Word; for that very Afternoon he, with his Gardiners

Opposite: *Early designs for the Wren Library, showing suggestions for a rotunda.*

and Servants, staked out the very Foundation upon which the Building now stands; and Dr. North saw the Finishing of it, except the Classes, which were forward, but not done, in his Time; and diverse benefactions came in upon that Account; wherewith, and the liberal Supply from the College, the whole is rendered complete; and the admirable Disposition and proportion on the Inside is such as touches the very Soul of any one who first sees it.

Few have dissented from the final remark. Nonetheless, the account is not entirely accurate. Although everyone was agreed on the site – at the western end of Nevile's Court – it took some discussion before the final design was determined. Wren at first proposed a rotunda, daringly experimental; but the Fellowship was more cautious, and practical. Costs were to be met by a public appeal, for the College had little spare money. Work on the building began in 1676. In the event it proved more difficult to raise the money than had been anticipated, and it was about 20 years before the building was finished thanks eventually to the Duke of Somerset, Chancellor of the University: we also owe to him the wonderful carvings by Grinling Gibbons. From the first appeal for funds, to which Isaac Newton was an early contributor, the College depended on benefactors for this project, at the time the largest single building in the University other than King's College Chapel.

Christopher Wren's library was a departure for Cambridge, where the University had some years before been unable to erect a new general library. From the external references to the work of Italian 16th-century architects working in the classical tradition, to the importance attached to good natural light, to the specially designed furniture, Trinity's was a building designed as a practical place to work and to keep books safely. Wren gave careful thought to the materials that were to be used, to the placing of windows well above the bookcases, and to access. In a letter to Barrow, he wrote of the 'middle ally' of the interior, 'paved with small marbles', whereas the spaces between the cases would be quieter if they were floored in wood. As for the furniture, 'the best way for the Students will be to haue a little square table in each Celle'. This strongly made furniture is still very much in use.

Not everything once thought of could be afforded. A south staircase, echoing the present one at the north, with its

spectacular plaster ceiling, was never built. The College waited until the mid-18th century before placing the plaster busts on the tops of the bookcases: classical figures on the east side facing modern ones on the west. The people chosen for the latter were by no means all members of the College. By contrast, the marble busts on the plinths, beginning with Sir Isaac Newton, Sir Francis Bacon, John Ray and Francis Willoughby, were chosen because they represented the best of Trinity's natural philosophers. Others were gradually assembled, including the lawyer Sir Edward Coke, Isaac Barrow and Richard Bentley. All of them, cut by François Roubiliac, Peter Scheemakers and others, were donations, and were part of a campaign to enliven the College with portraits of its past members. The great stained-glass south window of 1774, depicting Francis Bacon, Isaac Newton and King George III, drew attention specifically to Trinity's scientific bent in the generations immediately after Newton. Thorwaldsen's statue of Byron, rejected by Westminster Abbey, was placed in the Library in 1845. It stands not only as a focal point but also as a discreet protection for readers from the Library's everyday noises. Until the arrival of Thomas Woolner's bust of Tennyson (1857) all these sculptures were of the dead.

What of the books? Only three are known to have survived from King's Hall, and seven from Michaelhouse. If more were ever absorbed into the new college founded in 1546, they were either lost, destroyed or simply allowed to moulder away. In the turmoil of the brief reign of Queen Mary (1553–8) most of the libraries of the University – collegiate and private – were inspected, with a view to purging them of unacceptable authors. To add further to the destruction, as printed books replaced manuscripts so there seemed to be less need to keep the older copies. In Trinity, a new College library was installed at the end of the 1590s on the top floor of the north range of Great Court, west of the clock tower. Part of the room was still referred to in the 19th century as the Old Library, a reminder of the longevity of College memory.

The real growth of the library began at the end of the 16th century, as a succession of donors came forward, some of them successful businessmen, others from the Church. Why did these people, and others like them, give such books to the College? We

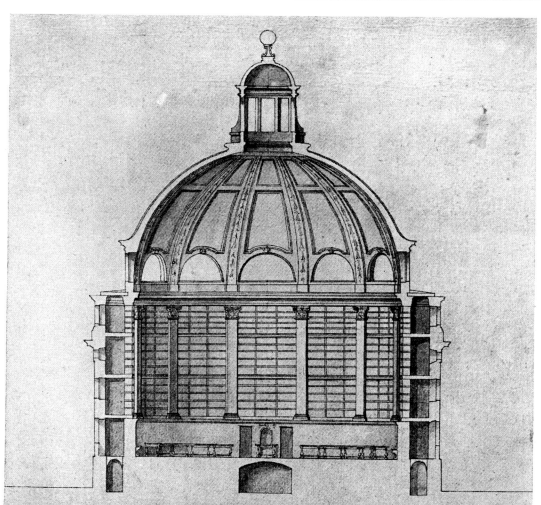

Wood carvings in the Wren by Grinling Gibbons.

cannot now know all the reasons, but some of them lay in a wish to see them preserved in safety, at a time when so much else had been destroyed. When Lady Anne Sadleir arranged for her 13th-century *Apocalypse* to come to Trinity, she was more explicit. It was, she explained, when Cambridge and Oxford should be restored to their 'pristine happines', and 'the Vulgar People to there former obedience'. So, with Charles II restored, the manuscript arrived in Trinity. She had inherited it from her father, Sir Edward Coke, Lord Chief Justice and a member of Trinity. The College was a place of sanctuary. It was – as it remains – a trustee for the past as well as a place of education, learning and research.

The College was also building up its collection of printed books, mainly by bequests and gifts, sometimes of cash, from Fellows and other members. Nevile's printed books had been mostly of divinity. English books began to appear on the shelves. John Speed's history of Great Britain was bought in 1613. Another bequest in 1618 was spent on a group of recent history books in English: of Spain, France and the Middle East. In the sciences, further bequests allowed purchases including Vesalius (1543) and Kepler (1609) in 1625, and Copernicus (1566) and Tycho Brahe (1602) in 1637. It was not until later in the century that the College began to try to keep up to date with the sciences as knowledge developed.

The Wren Library, opened in 1695, was vastly bigger than the College's immediate needs, but it rapidly filled up. There were plenty of well-wishers. For a while, Samuel Pepys thought of leaving his books to Trinity, before he decided on Magdalene. Soon after the Wren was finished, the books of Sir Henry Puckering arrived, including several that had once belonged to Henry, Prince of Wales, elder brother of Charles I. The famous Milton manuscript containing *Comus*, *Lycidas* and other poems came at this time. In 1738 Roger Gale presented about 450 medieval manuscripts collected by his father. It remains the largest such collection that the College has ever received. In 1779 Edward Capell gave his Shakespearean collection accumulated in the course of editing and commenting on Shakespeare's works. This included many early editions, among them one of the very few surviving copies of the first edition of *King Lear*, besides all four of the Folio editions from 1623 onwards. It was the existence of this collection that later enabled two Fellows of the College, W.G. Clark and William Aldis Wright, to produce the *Cambridge Shakespeare* of 1863–6, 'that rock on which all later Shakespearean textual scholarship has been founded'. But the 18th century was also remarkable for various gifts now often forgotten, at least in the Wren. These include a collection of articles from the first voyage of Captain Cook, in 1768–71, given by Lord Sandwich, First Lord of the Admiralty and a member of Trinity. They are now deposited in the Museum of Archaeology and Anthropology. So, too, are the Roman inscriptions and sculptures gathered from sites on Hadrian's Wall at the end of the 16th century by Sir Robert Cotton and given by one of his descendants in 1750.

In the 19th century this tradition of gifts continued, while at the same time the College increased its own buying. Several thousand books presented from the library of Julius Hare, Archdeacon of Lewes (d.1855), made the Wren one of the best places in the country to study late 18th- and early 19th-century German literature and philosophy. The number of 15th-century printed books (incunabula) was greatly increased – and greatly improved – with much of the library of William Grylls, bequeathed in 1863. Grylls was from a Cornish family, but had been closely in touch with the main London booksellers. His was a bibliophile's collection, that also added substantially to the College's collections of 16th-century books. And when William Whewell, Master since 1841, died in 1866, he left a vast collection on all manner of subjects, befitting a person who was reputed to be omniscient. Since the 18th century, undergraduates had been given more access to the Library than their equivalents in many other colleges; but it was only with the new reading room in the 1890s that there was adequate space both for modern books and to meet the needs of about 620 undergraduates and just over 60 Fellows.

By the beginning of the 20th century the College had become responsible for one of Britain's most prominent research libraries, with collections of manuscripts and early printed books of international importance. Over the past 100 years that has become still more true. In 1943 – in the midst of the Second World War – the Pilgrim Trust gave 859 volumes from the library of Sir Isaac Newton, which had survived together since his death. The collection of 18th-century books presented by Lord Rothschild in 1952 includes one of the best collections ever formed relating to Jonathan Swift. The several thousand books left by the economist Piero Sraffa (d.1983), rich in the history of Marxism, is among the best collections anywhere on the history of economics. To these must be added several major archives of correspondence from politicians, historians, literary scholars, philosophers, scientists and mathematicians from the 19th and 20th centuries, including perhaps most famously the papers of Wittgenstein. Today, the Library as a whole has to be a place for everyday study, a place for teaching, and a research library. It is also a library that is open on most days of the year to the public, anyone who wishes to see something of its treasures.

So, along with the daily needs of term-time are the daily responsibilities to those who wish to see inside a room that regularly features among the most photogenic libraries of the world. As I write this, the exhibition showcases include a series of medieval manuscripts beginning with a copy of the *Pauline Epistles* written in the eighth century; books printed at Nuremberg in 1493 and at Westminster by Caxton in 1477; Newton's own copy of the first edition of his *Principia Mathematica* (1687), annotated for the second edition that his friend Richard Bentley did so much to make possible; a notebook kept by Newton when he first came to Cambridge as a poor student in 1661, listing the costs of establishing himself (paper book, 8*d*; chamber-pot, *2s 2d*), the earliest surviving letter from Lord Byron, mentioning his pet rabbit; the so-called *Trinity carol roll*, a long parchment roll containing the music and words for 13 songs and dating from the first half of the 15th century; a vivid account by Otto Frisch (Fellow of the College, d.1979) of the first test explosion of an atomic bomb in the New Mexico desert in July 1945; and, of course, the manuscript of *Winnie-the-Pooh*.

The Wren still has the power to 'touch the soul'. While its appearance has changed slightly since it was first opened to readers, it is just one part of the Library, where on the main staircase a bust of J.J. Thomson leads upwards to Tennyson who in turn leads on to other figures and paintings. The reading room and lower library, with their more recent books, have a quite different mood. Throughout the Library we look to the future. The College has a long tradition of lending books to exhibitions round the world. We work constantly to make as much as possible available on the Web – catalogue records and images alike. There are some people who think that we will not long need libraries of this kind, and that the future is entirely electronic. It is much more realistic to plan for a mixed economy, where e-resources, paper and parchment exist side by side. Books are not only means of communication. They are also evidence of how we think, and of how people have thought in the past: of, literally, how we have handled knowledge. The world's methods of work change almost by the month. We will always need original evidence, not just surrogates, whatever the format.

THE MEDIEVAL MANUSCRIPTS OF TRINITY COLLEGE

Teresa Webber (1997)

Anyone fascinated by English medieval manuscripts is likely to view the portrait of Henry VIII in Hall with mixed emotions. It was Henry's dissolution of the monasteries that led to the dispersal and, in many cases, loss and destruction of the great medieval libraries housed within them. Yet, within less than 100 years, Trinity College – Henry's great foundation – was becoming one of the major custodians of manuscripts that had survived the dissolution, preserving crucial evidence of the religious culture and learning of the Middle Ages, including some of the masterpieces of English medieval illumination and book production. The collection has continued to grow, now comprising around 1,250 medieval manuscripts.

Although two manuscripts from the King's Hall survive in the British Library, none, other than the remarkable sequence of accounts, remains at Trinity, and nothing from the holdings of Trinity's other predecessor, Michaelhouse. The founders of Trinity's manuscript collection were two former Masters: John Whitgift (Master, 1567–77; Archbishop of Canterbury, 1583–1604) and Thomas Nevile (Master, 1593–1615; Dean of Canterbury, 1597–1615). Whitgift left around 150 medieval manuscripts to the College, and Nevile a further 126. Their example was followed on a somewhat smaller scale by other members of the College, all of whose donations were carefully recorded at the end of the handsome early 17th-century register of benefactors, known as the *Memoriale Collegii Trinitatis* (MS R.17.8). By 1667, when a comprehensive catalogue of the library was compiled following a fire that had destroyed the library roof, the collection had grown to around 500 manuscripts.

Most of these contained biblical and other religious texts, and a significant proportion had once occupied the book cupboards and library rooms of more than 40 different English religious communities. In many cases, the full history of these books between the dissolution of the monasteries (1536–40) and their acquisition by those who donated them to Trinity is unknown. However, over 50 of the books given by Whitgift and Nevile came directly from Canterbury, where they appear to have languished in benign neglect, evidently considered to

be of little value by the cathedral chapter that had replaced the former monastic community. Among these manuscripts is arguably the finest example of English monastic book production: the *Eadwine* (or *Canterbury*) *Psalter* (MS R.17.1), an extraordinary achievement of script and page design, from which modern web and graphic designers might learn a little. Each page accommodates no fewer than six different texts: three parallel Latin translations of the Psalms, one of which is surrounded

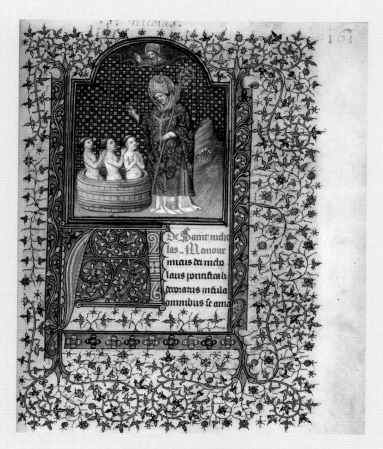

*Opposite and right: Early 15th-century book of hours
(MSS B.11.31-32), made in Paris and given to Trinity in 1861.*

by a Latin commentary, and, in tiny writing above the lines of each of the other two, vernacular translations in, respectively, English and French, together representing the trilingual culture of the learned classes in 12th-century England. Each psalm is introduced by a vivid, literal illustration in colour-tinted outline of images and episodes described in the psalm. The proportions of the multi-column arrangement, the harmony of all the scripts, differing in size to reflect the different status of each text, and the design of even the smallest details of style in the tracing of the individual letters, combine to produce pages of remarkable clarity and beauty.

Not all of these manuscripts were given by members of the College. Arguably the most spectacular, a stunning mid-13th-century *Apocalypse*, whose illuminations glow with gold and dense blues and reds, was the gift of Mrs Anne Sadleir, the daughter of a Trinity alumnus, the lawyer Sir Edward Coke. She had first made provision for this magnificent donation in 1649, in the troubled aftermath of the execution of Charles I, but waited for more peaceful times and the restoration of Charles II before handing the book over to the College in 1660.

Several decades after the building of the Wren Library, the manuscript collection was almost doubled in size through the largest of all donations of manuscripts to the library, that of the collection of some 450 volumes acquired by Thomas Gale and his son (the donor), Roger Gale, both of whom had been Fellows. This was a splendidly heterogenous collection, ranging in date from the eighth to the 18th centuries, comprising books from all over western Europe and all types of subject matter. Several, however, were long-dispersed books from English medieval monasteries. Among them is an early-12th-century copy of a group of texts by Jerome on the interpretation of the Bible, copied by a monk of Rochester Cathedral Priory (MS O.4.7). By happy chance, it can now be studied side by side with the exemplar from which it was copied: a manuscript produced just a decade or so earlier by a monk at nearby Canterbury Cathedral (now MS B.2.34), one of Whitgift's donations.

Although some of the Trinity manuscripts, like the *Eadwine Psalter* and the *Trinity Apocalypse*, are very well known and have often been exhibited within and outside the College, others

have remained obscure even to specialists. It was in recognition of the hidden treasures in the Cambridge college and University collections that a major exhibition, entitled *The Cambridge Illuminations*, was held at the Fitzwilliam Museum and the University Library in 2005. Among the many Trinity manuscripts exhibited was one such neglected book, which had been given to Trinity in 1861 by a Fellow, Augustus A. Vansittart. It is an exquisite and sumptuously illuminated early-15th-century book of hours (MSS B.11.31–2), made in Paris, and later owned by Anne of Austria, mother of Louis XIV of France, and more popularly famous from her depiction in Alexandre Dumas's *The Three Musketeers*.

It is to be hoped that, in the future, the medieval manuscripts of Trinity may become available in digital form online. Nevertheless, the digital image can only be a surrogate not a substitute for the books themselves; it cannot replicate their physical structure and texture, or the dynamic quality of the handwriting. The Wren Library will, therefore, remain a magnet to scholars and visitors, as it was to me, when first I came some 25 years ago as a graduate student from Oxford to study the *Eadwine Psalter*. As a Fellow of Trinity, I feel immensely privileged to have such ready access to so magnificent a collection of medieval books.

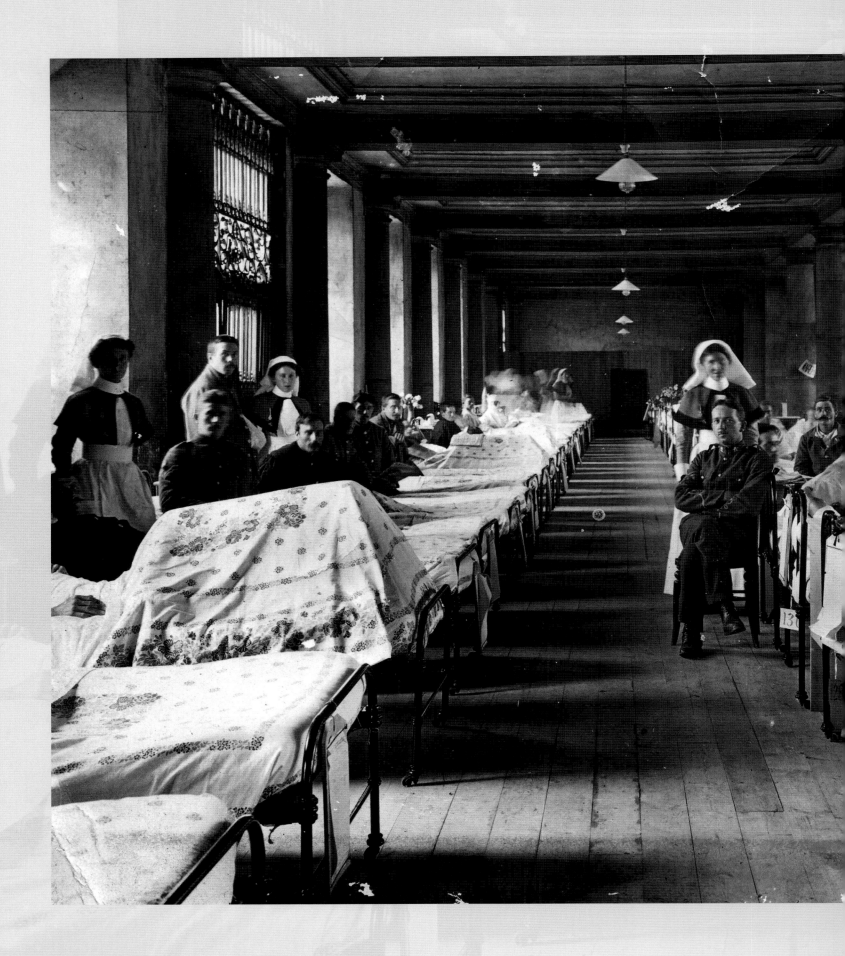

CHAPTER 14

Trinity at War

Trinity and remembrance of the dead of two World Wars

JOHN LONSDALE *(1958)*

On our Chapel walls are named 615 Trinity men who died in the Great War and 381 who died in the Second World War. Of the many sermons that will have commemorated them on Remembrance Days, two by the Rev. F.A. Simpson (Fellow, 1911–74) are most often quoted. Fellows remember Simpson himself each year on his birthday, 22 November, when they enjoy free champagne in the parlour thanks to a benefaction he made for that purpose in 1957. He preached the first of the two sermons as Lady Margaret's Preacher, at the Commemoration of Benefactors, in Great St Mary's Church on Sunday 6 November 1932. Most of the sermon remembered past benefactors in general. But he ended:

> *I would have you let your thoughts range outward to include all other benefactors who in this place have served God in their generation, and as we hope have entered into His peace. Let them include – for how shall our memories not include them – let them include those whose bright dawn no noon awaited here; those who would have been the light and lamp of our own generation, which now halts and stumbles, robbed of its natural leaders, towards its night … 'Leaders of the people by their counsels, such as bear rule in kingdoms,' that they can never be for us now: but 'the glory of their times,' that they would have been and are.*
>
> *'Remember your leaders,' said the Epistoler to the Hebrews. Well, the chief thing to remember about our leaders in the dozen years ahead of us is this: that most of them were not meant to be our leaders at all. They are only the last and worst of our war*

Previous pages: *First Eastern General Hospital, Nevile's Court, 1915.*

Right: *The Reverend F.A. Simpson.*

substitutes. Our true leaders, as well in literature and the arts as in public life – but most of all I think in public life – our true leaders were taken from our head now nearly 20 years ago: when a generation was not decimated but decapitated; not mauled at mere haphazard, but shorn precisely of its grace and glory, of its most ardent, its most generous, its most brave. And what happened to us happened to the greater part of Europe: happened that is to the greater part of the civilised world. Our born leaders are dead. That is why you must make ready to help quickly. There is small help or leading left in the generation ahead of you. You will have to save yourselves and us. And to do that at all you may have to do it soon. Meanwhile you must not too much wonder or be dismayed if, by the truncated remnant of a generation, Europe should be ruled with something less than the little wisdom – the quantula sapientia *– with which it has commonly been governed hitherto. Nor should you be afraid with any amazement though in the interval you should see small men make shift to fill big places in Church and State. For most of the big men a very little room suffices now.*

The second of Simpson's commemorative sermons, which he called 'A Last Sermon', was preached in our College Chapel on Remembrance Day 1948. Its text was twice reprinted to meet the demand from Trinity's ex-servicemen. The extracts reprinted here represent the beginning and the end of the sermon.

We are called upon today to remember our dead in two great wars. And it is natural perhaps that one, charged with the task of addressing you on such an occasion, should find himself in preparation for it turning over not only old memories, but old letters: letters received in both those wars from members of this College then far sundered from it: from men in France and Italy, Asia and Africa; from barracks, and billets, and hospitals, and from prisoners of war. They were letters naturally of every type and form: some on the crisp and crested paper of newly joined regiments in England; others scribbled in pencil on flimsy sheets from the trenches, reaching me sometimes after the writers were dead. But differing so much in so many ways, these letters were in one thing alike. It was clear that those who wrote them were constantly remembering this place, which they would not see again – for in

general I seem only to have kept the letters of those who did not see it again – and it is clear too that in that hour, when they remembered it, they were glad of it. Even as we, when we remember them, are in a sense not only proud of them, but glad of them.

Their thoughts, indeed, during those ten years of war, came flocking back to this place like homing pigeons … And besides their own letters and their fathers', were others perhaps more moving still, from those who would have been, but never were, their brides; more than one of whom I was to have married to these men, in short leaves that never came. From these it would obviously be improper for me to quote. But since without some sacrifice of reticence one cannot preach at all, I will allow myself – or force myself – from just one of their own letters, to read a single sentence; since it seems to me to comprehend the spirit of them all. It was written by a scholar of this College, a month or two before he was killed. 'The war', he wrote, 'has done one thing for me; it has shown me again, what I really knew already, what a grand thing it is to have known and loved people like all of you.' With how much greater reason may we say that of them. They have shown us again, what we too really knew already, what a grand thing it is to have known – and loved – people like all of them.

A grand thing, yes, but a very grievous thing: rendered more grievous still by the fact that in both wars, but especially in the first, death did not take toll haphazard, but chose the very best. Almost one found oneself predicting for that reason, after the

216

final handshake, 'Well, whoever comes back, he will not.' And too often we were right. And looking then at our deserted courts, and remembering them as they were on the eve of the First War, thronged as perhaps never before or since with the very flower of the race, we were tempted to add: 'Never again can such men fill this place.' 'Never, never more shall we behold the unbought grace of life' – and the rest of it. But there at any rate we were wrong. The genius of the place, and this happy breed of men, were not exhausted: God was able of these stones to raise up children unto Abraham …

But a man is vulnerable not only in his affections, but in his hopes. And though both wounds hurt, yet we would not have it otherwise; for to be invulnerable is not to be immortal: it is merely to be dead. But what then, what of our hopes? What of their hopes, whose sacrifice we commemorate today?

Three years or so after the First War, when wreaths at the foot of the Cenotaph were already becoming few, I chanced to pass it on a day when there was only one. At any rate I only noticed one. Upon it were five words written: 'Not in vain, my darling.' Would any of us, at this same interval after the Second War, dare to word a tribute so?

Simpson went on to contrast the hopes of the 1920s in the League of Nations, 'aiming at the reign of justice and law', with the then current fears of the late 1940s, at the beginning of a

Cold War when 'a far larger portion of Europe lies under an alien tyranny than on the eve of it; subjected to a despotism by the side of which the Turk was merciful, and the czardom liberal and humane. Was it all then but wasted labour? Were these lives then given in vain?' Simpson dared to hope that that was not so, and ended by reminding his congregation that 'this most evil thing', communism, was 'a corruption of things most good' – by which he meant the reinterpretation of English socialism by Marx and Engels. He concluded:

I will choose a valediction on these our dead a passage from one of the nobler line of English Socialists, before their doctrines had been rewritten in terms of hatred and class war, by men whom England sheltered, but did not breed. Those English Socialists were inspired by love of the many, not by hatred of the few; and though they had fire in their bellies, and indignation to match their eloquence, that was because they too, like another before them, had compassion on the multitude. 'Yea, forsooth' – these are words which the last great English Socialist [William Morris] put into the mouth of the man he imagined to be the first of them – 'Yea, forsooth, once again I saw, as of old, the great treading down the little, and the strong beating down the weak; and cruel men fearing not, and wise men caring not, and the Saints in heaven forbearing, and yet bidding me not forebear. *Forsooth I knew once more that he who doeth well in fellowship shall not fail, though he seem to fail today; but in days hereafter shall he and his work yet be alive, and men holpen by them to strive again and yet again: and yet even that was little, since to strive was my pleasure and my life.'*

It was their pleasure and their life: it was their pleasure and their death. And like Lincoln, half way though his war against slavery, *we too here highly resolve that these dead shall not have died in vain. We resolve, God helping us, that their purpose shall not fail, though it seem to fail today: today when yet once more we see cruel men fearing not, and kind men daring not – and wise men caring not. We resolve that in spite of all these things those three words 'not in vain' shall still be an epitaph their loved ones may apply to any one of them.*

Yes, those three words, even when they are also a portion of those five: 'Not in vain, my darling.'

From *A Last Eccentric: a symposium concerning the Rev. Canon F.A. Simpson* **(London, 1991)**

Eric James (Chaplain, 1955–9)

In early life Simpson had travelled a great deal in Europe, and had flown across the Channel in his own Gipsy Moth, but in later years he rarely ventured out of Cambridge, spending much of his time roaming the College gardens, armed with a formidable pair of secateurs. He was unmistakable out of doors, because of his blue-grey woollen scarf slung over one shoulder – in winter over a shabby raincoat; on his head, most days, winter and summer alike, an equally shabby cloth cap … Simpson was a man of strong likes and dislikes, which were not always of long duration. He had decided to like me when I went up to Trinity, as chaplain; and on my first day in Cambridge he knocked on the door of my rooms, immediately entered, introduced himself without removing his cloth cap, and, with a shy writhing, holding an envelope well away from him, presented it to me. 'I am Simpson,' he said. 'You come, I understand, from a background from which none of our previous chaplains has come. Pray do me the kindness of keeping entirely to yourself the contents of this envelope.' He then stepped backward a few paces, crooked his arm in farewell, writhed again, arm extended, executed a few more lurching steps backward toward the door, and left the room as suddenly as he had entered it. The envelope contained a most generous cheque.

Simpson sometimes suggested it was for difficulties of belief that he had virtually ceased to preach. 'How can one believe in the divinity of Our Lord', he would characteristically ask, 'when he was so unconscionably rude to His mother?' On the rare occasions that he preached, even in these later years, it was likely to be the same sermon, on the subject of the Good Samaritan; but it was a remarkable sermon, which many undergraduates made a point of hearing while they were up in Cambridge.

On one occasion he preached this sermon on succeeding Sundays in the chapels of Corpus and King's. The then Dean of Corpus, Roland Walls, is unlikely to forget the occasion, for Simpson had asked him to read as the lesson the parable of the Good Samaritan, but the Dean had read an entirely different passage. Simpson reminded the congregation continually of the Dean's failing, throughout the sermon. 'If only the lesson I had

asked to be read had in fact been read, you would now be able to recall …' The Dean wrote immediately to apologise, but Simpson returned his letter on the ground that it was 'insufficiently abject'.

The next week he spotted in King's some of the undergraduates who had heard him in Corpus, and prefaced his sermon with the words; 'I see some here today whom I saw in another place but a week ago. To them may I say: it is better to hear a good sermon twice than a bad sermon once.'

The Rt Hon. J. Enoch Powell PC (1930)

On the eve of my classical Tripos finals in June 1933 I was taken so seriously ill that it seemed likely I would have to be content with an *aegrotat* degree instead of honours. In the event I sat the seven papers in the Evelyn Nursing Home, with a special invigilator sitting in the bedroom throughout. At that time my rooms at Trinity were in Great Court above those occupied by the Rev. F.A. Simpson, of whom I had hitherto been aware only as a strange figure occasionally seen covertly pruning the ampelopsis at the mouth of the staircase – not necessarily, as malicious rumour reported, with nail scissors – and also because he had the annoying habit of slamming his door under my study with full force whenever he entered or left.

What had happened was that on the crucial Sunday the bedmaker took it upon herself to tell Simpson about the predicament of 'the young gentleman upstairs', who was by then in bad shape but still determined somehow to show up at whatever risk in the examination hall. Apparently Simpson went straight to my tutor, Mr Dykes, insisted that arrangements be made for me to take the papers in hospital, and pushed the matter as far as a personal and acrimonious altercation with the chairman of the examiners, Professor F.M. Cornford. From beginning to end no personal communication passed between Simpson and myself and I learned only afterwards indirectly what had happened.

It was after I came back into residence as a Prize Fellow in May 1935 that I became habitually caught up in the vast conversations which Simpson conducted at High Table dinner, conversations which extended at least three places to left and right of him and opposite and in which there took part among others Professor Hardy and the Russian mathematician, Besicovitch ('Well, I always regretted the old pronunciation of Latin, but it is splendid to hear

Hut 6 at Bletchley Park, where the Lorenz code was broken.

French in the old pronunciation again' – Simpson). Professor Hardy and Simpson were regular sparring partners. Professor Hardy sustained a long-running cricket fantasy, in which Simpson and he were captains respectively of the God Eleven and the No God Eleven. Being at that time rated a 'pure 100 per cent atheist' (Hardy), I was supposed to be one of the leading batsmen in Hardy's team. The competition was conducted only by losing runs through inadvertent acknowledgements of the position of the other side, as occurred when the Junior Bursar, de Bruyne, improved the heating in the College Chapel and had to be dropped in consequence from the No God Eleven altogether. I forget how it came about that I showed to Simpson the poetry I was then writing; but he spontaneously gave me £100 to publish *First Poems*. After the war I was able to repay him the sum out of the sales of *Casting Off*, and he used the money to plant cherry trees along the Coton footpath behind the Fellows' Garden.

Bletchley Park Memories
introduced by John Lonsdale

It is well known that four Trinity men – Burgess, Blunt, Cairncross and Philby – were among the 'Cambridge Five' so-called 'Russian spies'. That men from Trinity were also vital to the work of breaking German military codes at Bletchley Park (BP) is scarcely known at all. The memories of Keith Batey (who died shortly after submitting this reminiscence) and Rolf Noskwith, two of the many Trinity men who worked there, will put that right. They mention three Trinity men more senior than they at BP. Stuart Milner-Barry (1925) had read classics and had represented England in international chess competitions – with three opening variations named after him. After the war he rose through the ranks of the Treasury and on retirement took over the administration of the honours system. Knighted in 1975, he died in 1995. Bill Tutte (1936), son of a Newmarket gardener, read chemistry at Trinity

219

A Lorenz cipher machine.

but after the war returned to do a PhD in mathematics, the field in which he distinguished himself in the Canadian universities of Toronto and Waterloo; he died at Waterloo in 2002. His reconstruction of the Lorenz encoding machine, used only by the German general staff, was one of BP's most outstanding cryptographic achievements. Gordon Welchman (1925) was a mathematician. A Fellow of Sidney Sussex before the war he led – until 1943, when Milner-Barry succeeded him – the department that successfully read the Luftwaffe's Enigma traffic. After the war he worked on computer security in America, where he died in 1985.

AFTER COMPLETING THE MATHS TRIPOS IN 1940 WHILE THE Germans were storming across Belgium, I went home to await instructions. We had all been, in effect, conscripted and had to do whatever war work it was thought we could best do. In mid-June I got a very unofficial-looking letter from Gordon Welchman, offering me a job. He could not say what or where it was, but assured me that it was interesting and important, with 'lousy' pay. However, such was the secrecy surrounding the affair that among mathematicians of my year it was common knowledge that in January 1940, Welchman, then a don at Sidney Sussex, had recruited three of his pupils to work on codes. I wrote accepting Welchman's offer and some two weeks later was told to report to Bletchley Park.

I reported early in July but have no recollection of my arrival there or of what must have been a fairly lengthy admission process. My earliest memory is of being in a large room in Hut 6 with two other new entrants listening to a talk by Stuart Milner-Barry on the radio communication systems used by the German army and Luftwaffe. After an hour with him we were handed over to Hugh Alexander, who told us that we were to work in Hut 6, of which Welchman was head, on a German cipher machine called Enigma. He went on to explain how it worked with the aid of a specimen on the table in front of him. His explanation would have been more helpful had the machine had a battery and been working. It was, however, judged sufficient for one of us to be added to each of the three teams on the cryptographic staff of Hut 6, bringing the strength of each team to three.

To communicate via Enigma German servicemen had to know what wheels to use, the order in which they were mounted, the ring-clip settings and plug connections. These all provided the 'key' for transmission. Each German network had a list of keys and dates, each day using a different key. Hut 6 had the task of finding the daily key for each army and Luftwaffe network. By the time I arrived the main Luftwaffe key, called 'Red' by Hut 6, was being solved daily but the main army key, 'Green', had not been solved and was broken once only before I left Hut 6 in October 1941. Navy keys required a different approach and were Hut 8's responsibility.

While I was there, Hut 6 decodes provided comprehensive information on all aspects of Luftwaffe operations. Its success against the 'Red' key was complete, thanks to an electro-mechanical device, the bombe, invented by Alan Turing and much improved by Welchman, whose energy, drive and foresight were central to Hut 6's development. A second Luftwaffe key, 'Brown', had not been solved since May 1940 but was broken that September. It gave information about the radio beam settings that guided bombers to their targets. I clearly recollect our saddest failure. In early November 1940 Luftwaffe messages were giving notice of a special operation codenamed Mond. We knew no more than this and, to our dismay, failed to break any key for several days before 14 November. The result was the unhindered and disastrous bombing of Coventry. We could not explain our earlier failure when the missing keys were later broken.

In October 1941 I was moved to ISK (Intelligence Services Knox) to help solve the Abwehr (secret service) traffic enciphered on a different Enigma. Its mechanism and wiring had just been brilliantly discovered by Dilly Knox from intercepted messages. Before the end of the war, having broken three other Abwehr Enigmas, we had solved 140,000 messages from every country of strategic importance from South America to the Far East, and from Scandinavia to Africa.

The course of history was changed when America came into the war and plans could be laid for liberating Europe rather than just defending our shores. Our penetration of the German secret service gave Churchill a trump card – to provide a 'bodyguard of lies' for protecting allied invasion plans. Captured German agents were played back against their controllers in neutral countries, usually in Madrid or Lisbon, deceiving them with false intelligence through the 'double cross system'. Our ISK decrypts showed both what information was passed to Berlin and, from Berlin's replies, whether or not it was believed. Successful amphibious landings were made in North Africa in 1942, the Germans being convinced that the Allied fleet's destination was the eastern Mediterranean, and again in 1943 when they believed the landing in Sicily was to have been in Sardinia. Most important was the strategic deception carried out before the Normandy landings in 1944, when Hitler was made to believe that the main attack would be at the Pas de Calais, where he kept two panzer divisions waiting.

In July 1945 General Eisenhower wrote to the Head of MI6, who was also Head of Bletchley Park. The General acknowledged the value of the material circulated from Bletchley, derived from decryption of all the high-grade ciphers used not only in the Enigma traffic but also that from the Lorenz machine which carried messages between Hitler and his Generals – very cleverly broken by Bill Tutte. Eisenhower asked that all members of the Bletchley Park staff be told of 'his heartfelt admiration and sincere thanks for their very decisive contribution to the Allied war effort'.

Keith Batey (1937)

I WENT UP TO TRINITY IN OCTOBER 1938 WITH A MINOR scholarship in natural sciences but switched to the mathematical Tripos. I also abandoned pacifism and joined the artillery survey section of the Officers' Training Corps.

When war broke out the University set up a recruiting board for undergraduates. At my interview I mentioned my knowledge of German and suggested that, combined with mathematics, I might be qualified for 'decoding'. The board agreed and recommended me for both artillery survey and decoding. There was then a setback when I failed two medicals.

Early in 1940 I was interviewed by Gordon Welchman and another man from what I later recognised to be Bletchley Park. They wanted to recruit me but my appointment was vetoed because of my foreign birth. In 1941 I was interviewed again by C.P. Snow, who was then a Civil Service Commissioner, and Hugh Alexander (King's), the former British chess champion. The rules had changed and I was appointed as a junior assistant at the Foreign Office, which had jurisdiction over the Government Code and Cipher School (GCCS).

I arrived at Bletchley on 20 June 1941, the day after my 22nd birthday. Alexander met me at the station and took me to one of the huts in the nearby Bletchley Park. This was Hut 8 of which he was acting head. It was only then that I learned that the task was to break the German navy cipher. In my first few days at Bletchley Park I shared a billet with Bill Tutte whom I knew from Trinity. I remember his sharp eye for four-leaf clovers on our walks in nearby fields.

Despite my talk of decoding I knew very little about codes and ciphers so that I entered a completely new world when I met Enigma, the machine with which the German Navy encrypted its messages. Enigma had a keyboard and a panel with the letters of the alphabet. Each letter of a message typed on the keyboard activated an electric current that passed through wheels inside the machine to light up a letter on the panel. The sequence of letters so lit formed the encrypted text. The combination of wheels and other elements which determined the path of the current changed every day. We had to break this daily changing combination or 'key', and then go on to find the position of the wheels for each message.

Alan Turing and others had worked out how to break the key before I joined Hut 8, helped by the fact that the Poles had broken the main Wehrmacht machine in the early 1930s. The essence of the method was to make a 'crib'. This was a guess of what a passage of from 15 to 20 letters in a particular message might be saying. An electronic machine called a 'bombe' could rapidly test the crib against the vast number of permutations of variables in the key. If the guess which produced the crib was correct the bombe was likely to find the correct permutation.

I joined the crib section and remained a 'cribster' until the end of the war. Another section of Hut 8 was engaged in a mathematical process called 'Banburismus'. This reduced the number of permutations for the bombe to test. In my first six weeks we had in fact no need for codebreaking since we had got the keys for June and July 1941 from a 'pinch', the capture of a small German weather ship in the North Atlantic.

The decrypted messages helped us to identify possible cribs for future use. The most consistent messages were the weather reports sent twice daily from stations along the Channel coast. The German operators had instructions to vary the text but they were often lax and repeated similar wordings. Other possibilities included warnings about mines so, later on, the RAF dropped mines in specified locations in order to generate appropriate warning messages.

From 1 August 1941 until 31 January 1942 we demonstrated the potential of cribs, Banburismus and bombes by breaking the key for all but two days, sometimes very quickly. We were told that this success contributed to a dramatic fall in the number of merchant ships sunk by U-boats.

I was made responsible for trying to break top secret, or 'Offizier', messages. These had been encrypted twice, once by an officer with a special key and then again with the ordinary key of the day. I tried a variety of cribs; eventually one of these produced a promising result on the bombe just as I was about to go home on leave. I was promised a telegram: the mention of a fish would mean success. A mysterious telegram duly arrived, containing the word 'pompano'. The dictionary was needed to confirm that a pompano is indeed a fish.

On 1 February 1942 the Germans introduced a separate key for U-boats. This used an Enigma machine with four wheels, not three. The increased number of permutations made the bombes ineffective and put an end to Banburismus. Our inability to break this key during most of 1942 resulted in a dangerous increase in the number of sinkings. We were still breaking the key for other traffic, including the U-boats on the Arctic route to Russia. We started to break the U-boat key again from December 1942, thanks to some brilliant work in which I was not involved. Victory in the Battle of the Atlantic followed in May 1943, when Admiral Dönitz withdrew his surviving U-boats.

A new phase began in mid-1943 when we had a growing arsenal of more powerful bombes, mostly from the United States. These could rapidly test cribs for four-wheel and three-wheel messages, making Banburismus unnecessary. In the last 12 months of the war I was one of four cribsters – working in shifts around the clock – responsible for all naval keys, apart from some transferred to the US. There had been a proliferation of different keys for different areas: with very rare exceptions we were able to break them all every day. To some extent the work became routine but there were still highlights like D-Day in June 1944 and the sinking of the battleship *Tirpitz* in November 1944. There were also periodic challenges whenever the Germans changed procedures.

My time at Bletchley left a lasting legacy in the form of close friendships. Unlike many of my contemporaries I spent the War in safety and comfort doing fascinating work. I know how lucky I was.

Rolf Noskwith (1938)

E.J. Kenney (1946) writes: A.S.F. Gow. Before his increasing immobility finally led to his retiring to the Evelyn Nursing Home, he would on fine days sit in a chair in Great Court outside his rooms. Visitors, regarding him as a characteristic feature of the scene, would sometimes photograph him and try to chat him up. When asked about these conversations he is said to have replied: 'They always ask the same three questions, and I always give the same three answers. The first is, "When was the College founded?" I say I don't know. The second is, "Where are the lavatories?" I say, "There aren't any." The third is, "Which is the way out?" I always tell them that.'

Letters from Cambridge 1939–44 (Jonathan Cape, 1945)
A.S.F. Gow

1st letter, 8 September 1939

We have sent away some of the more important pictures and books, the Porters' Lodge at the Great Gate is strutted and sandbagged as our chief Wardens' Post, cellars in Whewell's and Nevile's Courts have been made into quite good shelters, and something is being done to the cellar under Hall which isn't so good for the purpose but will serve at a pinch.

I go to bed, but have disposed at hand clothes suitable to the purpose [Air Raid Warden] and can get to my post in about three minutes with my gas-mask, a tin hat (much too small and very uncomfortable, but there is a shortage of larger sizes) and in my pocket a copy of the *Inferno*, which seemed a suitable book for reading while waiting for something to happen.

14th letter, 29 September 1940

My time for the past ten days has been entirely occupied with such things as the protection of Hall windows and various skylights, devices for getting people out of Hall in an emergency, provision of sleeping quarters for the Fire Party (who don't fancy sleeping every night in a cellar), painting the lead on the Library roof (said to be too conspicuous from the air), etc., etc.

26th letter, 28 September 1941

Vegetables grow in certain other unwonted though more secluded spots (the lawn in the Botanic Garden for instance), but they have not as yet invaded our gardens, and the grass in our courts, unusually green for the time of year, is kept in order mostly by Besicovitch, who may be seen daily taking exercise in a pyjama jacket behind a man-powered mowing machine. [College playing fields are, however, cultivated.]

39th letter, 14 November 1942

It is, by the way, something of a mystery to me where the Bedmakers and Helps have gone to, for I cannot readily picture the absentees disguised as Wrens or Waafs, or even Land Girls. [He concludes they no longer need the money because so many members of their family are either away or earning through war work.]

62nd letter, 14 October 1944

… the only novelty of the last 12 months, if indeed it is not older, is, I think, the numerous parties, mostly of American airmen, being taken on tours conducted by various eminent persons. In this College, the Master or Vice Master may be seen on most afternoons showing a party round, and to judge from the number of Americans whom I catch photographing their buddies or cuties (if I have the terms correctly) in front of the fountain or sundial, these objects must now be pretty familiar in the States. [He goes on to report asking the Master whether he is getting rich on tips, but is told the airmen only offer cigarettes.]

[NB: The low point for Trinity was 1942 when there were fewer than 300 undergraduates in residence during the Michaelmas Term.]

Opposite: *The memorial to the dead of the Second World War in the Ante Chapel.*

IN THE SUMMER OF 1942, I WAS DOING SOME COURSES IN NATURAL sciences to complete the requirements of a wartime two-year course. My College rooms were in Whewell's Court, very near the gate out onto Bridge Street. The rooms were on the first floor and the windows looked down Jesus Lane. In the early hours, a German bomber sent a stick of bombs down, the first of which fell in Jesus Lane very near its start and just below my bedroom window. This bomb sent a small piece of pavement through the netting on my bedroom window into the plaster over my head. Apart from being woken up, I was quite unharmed. The exterior stonework of the Court also suffered some chips, but no real damage was done. The blast also sent all the soot in my chimney out into the fireplace and carpet in the living room; much to the horror of my bedder! In our bill for rooms every term there was an item for 'Chimney Cleaning…2/6'. I have often wondered whether the chimneys really were cleaned every term.

More damage was done by the other bombs in the stick, and three people were killed in the houses off Jesus Lane. None of the other nearby rooms in the College received any significant damage; few of them were occupied at that time, although the rooms at the top of my staircase were then occupied by Dr Wittgenstein, and the ones below him by Charles Kemball, then a fellow undergraduate, later Junior Bursar of the College.

David Le Cren (1941)

I CAME INTO RESIDENCE IN 12 WHEWELL'S. AN EARLY ENCOUNTER was with Mrs Brown, the bedmaker on that staircase, who would wake us in the morning bringing a jug of hot water into the bedroom: 'Quarter to eight if you please, Sir.' She cleaned the rooms and laid the fires, for each of the six sets on the staircase. Our shoes, if left outside the door, were cleaned for us by Charlie Finch who was small, white haired and willing.

During the war the College staff necessarily consisted of older members, the young being recruited into the forces. This came especially to my attention on one occasion when I was talking to one of the porters in the Whewell's Porter's Lodge and found that he had served in the Boer War.

The College having appropriated our ration books, all meals were taken in Hall, and we were fed, for wartime, remarkably well. In the kitchen office in the southwest corner of Great Court hung a large and impressive notice listing the 40 or 50 types of cooked eggs which could be included in the breakfasts sent out to the rooms of any undergraduate who chose to eat in his rooms. This was a purely historical document! In 1941 breakfast and lunch were set meals served at the buffet in Hall. Dinner was served at tables in Hall, and occasionally one would find the familiar hand of Charlie Finch, slightly cleaned up, coming over one's shoulder with a bowl of soup.

While meals in one's rooms were not possible, one could invite friends to tea or to coffee after Hall. Cakes were at a premium, but one's bedmaker would occasionally bring in for sale a substitute made by a firm called Grodzinsky trading somewhere in the back end of town. These were remarkable dry and dusty products decorated with something that looked like icing and it was acceptable to serve them to one's friends: 'Come and have tea; I've got a Grod.'

Having been in the choir in my parish church at home, I joined the College Chapel Choir under the College organist Dr Hubert Middleton. He was a Cambridge Doctor of Music and FRCO, had been organist of Truro Cathedral for a time, and had then gone on to Ely Cathedral, whence he came back to Trinity about the beginning of the war. He was a man I greatly liked and admired. He was short and stocky, with abundant white hair, a nose that looked as though it might have been broken in a prizefight, and a cheerful disposition.

I also joined the College fire party, which operated a fair-sized petrol-driven pump on a hand-drawn chassis. It had a full-sized fire hose and suction hose and could be drawn to any part of the College, obtaining water from one of the fire hydrants or from the river if handy. On practice evenings in winter we delighted in swamping the College lawns with water so that the dons, privileged to walk on the grass, might find it slippery in the morning. We were able to reach the College roofs, so that by hoisting the hose up and deploying a branch (the technical term for a nozzle) we could fight fires over a useful range of College buildings. Our only obstacle was that there were no fires in my time, nor I think during the rest of the war. Nevertheless it was a great joy to reach the roof of the Wren

Library and see Nevile's Court in clear moonlight with no light pollution. The fire party was organised by Andrew Gow, a Fellow and classical scholar and a retired tutor.

Donald V. Osbome (1941)

LIFE IN THE COLLEGE DURING THE WAR AND IN THE IMMEDIATE post-war years was very different in many ways from the present day. First, there was a severe and persistent shortage of food, as almost everything was rationed. The College took possession of our ration books so by necessity we had to eat all our meals in Hall every day. The *Trinity Magazine* of June 1947 records 'the difficulties of a Kitchen Manager called upon to supply 12,000 meals a week'. Whalemeat was served regularly at dinner, meaty in appearance but fishy in flavour, as this was one of the few things not on ration. Indeed, it appeared so frequently that a rumour spread among the undergraduates that the College must have bought the carcass of a whale, keeping it in the Cam and hacking off pieces as required.

The College buttery provided about 300cc of fresh milk daily, which could be collected by each undergraduate in a jar or jug. Monthly allocations of soap coupons and tea coupons were also available on request, although they rarely lasted until the next issue. Since all jams and curds were on ration they were unavailable to the students, but for some reason fish paste was not rationed and became the staple diet of the students for tea. Eggs were a rarity; I see from an entry in my diary that on 8 February 1943 'I had a real egg for lunch', which was a great treat as most egg dishes were made from reconstituted egg powder from the US.

Even in the years after the war, bread was rationed and supplies of buns, tarts and cakes of all kinds were very scarce; each day hundreds of hungry students joined the long queue that formed outside the Lyons shop in Petty Cury until all the stock was sold.

The College suffered from a dire shortage of accommodation as the whole of New Court and Bishop's Hostel were occupied by members of the Civil Service evacuated from more vulnerable areas, so men in their first year were mostly allocated to lodgings. Those living in College faced various difficulties: there was no water supply in most rooms, so you had to go to the nearest tap on your staircase, where a gas ring was also provided for heating

The visit of the Regent of Iraq to Trinity during the Second World War. Imperial War Museum.

a kettle. Every morning you were awakened by your bedder bringing you a jug of hot water for washing and shaving; if you were slow to get up, the water would be cold.

A coal fire was the main means of heating rooms in College but the weekly ration, fetched in buckets from the coal-heap stored under the Wren Library, did not last more than a few days and many undergraduates spent their evenings in the College Reading Room to keep warm. Very few sets were wired

N.J.F. Earle (1944) writes: I was up twice: in 1944–6 to read mathematics (essential for a cryptographer), and 1948–50 to read theology (sadly, not essential for the Anglican priesthood). I feel I ought to bear witness to one of the peculiarities of that most endearing and eccentric of maths tutors, A.S. Besicovitch (above, cutting the grass during the war). From my rooms in Nevile's Court (C3), I was often able to observe him on a summer's evening come down his staircase opposite, armed only with a table fork and a chamber pot, and solemnly remove from the lawn, which is, as you know, part of the Court's glory, what he believed to be 'weeds'. It impressed me deeply not least by its obvious devotion to the place.

for power, so electric fires and heaters were useless. Hot baths, available only mornings and evenings, were sited in Lavatory Court, if you could find them through the clouds of steam.

The regulations concerning music in College were very strict. Only pianos and violins were allowed (any other instrument needed the permission of the Dean of College). Play was limited to the hours 1pm to 10pm weekends and 1pm to 5.30pm and between 7.30pm and 10pm on other days, and gramophones and wireless sets with loudspeakers were subject to the same hours. The Clerk of Works had to be informed whenever a radio receiver was installed in a College room and a receiving licence obtained from the Post Office.

In 1942 academic dress of cap and gown had to be worn at University lectures and exams, in the University Library, when visiting one's tutor or director of studies, at dinner in Hall, and in

the streets of Cambridge after dusk in all parts of the town. The regulation on wearing the academic cap or 'mortarboard' was relaxed from 2 March 1943. During the war, all undergraduates had to join the Home Guard and attend twice-weekly training sessions in full army uniform, which was also often worn on those days at lectures and meals.

John Hicks (1942)

I RETURNED TO TRINITY AFTER WAR SERVICE IN JANUARY 1946. Although the war was over, its problems and shortages were certainly not, particularly food and clothing and, most important of, all coal and electricity. Power cuts frequently affected us. I well remember having morning cups of tea (costing only a penny or two) in the then Lyons Tea Shop in Petty Cury. The shop was often plunged into darkness leaving life to continue just with candles.

Early 1947 was a long and bitterly cold winter with snow on the ground until late March. I now find it hard to believe that I posted, in brown-paper parcels, some of my Trinity College coal ration to my parents who were short of fuel in London.

Edward Vincent (1940)

Our 'Russian spies': treachery and idealism
Julian Hunt (1960)

Trinity can be proud of the many fine people and great ideas it has produced. It is also infamous for some of its spies. Most of the spies and secret agents educated at Trinity are inevitably less well known, including its code-breakers at Bletchley Park. There can be no question about the patriotism of the tight-lipped boffins of Bletchley. Our 'Russian spies' by contrast excite opposing views.

A majority probably see Guy Burgess, Kim Philby and Anthony Blunt – the best known – as traitors who betrayed the lives of British agents and servicemen and disgraced the College. They were not the only 'Cambridge spies'; Donald Maclean was at Trinity Hall. Two other Trinity men were also involved: John Cairncross, later unmasked as 'the fifth man', and the American Michael Whitney Straight, whom Blunt recruited when he was in mourning for his Trinity friend John Cornford, killed when fighting for the Republicans in the Spanish Civil War.

bitterly that power remained in the hands of the landed gentry and their collaborators. He protested, 'My friends, the heart of England does not beat in stately homes and castles. It beats in the factories and on the farms …'

Fascism was a growing threat both on the continent and, to a lesser extent, in Britain. Continental communists were active on the streets, fighting the anti-semitic and anti-trade union actions of fascist groups or fascist governments. In Britain the Party attracted leading intellectuals and, through such secretive organisations as the Comintern, connected them with Soviet agents.

Trinity was one of the many British institutions that benefited from the continental turmoil. Among others, Besicovitch, the distinguished mathematician, and Wittgenstein, to many the most important 20th-century philosopher, came to work at Trinity. Apparently they were inducted into their Fellowships on the same day. 'I, Abram Samoilivitch Besicovitch, promise to abide by the statutes and ordinances of Trinity College …' 'I, Ludwig von Wittgenstein …' The senior tutor was heard to mutter, 'Two fine Anglo-Saxon names.' Besi once told me it was easier to teach under the czar than to do the regular stint of a Trinity teaching Fellow. He should have known; he had done both.

In the 1930s many undergraduates and some dons were either members of the Communist Party or active sympathisers –

The contrary view holds that young men at Trinity and Cambridge, naturally fired by student idealism, saw in Soviet communism the only progressive alternative to fascism. During the 1930s Depression social democracy lacked all conviction. Cambridge had in any case long been known for its sceptical views on patriotism, epitomised by E.M. Forster (King's 1897): 'If I had to choose between betraying my country and betraying my friends, I hope I should have the guts to betray my country.'

It was a period of political unease and conflict. The First World War hung heavy in the memory; economic collapse had brought mass employment, embodied in hunger marches. Stalin's Russia had many European admirers. Even Russia's own intellectuals suspected little of the horrors enacted in farm collectivisation and the punitive *gulag* of the labour camps.

Nor did there seem to be a parliamentary answer to economic and social misery. Ramsay MacDonald's first and second Labour governments had collapsed. Philby reflected

Maurice Dobb's wartime identity card and civil defence handbook.

fellow-travellers as they were known. Some were so committed that they died for the Republican cause in Spain, not only Cornford but also, from King's, another poet, Julian Bell. Some openly joined the Party and remained lifetime members. Among these were two Fellows of Trinity, James Klugman – in SOE in the war and historian of the Communist Party of Great Britain thereafter – and Maurice Dobb. Dobb taught economics at Trinity all his life, a charming and kindly don who helped many students and never forced his views on any of them.

Philby, Burgess and Blunt were different. They joined the Party not openly but in secret, were soon in touch with Soviet agents, and prepared to recruit others to the cause. They saw Soviet communism as the best model for British society and natural ally of those wanting a British revolution.

If you listen carefully to the creaky panelling on C staircase, Nevile's Court, you might perhaps fancy you can hear whispered voices scheming and recruiting, against a background of anxious discussion about how to be a man in inter-war Britain. You might hear Blunt from C2, Dobb from C1 and Cairncross in C4. C Nevile's is as important in history as Isaac Newton's E Great Court or the New Court stair that witnessed the earliest agreement on the rules of soccer in 1848. In the 1930s homo- or bi-sexuality was a more common bond than football, at least for some among the educated classes. Friendships were also cemented in the secret dining club, the Apostles, which continues in Cambridge to this day.

To disguise their activities, Philby and Burgess openly associated with right-wing pro-fascist organisations. Blunt devoted himself mainly to scholarship in art history. After his Trinity Research fellowship he moved to London, where he later became Professor at London University, the knighted Keeper of the Queen's Pictures, and finally an Honorary Fellow of Trinity – the highest honour the College can bestow.

In the Second World War many dons and journalists were taken into British Intelligence. Philby and Blunt seemed sufficiently respectable to be accepted. Even the promiscuously homosexual Burgess was able to join the Foreign Office press department. All ex-public school types, they were recruited along the old-boy network. This had then no need of a tutor's

A Meeting of the Apostles, c.1934, from the Trinity Review *of 1984.*

reference. It does so now. According to Patrick Duff, our Vice Master after the Second World War, Trinity was never consulted about Burgess's extraordinary appointment.

From 1941 to 1945 the Soviet Union was our ally and indeed took the brunt of the war's casualties. The public revered 'Uncle Joe'. Philby, Blunt and Burgess et al. did not therefore spy on behalf of an active enemy – not even after 1945. Their actions were treasonable in the strict sense of violating their allegiance to the state, not in the popular sense of helping an enemy at war with the state, although there is strong evidence that Philby's actions led to the deaths of many NATO intelligence agents working in post-war Eastern Europe.

Blunt helped Burgess and Maclean, both in the Foreign Office, to escape to the Soviet Union in 1951. He tipped them off – something Forster would have approved. He eventually confessed his questionable past to the British security services in 1964 but he was not prosecuted, nor did the establishment publish his misdeeds. He retained his position of Keeper of the Queen's Pictures, and his knighthood. For his scholarship, particularly on the paintings of Poussin, Trinity elected him an Honorary Fellow in 1968.

Philby, the arch spy, was also involved in the flight of Burgess and Maclean. He became a newspaper correspondent and fled to Moscow himself in 1963 when he was exposed by Russian defectors to the West. While Philby and Blunt worked for British Intelligence as Britons, they also passed information to the Soviet Union as communists. They were in both British and Russian espionage. Yet they are known only as 'Russian spies'.

How did all this affect Trinity? The big questions about treachery, scholarship and idealism came up in 1979 soon after a new master, Sir Alan Hodgkin, had been installed. Thanks to information from the US, through their Freedom of Information Act, it became known that Blunt had been the 'fourth man', involved with Philby, Burgess and Maclean. The new Prime Minister, Mrs Thatcher, confirmed the facts. The Queen, who had known earlier about Blunt's confession, could now withdraw his knighthood, originally given for personal service to her.

The press wondered what Trinity would decide about the Honorary Fellowship. The College Council met on Friday 16 November 1979. The Master, who knew Blunt, asked each member of the Council in turn how they thought the College ought to react, a procedure followed only for the most serious of issues. Every other member of Council wanted Blunt to resign or to force him to do so. Some said he was a traitor. I disagreed. I said we should do nothing, since his Honorary Fellowship was a tribute to his scholarship, not to his politics. Furthermore, he had not worked for an enemy engaged in open warfare with this country.

The Master wound up the discussion by suggesting that a historical perspective might be helpful. In the 1650s, as he reminded us, many distinguished English scientists who later helped to found the Royal Society had fled to the Netherlands with Charles II and his exile regime. They were in effect working with an enemy with whom we were at war, the Dutch. But we remembered them as scientists, and respected them for their contribution to the country.

The Master had already given an interview to the *Cambridge Evening News*. This ran big headlines on that same Friday. It reported Sir Alan as saying that 'the Honorary Fellowship is a

reflection of his scholarship and I do not think the PM's statement questioned this. It is most unlikely that the College would take any precipitate action.' On the next day, Saturday, following the Council meeting and a judicious leak by a person or persons unknown, the bemused readers of the *CEN* met a contradictory headline: 'Moves to strip Blunt of College Fellowship.'

Blunt gave an extraordinary interview to *The Times* newspaper a few days later. He justified his past actions and regretted 'the idea of losing my Fellowship at Trinity'. All that week there was hectic discussion and lobbying both at Trinity and in the press. Some dons felt Trinity should stand firm in its recognition of Mr Blunt's expertise and allow him to keep his honour. Even some Trinity men who had been in the secret service took that view. Others felt otherwise.

The following Friday the Master told Council that he had accepted an offer from Blunt to resign his Honorary Fellowship. Subsequently the Universities of London and Oxford, respectively, agreed to revoke neither his Emeritus Professorship nor his Honorary Degree, having rejected arguments for revocation similar to those heard at Trinity.

It must have seemed to Blunt when he decided to resign his Fellowship that his old College had joined in the clamour to strip him of his academic honours. Trinity appeared to have learned nothing from its decision in 1916 to sack the philosopher Bertrand Russell from his lectureship after his conviction for the crime of pacifism. At the insistence of many Fellows that most unfortunate decision was rescinded after the Great War. But in 1979 Trinity had, or so Blunt must have thought, reverted to the position that loyalty to the state was more important than that owed to scholarship and the free expression of ideas.

Trinity gladly accepts that its privileges bring with them responsibilities, not least to British citizens whose taxes help to pay for what the College spends on education and research. As a scientist myself I have tried to ensure that my research is also of practical benefit. But this duty does not require unconditional loyalty to the state. In the critical world of a University the terms 'traitor' and 'treason' should be used only with caution, after full and cool consideration of the evidence – as indeed Sir Alan Hodgkin reminded the College in the heat of the debate in 1979.

Abram Samoilovitch Besicovitch.

A safe haven in turbulent times
Béla Bollobás (1963)

Until the First World War, Fellows of the College were almost exclusively of British stock. This started to change when the College gave refuge to some academics escaping from the two main evil tyrannies of the 20th century, communism and fascism. The honourable behaviour of the College in welcoming the refugees did not, as many had feared at the time, harm the College; on the contrary the newcomers enriched its life in many ways.

I myself was fortunate enough to have found refuge in Trinity: my crime was not that I was considered to be anti-Soviet, rather that I overstayed my permitted time in the West. While the Nazis occasionally allowed 'undesirable' people to leave their empire, the Soviets did not make this mistake, and in effect turned the entire Soviet bloc into a huge prison. When in 1966 I won a Fellowship from the Mathematical Institute in Oxford, my repeated applications for permission to take it up were rejected. Eventually, in early 1969, when I was 25, I was allowed to leave Hungary for a year. Cutting short my Fellowship in Oxford, I took up a scholarship I had been awarded by Trinity some years earlier. The Hungarian KGB put much pressure on me to leave Cambridge and return to Hungary. When I refused to do so, there was a show trial in Budapest at which I was sentenced *in absentia* to three years solitary confinement: the only Hungarian

academic honoured in this way. For years, I had nightmares in which a flight I was on was hijacked and flown to a communist country, where I would be put in prison. These nightmares only stopped in 1989, with the fall of communism in Hungary. In all these years, Trinity has been a wonderful home to me, enabling me to do mathematics in a splendid environment.

The College's greatest philosopher, Wittgenstein, was the most famous of Trinity's refugees, but he became a refugee only decades after his arrival in Cambridge. When he first came to Trinity in 1911, he was far from penniless or homeless, but with the rise of the Nazis in Germany and the *Anschluss* in 1938 he found himself a man without a country. Similarly, Leon Radzinowicz (1906–99) arrived in Cambridge from Paris in 1938, ostensibly to report on the English penal system for the Polish government. A year later, the Nazis invaded his homeland and he wisely decided to remain in Cambridge. Most of his colleagues at the Law School at the Free University of Warsaw were massacred. He was naturalised in 1947, elected a Fellow of Trinity in 1948 and over the next 40 years published his five-volume masterpiece, *A History of English Criminal Law*. He became in 1959 the first Wolfson Professor of Criminology at Cambridge in the Institute founded by him at the instigation of the then Home Secretary and future Master of Trinity, Rab Butler. Under Radzinowicz, the Institute maintained a close relationship with the Home Office, researching penal policy and contributing to the debate on the abolition of the death penalty. One of 'Radzy's' first tasks as its director had been to create a world-class research library, which, on his retirement in 1973, was renamed in his honour.

The first refugee given shelter by the College was the mathematician Abram Samoilovitch Besicovitch (1891–1970), who was born in Berdyansk on the Sea of Azov in the Ukraine. In 1920, after the communists had taken power, Besicovitch was appointed Professor in the Pedagogical Institute in Petrograd (St Petersburg), where he taught classes of workers with no background in mathematics. The times were harsh: he survived the famine of 1918–19 by eating chunks of a horse he had buried in the ground.

In 1924 Besicovitch was awarded a Rockefeller Fellowship to work in Copenhagen with Harald Bohr, but the Soviets

Piero Sraffa's certificate of registration as an alien. It has stamps in it recording a stay in the Evelyn Nursing Home in June 1940, prior to a brief incarceration in the Metropole Camp, Isle of Man, from which he was released in October 1940.

repeatedly refused to give him permission to take it up. Eventually, he was smuggled across the Baltic Sea in a small boat and safely reached Copenhagen. To their credit, the Rockefeller Foundation covered all his expenses, including the bribe to the smugglers. In 1925 Besicovitch spent a few months in New College with Hardy, who was so impressed by him that he secured for him a lectureship at Liverpool and then at Cambridge. In 1930 Littlewood, strongly supported by Hardy, put Besicovitch up for a Fellowship at Trinity. Although the case was a very strong one, the Master's casting vote was needed to win the day. Littlewood immediately dispatched a postcard to Hardy: 'ASBOKQTJEL' (A.S. Besicovitch OK, quiet, J.E. Littlewood).

As a Teaching Fellow of Trinity, Besicovitch ran a weekly problem competition for his undergraduates. The undergraduates loved this: the better ones got their first taste of research. In 1950 he succeeded Littlewood in the Rouse Ball Chair, which he held until his retirement in 1958.

Besicovitch was an exceptionally open-minded mathematician, who was ready to consider the most unlikely options; this enabled him to prove several very surprising results. His most famous theorem is a good example of this. In 1917 the Japanese mathematician Kakeya asked for the smallest area in which a needle (a line segment) of length 1 can be turned around completely. In 1928 Besicovitch proved the paradoxical result that there is no minimum area: domains with arbitrarily small areas can be constructed in which our needle can be rotated through $2\prod$. Although at the first glance this result is a curiosity,

this is far from the case: the result is closely related to numerous deep questions studied today by some of the best analysts. Bohr and Besicovitch were the founders of the theory of almost periodic functions – another area alive and well today.

Throughout his career Besicovitch was attracted to seemingly intractable problems needing ingenious and intricate constructions, so his proofs tended to be very complicated, occasionally unnecessarily so. His achievements were not diminished by simpler proofs found later – often by himself. Quoting him exactly, 'mathematician reputation rests on number of his bad proofs'.

Piero Sraffa (1898–1983) was born in Turin to a wealthy Italian–Jewish family. After a degree in law from his local university, he spent the academic year 1921–2 at the London School of Economics, after which he worked in Milan, Perugia and Cagliari as an economist. Sraffa became a staunch socialist, and befriended the influential politicians of the left, Antonio Gramsci and Filippo Turati. Soon after his march on Rome in 1922, Mussolini attacked Sraffa for his articles on economics. By 1927 his position in Italy became untenable, and he accepted Keynes's offer of a lectureship in Cambridge. He was a Fellow of Trinity from 1939 until his death, and supervised generations of students. While at Trinity, he greatly influenced Wittgenstein's later philosophical investigations.

Sraffa spent over 20 years collecting and editing the papers of David Ricardo, the great English economist. This was a monumental enterprise he undertook on Keynes's suggestion; as Stigler wrote: 'Ricardo was a fortunate man … And now,

Below: *Otto Frisch was a keen cartoonist. These were published in the* Trinity Review *in 1957: ASB is A.S. Besicovitch, GMT is the former Master, G.M. Trevelyan, ARGO is Alan Owen, the mathematician and parapsychologist; 'A Past Fellow' has not been conclusively identified.*

130 years after his death, he is as fortunate as ever: he has been befriended by Sraffa.' In 1960 he published his only book, *The Production of Commodities by Means of Commodities*; with this slim volume he founded the Neo-Ricardian school of economics. Samuelson, the Nobel Prize-winning economist, doubted whether any scholar had had as great an impact on economic science as Sraffa, in so few writings.

The mathematician Hans Heilbronn (1908–75) was born in Berlin into a cultured German–Jewish middle-class family, which had been thoroughly assimilated into German life. He fully immersed himself in the life of a German student: he even fought a duel, whose scar he carried for the rest of his life. In Göttingen he was the star pupil of Landau, the great number theorist (and a friend of Hardy and Littlewood), receiving his PhD in 1933.

From a Don's Notebook

by FRISCH

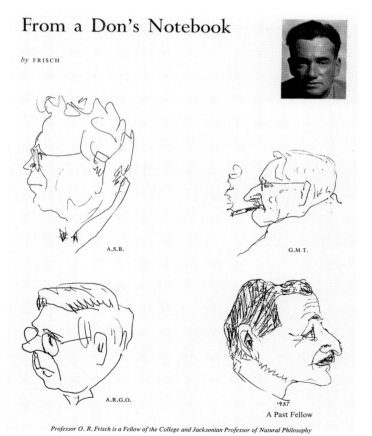

A.S.B.

G.M.T.

A.R.G.O.

'1957

A Past Fellow

Professor O. R. Frisch is a Fellow of the College and Jacksonian Professor of Natural Philosophy

After the Nazis had come to power, Heilbronn, like all Jewish scientists in Germany, lost his position. At the beginning of 1934, the combined efforts of Hardy, Hassé (the Head of Department at Bristol), the Academic Assistance Council, and the Jewish community in Bristol enabled Heilbronn to leave Göttingen for Bristol. In England he struck up lifelong friendships with two slightly younger mathematicians, Harold Davenport (of Trinity) and Paul Erdos (in Manchester at that time).

Hardy, who worked tirelessly on behalf of the Jewish mathematicians who had to flee from the Nazis, thought especially highly of Heilbronn. In May 1935, at Hardy's insistence, Heilbronn was elected to a Fellowship at Trinity. Heilbronn spent five happy and productive years in Cambridge; he even brought his parents and sister over from Germany. In 1940 the College Council decided to continue Heilbronn's salary and rights, but he could not take advantage of this: like most other anti-Nazi refugees, he was interned on the Isle of Wight as an 'enemy alien'. After his release, he served with the British Army until the end of the war. Shortly afterwards, he returned to Bristol, where he built up an excellent department of mathematics. In 1964 he moved to Toronto, where he stayed until his death.

Heilbronn made important contributions to number theory. In particular, shortly after his arrival in England, he shot to fame when he proved a long-standing conjecture of Gauss. For decades, he collaborated with Davenport, and he also wrote an influential paper with Erdos. Although after leaving Bristol for Toronto he never revisited the College, he bequeathed a large sum to the mathematical Fellows.

The Academic Assistance Council was founded in 1933 by William Beveridge, Director of the LSE. He persuaded two well-known Trinity men, Ernest Rutherford and Archibald Hill, to become, respectively, its founding President and Vice President. In less than eight months, they had raised £10,000 for the assistance of Jewish academics dismissed from their posts in Germany and Austria. In 1936, the Council was expanded and became the Society for the Protection of Science and Learning after it became clear that its work would be required for more than a temporary period. By the outbreak of war, it had assisted

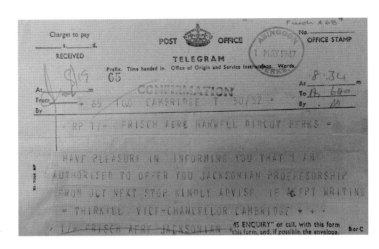

A telegram from the Vice Chancellor, Henry Thirkill, offering Otto Frisch the Jacksonian Professorship, May 1947.

900 academics, its profile greatly enhanced by the involvement of such respected scientists.

For several eminent refugees from the Nazis, such as Otto Frisch and Hans Lissmann, Trinity offered a final safe haven after years of rootlessness. The experimental physicist Otto Robert Frisch (1904–79) was born in Vienna, the son of Austrian–Jewish parents. After his doctorate he spent three years in Berlin at the physical laboratory there, and started to work with the great physicist Lise Meitner, his aunt, with whom later he did some of his best work. After the introduction of the race laws in 1933, he had to leave Germany; a grant from the Academic Assistance Council enabled him to go to work with Blackett at Birkbeck College. From then on, until his arrival in Cambridge in 1947, Frisch moved from place to place – Copenhagen, Birmingham, Liverpool, Los Alamos and Harwell – staying only for a short while at each location. Otto Frisch was first to realise with Meitner the possibility of neutron-induced fission of uranium. He also designed the first detonator of the atomic bomb while at Los Alamos.

In 1947 he was appointed to the Jacksonian Professorship of Natural Philosophy in Cambridge, and became a Fellow of Trinity. With this, Frisch's peregrinations were over: Cambridge was his first permanent home since Vienna. His parents joined him in 1948, and his beloved aunt, Lise Meitner, in 1960. He revelled in his life in Cambridge: not only did he take much pleasure in doing physics and having excellent students, but he also enjoyed the abundance of music and visual arts Cambridge offered.

Although the zoologist Hans Werner Lissmann (1909–95) was born near Odessa, both his parents were German and the family returned to Germany after the First World War.

In 1932 Lissmann obtained a doctorate in Hamburg for a dissertation on Siamese fighting fishes; this led to a grant to work at the Hungarian Biological Research Institute in Tihany on Lake Balaton. When Hitler came to power, Lissmann made it clear that he had no sympathy for the Nazis; as a result, his German grant was revoked, and the Institute was even pressured into dismissing him altogether. His idea of producing an anti-fouling paint for boats took him to Calcutta, where he received a letter from James Gray with an offer of a meagre grant to work

in Cambridge. This led to his outstanding work with Gray on the locomotion of leeches and earthworms.

At the outbreak of war, Lissmann was interned as an 'enemy alien', released and then interned again; eventually he was transferred to Canada. On his return to Cambridge in 1943, he continued his research. The highlight of his scientific career was his work on the electric eel and other fishes that can deliver powerful electric shocks. This work earned him a Fellowship of the Royal Society in 1954, and a University Lectureship the following year. The same year he became a Fellow of Trinity and a Director of Studies.

Fate in many respects had been most unkind to Lissmann until his Fellowship in Trinity: his adventures up to then (in Russia, Germany, Hungary, India, Ghana and other places) seem to be from a thriller. His vicissitudes turned him into a most attractive individual: he was quiet, kind and gentle, with a wonderful low-key sense of humour. He was fluent in Russian,

Walter Ullmann.

Hans Heilbronn.

Mohammad Hashem Pesaran.

French, German, Tartar, Hungarian and English. He was all one could hope for in a refugee in Trinity.

The historian Walter Ullmann (1910–83) was born in Palkau, in Lower Austria. In 1929 he entered the University of Vienna to read law but, finding his professors remote, he transferred two years later to Innsbruck. From 1935 he was a pre-trial investigator in Vienna, the youngest of his rank in Austria. As he relentlessly pursued Nazi thugs within the jurisdiction of his court, he fell foul of the Nazis, especially after it was discovered that one of his grandfathers had been Jewish. After the *Anschluss* in March 1938 and the establishment of a puppet regime, Ullmann refused to take the oath of allegiance to the Führer; with that, his position became untenable, and he had to flee Austria. As he said later, the Gestapo was 'far too busy with the big fish to deal efficiently with such small fry as myself', so that he could get four weeks of study leave, which he spent in Cambridge.

It would have been foolhardy to return to Austria: the Cambridge Refugee Committee made it possible for him to stay in Cambridge. He established contacts with several academics, and made use of the libraries to start to work on 14th-century jurists. In 1940 he was interned as an 'enemy alien' but was allowed to join the Pioneer Corps on his release. Already in 1942 he published a paper on medieval law, but after his discharge from the army his research intensified, so that by 1946 he could publish his first major book, on Lucas da Penna. His book on the election of Pope Urban VI in 1378 and the start of the Great Schism appeared while he was a lecturer at Leeds. A year later, in 1959, he moved back to Cambridge, where within a few

months he had four research students. He became a Fellow of the College in 1959, and in 1972 was elected to the Cambridge Chair of Medieval History.

In Cambridge, Ullmann was very productive, doing much work on the Papacy. Perhaps his most important books were *The Growth of Papal Government in the Middle Ages* and the very ambitious *Principles of Government and Politics in the Middle Ages*. In keeping with his belief that scholarship should be made available to the general reader, he wrote a very successful popular book, *A Short History of the Papacy*. Ullmann's passion for medieval history made him a legendary figure. He was devoted to the College; he never tired of supervising hosts of students, giving his last supervision a few days before his death.

After the defeat of the Nazis the stream of refugees escaping persecution and death became a trickle. Although the College has more and more foreign-born Fellows, very few of them arrived in Cambridge as refugees. The economist Mohammad Hashem Pesaran is one of these recent refugees. He was born in Shiraz, Iran, in 1946, and arrived in Cambridge in 1968 to start a PhD. After a year at Harvard, he became a Lector in Economics at Trinity a year before his PhD was awarded in 1972. In that year he returned home to take up a position at the Central Bank of Iran, which had financially supported his education in England. In 1975, 'out of the blue' he received a letter from Lord Butler offering him a College Lectureship in Economics. This he could not accept as he still had to complete his military service; amazingly, the College persevered and told him that their offer would remain open until 1979.

With the start of the revolutionary upheavals in 1978, Pesaran's position in the Ministry of Education became a liability. He soon realised that life in Iran was no longer safe for his English-born wife and three young children, whom he sent back to England. Eventually, he managed to resign his position and returned to Cambridge; generously, the College provided the Pesarans with a home and other support even before he took up his Fellowship in January 1979. Hardly a fortnight later, the Shah was forced to leave Iran; with the subsequent return of Ayatollah Khomeini, Iran became an Islamic Republic and had no use for the officials of the Shah's ministries.

Opposite: *Nevile's Court.*

I READ ECONOMICS AT TRINITY UNDER PROFESSOR SIR DENNIS Robertson, who roomed in Great Court. My Director of Studies in my final year was Pierro Sraffa: both renowned economists in very different ways and both charming and caring teachers. On seeing my name in the lists pinned up at the Senate House, I ran at great speed to the rooms of Dr Sraffa in Nevile's Court. Breathless, I banged on the door and barged in. 'Sir, Sir, I am now a graduate of Cambridge University!'

'So?' questioned Dr Sraffa.

'You said I would fail or just pass, Sir.'

'Sit down. Sit down. Here, have a glass of sherry. You see, my young man, you are stupid but the examiners even more so.' All in a strong Italian accent. Then he hugged me. As I left, I turned to look at this amazing man who threw all my supervisions into the fireplace. His tears were better concealed than mine.

It is a moment which defined my entire stay at Cambridge and, on my visits, I always stand for a moment outside the same door.

Nawshir Khurody (1955)

I TOOK THE ENTRANCE SCHOLARSHIP EXAMINATION TO TRINITY in December 1941. I remember the date well, because the Japanese attack on Pearl Harbor, and the US entry into the Second World War, happened in the course of the examination. I gained a scholarship, and went up to Trinity as a 'bye-termist' in January 1942, to read for the natural sciences Tripos. My favoured subject was chemistry, but when I mentioned this to my Director of Studies, the nuclear physicist Norman Feather, he said, 'Nonsense – you did an excellent physics paper, and the country needs physicists, so your Part II subject should be physics,' to which I meekly agreed. After doing well in the prelims to Part I, we were allowed to go on to Part II of the Tripos, but most of my fellow students were called up in the course of their studies and (as I learned later) sent to Canada to work on uranium isotope separation. As I was not a British subject at that time (I had come to England as a refugee from the Nazis in 1936), I did not qualify for this top-secret work, and was allowed, as one of two, to finish the degree. We were allowed an extra term, so took the Part II examination in December 1943.

Having taken Part II, I was assigned to some work in Cambridge, for which I was quite unsuited. I continued to live in College, most of the time, and to eat in Hall. The food, as I recall, was quite adequate, and the College cellars continued to be richly stocked. One evening remains in my memory, when we smuggled a woman student, dressed as a man, into the all-male dinner society. Halfway through the dinner we realised, with alarm, that nothing had been done about the lady's painted fingernails. The waiters were surely aware of what was going on, but said nothing.

Having, with some difficulty, extricated myself from this work at the end of the war, I started to work for a PhD in theoretical physics under the direction of A.H. Wilson (Fellow, 1933–45), who was research director at the textile firm Courtaulds, but wanted also to continue with pure science; my tutor at the time, John Burnaby, who was not in favour of academics going into industry, rather reluctantly agreed to this. And the College awarded me a research scholarship (there were no state grants in those days); I believe the scholarship was really intended for sons of clergymen from Staffordshire, and I was the nearest the College could find to fit that description. Wilson suggested a problem in the theory of metals which was worthy and involved laborious calculations. I spent much of the hot summer of 1947 bent over a desk calculating machine, having ascertained from Maurice Wilkes that his computer would not be up and running for a further two years. Fortunately the results came out much as they should. The previous winter had been notoriously long and cold, with little fuel available for heating; but the Cavendish Laboratory stayed warm, so I spent most of my waking hours there and got much work done.

I submitted all my work in the theory of metals to the competition for a Research Fellowship at Trinity, and was fortunate to be successful in 1948. I had by then accepted a year's Fellowship at Bristol, under Nevill Mott, but spent happy weekends at Trinity. This was followed by a year in the US. On my return I married Janet, a historian at Girton College, and we lived for a year in a College flat above Hobbs sports shop in Trinity Street. Janet supervised history students at Trinity (one of them was Douglas Hurd, now Baron Hurd of Westwell), and taught at Girton. I count my years at Trinity in the 1940s as perhaps the happiest of my life.

Ernst Sondheimer (1942)

CHAPTER 15

Scenes From College Life (1980s–2000s)
TCSU, RAG, the Magpie and Stump

To Amiens and back with Norman Stone

It was towards the end of February 1983, my second year at Trinity. I had been supervised in my first year by Norman Stone, and we had hit it off, despite a near disastrous start to my first supervision. (I had expressed admiration for Louis Napoleon – Norman thought him unutterable, and his ejection after Sedan 18 years too late.) I went round mid-evening for a drink. The whiskey flowed, and at about 10.30 Norman suddenly asked if I would like to go to Amiens with him. 'I'm having a book published tomorrow,' he said, 'and it always brings me good luck if I go there and buy a cigarette lighter with a picture of the Cathedral on it.' 'Why not,' I said. 'But you'll have to drive,' he said. There followed a slightly convoluted story about a Polish friend, another woman, sudden illness, his obligation to drive one, or both of them home after a boozy party, and an inevitable meeting with the police, etc. 'That's fine,' I said. So at 11pm we called Marshall's, and somehow managed to get a car. On the way out, Norman left a note on his door for his next day's supervisees letting them know – in German, perhaps slightly unhelpfully – that 'Mr Stone had passed away in the night.'

After picking up my passport, and encountering several rather sceptical friends, we arrived at Marshall's where, somewhat to my surprise, they rented us a car (Norman's cherished gold card, my licence). We set off south at midnight. The M11 had just been opened, but not the M25, so we felt our way round London and on to Dover. Norman entertained by running through the members of the history faculty that he liked (a relatively short list, mostly Trinity Fellows) and a rather longer list of those he valued less highly (the foibles of this latter group being illustrated by the addition of some colourful but perhaps unnecessary horizontal details). We made it to Dover at 3.30, where we discovered that the exceptional sluggishness of the car could be explained by the choke having been out all the way from Cambridge. We parked in a side street and bought ourselves tickets for the next ferry.

After a breakfast of lager and crisps, we got to Calais around 8am, and found another car rental desk (equally happy to see Norman's gold card, somewhat less happy to see my licence). We set off from Calais and promptly got lost in Boulogne. After a couple of circuits round the town centre, we stopped to see if a little Calvados might make things clearer. It didn't, but back on the road, eventually, some centripetal force propelled us out of Boulogne and we headed for Amiens. Having exhausted Cambridge topics, Norman spoke movingly about his childhood, and, particularly the loss of his father, a RAF pilot, in the Second World War.

As we approached Amiens, Norman started to worry. What if the bar by the Cathedral was closed? What if it no longer stocked the lighters? (That's the downside of superstition.) But the bar was open, and there was an entire carton of lighters. Norman bought four just to be on the safe side. After a little more celebratory Calvados, we went outside to record the great event. I've still got the very blurry photographs in the front of the great west door of the Cathedral. Norman's grin tells it all.

It seemed silly to come to France and return empty-handed (excepting the lucky lighters, of course), so we went next to the local hypermarket, where Norman bought four cases of wine and a lot of cheese. Then back into Amiens for a late lunch of couscous and wine (the hour(s) for Calvados, thankfully, having come and gone).

We headed back to Calais, and, unable to find the Hertz office, parked the French car on the quayside (Hertz charged Norman for the extra day it took them to find it). At Dover, however, we were faced with a problem. How were we to get four cases of wine to the English car? We got the wine onto the quayside, and Norman then disappeared. He reappeared a few minutes later, followed by a forklift truck and bemused driver.

Having settled up with Customs, the forklift obligingly dropped us at the main gate.

The drive back to London was uneventful – until it became clear that we had missed the turn for the Dartford Tunnel. So, with no London driving experience at all (and no sleep either), we went round Hyde Park Corner during the evening rush hour. To celebrate our survival, Norman suggested we stop at his favourite Chinese restaurant in Hampstead. Once we'd sat down, Norman asked if I'd like a drink. 'What do you drink with Chinese food?' I asked. Norman clearly regarded this as a rather stupid question. 'Whisky, of course,' he replied. So whisky it was.

On the road to Cambridge at around 11pm, lack of sleep eventually caught up with me. Amazingly, however, Norman was wide awake and caught me and the car before we drifted too far. After that, I also was quite awake, and at midnight, almost exactly 24 hours after we had left, plus the lucky lighters, we got back to Cambridge.

And, yes, the book was a triumph.

William Morris (1981)

DURING MY SECOND YEAR AT TRINITY (1984–5), I BECAME AWARE of a decoy duck, mascot of dining society The Mallards. I'm told it was traditional for the incumbent president to challenge the successor by placing the duck in a devilishly inaccessible place – in this instance, high in the rafters of Hall together with a prominently displayed sign announcing the bird's name, 'Sir Francis Mallard'. After some months, noting that the challenge was not being met, I conceived the ridiculous notion of attempting to retrieve Sir Francis myself.

The obvious way to gain entry to Hall late at night – 'carding' the door to the Minstrel's Gallery on the staircase leading up from the JCR – proved unnecessary when I encountered the door unlocked, permitting an easy (but very naughty) climb down the ornate woodwork into Hall. I realised after some experimentation however that reaching the rafters would be very difficult and dangerous, and I adjourned. It was too big a challenge to take on alone.

While discussing the duck with a friend (whom I shall not name out of good manners), I learned that he, too, had

Sir Francis Mallard. He was removed from the Hall during renovations in 2000–1, but a replacement decoy made an appearance after the May Ball in 2001. It was knocked down and confiscated in 2006.

infiltrated Hall late at night via the same door, with the same aim, and had drawn the same conclusion. We joined forces and hatched a plan to return to Hall with suitable equipment. A soft fabric juggling ball was thrown over one of the rafters with a length of cotton attached, allowing us to pull up some thicker string. The string in place, a copious amount of climbing rope could then be hoisted, paving the way to a safe(ish) climb. In fact, the knot joining the cotton to the string became badly snagged, and a sharp tug then broke the string, forcing us to abandon the attempt. On taking breakfast in the morning, we observed the highly conspicuous 20-foot length of string dangling over the heads of breakfasters.

We returned several nights later with superior equipment. I climbed to a ledge above the wood panelling and was handed a lightweight bamboo punt pole, with a loop of string at one end, through which we had fed the climbing rope. The pole was employed like a fishing rod to dangle a weight (unicycle pedal cranks, as I recall) over the lowest point of the rafters. Releasing tension on the rope allowed the weight to draw it over. My friend then made the ascent while I, being heavier, stayed the rope at

ground level. The sole impediment now being umpteen years of accumulated dust, Sir Francis was soon safely down, whereupon to our surprise he turned out to be made of plastic, not the wood we were expecting.

My wardrobe in B13 Butler House served as his storage location for several months while we considered where to put Sir Francis. Eventually the location suggested itself: renovation work in Nevile's Court meant that the roof over the BA Room was shrouded in scaffolding. We had only to climb out the window late at night, whereupon we gained access to an exceedingly long ladder being used in the renovation. After an hour or two of careful and quiet manoeuvring, we had managed to move the ladder through the maze of scaffolding and slowly raise it into position against the western roof of Hall where, by a wonderful coincidence, it reached within an arm's length of the Lantern. I climbed the ladder, eased open a window and located the window-opening cord inside. Having attached Sir Francis to the cord via a key ring, I lowered him to his new nose-down resting position inside the Lantern.

I am not certain how long he remained there. My last sighting of him was on a visit in the 1990s. The College's Wikipedia page says that he was knocked down by pigeons in 2003 and has since been resident in the Junior Bursar's office.

Mike Day (1983)

I AM A LITTLE ASHAMED NOW TO RECALL THAT MY MAIN AMBITION on coming up to Trinity was to live in Great Court. Thanks to the vagaries of the ballot, I achieved it in my third year. I6 was a low-ceilinged double set, above the shower block. But to me, it was a palace. We had an upright piano, the use of a double electric cooking ring, and, most wondrous of all, three windows through which we could crawl onto the battlements.

It was there, in the summer, that I used to conduct most of my daily – and nightly – life. I'd take a cushion, and a couple of books, and sunbathe while revising post-Keynesian econometrics. As the sun started to set, a bottle of wine would come out and a couple of glasses, and often, a handful of friends and neighbours. Having mild vertigo, I wasn't a committed roof-climber, but I knew a lot of them, who would invariably drop in for a drink

Right:
Samantha Weinberg on the roof outside her room.

Far right: *The Cuppers-winning athletics team, 1985.*

after negotiating the Hall and Chapel, or perhaps on their way to tackle the Senate House Leap.

None of us ever fell off, thank God, but it's left me with an enduring yearning for a courtyard of my own, another ambition that I will, I hope, one day achieve.

Samantha Weinberg (1985)

WE SCRIBBLED OUR WAY THROUGH TRINITY JUST BEFORE COMPUTERS went from novelty to necessity, quaintly penning essays in a single late-night sitting. We arranged our lives in advance or relied on chance encounters, just before cellphones made communication so simple. And, for those of us in Bishop's Hostel, we arrived just before bathrooms.

Not that it was all bad. The icy dash in dressing gown and flip-flops to New Court on a January morning beat any espresso for jolting us awake – as long as we did not find a full bathroom, and a draughty wait the other end. On warm summer mornings, our walk round the corner simply added to the romance of student life.

Sometimes, however, it turned into a longer journey. I would return from a shower to find my door locked and my key on the wrong side. That meant a walk of shame. Not the glamorous variety, sporting white tie the morning after a May Ball, but a bleary-eyed trip across Great Court in a tatty robe.

Invariably, a group of the tourists would be crowded under Queen's Gate to enjoy sweeping views across to the Chapel. There was nowhere to hide. So rather than skulk round the edge of the Court, the best choice was to stroll past the fountain and appreciate Trinity through their eyes. I still have rich images of blue sky against warm yellow stone and green, manicured grass. The mundane reason for my walk, and an awareness of the many curious eyes behind me, hammered home the privilege of living inside a world that people had travelled so far to peer into for a fleeting moment. Out of the spotlight, below Great Gate, the porter would hand me the spare key with a look of pity, disdain, or, if I was lucky, a grin, before I broke cover again to face the tourists head on.

Perhaps the need for my key-retrieval journeys was simple forgetfulness or the result of too many late nights. Either way, they left me with a mental album of images showing Trinity at its best. And while I was there, gave me a reason to slow down and stare.

Thorold Barker (1990)

ON MY ELECTION TO THE FELLOWSHIP, MICHAEL ATIYAH HAD to introduce me and the other new Fellows in his speech at the Fellowship Admissions Dinner. He noted that 'as an expert on dinosaur feeding behaviour, Dr Barrett is likely to have an interesting time as a new member of High Table'.

Paul Barrett (1990)

Above: *Simon Naylor's invitations, October 1993.*

Right: *The rich variety of student social life in the 1980s.*

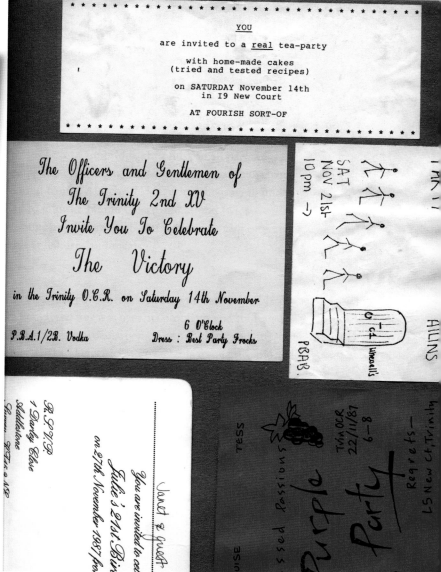

'TRINITY MATRICULATION MENU' IS ONE OF THE EARLIEST memories of the College which has lingered with me, and a rather apt introduction to the world of Trinity. What struck me more than anything else at the time was that the College was serving wine to the students which was of the same vintage as most of the students themselves, followed by port which was definitely older. Of course now I understand that because Trinity has such a long-term view of the world, it can invest in wine at very low cost, store it for years in the cellars, and then produce it like magic for the Fellows and students. I spent years as a student fascinated by the heavily locked doors around the College which were rumoured to lead down to wine cellars, forming a huge labyrinth secretly hidden below the bustle of Cambridge. To this day I don't know the true extent and size of these cellars, which seem to be more heavily guarded than the silver vault (which I have now seen).

'Invitation to Lodge 1993' is an invitation of the sort which all students must have received in their time to meet the Master during their first term. In my days the Master was Professor Amartya Sen, who is always going to be 'The Master' for me. By far the strongest memory however is meeting the Master's wife, who has a fantastic memory and is rumoured to have memorised most of the students' names and photographs prior to our arrival at the Lodge. To meet someone for the first time who already knows who you are, in a room full of other new students, is both amazing and somewhat unnerving.

Despite the College's size and reputation, during my time we had the smallest college bar that I knew about, with a floor you stuck to, but always the friendly face of Norman ready to serve. Then there were the 'Sweaties' in the basement of the Wolfson building – a small basement room that was so full of people that it started to rain sweat at a certain time in the evening.

I now work on the Science Park in Cambridge and exercise at the Trinity Centre after work. It will never cease to amaze me just what influence a 'small college' can have to both me as an individual and the world as a whole.

Simon Naylor (1993)

I WAS 18 WHEN I FIRST LEARNED ABOUT THE EXISTENCE OF my parents. My mother, Rachel, wrote me a letter. I can still remember the advice she offered in those handwritten paragraphs: throw yourself into everything on offer, try your hardest and don't worry when you find that for everything you do, there is someone in Cambridge doing it better than you. It was advice that was reinforced by my father, when I eventually met him in late September of 1998.

The league tennis team, 1997.

I am referring, of course, to my 'College parents'. There was – and I hope, still is – a tradition within Trinity whereby second-year students would pair up and foster one or more freshers, creating pseudo families within the College. In some cases, the parents' role ended shortly after the first week of Michaelmas term, once they had shown the younger students the short-cut to the College bar and bought them a curry on Castle Hill. My parents, however, remained supportive for the duration of our time together at Trinity and even now, over a decade later, they continue to be close friends.

Initially, I was a disappointment to my College mother. As a second-year tennis blue who represented her College in rowing, hockey, football, lacrosse, tennis and squash (and possibly others too – I lost track), she evidently expected her 'daughter' to follow in her footsteps. I would have done, too, had my leg not been wrapped in a plaster cast following a serious car accident. For the whole of the first two terms, I was simply known as 'the girl on crutches'.

All was not lost, however. My College father, Matthew, was a social and political sciences undergraduate and a talented pianist. He spotted the violin case in my room and set about finding me orchestras and groups to join. He introduced me to a friend of his, Celia, who played cello to an exceptional standard and before long, a string quartet (dubiously named No Strings Attached)

was formed. More than ten years later, we are still playing semi-professionally up and down the country, still with the original four members. Violin playing, at least, is something that can be done with a broken leg.

Very quickly, Michaelmas term turned to Lent, and then Easter. The crutches and plaster cast were finally replaced, on my College mother's insistence, by tennis racquets and shorts, and my time became filled with sporting activities, social events and the raft of musical pursuits I had taken up in the first half of the year – as well as the occasional foray into engineering, my degree discipline. I found myself running the University symphony orchestra, learning to ballroom dance and, at one point, volunteering to pole-vault for Trinity. Thankfully, the event was rained off. Without having time to acknowledge it at the time, I was following the advice of my College parents: throwing myself into everything.

The year drew to a close in a whirl of May Balls, concerts, parties and tournaments and before long, it was time to take on a brood of my own. With Faisal, my College husband, I was granted two sons and a daughter and, as Rachel had done for me, I wrote them a letter. In it, I advised them to throw themselves into everything, to try their hardest and not to worry when they found that for everything they did, there was someone in Cambridge doing it better than them – because my College parents were right. I was grateful to them at the time, and I am still grateful to them now. I hope that the Trinity tradition of fostering first-year undergraduates is one that goes on for a very long time.

Polly Courtney (1998)

RAG
Laurie van Someren (1958)
RAG Day was a very big event during the period I was an undergraduate (1958–61). The goal was to raise money for Poppy Day, and there was a competition to see which college raised most. Trinity tended to win because of its size, and I remember figures of around £11,000 being raised, though I cannot say whether that was by the University as a whole, or just Trinity. Since the retail price index then was about a twentieth of now, it was a significant sum.

The Cambridge Highland Band play in a Poppy Day parade on Trinity Street, 1950.

A resurgence of student philanthropy
Immanuel Kemp (2006)

In 2009 the Cambridge Students' RAG Appeal celebrated its 50th birthday as a recognised university society. Student fund-raising across Cambridge under the acronym for 'Raise and Give' has been going for much longer. Within Trinity, the charity-spirited activities of RAG have permeated the fabric of College life for years to some greater or lesser degree, where they always found a warm reception. However, in recent years, Trinity RAG, the College branch of the wider student organisation, has become a burgeoning powerhouse of student fund-raising that pales its earlier efforts by comparison.

Alan Barker and I ran a barbecue on Midsummer Common in 1959 for about 5,000 people. Like other RAG Day events this had a huge amount of cooperation from the City Council, in matters like providing fencing and electricity for lighting the tents where bands played for dancing, providing some policing and simply letting an adequately organised bunch of students do what they wanted with a public open space for a few days.

One of my pleasant tasks was to go to all the bakers I could find in Cambridge and sample their rolls, with a view to placing a large order. I remember the filling bicycle basket as I rode around, and the full sensation after I had done the necessary taste testing; I can't remember the fortunate supplier.

A less pleasant task was screwing down 4×8ft plywood sheets onto a substructure of 2×4 to make a good big dance floor. Buying the woodscrews was easy, but it soon was clear I must go back to the hardware shop and buy screwdrivers too; the available ones were pathetically inadequate. The wooden-handled one which I kept afterwards I still use now. In those days the Marketplace had useful shops around it and the hardware shop supplied anything from one picture hook to a gross of woodscrews with screwdrivers to match.

Amongst the attractions was an ox roast; it takes a long time to roast a whole ox and I think they started on Friday before the event – 'they' being professionals brought in for the purpose, who also knew how to carve it into pieces big enough to satisfy students and small enough to satisfy most of those attending.

Another of my responsibilities was to spend the night there, in a marquee, with the electric-light master switch to hand, in case there were any intruders. There were not, and I left around 6am and told the porters at the Great Gate where I had been overnight on my way back to bed; they were calm about it.

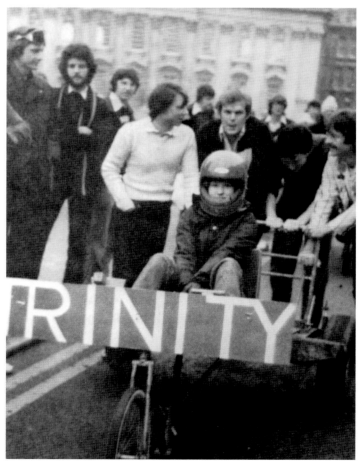

Trinity participants in the 1981 RAG kart race.

MAGPIE AND STUMP

Robert Thomas (2006)

The Magpie and Stump debating society was founded in February 1866 in the rooms of John Chaigneau Colvill on F staircase, Great Court. It celebrated its 1,000th meeting with a grand dinner in 1912 and a former member, the Rev. C.L. Ferguson, published a history of the society in 1931. In it, debates and resolutions are recorded, although it should be noted that the major decision of the first 40 years was that members should be permitted to take snuff at meetings. Members in those early years included Stanley Baldwin, Erskine Childers and Bertrand Russell.

Debates never strayed into the realms of the serious and, since the 1960s, the word 'comedy' has been included in its title. Since 2009, the society has become the Magpie and Stump Comedy Society, with the debating format sometimes eschewed entirely in favour of stand-up comedy. This development has led to the society's recent successes, including performances at a number of May Balls and a week-long run at the Edinburgh Fringe Festival. These developments have been made possible by a renewed enthusiasm for the society within College, and a committed and talented group of new joiners each year.

Quite why, each year, fresh-faced students are so willing to cast their dignity aside for the warm (often lukewarm) applause of their peers is mystifying. His Majesty, the Bird, remains stoically silent on this point. However, new speakers continue to fill the society's meetings, with their wit, their wine and their whipped cream.

Although the society has had its ups and downs, narrowly avoiding closure in 2007, the 'Magpiety' survives and presents stand-up comedy every other Sunday during term time. He remains ably assisted by His Majesty, the Bird, who has recently been rehoused in a new case fitted with safety glass (rumours of assassination threats abound). His Majesty's new home neatly parallels the new growth of the society, which we hope will continue for years to come.

Inset: *Magpie and Stump poster, 1986.*

Left: *The Magpie and Stump Committee, 1900.*

This metamorphosis has been made possible not only by the cluster of dedicated student volunteers at the helm since 2005 but by the ever-present generosity of the wider College community and the support RAG enjoys from the College authorities which makes its fund-raising events possible. In recent years RAG and the College catering have arranged an annual 'Fellows Formal' in which senior members of College such as the Vice Master, Dean and Senior Tutor serve dinner to the undergraduates, who pay RAG for the privilege, while the College departments and officials have supported the annual charity auction with such donations as Trinity's famous in-house brand of ice cream, samples of the wine cellars' finest and the iconic bowler hat of a Trinity porter.

In the context of the University RAG, Trinity volunteers are often to be seen around College selling tickets to Cambridge RAG events or on the streets of Cambridge with buckets and silly costumes to raise funds for various charities, and former College RAG organisers frequently fill posts on Cambridge RAG's central committee – a tradition which culminated in 2007 with both the chairman and president being Trinity mathematicians. In the academic year 2006–7 it was Trinity College that took home not only the shield for the college with the highest fundraising total (an honour previously the unassailable territory of Gonville and Caius College) but also the award for top individual collector, and has defended both against all challengers since then. At present, Trinity is considered the dominant feature of the University RAG scene, and rightly so.

Trinity College Students Union
Oliver McFarlane (2007)

In many respects TCSU has an easy existence. Trinity never seems to make cutbacks or trigger any conflicts with its students. Those at other colleges may have seen room rents hiked by 30 per cent, been cleared out of their accommodation before May Week, or have had their wine restricted at formal – but we've had none of

this at Trinity. Jolly good all round, but it does leave a union of students which is somewhat short of issues to campaign on. Instead, TCSU has left behind political aspirations to embrace its current role as a service provider.

One of the most important tasks is to welcome all the new undergraduate members of Trinity every October, helping them to settle in and make friends – a tall task in such a large College. Freshers' weeks have been rising in profile across the country and while Trinity's does not grab any headlines (almost certainly a good thing), it is a solid programme of awkward mingling and red wine that seems to do the trick, despite lectures beginning halfway through the week.

TCSU even aims to help those yet to arrive, through its College-funded but student-organised access programme. School groups are guided around by those who know how life here really is, and interviewees are calmed by those who've been through it all themselves. Every Easter term a small group goes on tour, visiting schools on the 'Access Bus'.

Much of TCSU's work concerns welfare provision, working closely with College to provide general and individual support. The support available to Trinity students is phenomenal, though it is a credit to the system's discretion that many will have come and gone entirely unaware of it. Perhaps some problems are exaggerated by the pressures of the Tripos system and the way terms are structured, but we wouldn't have it any other way.

Far more visible are the regular TCSU Ents, held fortnightly in the Wolfson Party Room and twice a year decamping to Burrell's Field for a far larger party. A strong tradition of fancy dress continues, as does a naive attitude towards turning a profit, keeping the night cheap and enjoyable for all.

Ultimately TCSU is run for the students, by the students – it isn't perfect and it never will be. Hopefully most feel it is of some use though, or at the very least provides a few welcome distractions.

MAY BALLS

First and Third Trinity Boat Club May Ball
Nicholas Chapman (2007)

As is clear from its official name, the First and Third Trinity Boat Club May Ball is traditionally connected with the College boat clubs. Arguably the first recorded prototype for the May Ball occurred in 1838, in the form of an unusually splendid post-race dinner at the Hoop Inn and held in honour of the 'First Trinity' team. The club paid for 47 bottles of champagne, 12 of sherry, six of Mosel, two of claret, six quarts of ale and £16 14s of punch; with only 38 Trinitarians present, it seems that the proportional alcohol intake was not dissimilar to that of today's May Ball, with its seemingly endless supply of vintage champagne served from ice-filled punts underneath the Wren Library.

Officially, the first May Ball was held in 1866 when the First Trinity team was head of the river, with Third Trinity second. The 20th century saw it evolve into the largest and most sought-after event on the student social calendar.

It may shock those who matriculated before the 1990s to learn that students in 2010 had to shell out nearly £300 for a double ticket. However, the fact that the ball sells out every year suggests that guests feel they get their money's worth. Held in sparkling white marquees on the South Paddock, students in their white tie or colourful ball gowns flit from tent to tent, where they hear some of Cambridge's finest talent performing a range of acts: big bands recapturing the days of Glenn Miller, string quartets playing Mozart and Haydn, the Footlights' unique brand of surreal wit, and even belly dancers. Great Hall boasts a Venetian masquerade, or a pseudo-Victorian music hall, while the Old Kitchens are turned into the University's most elegant casino.

In all of these venues, a mouth-watering display of food and drink is on offer. Hog roasts, chocolate fountains, oysters, gourmet pizza and ice creams, vintage cheese boards, port, gin, whisky, cocktails and fine wines are all on the menu throughout the evening.

Even with all this meticulously planned profligacy, most students rate the ball's success on two of its most transient events: the ten-minute fireworks and the 'main (professional) band'. With Trinity's reputation, the main act is usually the most difficult call of the entire ball. For all the effort that goes into the food, drink, aesthetics, security and logistics, it is the headliner which will cement itself into the minds of the ball-goers and fill the student newspapers the following morning. Thankfully, Trinity usually gets it right.

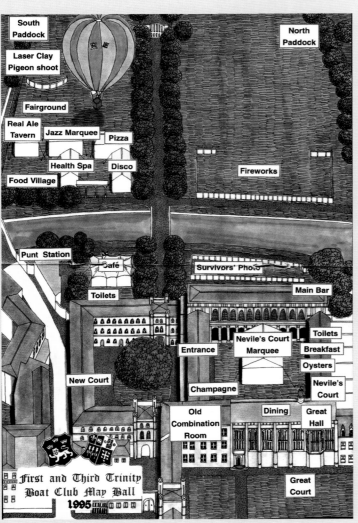

Trinity Survivors, 2002.

Those guests still standing as rosy-fingered dawn creeps over the Wren at 5am are ushered from their breakfasts towards the bank of the river adjacent to Nevile's Court in preparation for the traditional Survivors' photograph, before which they are serenaded by *a capella* singers drifting by on punts. The perennial popularity of the May Ball is testament to a night when Trinity students show their peers how to party with decorum and style.

I was Secretary of the May Ball in 1982. Running the ball was a fantastic opportunity for a third year student with a budget of £42,000 (a serious amount of money 30 years ago) but also a huge responsibility. It sounds glamorous, which indeed it was, but it certainly had its moments. The double tickets cost £42 and included food and bubbly as well as the chance to enjoy dancing to big name bands such as Bad Manners or Elvis Costello. Running the May Ball took over my life so you can imagine how I felt when the Thursday before the event a friend, now the Bursar of Trinity, reported that he had heard on the May Week party grapevine that the Bullingdon Club from Oxford had printed 100 (double) forged tickets and were planning on gatecrashing the ball. Gatecrashing balls was part of the game

but this was different. We enlisted the help of a big policeman and doubled our security. After about 20 minutes following the gates opening we spotted that the tickets from Oxford were slightly more heavily embossed than the real thing - and the Bullingdon crowd all turned up very early - so we were able to turn them away. The best thing was that their partners clearly didn't know they were coming on fake tickets so the rows and disappointment were ferocious! Only four couples got in.

The rest of the security worked well, with invaders on punts being rebuffed and students chased across the roof. At about three in the morning I came face to face with a friend who I knew had set himself the challenge to crash - he went white and issued an expletive. It had taken him four hours to get in - he'd been seen off by a porter on the bridge, fallen in the river and had to go back to his College to change and had only eventually managed it by taking an obscure route through the kitchens where he had been chased by a mad Italian chef with a meat cleaver! This was definitely part of the game so I took him up to the Committee room and treated him to a glass of proper Champagne.

Theodore Hubbard (1979)

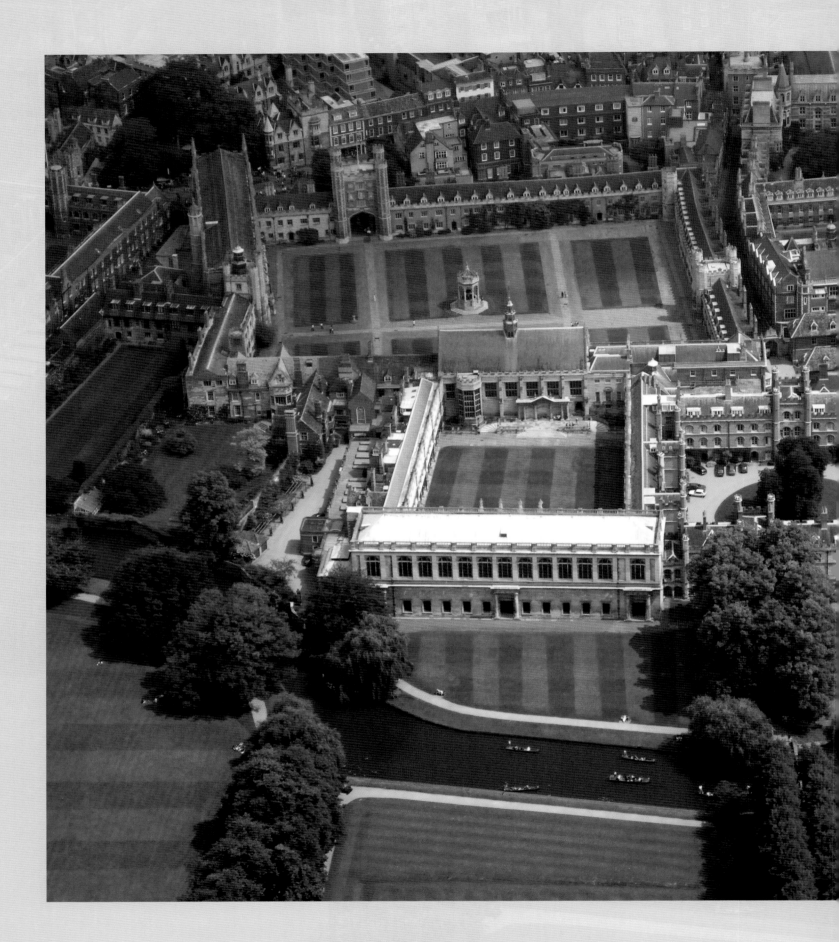

CHAPTER 16

Trinity, Political Life and the World

A place beyond politics

Oliver Letwin (1975), Conservative MP, Minister of State for Policy 2010– and Nick Butler (1973), Member of the Fabian Society, Special Advisor to Gordon Brown, 2009–10

In contrast to Trinity's clear and undisputed triumphs in other aspects of world affairs from science to economics, the casual observer could be forgiven for thinking that the College had largely absented itself from the political arena over the last century. The facts surely speak for themselves. No British prime minister since Stanley Baldwin; only one Trinity graduate sitting round the current cabinet table; and only six current members of the House of Commons. How different things were 90 years ago. In 1920 six of the previous 22 prime ministers had been Trinity men. And there were 37 members of the House of Commons who hailed from Trinity. Nor has this just been a matter of individuals failing to climb the greasy pole. Since the end of the Second World War Trinity has been largely absent from British ideological debate. Nothing to compare with the Keynesians of Kings or the Fabians of the LSE – nothing so distinctive as the Cowlingites of Peterhouse or the appeasers of All Souls. But does this mean that Trinity has become apolitical – a place beyond politics to which the unlucky or unworldly (like Rab Butler – in the opinion of many 'the best Prime Minister we never had') a retreat in search of tranquillity when the battles are lost?

There is some truth in that image of modern Trinity. The long sequence of scientific and mathematical pre-eminence has produced an atmosphere which discourages the passionate

Opposite: *Rajiv Gandhi with his grandfather, Jawaharlal Nehru.*

assertion of beliefs bereft of facts, disparages the artificial divisions produced by party allegiance and despises the black arts of presentation and spin that demean some of modern politics. True, at some levels, modern politics has had a place in Trinity. For example, there has been a strong and continuing tradition of links to international political leadership. Even if we have no recent British Prime Minister, we can boast the current Prime Minister of Singapore, Lee Hsien Loong, and two former Indian 20th-century Prime Ministers, Jawaharlal Nehru and Rajiv Gandhi. This is a trend likely to be strengthened by the sustained success of the Overseas Trust which, under Dr Seal's guidance, has brought thousands of hugely impressive overseas students into Cambridge over the last 25 years. Our frontier is on the Himalayas, not the white cliffs.

In intellectual as well as geographical terms, modern Trinity has contributed to global politics. Splitting the atom has had a more profound effect on the world of ideas – the atomic bomb, atomism, the belief in science, the pattern of international relationships – than any number of British political movements or British Prime Ministers. Trinity fully engaged in both the scientific breakthroughs and the subsequent discussion of their moral and strategic implications. Bertrand Russell may not have been a politician in the same sense as his distinguished ancestor, Lord John Russell, but he was certainly a part of the national (and international) conversation about the future of the planet. Certainly, also, there has been no shortage of cultural politics within the College. From time to time, there has been hand-to-hand, pen-to-pen conflict – as when Wittgenstein and the Wittgersnappers consciously and productively disrupted the moral sciences, or when John Robinson took on the ecclesiastical traditionalists. These global and local examples show that Trinity has never been wholly removed from the fray. But it remains true that Trinity over the last century at least has largely been at a remove from the immediate national political to and fro. This is not an accident. It reflects the fundamental, overriding objective of the College – an objective that has unified successive generations of Fellows rather more effectively than any passing ideological fashion. That objective has been the independence of the College from all external interference – an objective so

profound as to require no articulation; an objective beyond all normal definitions of politics where at least two views compete with each other for supremacy. No one speaks against the imperative of independence. Tacitly but consistently, the College has understood that partisan involvement in national politics represents a potential threat to that independence – a danger which cannot ever be completely eliminated but which has to be constantly managed.

To embrace one ideology would be to invite intrusion by those of different persuasions; so although many of an ideological turn of mind have passed through the College – from Enoch Powell to Maurice Dobb, from Francis Bacon to Piero Sraffa – no single ideology has ever been embraced. Instead, a continuing diversity – the product and expression of a long-instilled Whiggish liberalism – has been understood as the highest expression of the virtues of independence. Governments change like the weather, and ministers of every shade have found themselves enjoying the port on High Table. None are excluded but none are completely embraced. All are profoundly temporary. Independence cannot be bought, but critics and potential enemies can find that funds have been found from Trinity's substantial resources to make the arguments for external control – whether by the Old Schools or any Whitehall department – impossible to sustain. To reduce the independence of the College would create too many losers. Successive governments have paused and left Trinity alone. Beside the College's other great achievements, this preservation of independence may seem a relatively small matter. But in fact the independence – and the liberal diversity of intellect that sustains it – has helped to make possible all of those achievements. Modern Trinity's refusal to be partisan is not only part of its charm. It is also one of the sources of its distinction.

Trinity and Empire
John Lonsdale (1958)

Trinity's frontier, Oliver Letwin and Nick Butler observe, is on the Himalayas, not the white cliffs. Equally, for Trinity men the seats of power have stood on the banks of the Seine, Liffey, Ganges and Chao Phraya as much as by the Thames. For our

Jack Gallagher, Vere Harmsworth Professor of Imperial and Naval History from 1971 until his death in 1980, Vice Master and bon viveur.

prime ministers, poets and civil servants have played a central part in the life of the British Empire and the wider world while our historians, Jack Gallagher especially, have helped us to understand these global relationships anew.

Two of Britain's most controversial Prime Minsters, very different in character if both Conservatives, were Arthur Balfour (1866) and Stanley Baldwin (1885). 'Bloody Balfour' – 'Miss Nancy' to his Trinity contemporaries – earned Irish enmity in the 1880s when trying to kill Home Rule with misunderstood kindness; secured the *Entente Cordiale* when Prime Minister; and in 1917 famously declared a national home for Zionists, a promise redeemed only after Palestine became the most explosive of the Empire's many powder kegs. In the 1920s Baldwin took part in the decision not to reinforce the Singapore naval base – a matter on which it would be

interesting to hear the views of Lee Hsien Loong (1971), Prime Minister of Singapore – but conceivably saved Britain from disaster in 1937 by forcing the abdication of Edward VIII. Henry Campbell-Bannerman (1854) had earlier led the Liberal opposition to Balfour, appalled by the deaths of Afrikaner women and children detained in concentration camps during the Boer War, 'methods of barbarism' as he called them. When he succeeded Balfour as Prime Minister, however, his post-war settlement with the Afrikaners was arguably too generous, a sentiment they did not return.

Two Trinity Kashmiris, Mohammad Iqbal (1905), Pakistan's national poet, a romantic, and Jawaharlal Nehru (1907), India's first Prime Minister and convinced moderniser, did not quite meet in Great Court. Many would say Nehru was the father of today's multi-racial Commonwealth. Had India not joined this all-white club in 1947, surely no other former colony would have followed. His grandson Rajiv Gandhi (1962), India's seventh Prime Minister and, sadly, assassinated like his mother Indira before him, kept up his family's Trinity tradition, carried further when his own son Rahul came up to Trinity 30 years later.

One of our distinguished public servants, Andrew Cohen (1928), Ashkenazi Jew, Apostle, double First in classics, charged with the civil supply of Malta under siege in the Second World War, did more at the post-war Colonial Office than any other man to bring the Empire to a not ignominious end in Africa – although as Governor of Uganda in the 1950s he was responsible for deporting King 'Freddie' Muteesa II, that Magdalene man. But Trinity's reach is even wider than the Empire's. Anand Panyarachayun (1952), who played tennis and squash for Trinity, joined Thailand's diplomatic service and, as Prime Minister in the 1990s, introduced democratic reforms against the wishes of the generals who had put him in power. By contrast, Willie Whitelaw (1936), golfing blue, Normandy tank commander and Edward Heath's Secretary of State for Northern Ireland, failed to end 'the troubles' in one of the ex-Empire's oldest and most intimate family disputes. Some in the College wondered why he had not simply got on the phone to his fellow Trinity man south of the border, Erskine Childers (1924), then President of the Irish Republic.

To expect 'great men' to wield such power went clean counter to the new understanding of imperial history pioneered by Jack Gallagher (1937), Merseyside Irishman, tank driver at Alamein and Salerno, sleepless Dean of College in the 1950s, Vice Master in the 1970s, inventor of fantastical nicknames for his colleagues, and revered supervisor of research students in his 'Cambridge school' of imperial, principally Indian, history. For him high policy was always hobbled by low intrigue, central strategy by local crisis. One of his more surprising revelations was that France's ambassador to London during the 'scramble for Africa' – and previously prime minister in Paris – who tried vainly to preserve good relations between his country and Britain, was yet another Trinity man, and possibly the first Frenchman to row against Oxford, William Henry Waddington (1845). Trinity's nearest frontier is not so much the white cliffs as *trans Manche*.

—— ·•· ——

IN RECENT YEARS, I HAVE BEEN INVITED TO SIT ON THE SELECTION panels for post-graduates from all over the world who are applying for Gates Scholarships at Cambridge and also to interview Nehru Memorial Trust scholars from India. It is inspiring to hear how much these candidates (all incredibly bright) want to come to Cambridge – and how a place at Trinity means so much to them. During the interviews, I am always a bit apprehensive if one of the candidates asks me: 'What did you read?' I can't remember reading anything.

It was, in our day, a little easier to drift into Cambridge. The housemaster at school, in discussion with parents, played a larger role in making and shaping the application. The process seemed more casual. There were no interviews. I received a courteous letter offering me a place in response to my request. I can't remember making a request.

We had all done an obligatory two-year 'gap' as National Servicemen. Coming up was a marvellous experience. We were moving out of a decade of severe austerity and rationing – and entering a time of more relaxed authority.

This commitment to enjoyment was reflected in my Part 1 results (modern languages). My tutor, a lovely man, H.O.

Evennett, considered these results. He chose his words carefully, with agonising pauses. 'Fewest people [pause] seem to fail [pause] reading history.' I might have been a bit dim, but it didn't take long (only a few days) to interpret this. I didn't regret the change – and I have been reading history ever since.

We were somewhat suspicious of those who might get a First. There were fewer of them about in our day. The most desirable degree was thought to be something called a Fourth (or Special). Whether such a degree existed didn't matter. It was taken to indicate sheer idleness, but with some recognisable hidden value. It was clearly a far rarer degree than a First – and confirmation that there was no danger in burning out early.

I signed up to attend the University OTC in order to ensure that I clocked up the obligatory TA drills during term time, so that I could leave the Long Vacation free. We were not very effective militarily. There were 119 ex-National Service 2nd Lieutenants on the strength of the Infantry Wing and only one cadet. He got a lot of training. We did a lot of drinking.

The ladies in our day seemed to feature either as skilful night-time climbers or as stars on the stage. I spent much time in minor roles at the ADC and in the Marlowe gazing at these desirable individuals. I also like dressing up, which is probably why I rejoined the Army.

Field Marshal Sir John Chapple (1951)

I ENTERED TRINITY COLLEGE IN THE AUTUMN OF 1952. AS A young student from Thailand, I recall feeling quite overwhelmed by the history and rich academic tradition of the College. Arriving at the College for an interview before admission, I remember walking through the Gate to the Great Court and being totally captivated by the serenity and tranquillity of the campus environment. Fortunately, unlike Oxford where either Greek or Latin was obligatory, Cambridge displayed leniency in admitting Thai as a 'classical language'.

Later on, disappointment set in when I was informed that due to lack of space, first-year students would be put up in 'digs'. Fortunately, my 'digs' were at 28 Park Parade facing Jesus Green and not too far from Trinity and the lecture halls.

Lord Adrian hosting King Bhumibol and Queen Sirikit of Siam, who were visiting Trinity with Princess Alexandra of Kent during the summer of 1960.

The digs were also a conveniently short distance from the squash and tennis courts, the two sports at which I represented my College. As a foreigner from a tropical climate, I certainly did not relish the idea of walking or bicycling in the windy, rain-soaked or freezing Cambridge weather.

Another preoccupation was the quality of food served in College Halls. Peterhouse and Magdalene were reputed to offer a reasonable fare. Trinity food was then one of the least appetising. We were obliged to sign in for at least four dinners a week. Many a time I would walk into the dining hall, sit down and leave soon after the plate was placed before me. Then I would find refuge in either a Chinese or Indian eating place. At that time, of course, Thai food had not yet been discovered in the Western world.

My tutor, Mr Francis Henry Sandbach, known as Harry, was a charming and affable gentleman. He had an impish smile and a dry sense of humour. Some years ago, I was visiting Trinity and asked for an appointment to see him. He was still recuperating from a hip operation but arranged for me to call on him at a ground-level office in the Great Court. After a very pleasant visit, I said goodbye and started to walk on the path towards the Gate, when he gently directed me to walk on the lawn – a privilege reserved for College Fellows and those who have graduated. It was the first time that I exercised that sacred right!

I was an average student, but worked hard, well into the night. Because of my late-night studies, I frequently missed the 9 o'clock lectures. Of those that I attended, my favourite was a Mr Barnes, whose witty and colourful lectures on criminal law made interesting hours. Professor Elihu Lauterpacht's lectures on international law were always learned and scholarly, but at times difficult to comprehend and follow. His son, my supervisor on the same subject, was more lucid and approachable.

Throughout my three years at Trinity, studies and sports occupied most of my time. I did not lead an active social life, attending occasional tea and sherry parties, and hardly participated in University or College group activities, but my years at Trinity College had significant bearing in shaping my values and beliefs. As a boarder at Dulwich, I had been used to a supervised and regimented life. At Trinity, I was free and independent. It was here that I learned the importance of self-discipline, responsibility and accountability. I was not a native speaker so I had to work harder than the others to meet the mark.

What did I gain from three years at the College aside from a law degree? Most importantly, I acquired a set of values, based on hard work, discipline and diligence which continues to shape and influence my life to this day. For that, I am eternally indebted to Trinity College.

Anand Panyarachun (1952)
Former Prime Minister of Thailand

As a young regular soldier I was extracted from the Malayan jungle in 1952 to act as ADC to an important General in Singapore. As the Foreign Office telegrams and strategy papers passed across my desk on the way to my boss, I decided that I should try for the Foreign Service which meant that I needed a degree.

I wrote to Trinity on the recommendation of colleagues and received a charming letter in Malaya almost by return from J.M.K. Vyvyan, saying that Trinity would welcome a former

Gurkha officer. I never took an exam or had an interview. I paid my way through Cambridge with the generous army food and language allowances that I had saved by eating curry in the jungle and speaking to my men in Gurkhali.

I resigned my Commission and arrived for my first term in the autumn of 1956. It was the occasion of the Soviet invasion of Hungary and the British invasion of Suez. I was passionate for the Hungarians and appalled by many of my Trinity colleagues who supported Eden's adventure. Cambridge was in turmoil. Chance set me on the road to politics when the then President of the Union decided that he wanted a freshman undergraduate to propose the motion on Hungary, namely that 'This house would risk a third world war for a Communist satellite in revolt'. Undergraduates showed their collective wisdom by rejecting the motion by 301 votes to 271. It was the only serious speech that I ever made in the Union, even subsequently as President.

Although I lived comfortably in Great Court and Bishop's Hostel, my only direct involvement with Trinity's own activities was as a follower of the Trinity Foot Beagles and as a participant in the affairs of the Magpie and Stump, a much more prestigious and enjoyable institution than the Cambridge Union.

I found Cambridge rather claustrophobic after the army. I had no academic pretensions, did no work and never once went to a lecture. Deservedly I received a Second. I am proud that I went to Trinity and I am so glad that Trinity is rich and cannot be messed about by governments. But I was never an aspirant for a Nobel Prize and have often wondered whether with its academic pre-eminence it was really the right college for an ex-soldier like me.

Sir John Nott (1956)

WHEN I WENT UP TO CAMBRIDGE SOME OF MY MORE GLOOMY friends warned me that Trinity was a large and impersonal college, divided between a large contingent of hearty and arrogant public-school boys and an equally large group of boys studying science from northern grammar schools, who were ill at ease and rarely seen, because they led a troglodytic existence, working away in their rooms and labs.

It took me less than a week to learn that this was an absurd caricature. Of course it was not difficult to find people answering to both descriptions, but what really made Trinity distinctive was that an enormously diverse group of people were thrown together, and given the opportunity of meeting fellow undergraduates who differed enormously in background, interests, ability and character. The size of the College meant that this did not come about because we were huddled together in an artificially cosy environment. If you wanted to you could hang around exclusively with people of your own type, but you had a great opportunity to mix widely, and most people availed themselves of that opportunity with enthusiasm.

The institution of semi-compulsory dining in Hall was one of the major features of College life which enabled that to happen. Within a few days, I found myself, for example, sitting next to somebody who responded to my admiration of the panelling by saying that yes, it was good, but it was better at his home. The next

Leon Brittan, President of the Union Society, 1959.

day I was chatting to a scientist son of a fruit farmer and the day after I was learning about the medieval battles between the Papacy and the Empire from an enthusiastic historian who went on to become an extremely distinguished human rights lawyer.

The teaching was similarly diverse. I was mildly surprised, for example, to find that my first supervisor in English was a Spanish refugee from the Civil War, Juan Mascaro, whose interest was oriental religions. He began by bemoaning the level of aircraft noise that distracted his peace and studies and said to me: 'Lord Tedder, the Chancellor of the University, he is an airman, why can't he stop all this noise?' Others who taught me were less eccentric, but just as interesting and unfailingly helpful.

Having switched from English to law, I decided that I wanted to go to the Bar and needed to get a pupillage. It is only in retrospect that I realise how incredibly arrogant I must have seemed when I turned down two offers of pupillage obtained for me in very eminent chambers by Eli Lauterpacht and Bill Wade, respectively. I deserved to be told to fend for myself. But instead Eli fixed me up with David Hirst, who later became a Lord Justice of Appeal and a lifelong friend, saying, 'David is interested in politics, and libel practice is more dramatic than charter parties or Chancery work, what about that?' I graciously accepted!

My interest in politics, too, was advanced in curious ways by being at Trinity. I am sure all my Trinity contemporaries were brilliant debaters, but when it came to the Union elections it did no harm to be at a college so large in size and so close to the Union. Of course we weren't allowed to canvass votes or mobilise the Trinity 'crocodile' to the Union. But even now I vividly remember helping a subsequent Secretary of State for Defence remove the bicycles at the Great Gate which were covering up the notice of the Union elections that showed how many of the candidates were from Trinity.

I am not sure if my academic success was materially advanced by a later supervisor in English who told me that whether I got a First or not would depend not so much on how much work I did, but on what I thought about when waiting for a bus. The problem was that from Trinity it was almost always much easier to walk!

Leon Brittan (1957)
(The Rt Hon The Lord Brittan of Spennithorne QC DL)

In 1960, my second year, Cambridge students responded with enthusiasm to the call by chief Albert Luthuli, president of the African National Congress, for a boycott of South African goods. The chief supplier of undergraduate provender was Matthews, in Trinity Street, where Heffers now stands. One day David Robertson (also 1958), whose nickname 'Granny' had followed him from his national service in the navy, asked a Matthews assistant, 'Are you suffering from the South African boycott?' before going to the cashier to pay his bill. On his return, to pick up his Horlicks, he found the assistant indignant. 'WHAT did you say I was suffering from?'

Ten years later I had recently returned to Trinity from my first teaching job, in Dar es Salaam, Tanzania. Ted Heath's Conservative government was contemplating an arms deal with South Africa, contrary to a United Nations resolution. I acquired from the Anti-Apartheid Movement a bright red sticker for my car's rear window that demanded 'No Arms for South Africa'. Mollie Butler was delighted. I got her a sticker for her own car. 'Rab' Butler, our Master and a former Conservative Foreign Secretary, was not pleased.

John Lonsdale (1958)

In my second year I was elected President of the JCR and was shortly confronted with a dispute about whether the College should be asked to ban food from South Africa. There was an emotional College meeting for undergraduates and research students with about 60 or 70 people present. Passionate speeches were made on both sides, and eventually someone asked what I hoped I would be asked: 'How much food from South Africa does the College buy?' I was the only person there who had bothered to ask the catering manager, who had told me that South African food was far too expensive and the College did not buy any. When I reported that fact there was momentary silence followed by near-hysterical laughter, and we then passed a motion almost unanimously saying 'In the unlikely event of the College buying food from South Africa a separate table would be provided for those who did not wish to eat it.' To this day I do not know whether the then catering manager had told me the truth.

Bob Reiss (1964)

Chris Morley, former Vice Master, by the portrait of Sir Muhammad Iqbal at a conference held in College in 2008 to celebrate the centenary of Iqbal's stay in Europe.

It wasn't until my second week that I began to think that I might just be the only Hawaiian here. No one else wore a daily uniform of shorts and flip flops. And I remember fondly an elderly porter, affectionately known as Mac, explaining, 'We wondered about you wearing your flowery underwear in Great Court. But then we heard you were Mr "Loo" from Hawaii. Ah … a native!' It was a splendid introduction to the discretion and tolerance of Trinity society.

New acquaintances were apparently confused over whether I fitted better into an Asian cubby hole or an American one. The American one was convenient when visiting the IRA pub up the hill towards Girton. These were times when the conflict was very, very serious. One opened the pub door to the imposing sight of a beefy matron with her arms crossed. If you were American, there was a smile on her face and a friendly nod to the bar under a portrait of John Kennedy. Patrons murmuring in a mysterious dialect ignored us completely. If you were English, she had a scowl and the room went silent, all pairs of eyes staring with menace. To this day, I still marvel at how Britain's different cultures manage to flourish so well together. To foreigners from vast homogeneous new cultures, such things give great optimism about humanity.

I wish I could present a list of accomplishments from my Trinity years. But I can't. The most remarkable was being thrown in the fountain for organising Trinity's last boat during an unusually lean Lent Bumps (which I suppose allowed me to share the same aquatic experience as Lord Byron).

The glories of both past and present are always partly squandered on immature youth. Yes, I did react with proper embarrassment when I nearly ran over Professor Stephen Hawking near the Cavendish Laboratory with a bicycle. But I also remember a midnight raid on what was assumed to be Newton's apple tree just outside the Porters' Lodge to snatch a cutting as a departure gift for a physics major. It was only many years later when reading *Principia Mathematica* in translation that I began truly to appreciate Newton's unique genius.

In spite of (or is it because of?) this foolishness, Trinity left many marks of which I still carry at least two today: I know people from around the world doing an amazing variety of worthwhile things who, given our advanced ages, can rightly be called lifelong friends; and, once given a taste of how people live such different lives, I never settled back in Hawaii.

It is with some sadness that I read about perceptions that US President Barack Obama is somehow distant from Britain because of his background. The President was born and raised in Hawaii. Indeed, he was raised about one block from me, and we went to the same school (although because I am four years older, we did not know each other). We both know how the Kingdom of Hawaii was protected by Britain before the islands became one of the first pawns in a belated American colonial thrust. Captain James Cook, Britain's great pre-Nelson nautical explorer, discovered and then was killed in Hawaii over a quickly settled misunderstanding. Hawaii is the only US state flag with the Union Jack in a corner. Hawaii's state motto, 'The Life of the Land is Preserved in Righteousness', was inspired after Britain twice sent warships to chase away putative colonisers.

So when visiting Trinity, I often pause in Great Court thinking of the knowledge and values that resonate in its ancient walls and of how they miraculously spread to some tiny Pacific islands on the other side of the world centuries before my flip-flops appeared. Regretfully, I am also reminded of one dull spot in this otherwise radiant history: Trinity obviously took in the wrong guy from Hawaii.

Wayne Lau (1979)

1980s May Ball Fashions. Alice Wallbank, Janet Lewis, Lucy Elston and Victoria Pollock at the 1988 May Ball.

Whewell's Court on the ground floor and very close to Trinity Street. I read in the 2009 annual record that all students now need electronic lock cards to get around the College, but back in 1989 our security was rather more lax. I used to leave my room key on the ledge above the door and would frequently return home to find a tea party in full swing. On Thursdays I had my weekly essay crisis and needed to post the completed work under my tutor's door in Great Court by 9pm, the same time that the Victoria Wine shop opposite Great Gate closed. I would drop the essay a couple of minutes early and celebrate by buying a bottle of gin and some tonic on my way back – the friends who I had kicked out from their tea drinking the day before seemed miraculously to reappear with glasses at the ready.

Vicky Ford (née Pollock)
MEP East of England (1986)

THERE HAS BEEN A POLLOCK AT TRINITY IN EVERY GENERATION since *c.*1800. My father (Anthony Pollock) sadly died when he was only 42. One of my last memories of my father is of him opening the letter from the College explaining they would now admit women – he was delighted and encouraged me to apply (I was only ten). I will always be indebted to my father's friends from Trinity days who helped to pay for my own education after his death and for their encouragement when I later did decide to attempt the entrance exam.

The most important thing Trinity gave me (other than the Cambridge degree that remains a passport to the world) was another exceptional group of friends, many of whom I am still in close contact with today. Back in the days before email and mobile phones, we used to communicate with endless notes pinned to doors or better still by regular rendezvous points – you could nearly always guarantee to find whoever you wanted to see at last orders in the bar or for a cheese roll and half of orange juice with lemonade at lunchtime (price together 52p). We didn't have TVs in our rooms but I remember that many hours were wasted away after lunch in the JCR watching *Neighbours* and *Countdown*.

There were also various rooms across the College that became 'open house'. In my final year I lived in the first part of

To be at Trinity was to be elect. Arrogant, probably. Fortunate, no question. Who else had Henry VIII guarding their college threshold with a chair leg, a wooden mallard hanging from the rafters in Hall as a shared in-joke, the most exciting wine cellar, most glorious, light-filled library, and did anyone mention those Nobels?

To be a woman at Trinity was a privilege. We shared huge camaraderie, dusted with the competitiveness which goes with everything Oxbridge. In the minority – in 1998 our year was split 60/120 – we had a certain power. The round of bops and mingles, balls, dinner parties and formal halls gave us ample opportunity to experiment: red lipstick and black dresses; bicycles and bluestockings; you could be anyone you wanted to be. By and large everyone switched easily between roles, and excelled at it.

My College mother was an Olympian in bridge. My room-mate was one of the more stunning, loved and intelligently articulate women I have encountered. She was also head of the Slappers, our non-sporting College women's drinking society. While Virginia Woolf was turned away from Trinity's library, we had the pass card and weren't about to waste it. That said, we less burned our bras than padded them.

It was pressured. But the pastoral system, like the tutorial system, was excellent, breaking down each annual intake to small

Professor John Lonsdale welcoming alumni at the Annual Buffet Lunch, 2009.

groups of people with a 'family' looking out for them. This was especially relevant to me. I went up in the final stages of chronic fatigue syndrome, having been deeply unwell the previous four years. The illness left me exhausted and in great pain, so my life would flip between days when light hurt my eyes and I was hardly able to hold a book, and weeks when I gradually felt myself recovering, desperate for T.S. Eliot's 'lifetime burning in every moment'. Trinity went to extraordinary lengths to support me, with a flexibility of approach I am sure I could not have found elsewhere.

The Eliot I studied with Eric Griffiths, our most colourful tutor, is etched into my mind. A bad supervision with him was bloody; two days before my deadline he refused me entry to his room, returning my work branded 'vile, execrable slop'. But if you found something to say which pleased him, he would put on Beethoven, pour a glass of white Burgundy and tease your understanding to points where the words made sense in a different way.

While we were students, communication switched from the old note-in-the-pigeon-hole system to email. Most people had a PC in their room and were each connected to the Cantab web. This intra-university network had a stalker feature which allowed you to see if your email had been read, a handy dating aide which knocked hours off useful work time. But modernisation was by no means uniform. We still, for example, made the mid-morning dash across New Court to find a staircase with a shower, running the gamut of the camera-happy tourists.

It was at a Trinity Wine Society that I made the first step on my career in journalism. I was seated next to a reputed columnist who, over generous quantities of Chateau Margaux, asserted the best way into newspapers was to be a diarist. When Charles Moore (another College alumnus, then editor of the *Telegraph*) spoke at the Union the following week, I latched on to him until he was kind enough to give me diary work experience.

In my early days as a reporter I spent a great deal of time interviewing London's literati. I was astonished to discover how many of them had been taught by my director of studies, Adrian Poole; he was a man of great warmth, who inspired universally fond memories. I continue to encounter and befriend Trinitarians and find huge pleasure in what is less some coincidental old boys' network, more a cobweb of inspirational people with a shared vernacular. A snapshot memory of Trinity must include its architecture – the sweep of the ceiling in Chapel, the fountain, the arched colonades in Nevile's Court – and touch on its remarkable facilities, and the bursaries and grants enabled by its wealth. But the singularity of the College is in its alumni. When we signed in, an older Matriculation book was open to the page with Isaac Newton's signature. Amartya Sen, then our humble and brilliant Master, continues to bestride the economic world. Already, our generation is excelling, at the bar, in maths and in the arts; it is exciting to watch younger talent blossom and a privilege to be part of the flowering whole.

Rebecca Newman (1998)

List of Subscribers

This book has been made possible through the generosity of the following subscribers.
The only dates given are of matriculation.

John Abbott	1961
Christopher B Abela	1994
Dr Jack Abramsky	1961
D M Adam	1951
Paul Adams	1959
Canon Peter Adams	
His Hon. Roderick Adams	1956
Peter Mark Adlard	1951
Jonathan Agnew	1960
Dr Abigail R A Aiken	2002
Dr Catherine E M Aiken	1999
Anand Aithal	1986
Dr J E Aitken	1966
A Aldred	1964
Hugh John Alexander	1971
Patrick Alexander	1964
Dr Harold Allan	1939
Nicholas Allan	1976
Roger Allen	1980
Tim Allen	1963
Tony Allen	1969
G O C Allhusen	1960
Dr John Anderson	1947
Philip Edward Anderson	1956
Jared Andrews	1987
Vanessa Andrews	
(née Hannah)	1987
Saleem A Ahmadullah	1959
Joseph Antebi	1953
Sir Raymond Appleyard	1941
Thomas J Arneson	1981
Jock Asbury-Bailey	1949
Robert Ascott	1961
A Ashbrook	1944
H G Ashton	1950
Bishop Jeremy Ashton	1950
Sir Michael Atiyah	1949
Martin Atkin	1976
Professor Tony Atkins FREng	1961
The Rt Revd Robert Atwell	
Rachel Jane Avery	1998
David A B Babington-Smith	1986
David Baggaley	1953
R H Bailey	1957
Tristan Bailey	1965
Edward Baker	1973
Professor Shankar Balasubramanian	
Kenneth Ball	1976
Professor L A Balzer	1970
Mr Hans C Bang	1956
A Bannard Smith	

Dr Raymond V Bar-On FSS FTS	
	1944
Professor John Barbara	1965
Robert Barbour	1973
D M Barclay	1971
Richard Barclay	1946
Stephen Barclay	1975
Cath and Jules Barker	2001
Leonard Barkey	1953
Peter Barnard	1975
Simon W S Barnes	1967
Mark D Barnett	1989
Gavin Barras Reed	1955
Mr Brian J Barrett	1984
Dr Michael Barrett	1970
Dr Paul M Barrett	1990
Martin Barry	1980
John Vernon Bartlett	1945
Marshall P Bartlett	1965
M P A Bass	1986
Ian Bateman	1955
Brian Bates	1956
C D J Bathurst	1968
S D Baxter	1995
Dr A R Beal	1967
Trevor Beale	1955
J H W Beardwell	1957
Dr Nigel Bee	
David Beeden	1976
W M Beese	1965
Aurelian Bejancu	1995
Toby J Belfield	1991
S C J Bell	1988
C V Ben-Nathan	1983
Rachel A J Bennett	1997
Geoffrey H L Berg	1974
M L Berger	1952
Conway Berners-Lee	1940
Sir Michael Berridge	
D Berrington Davies	1959
W G B Bevan	1976
Bhupendra N Bhagat	1948
Sandeep Bhargava	1984
Bryan Birch	1951
Alec Bird	1944
Bill Bird MBE	1970
Dr George Bird	1976
Philip Bird	1955
Rolf Blach	1949
Alan Gordon Black	1989
Ms Paula J Black	1994

Miss Tamara Black	2002
Simon Blackburn	1997
Tim Blenkin	1966
Robert Blower	1984
R A Blythe	1949
Richard Boggis-Rolfe	1969
A D Bolingbroke	1935
Christopher Bond	1996
David Bonser	1968
John F Booth	1963
Ansy Boothroyd	1983
C Boreham	2007
H M W Borrill FSA	1974
C J Bosanquet	1967
Peter Bottomley MP	1963
Nicholas Bourne AM	1973
Brian Boutel	1959
David Bowden	1965
J H Bowman	1971
Michael Boxford	1960
Pollie and Paddy Boyle	
	1992 and 1993
J V Boys	1955
Dr J S Bradbrook	1967
John Bradfield	1942
Philip Bradfield	1960
Alan Bradley	1961
Dr Stephen Bragg	1942
L A A Bramwell	
Gillian Brander	1999
Michael Brandon	1946
P A Brandt	1951
J T Braunholtz	1948
Timothy Frederick Desmond	
Bravington	1953
Gerald Bray	1972
Revd Denis I A Brazell	1961
Abigail Breary	2006
David John Brecher	1948
John Breeze	1961
Mr Michael J Brett	1953
Richard Brett	1970
R A Bride	1942
K A Briggs	1967
Robert Bristow	1980
Dr Dominic and	
Mrs Georgina Brittain	1999
Lord Brittan	1957
Fiona L Britten	1988
Stuart G Broadfoot	2004
David Brock	1990

Christopher J Brocksom	1957
Ms Natasha Brook-Walters	1993
Greg Brooks	1963
Gerald Brough	1952
Robert Broughton	1973
Chris Brown	1963
Christopher R B Brown	2000
Dr Geoffrey Duncan Brown	1981
Nigel C Brown	1960
Ben Browne	1972
Mr A J Browning	1973
Richard J Bruce	1982
David C Brunt	1981
Dr Peter Brunyate	1963
Dr Chris Bruton	1963
Sir Andrew Buchanan	1958
G L Buchanan	1959
Very Revd Philip Buckler	
Sabine U Bueckmann de Villegas	
	1980
E A W (Tony) Bullock	1947
Mr M T C Burkitt	1952
Mr Alexander John Burn	1967
Geoffrey Burnaby	1951
Muhammad Salman Burney	1974
Philip Burnford	1954
Sir Andrew Burns	1962
Thomas A L Burns	1996
Bob Burrage	1965
John Burridge	1974
Dr David Bush	
Peter Butenschon	1963
Dr Brian Butler	1961
Nick Butler	1973
R C Buxton	1940
Sir Dominic Cadbury	1959
Sir Andrew Cahn	1970
Graham Caldbeck	1968
Iolie Calochristos	2004
Glenn Calvert	1974
Mr Jehangir Cama	2009
Andrew Cambridge	1977
David B Cameron	1988
Cyrille Francis Camilleri	1992
Arthur P Campbell	1967
Dr Edward Keith Campbell	1972
G H Campbell	1948
Patrick J Campbell	1988
Michael Campling	1948
Donald Candlin	1952
Stephen Cannon	1968

Thomas N Cappie-Wood	1947	Dr John Cooke	1972	Dr John Stewart Davies	1963	Mike Evans	1964
Charles Edward Carey	1955	Stephen Cooper	1977	Rod Davis	1960	Martin R Evers	1967
Dr Pierre A Carlotti	1998	Charles Richard Rainford Corbett		Lucy Davison	1978	Simon Every	1949
Professor J W S Cassels	1946		1963	Nigel Daw	1953	John Fairbairn	1954
Sir John Cassels CB	1948	L Alberto Cordero-Lecca	1977	Elliot W Dawson	1955	Mr M G Falcon	1960
Mr Michele Castiglioni	2010	Emma Cory	2008	Cheryl Louise Day	2003	Richard J Falder	2007
Marcus A M Cavalier Esq	1987	Pieter Coulier	2009	Dr D W Day	1963	Dr Tony Falkner	1958
W H T Cavendish	1960	D J I Coulson	1982	Kylie Day	2000	Richard Fallas	1968
Michael Farinton Challis	1964	Michael Coultas	1970	Mike Day	1983	Nigel Falls	1964
Cheow Thia Chan	2009	Dr Jonathan Couriel	1967	Richard C Day	1960	Eric Farge	1958
William Chan Guang Yu	2008	Julien Courtauld	1958	Leonardo de Arrizabalaga y Prado		Dr James Farmer QC	1966
Dr Gopal Chand	1987	The Revd Christopher Courtauld			1964	Michael Farrow	1954
Malcolm G Chandler	1962		1953	Robin de Beaumont	1944	Dr William Fawcett	1968
R G Chapman	1947	Roger Courtney	1964	Maurice de Bunsen	1963	Nicola Arlette Ann Fearns	
Field Marshal Sir John Chapple		Charles Covell	1973	Sunith Dilantha de Fonseka	2006	(née Piek)	1995
	1951	Siobhan L Cox	2004	Visc. Hubert de Marcy	1946	Dr I W Fellows	1971
Michael Charlesworth	1949	Mr J F A Cox	1967	D L de Rothschild	1974	Roger Felstead	1955
Dr David Chart	1990	Adrian Crampton	1978	Camilla de Sousa Turner	1983	Hugh Anthony Fenn	1961
R J C Chartres	1965	L A (Tony) Crapnell	1957	J C de Swaan	1993	Caroline Fentem and Thomas Judd	
Nigel E Chase	1995	Lord Crathorne	1960	Sir Oscar de Ville CBE PhD	1942		1980
Suli Chen	2000	Richard Craven-Smith-Milnes	1955	Dr J N de Villiers	1964	Roger William Few	1970
Colonel W J Chesshyre	1963	Douglas Crawford	1950	Guy Dear	1973	Peter Fickling	1968
Anson Cheung	1999	Neville Creed	1975	J C Demmar	1953	Christopher Field	1959
Alison Child	1982	Philip Crewdson	1983	Brian Timothy Denvir	1959	David Fielding	1969
Graham Chinner	1984	Lord Crickhowell		Jonathan Desler	1991	Tony Finch	1994
Tae-Joon Cho	2003	(Nicholas Edwards)	1954	Professor Ronald B Dew		Dr Jervois Firmin	1947
Nicholas P Chotiros	1970	Professor Frank Critchley	1968	Stephen D Dias	1971	Alastair C Fisher	1994
William E Church	1962	Peter Croft	1968	Professor Jeremy Dibble	1977	Dr Crispin A H Fisher	1981
Edwin C Clark	1987	David Crowe	1977	Howard Dilley	1964	Mrs Kari Fisher (née Jones)	1980
Edwin F Clark	1945	J S Crowhurst	1972	Stephen Dilworth	1977	Luke Fisher	2008
Dr Chris and Revd Dr Alexandra		Sir Brian Cubbon	1946	Mr Konstantinos Dimitriou	1997	Mark Fitzgerald	1995
Clarke (née Luff) 1986 and 1993		David Cuming	1953	James Dixon	2007	R J M FitzHugh	1994
J G Clarke	1970	Loveday Cuming	1991	Michael Dobson	1970	John G Fleming	1943
Steve Clarke	1965	David Cumings	1961	Roger Dobson	1956	G J Fletcher	1947
Richard S Cleary Jr	2009	Peter Cummins	1981	Michael P Drazin	1947	Sir Christopher Floyd	1970
Dr Alan Clements	1951	David Cundy	1962	James N Dreaper	1950	Paul Flynn	1984
Peter Clifford	1976	Susan Cunningham		Dr Christopher Drouet	1949	Vernon Flynn QC	1986
David Clissitt	1978	(née Kirkpatrick)	1985	P M E Drury	1951	John Fooks	1952
W B Close	1969	Dr Andrzej J Czernuszewicz	1980	Helena Drysdale	1978	Richard M Foote	1972
Iain Clough	1983	Marc d'Abbadie	1997	Ken Dudeney	1964	Richard G Forbes	1960
Douglas Clyde	1952	C Daintree	1948	Euan Duff	1969	Dr Matthew Ford	1995
Benjamin Jonathan Coates	2001	Dr K W Daisley	1950	John S Duffield	1980	Michael De La F Ford	1950
Clare Gye Coates and		Michael Neale Dalton	1964	Dr Peter W Dufton	1963	Vicky Ford (née Pollock)	1986
Stephen Coates	1991	Richard John Edward Dammery		Peter Dulson	1969	Dr Peter Forder	1968
Dr Alan B Cobban	1961		1987	Dr John V Dunworth CB CBE		Dr Roger Forder	1965
Jim Cobbe	1965	Leo Damrosch	1964	Professor Gareth Dyas	1961	Roddy Forman	1957
Richard R Cockroft	1957	George Danker	2009	D S M Eadie	1935	A Robin Forrest	1965
Adrian Victor Cohen	1947	S J Dann	1986	W H Earle	1942	Michael Forrest	1951
Jeremy Cohen	1950	D S Dannhauser	1973	Mr H J Easterling	1952	Jonathan Forsyth	2004
B K Cole	1958	J R A Dannhauser	2002	Stephen Eccles	1956	David Foster	2007
David R B Collins	1964	D Darley	1994	Mark J T Edwards	1976	Dr F H Foster	1957
Stephen Paul Collins	1969	Marc Dassesse	1973	Charlie Egerton-Warburton	1980	Ian C Fowler	1954
Steven Collins	1985	Professor J F Davidson	1944	John Ehrman	1938	Howard Fox	1956
Michael Combes	1963	Nicholas Davidson	1969	Dr A Eisinger	1957	J Victor Fox	1950
David P Condit	1973	In memory of Rollo Davidson	1962	Professor David Ekserdjian	1974	Michael Fox	1950
Peter H Conze Jr	1965	Dr Alun O Davies	1954	Richard S Eley	1977	Guy Francis	1957
Lyndsay Coo		Barry and June Davies	1956	David Elias	1994	William R Franklin Phd DIC	1972
William Cook	1951	C Barry Davies	1982	Julian Ellison	1976	A R G Frase Esq	1973
David Cooke	1975	Edward C Davies	1965	Elisabeth Ann English	1980	Dr David Freeman	1951
H G W Cooke	1941	Harold Gordon Davies	1950	R D English		George Freeman	1962

Name	Year
Professor K C Freeman FRS	1962
The Revd John Friars	1952
Dr Roger Frie	1989
Michael J Friedman	1965
Sophie Friese-Greene	2009
N J Frobisher	1976
Dr Christopher D Frost	1987
David Fullagar	1960
Dr Patrick Furniss	1960
Ms Carolyn Fyall	1989
Dr Hugh Gallagher	1988
Diane Galloway	1979
Richard Mark Gardiner	1966
Professor C H B Garraway	1968
Dr C G B Garrett	1943
Richard J Garrett	1961
Miss Jennifer Gates	2001
Howard C Gatiss	1977
Jeremy Gaunt	1973
Jacqueline Gazzard	1987
Andrew George	1973
Professor Andrew George	1981
A E H Gerry	1958
Mr Satyajit Ghosh	1971
Anthony Gibbs	1956
Dr Ian Henry Gibson MA (Cantab) MSc	1956
Professor Valerie Gibson	
Christopher Gilchrist	1967
Dr C R Gillham	1993
Konrad Ginther	1958
Debora Di Gioacchino	1989
Derek Glenton	1952
Ian M Glynn	1946
Professor Sunthara Gnanalingam	1946
Tim Goatcher	1989
Nicolai Goeke	1997
Dr Peter Goldberg	1973
Richard Gompertz	1951
C A E Goodhart	1957
Sir Philip Goodhart	1947
William Goodhart	1953
David W Gooding	1947
D J Goodwin	1983
Dr A D Gordon	1969
Cameron M Gordon	1963
Campbell Gordon	1975
Dane R Gordon	1948
J Ian Gordon	1961
Martin Grabiner	1972
John M Graham-Campbell	1960
F P and R W Graham-Watson	1976 and 2008
J Graham	1986
Sir John Graham	1947
Mr Philip Grainge	1996
Brian Gray	1957
Brian Gray	1983
Professor K J Gray FBA	
Michael Robert Gray	1972
Peter Gray	1958
Mr Simon Gray	1986
C J B Green	1955
Christopher J Green	1954
Dr Edmund Green	1984
Laurence Green	1969
Professor Peter Green	1947
Samuel Green	2002
Laura H Greene	
Martin Greenhalgh	1970
Lt Col R C Gregory	1958
Mark Griffiths	1960
Peter Grove	1967
Jonathan Groves	1971
Professor Tony Guénault	1954
Cyrus Guzder	1964
Michael C Gwinner	2008
Dr Andreas Haaf	1994
Philip Haberman	1974
Reinmar Hager	1999
The Revd Richard Haggis	
Ranald Hahn	1975
Roy Haigh	1950
J J Hall	1959
Michael Hall	1952
Michael A W Hall	1963
Mr N J Hall	1982
L Jane Hamblen	1976
Henry Francis Hambly	1963
D C Hambidge	1952
Canon Peter Hamel	1966
Malcolm Hamer	1958
Eben Hamilton QC	1957
Dr Paul S Hammond	1975
Harry Hampson	1984
Peter F Hanbury	1937
Christopher Hancock QC	1979
Malcolm C Hancock	1963
Eric Handley	1943
Dr David Handscomb	1951
Roger Hanna	1941
Philip Hardie	
J G R Harding	1954
Dr John R Hardy	1952
Dr Anthony Harker	1967
Mr Leonard Harpum	1953
Christopher Harris	1971
H C E Harris	1956
Miles Harris	1997
Dr Susie Harris	1983
Lord Toby Harris	1971
C E P Harrison	1953
C Roger Harrison	1967
G Ainsworth Harrison	1948
David Hart	1968
Debbie Hart	
P M Hart	1963
Professor Brian S Hartley	1944
Keith G Hartley	1958
R Hartshorn	1956
Dr Stuart Hartshorn	1995
Guy Harvey	1969
Keith A R Harwood	1967
Dr Patrick H Hase	1968
Sir Mark Havelock-Allan Bt	1972
Joanna Heath	2005
Dr Michael Ambrose Heather	1964
John M Heaton	1944
Dirk van Heck	1995
David Helm	1976
M S Henderson	1962
Peter Hensman	1967
Mr G A Hepworth	1949
Mr Dominic Herbert	1990
Ivor Herbert	1947
Robert Herries	1975
John P Hess	1954
R R Hetherington	1969
M R M Heyes	1954
B C Heywood	1943
Graham Heywood	1995
M G Hickford	2007
J P Hickman	1982
John Hicks	1942
Professor P J Higgins	1943
Christopher Hill	1953
Grace Lee Hill	2007
J E Hill	
Matthew Hill	1971
R M Hilton	1958
E J Hinch	1965
C E Hindson	1945
Sir David Hirst	1947
S G M Hirtzel	1985
Mark Hoffman	1959
John C C Holder	1954
Donald C Holdsworth	1972
J J Hollis	1965
R Hein Hooghoudt	1973
Rashid Hoosenally	1989
Professor Theo Hoppen FBA Hon. MRIA	1963
Ian Hopwood	1973
Graham S Horn	1993
Robert Horner	1957
Graham Hornett	1956
Nigel Horsford	1962
David J Horton	1974
R B Hoskyn	1940
Mark Hough	1999
Peter J Houghton	1953
S M Houghton	1997
Denzil How	1963
Barnaby J Howard	1945
Mr Christopher Howe	1985
Malcolm S Howe	1959
R Howie	1946
Dr Ken Howlett	1967
Theodore Hubbard	1979
Nigel Huckstep	1974
Alex H Hughes	1957
Revd David Hughes	1946
Richard Hughes	1987
T R Hughes	1980
Vanessa Hui	1991
Christopher Hulse CMG OBE	1961
J C R Hunt	1960
Tony Hunt	1965
Gavin Hurley	1996
Robert B Hutton	1946
Peter Huxtable	1962
Sir Robin Ibbs KBE	1944
Chris Ignatowicz	1969
Susan Imgrund (née Moss)	1978
Rachael Ingall	1993
John Inglis	1964
Malcolm Innes	1959
Antonis Ioannides	1986
Paul Isaacs	1969
John (Smiler) Isherwood	1974
Douglas Isles	1993
Sir Raymond Jack	1962
J S Gyakye Jackson	1957
Peter J Jackson	1958
Robin Jacob	1960
Dr W R Jacob	1961
Catherine Jagger	1994
Hywel James	1954
David S B Jamieson	1957
Dr Lara Jamieson	1999
Jonathan Janson	1952
Lisa Jardine-Wright (née Wright)	1994
David Jeffreys	1954
J V Jenkins	1955
Guy Jennings	1941
Nerys Elizabeth John	1996
Andrew Johns	1969
Sir Ian Johnson-Ferguson Bt	1950
Dr Julia Johnson-Ferguson (née Getley)	1984
Lt Col Mark Johnson-Ferguson	1984
A H S Johnson	1965
Gordon J Johnson	1954
Professor John Johnson	1960
Lucy Johnson (née Pollock)	1984
Steve Jolley	1978
J A Jolowicz	1948
A C Jones	1941
David Jones	1958
Elizabeth Jones	1992
Professor Gareth Jones	
Gareth Jones	1973
J P M Jones	1963
R Glyn Jones	1963
Raymond C F Jones	1967
Dr T P H Jones	1976
Dr Anthony P Joseph	1955

Bryan Joynes	1951
Ryo Kaiami	2006
Dr Oussama Taher Kanaan MSc (Cantab)	1986
Dr Taher Hamdi Kanaan	1958
Joseph Kanon	1968
Cary Berkeley Kaye and Nigel Kaye	1993 and 1994
Michael Kaye	1954
John F Keighley FACP	1945
Chris Kelly	1976
Immanuel Kemp	2006
Graham Keniston-Cooper	1977
D P Kennedy	
Edward John Kenney	1946
Alan Kenny	1972
D A Kenrick	1958
Murray Kenyon	1965
Wesley Kerr	1976
Alan Kershaw	1965
Laura Keys	2009
Ameer Hamza Khan	2005
Ansar Khan	1983
Nawshir D Khurody	1955
Michael Kibblewhite	1963
Patrick Kidd	1995
Mr Charles Kimmins	1990
Basil King	1959
Donald Stuart King	1957
Dr Nigel Kingsley	1965
John F Kingston	1951
Cyril Kinsky	1972
Mike Kipling	1975
Jonathan Kirk	1981
Mr Vinay Kishore	1996
Steven Knapper	1990
J F L Knight	1942
Lionel Knight	1959
Naomi L Knight	2007
Viscount Knutsford	1948
Dr Michael Koehler	
T Yung Kong	1978
Justin Anthony Kornberg	1947
Andy Krajewski	1975
Oliver B Kroemer	2004
Antonina Jelena Kruppa	2007
Sarah Kummerfeld	2002
Sabine M Kummutat	1996
John Chun Ting Kwan	2009
William Kynan-Wilson	2004
Peter Lachmann	1950
Rodney J C Laing	1977
Godfrey Lam	1988
Professor Harold Lambert	1943
Ian T G 'Brother Damian' Lambert	1979
James A Lancashire	1989
Andrew Lance	1962
Ms Jacqueline Lane	1987
Dr B W Langley	1945

Brian Langton	1958
A P Lanitis	1952
P S Lansley	1953
Solly J Laredo	1948
François J Larocque	2002
Catalina Laserna	1977
Queenie Lau	2001
W C W Lau	1979
Sir Elihu Lauterpacht CBE QC	1945
Minal Lavingia	2002
John P Lavis	1976
Dr Geoffrey P Lawrence	1972
Peter Hugh Lawrence	1972
David Lawson	1956
Paul Lazenby	1961
E David Le Cren	1940
Ed Le Quesne	1960
Dr Gregory Leadbetter	1993
John Leaf	1948
Gordon Lee-Steere	1960
Michael Lee	1972
Szu-Hee Lee	1969
Thomas Lee	2000
Xenon Lee	2006
Anthony J Leech	1974
Richard Lees	1964
John P Lefroy	1959
Professor Angela Leighton	
David Leith	1981
Eugene E Lemcio	1973
Venetia Leng	1984
John Lethbridge	1948
Eric Gilbert Lever	1970
Professor Jeffrey Lever	1941
Peter Levitt	1955
Christopher J Lewis	1952
Dr M G H Lewis	1941
Matt Lewis	1978
Michael Lewis	1975
Peter Lewis	1968
Clive Liddle	1965
Ryan Y H Lim	2009
Peter Linnecar	1972
Trevor Linnecar	1964
Alan Lloyd	1962
Captain John Lloyd MC DL	1947
Rt Hon. Lord Lloyd of Berwick	1949
Mark Lloyd-Price	1964
Adrian Longley	1947
F M Longmaid	1958
Dr Elinor Longridge	1992
John Lonsdale	1958
Dr Patrick Loo	1994
Julie Louette (née Rollison)	1980
Gerard Loughlin	1980
David Lowish	1995
John B H Lucia	1963
Amy Claire Ludlow	2005

Ken Ludwig	1973
Guy L Lyster DL MA	1947
Sir Richard MacCormac	1959
A W MacDonald	1950
Ian C Macdougall	1967
J B MacGill	1950
Dr John MacGinnis	1982
David Machin	1954
Neil MacInnes	1963
Lord Mackay of Clashfern	1950
Andrew Mackay	1970
Andrew D Mackay	1977
J Mackay	
Fiona Jane Mackenzie	2010
J M B Mackie	1936
J R Mackowiak	1996
Ewan MacLeod	1957
Sophi MacMillan (née Farley)	1982
Ewen Macpherson	1949
Ian Macpherson	1960
R W Mackworth-Praed	1957
Marcella Maura Madden Austad	
Brendan Magee	1973
Ewan Makepeace	1983
John B Makinson	1950
Andrew Makower	1980
Peter Makower	1952
Stanley Victor Makower	1890
Timothy Makower	1983
Andrew Malec	
In memory of Jalal Malik	1926
Damien P S Maltarp	1993
Guido Manca	1976
Sir Nicholas Mander Bt	1968
Sateesh R Mane	1978
Katherine Mann (née Dunstan)	1990
Michael Manson	1972
Peter Mantle	1970
Samit Mapara	2004
Lord Marlesford	1951
Dr Hedley Martin	1954
D N N Martineau	1960
John Mathieson	1978
Janet Lewis Matricciani	1985
Geoffrey Matthews	1978
Roger K F Matthews	1971
Catherine Temperley Mattison	1996
Robert May	2009
C A W McCalla	1965
Geoffrey Ian McCauley	1976
B M McCorkell	1977
Chris McCracken	1979
Mr J McDonnell	1969
Rachel McDowell (née Webster)	1988
Hugh McGarel-Groves	1970
Austin McHale	1972
Michael McLoughlin	1951
Keith A McLusky	1958

Mark McMullen	1983
James David McNamara	2009
Dr M P McOnie	1958
Henry Meadows	1959
Sophia Mealy	1998
Christopher H B Mee OBE	1954
Douglas Melton	1977
Mark Menhinick	1965
Peter Mennie	1992
Frederick W L Meredith	1955
Canon Roland Meredith	1952
John Messenger	1956
Lt Col and Mrs Andrew Methven	1988
Tim Meunier	1977
Dominique Michaelis	1968
Francis Miller	1978
Guy Miller	1983
Mr I E G Miller	1962
Richard Millington	1959
Dr Helen R Milner	1996
J K Milner	1953
Roger Mitchell	1957
Chris Mole	1979
Dr Simon Mollett	1973
R E M Momber	1949
Euan Montgomerie	1940
Kenneth B C Montgomerie	1953
Richard Gillachrist Moore	1951
Mr David Moore-Gwyn	1966
Mike Moran	1992
Ray Moran	1965
T S Moran	1967
Bernard Morgan	1950
D L Morgan	1953
Professor H Gethin Morgan	1952
Dr Daniel Morgenstern	1993
Revd Chancellor M G R Morris	1960
William Morris	1981
Colin F Morsley	1966
John Morton	1959
Vernon Morton	1953
Graham Y Mostyn	1972
Peter D A Mothersill	1976
Professor Orest Mulka	1969
Dr J Mulvein	1957
Kenneth Munday	1954
Rachel J Munro	2002
Nick Murphy	1974
P M K Murphy	1962
R V Murphy	1949
Allan James Murray	1984
Euan and Emily Murray	1995
David Muxworthy	1957
Jo Myers	1979
S L Mynott	2004
Dr S A C Napier	1983
Bruce Ivor Nathan	1951
Simon J Naylor	1993

Name	Year
John Lawrence Nazareth	1964
Professor Bernard Neal	1940
Professor Michael Neuberger	1971
David and Helena Neville	1990
Derek and Carolyn Newman	
Professor Edward Ng	1987
Stuart Niman	1981
George Nissen	1950
P J Nkambo Mugerwa	1957
Jonathan Noakes	1982
Charles Noel	1966
William Marden Nolan	1937
Revd Canon William Norman	1947
H C B C S Northcote	1958
Sir John Nott	1956
Dirk Notz	2002
Rob Nowell	1973
J R L Nuttall	1944
James O'Connor	2000
Angus O'Neill	1979
Mr D C Odendaal	1971
Dr Martin Ogle	1958
Robert Oliver	1982
Andrew Ollivant	1974
Jeremy Oppenheim	1980
Donald V Osborne	1941
Richard H A Osmond	1972
Bojosi Otlhogile	1983
Hisashi Owada	1955
Dr John Oxbury FRCP	1954
Michael Pacold	1999
Neil Page	1967
Malcolm Palmer	1960
Ian Pankhurst	1969
Michael Pannett	1952
Richard Pannett	1966
Richard Park	1953
Ben Parker	1956
Colin Parker	1955
Lorna Parker	1978
N G Parker	1952
Roger M Parker	1963
Derrick Parkes	1972
Neil Parrish	1986
Laurence Parrott	1986
Philip J Parsons	1960
Ian Partridge	1976
Jon Pasfield	1959
Tom Pasfield	1993
Dr Ian Paterson	1980
Mike Paterson	1961
Ronald Paterson	1975
Hamish Paton	1995
Mark Pattinson	1952
Dr Surendra C Paul	1967
J M Payne	1951
Cedric Peachey	1966
David G Pearson	1959
Gordon E Peckham	1957
Derk Pelly	1949

Name	Year
R H Pelly	1947
Nigel Pemberton	1953
David Peppercorn	1951
Professor M B Pepys FRS FMedSci	1962
Vicki Perrin	2009
Deborah Lily Perry (née Whitton)	1984
George Perry	1954
Mr J N Perry	1985
Mrs Jane Petkovic	
Graham Petrie	1949
Richard Petrie	1978
Colin Philpott	1976
Hilary Philpott	1978
Wesley Kym-Son Phoa	1988
Nellie Phoca-Cosmetatou	1992
Alex Phocas-Cosmetatos	1994
Chris Phylactou	1950
Simon Pickard	1989
Ian Pickering	1974
Natalya Pilbeam	1992
Roger Pilgrim	1975
Rt Hon. Sir Malcolm Pill	1958
George Richard Pinto	1950
Daniel Jeffrey Plaine	1965
M R C Plaister	1948
Stephen Plaister	1942
Professor Peter H Plesch	1936
W G Plomer	1949
Roger Plumb	1975
Mervyn Pocock	1967
Mrs Norika Podolska	
N R V W Pointon	1990
John Polsue	1970
R C Ponniah	2001
Patrick E Poole MD	1954
Helen Pooley	2007
Michael H Pope	1943
Nikolai Alexander Popescu	2001
Don Pople	1948
Sue Porter	1978
Witold K Potempa	1982
Dr Brian D Powell	1944
Dr Mark E Powell	1985
R J Pratt	1947
Anthony Preiskel	1965
Philipp Preiss	2006
Robert Prendergast	1960
Revd Martin Preston	1952
Margaret Priaulx (née Hall)	1979
Charles Price	1967
David R Price	1959
Sir David Price DL	1946
Dr Peter C Price	1949
Charles Priestley	1964
Professor Michael Proctor	1968
Laura Profumo	2010
Revd R H K Prosser	1950
Christopher Proudfoot	1966

Name	Year
Lewis R Proudlove	1981
Dr M J Provost	1973
Peter Pucill	1948
Professor David Punter	1956
Christopher Purchas	1962
R A G Raimes	1953
Lydia R E Rainforth	1999
Thomas Ransford	1977
Roger C Rawcliffe	1954
Mr J B Rawlings	1965
Francesca Rawlins	2005
Roger Rayner	1974
Jack Read	1955
A L J Redfern	1972
E N Reed	1988
Brian Rees	1949
Dr M J Reeves	1985
Donald S Reid	1951
Graham Reid	1990
W H Reid	1951
Sir William Reid	1954
Mark Reilly	1992
Canon Robert Reiss	1964
Dr C J C Remfry	1983
Max Rendall	1953
Paul Renney	1981
Martin Rennison	1949
Dr Ralf Retter	2005
Michael T Reynolds	1990
John R Rhodes	1955
Stephanie E Richards	1999
Charles Richmond	1962
Timothy Ridley	1966
Warren Rieutort-Louis	2005
Dr John Rigby	1950
Dr Nicola M Riley	1988
W F J Ritchie	1952
Alexander Friedrich Ritter	2000
Christopher Rivington	1938
David Rix	1970
Professor Andrew D Roberts	1957
David Roberts	1975
David L Roberts	1976
Dr John D Roberts	1954
Kerrin Roberts	1984
Frederick Douglas Robins	1961
D Keith Robinson	1947
F C R Robinson	1963
Dr Kevin St John Robinson	1964
Michael Robinson	1954
Steve Rogers	1964
W R Rollo	1974
Michael John Rose	1960
Jim Roseblade	1956
Gary L Rosenthal	1971
J L W Roslington	1996
Professor Angus Ross	1951
J Nicholas Ross	1959
Jack R Ross	1951
Nicos Rossos	1946

Name	Year
Sir David Rowland	1952
Charles Roxburgh	1978
Dr John F Rudge	1999
I A Rudolf	1961
Professor Martin Rudwick FBA	1950
Philip Rushforth	1991
Paulina Rychenkova	1994
Marcin Sablik	2005
Natasha Sachsenmeier	2007
Waq Saigol	1994
J B Sampson	1959
Dr Henry A Sanford	1944
John Saumarez Smith	1962
T E Savage	1955
Kenneth J H Saxton	1948
Latif N Sayani	1976
H F H F Schlichting	1969
Julian Schmidt-Kluegmann	1997
Professor Dr Peter Schnyder	1994
Dr Julian Paul Schofield	1988
Raymond Schonfeld	1962
Judge Stephen M Schwebel, Fellow	1950
K J F Scotland	1957
Revd Dr J F Scott AO	1946
Sir James Scott Bt	1971
Dr James G Scott	2004
Peter H Scott	1968
Peter O Scott	1967
Revd Hugh A Scriven	1977
S E Scrope	1955
William and Alexandra Seager	1999
Mark Seaman	1980
Christine Sears	1987
Anthony M Seddon	1965
Markus A Seeliger	1999
Dr A O Sergiades	1951
M T J Seymour	1972
Dr Peter Shahbenderian	1951
John Shakeshaft	1972
Michael St J Shallow	1972
Andrew Sharpe	1979
Professor Richard Sharpe FBA	1973
Stephen Shaw	1968
Charles Simon Camac Sheller	1951
Charles Shelton-Agar	1960
Gillian Sheridan (née Nattrass)	2001
A J Sherlock	1957
Nigel Sherratt	1971
Ajit Shetty	
A F Shewan	1962
Ken Shibata	1960
Mark Shillam	1979
Alastair Shore	1982
Henry S Short MA BSc	1950
Terence Shutt	1954
Dr Toufiq Siddiqi	1955
Jennifer Siggers	1995
Bruce A Sikora	1966

Sir Stephen Silber	1966	Professor Keith Straughan	1994
Jonathan Silver	2007	Michael Streat	1981
Mr Nicholas Sim Keyi	2009	Dr Clive Stubbings	1967
Andrew Sinclair	1965	Sarah Xiaoman Su	2005
Mark Peter Brian Sinclair	1998	Pauline and Brian Sugarman	
Rabinder Singh QC	1982	Alex Summers	2002
Mr C R J Singleton	1961	Professor Chris Sutton	1960
James Wallace Sleigh	1991	David Swain	1961
Dr Tomaz Slivnik	1988	P W Swales	1965
Richard Slynn	1980	Christopher Swan	1985
Simon N G Small	2003	Annabel Sykes	1979
Ian Smallbone	1984	Phil Sykes	1958
Rod Smallwood	1968	Nicholas Paul Tait	1972
Andrew Smith	1968	Reginald B H Tan	1986
David B Smith	1964	Tin Wee Tan	1982
Michael H A Smith	1956	Dr Sarah Tang Yu Weng	2004
N V Smith	1958	Andy Taylor	1969
Owen S Smith	1984	Beverley Taylor	
Sir Robert Smith	1947	Dr Joanne E Taylor	1982
Dr Roderick A Smith	1967	Katherine Taylor	
Ross Smith	1967	(née Tunnicliffe)	2001
J Smithson	1954	Stephen J Taylor	1971
Professor Stephen Smye	1976	Robert-Jan Temmink	1992
Professor John F Smyth	1964	Vei Kim Teo	1996
Dr J K Snell	1947	Paul Terry	1971
Dr Mark Snellgrove	1995	Sven L C Tester	1953
John Snook	1972	David Thatcher	1958
Colin B Snowdon	1959	A J Thompson	1961
Claire Soares	1996	J R Thompson	1956
Mark Solomon	1982	Jack Thompson	1957
Professor Ernst Sondheimer	1941	Michael H Thompson	1954
Mark Soundy	1983	Dr S J Thompson	2002
Richard Southwell QC	1955	Sir John Thomson	1944
Jacqueline Spayne	1981	P F Thomson	1957
Eur Ing Richard G B Spencer	1995	John Thornton	1948
Sir Donald Spiers	1954	Professor S A Thorpe FRS	1958
Dr Chris Spink	1971	Brian Threlfall	1947
Jan Sramek	2006	J S Tilley	1966
Ljiljana Stancic		Jonathan David Tims	2007
(née Mihajlovic)	1999	Toh Hoon Chew	1991
Lucy Stannard	1999	P R Tombling	1954
Stuart (Jimmy) Steele	1950	David Tomlinson	1957
Peter Stefanini	1965	G H Topple	1954
John Nicholas Stevens	1950	Mr M R Trace	1966
N E Stevenson	1988	Charles Tracy	1963
Barbara Steward		Stephen Tracy	2006
Professor Cleveland		The Viscount Trenchard DL	1970
Stewart-Patterson	1952	P J C Troughton	1966
John Massey Stewart	1953	Robert Tulloch	1991
K H Stewart	1939	Derek Tunnicliffe	1944
Paul Stickland	1951	Julian Tunnicliffe	1977
Brian Stock	1962	Mr C M Turk	1969
Jeffrey Stokes	1955	Dr C R Turner	1989
Chris Stone	1998	Simon Turnill	1987
Jacopo Stoppa		John Tusa	1956
Sir Richard Storey Bt CBE	1957	Stephen Twilley	1965
Mrs J Stourton		Surg. Cmdr J C Twomey	1951
Tony Stowell	1956	Michael E Tzartzouras	1991

Sami Uljas		Kate Whyte	1986
W Ungerer	1990	Stuart Whyte	1947
Robin Upton	1950	James Widdowson	1993
Dr Anton van Dellen	2007	Dr Hervey Wilcox	1967
Laurence van Someren	1958	Sharon Marie Wilkins	2003
Dr Archana Vats	1987	James Wilkinson	2004
David Vaughan CBE QC	1959	Ralph Wilkinson	1972
Mr Ashok Venkatesh	1983	Dr Ronald Wilks	1954
Edward Vincent	1940	Anthony Williams	1974
Mr G A Vowles	1953	Paul G L Williams	1964
The Hon. Robert A M Wade	1962	Mr R G Williams	1941
A Wailes-Fairbairn	1948	R W B Williams	1968
Mr R B Waite	1961	Rowland Williams	1948
Michael J Waldron	2006	Miles Williamson-Noble	1962
Andrew Wales	1987	Charles H K Williamson	1978
Dr G Walford		H G M Williamson	1966
Colin Walker FRCOphth	1943	Paul Kenyon Williamson	1943
Lord Walker of Gestingthorpe	1955	Geoff Wilsher	1959
Ian Walker	1977	Christina I Wilson	1996
Geoffrey Wall	1966	Professor Pelham M H Wilson	
L G R Wand	1941	Robin Wilson	1952
A and H Warburton	1942	Rohan Wilson	1965
Clare Warburton	1981	Michael Windle	1961
John W Ward	1960	Professor Alan Windle FRS	1963
Peter E Ward	1958	Jonathan Windsor	1989
Roger Ward	1971	Rob Winterbourne	1974
J P M Wardell Esq	1944	Andrew Wise	1967
Dr Paul Waring	1976	Neil Wiseman	1971
Josh Waters	2004	Paul Withers	1975
Sir Alan Waterworth KCVO	1951	Joeri Witteveen	2008
Dr Alan R Watkinson	1971	H C Wolstencroft (née Adams)	1984
C John Watson	1950	Cherry C W Wong	2003
Dr Elizabeth Ann Watson	1977	David J Wood	1964
Eric Watson	1942	Mike Wood	1974
Nigel M Watson	1951	Percy Wood	1953
Peter Watson	1969	Tim Wood	1974
Marilyn Watts	1979	Denis Woodhams	1952
J Howard Webb	1953	Robert Woods	1965
Reverend Richard Graeme		Edward A Wright	1997
Webb	1995	Michael Wright	1960
A J Wedgwood	1962	Robertson Wright	1980
N P E Weeds	1988	T John Wright	1939
Brian H Weight	1969	Yang Xia	2003
Peter J Welbank	1950	Professor Jer-Ren Yang	1984
Richard Wells CBE	1961	Puzhong Yao	2004
Pascal Wenz	2009	Benjamin Yates	2005
Professor Francis West	1949	Mrs Rebecca Yates	
Charles Westgarth	1944	(née Daldorph)	1989
Brian Westwood	1958	Nicholas Yates	1991
Bernard Wheeler	1981	Roger Alan Yates	1965
Colin Whimster	1956	Andrew Yeomans	1973
Nicholas White	1987	Graham Young	1956
Sasha White	1986	Richard Young	1989
Guy Whitmarsh	1949	Shahid N Zahid	1971
Dr Alan J Whitton	1985	Fisseha Zewdie	1967
Andrew S D Whybrow	1962		
Chris Whymark	1973		
James Whyte	1993		

Index

Acknowledgements

Publishers' Note:

The Publishers would like to thank all those who have contributed to this book and acknowledge an additional debt of gratitude for their help to several members of the College, including Jonathan Smith, Paul Simm, Richard Glauert, John Easterling, Mike Proctor and Chris Morley. We are also grateful to Rod Pullen, Junior Bursar, for facilitating photography in College. We would like to thank the following for their advice, help with images and the loan of personal material: Alan Bain, Antony Barrington Brown, Paul Brackley (Cambridge News), Sir John Bradfield, Debbie Coe (Port of Felixstowe Commercial Dept), Chris Elliott (Cambridge News), Kelvin Fagan, Patricia Fara, Marina Frasca Spada, Peter Goldberg, George Gordon, Boyd Hilton, Hugh Hunt, Chris Jakes (Cambridgeshire Collection), Manny Kemp, Tristram Kenton, Catalina Laserna, Tom Lovering, John Macgill, Janet Lewis Matricciani, Selene Mills, Hugh Osborn, Sir David Price, Hannah Schmitz (Complicité), Amanda Talhat, The Warden and Fellows of All Souls College, Oxford, David Wykes. Finally, we would like to thank our photographers, Sir Cam, Stephen Bond, Adam Smyth and Douglas Atfield.

Picture Acknowledgments:

Images identified by page reference here are either copyright to or the property of the persons or institutions listed. While every effort has been made to identify sources, the publishers will be delighted to acknowledge corrections or any further information in future editions.

Courtesy of 5th Studio Architects 168; Phyllis Agbo 77B; Courtesy of Warden and Fellows of All Souls, Oxford 209; Stephen Allan 245L; Douglas Atfield 58B, 142, 143, 192R; BA Society 74; Alan Bain 84B; Antony Barrington Brown 123, 174R, 223, 231; Jeremy Bays 170; Courtesy of Bidwells Ltd 128T; Stephen Bragg 106T; Peter Brandt 184; British Museum 44; Douglas Brumley 66–7, 75; Sir Cam 4, 8, 19, 37, 63, 78–9, 81, 118–9, 132T, 139, 140, 144–5, 161, 164–5, 171, 225, 259, 261; *Cambridge News* 177T; Cambridge University 7; Cambridge University Library 47, 180, 192L; Courtesy of the Syndics of Cambridge University Press 151; Cambridgeshire Collection 22TR, 30–1, 217; Cavendish Museum 86–7, 92–3, 93, 96; Complicité 56; John Cox 187L,R; Matt Crypto 220; frscpd 169; Ian Galloway 100L; Getty Images 194, 196L, 219, 252; Richard Glauert 28, 32TL, 128B, 132B, 133, 134–5, 138, 175; Peter Goldberg 198; Les Goodey 17, 204–5; Richard Hall 188R; from Boyd Hilton 167; Hugh Hunt 98, 100R; Imperial War Museum 226; Manny Kemp 247; Tristram Kenton 57; Wesley Kerr 27; Catalina Laserna 69; Janet Lewis Matricciani 243R, 246T, 260; Mark Mniszko 250–1; Chris Morley 185; Simon Naylor 243L; from Hugh Osborn 248–9; Colin and Hilary Philpott 68; Peter Plesch 106T; Courtesy of Port of Felixstowe Commercial Dept 136; Sir David Price 186T; Private collection 85; Charlotte Roche 182R; Royal Society 196R; W.G. Runciman 149L; Science & Society Picture Library 46, 49; Adam Smyth 33, 35, 38; Trinity College 6, 12T+B, 13T+L,T+R, 14, 20, 21, 24, 26, 29, 32, 34, 41, 45, 50, 65, 76, 77T, 82, 83, 88, 107R, 108, 110, 112, 117, 124, 125, 130, 135, 147, 149R, 152, 154, 155, 158–9, 166, 172–3, 176, 177B, 179, 183T+B, 188L, 199, 200, 201, 202, 206–7, 210, 212, 213, 214–5, 227, 228T+B, 232, 234, 235, 236, 238–9, 246B, 256; Trinity College/Stephen Bond cover, 2, 9, 10, 16, 36, 42–3, 72, 102–3, 104–5, 114, 115, 121, 126–7, 181; Trinity College/John Evans 101, 190–1; Trinity Field Club 182L, 242R, 244; Trinity Mathematical Society 58T; *Trinity Review* 53, 55L+R, 107L, 162, 174L, 178L,R, 229, 233, 241, 245R, 254, 257; Unknown source 62, 89, 216; Catharine Walston 48, 84T; Samantha Weinberg 242L; Matthew Wilson 97; David Wykes 186B

Trinity: A Portrait
2011 © Trinity College and Third Millennium Publishing Limited
First published in 2011 by Third Millennium Publishing Limited,
a subsidiary of Third Millennium Information Limited,
2–5 Benjamin Street, London, United Kingdom, EC1M 5QL

www.tmiltd.com

ISBN 978 1 906507 31 2

British Library Cataloguing in Publication Data. A CIP catalogue record for this book is available from the British Library.

Edited by	Catharine Walston
Design	Matthew Wilson
Production	Bonnie Murray
Reprographics	Studio Fasoli, Verona, Italy
Printing	Gorenjski Tisk, Slovenia